THE
GERMAN NAVY
IN THE
NAZI ERA

THE GERMAN NAVY IN THE NAZI ERA

Charles S. Thomas

Georgia Southern University

NAVAL INSTITUTE PRESS

Published and distributed in the United States of America and Canada
by the Naval Institute Press, Annapolis, Maryland 21402

Originally published by the Academic Division of
Unwin Hyman Ltd
15/17 Broadwick Street, London W1V 1FP, UK

First published in 1990

Library of Congress Catalog Card No. 89-64222

ISBN 0-87021-791-7

This edition is authorized for sale only in the United States and its
territories and possessions, and Canada

Typeset in 10 on 11 point Bembo and printed in Great Britain by
The University Press, Cambridge

Table of Contents

Naval Ranks

Kriegsmarine	United States Navy	Royal Navy
Leutnant zur See	Lieutenant (Junior Grade)	Sub-Lieutenant
Oberleutnant zur See	Lieutenant	Lieutenant
Kapitänleutnant	Lieutenant Commander	Lieutenant Commander
Korvettenkapitän	Commander	Commander
Fregattenkapitän	————	————
Kapitän zur See	Captain	Captain
————	————	Commodore
Konteradmiral	Rear Admiral	Rear Admiral
Vizeadmiral	Vice Admiral	Vice Admiral
Admiral	Admiral	Admiral
Generaladmiral	————	————
Grossadmiral	Fleet Admiral	Admiral of the Fleet

Introduction

In the wake of the unsuccessful attempt against his life on July 20, 1944, Adolf Hitler crowed: "Not a single one of these criminals belongs to the navy. Today it has no Reichpietsch in it."[1] The Führer had hit the nail on the head. The Kaiserliche Marine of Wilhelm II and the Kriegsmarine of Adolf Hitler reacted very differently to war and defeat. In the Great War, the High Sea Fleet largely rusted in port while the army bled in the trenches of France. Intra-service friction and inequalities led to a food rebellion in the summer of 1917 which, in turn, resulted in the execution of two sailors, Albin Köbis and Max Reichpietsch. One year later, the officers concocted a desperate sortie (Operations Plan 19) against the combined Anglo-American surface fleets in the southern North Sea in an attempt to salvage the officer corps' honor and to secure future naval funding; the affair ended in mutiny within the fleet and fueled the fires of revolution in Germany's major ports. Few officers died defending either their emperor or their ships, and in November 1918 William II, never at a loss for words, simply noted that the navy had deserted him "quite nicely." The fleet survived the war intact, only to be scuttled at Scapa Flow in June 1919.

How different was the situation in the Second World War! There was no apparent intra-service squabbling, no food revolts, and certainly no revolutionary manifestation in the navy to rival that of 1918. Instead, the warships of the Kriegsmarine duly went down to their watery graves as ordered by Erich Raeder and Karl Dönitz. In the end, far from feeling deserted by the navy, a grateful Hitler "rewarded" it by naming its commander his successor when he chose to exit the stage in April 1945.

What accounts for the vast difference in the performance between the navy of Wilhelm II and that of Adolf Hitler? Had the errors in the art of leadership (*Menschenführung*) of a previous generation simply been corrected? Or had the *Seeoffiziere* of the Third Reich fully embraced the tenets of National Socialist doctrine? Had Erich Raeder and his successor, Karl Dönitz, utterly Nazified the corps? And why exactly had Hitler, a man afraid of water and unsure of naval strategy, assigned an admiral as his successor when that man came from the very corps that in 1918 had ingloriously deserted its Supreme War Lord?

Or are we jumping to conclusions? Had the naval officer corps survived the National Socialist period by closing ranks against the Party, by maintaining the past tradition of remaining above politics? Had the corps simply decided to serve the fatherland regardless of the political developments in the years between 1918 and 1945? And had Germany's naval officers, as Dönitz later suggested to French journalists, sharply protested against any and all effronteries against the laws of the realm by the National Socialists when these became public?[2]

Obviously, there is a rather large gap between these two contrasting views of the naval officer corps. And other, less all-embracing questions concerning the relationship between the Kriegsmarine and the Party have proven to be equally controversial. What appeal, if any, did National Socialism exert in the eyes of the navy in the days before the Party came to power? What was the nature of the Service's relationship with the *Sturmabteilung* (SA) and the *Schutzstaffel* (SS)? To what extent did the leaders of the Kriegsmarine alter the navy's recruitment and training programs to meet the demands of the Party? How was the navy affected by the Party's anti-Semitic legislation and by its campaign against the churches? And finally, what was the nature of the naval commanders' relationship with Hitler? Did Raeder's view of the German dictator change over time, for example, and did Dönitz's succession in January 1943 bring any modification in the high command's dealings with the Führer? These as well as similar questions provide the starting point for the present study.

Clearly, in the experience of the navy, as in perhaps no other institution of the National Socialist era, a great deal of work needs to be done to unravel apologias and hagiographies in order to arrive at some sort of historical truth. Until relatively recently any attempt to bridge the gap between conflicting accounts of the navy's role in the National Socialist state was blocked by a number of obstacles. Immediately after the Second World War resentment against virtually all things having to do with the German military by historians of the formerly Allied nations ran so deeply as to render an objective assessment of the relationship between the Nationalsozialistische Deutsche Arbeiterpartei (NSDAP) and the Kriegsmarine difficult, if not impossible.[3] Veterans of the German navy, by contrast, were reluctant—understandably so in view of the charges preferred against their two former commanders at the Nuremberg Tribunal—to admit that the Service had been the least bit affected by the teachings and practices of National Socialism. Perhaps it was because of this that initial postwar studies of the navy by former Kriegsmarine personnel tended to concentrate on the operational side of the war and to ignore the larger political context of the campaign at sea.[4] When the subject of the navy's role in politics did come up, the debates that followed generally shed more heat than light on the issue of the navy's dealings with the Party. Already in August 1945, for example, Raeder, while vociferously denying any affinity between the navy and the NSDAP during *his* term of office, had decried the direction that developments had taken after January 1943 under the leadership of his successor, whom he styled the "Hitler Youth" Dönitz.[5]

By the mid-1950s, the would-be historian of the naval officer corps was beginning to confront a different problem. Almost a decade of confinement together at Spandau prison apparently convinced Raeder and Dönitz that it was better not to wash the navy's dirty linen in public. Accordingly, when the memoirs of the former *Grossadmirale* appeared in the latter part of the decade, all traces of Raeder's earlier accusation concerning the enthusiasm of at least a part of the officer corps for National Socialism had miraculously disappeared.[6] In turn, the carefully coordinated accounts of the Service's two surviving commanders would seem to have fueled at least a partial revision of the Kriegsmarine's role in politics that attracted adherents on both sides of the Atlantic. Indeed, this had reached the point that when the English translation of Raeder's memoirs appeared in 1960, an American admiral could applaud Raeder's relative success, compared with the other branches of the armed forces, in keeping the navy free of party influence.[7]

One final problem rendered a historical assessment of the naval officers' role in the National Socialist state exceedingly difficult. Although the Service's documents survived the vicissitudes of the Second World War largely intact, they were subsequently scattered over the globe as booty of the victor powers. A few papers eventually found their way to the National Archives in Washington; others presumably went to a Soviet repository. The bulk of the naval high command's documents, however, went to the vaults of the Royal Navy where, with but a few exceptions, they lay neglected for roughly two decades. To be sure, a few especially fortunate scholars occasionally gained access to the Marinearchiv. When they did, their findings often offered a tantalizing glimpse into the role of the naval officer corps in politics. In 1951, the British historian F. H. Hinsley published a pioneering analysis of Hitler's wartime strategy based largely on the written record of the Führer's conferences with his two naval commanders-in-chief.[8] Seven years later, another Briton, D. C. Watt, utilized the Marinearchiv for a valuable study of Anglo-German naval relations on the eve of the Second World War.[9] In 1965 the Swedish historian Carl-Axel Gemzell added a provocative look into the Kriegsmarine's role in the German decision to invade Denmark and Norway in 1940.[10] But as the seven-year hiatuses between the appearance of each of these three works indicate, the overall insights gained into the influence of politics on the navy in the Third Reich were relatively few and far between.

By the early 1970s this picture was beginning to change. The return of the documents of the Marinearchiv to West German custody by the United States and Great Britain in the mid- to late 1960s, and their central location at Freiburg, West Germany, enabled a new generation of historians, both German and foreign, to examine the navy's record under National Socialism. Moreover, the ongoing collection of the personal papers of numerous former members of the Kriegsmarine by the Bundesarchiv-Militärarchiv facilitated a revision of the historical record as established by Raeder and Dönitz. In 1969, Manfred Messerschmidt's *Die Wehrmacht im NS Staat*, while dealing primarily with the experiences of the army, nevertheless offered a number of insights into problems that the navy faced in common with the other two branches of the armed forces in dealing with the NSDAP and its leaders.[11] Works devoted exclusively to the history of the Kriegsmarine soon followed. In 1970 Michael Salewski delivered the first volume of his mammoth history of the Service's strategic planning in the period from 1935 to 1945, and the following year he extended his research backward in time with a very important article on naval and political leadership in the period 1931–1935.[12] In 1973, Jost Dülffer produced a masterful analysis of the interrelationship between political and diplomatic decision-making on the one hand and naval construction on the other between 1920 and 1939.[13] A fourth German historian, Gerhard Schreiber, added another contribution in 1978 with his meticulous evaluation of Italo-German naval relations.[14]

While none of these works was directly concerned with the naval officer corps as a whole, each shed valuable light on problems faced by the corps in the 1930s and 1940s. In addition, many of the innumerable accounts of the vessels and engagements of the Kriegsmarine in the Second World War proved to be of considerable value for the reactions of the *Marineoffiziere* to the strains of war. At the same time, however, the reader should be reminded that the subject of the present study is the political history of the naval officer corps, albeit somewhat broadly defined, and not that of the navy as a whole during this period, its ships, its armaments, or its engagements.

One final source of information—the numerous investigations of the navy in earlier periods of German history—proved to be especially useful for the present study. The books of the Canadian historian Holger H. Herwig and the American Keith W. Bird on the officer corps of the imperial and republican navies, respectively, suggested questions that might be asked in a similar study of the officer corps of the Third Reich and, just as importantly, revealed much about the *mentalités* of the officers of the Kriegsmarine who had served in Germany's earlier navies.[15] In similar fashion the studies of specific aspects of naval history by, among others, Jonathan Steinberg, Volker Berghahn, Wilhelm Deist, and Paul Kennedy for the Wilhelmian period and by Werner Rahn for the Reichsmarine between 1919 and 1928 offered insights into the way that Raeder, a veteran of both of the earlier navies and one of Alfred von Tirpitz's prize pupils, would administer the Service after he assumed command in 1928.[16] Nor ought one to forget those works which, through their longer view of certain aspects of the navy's experience, provide a link between the Kaiserliche Marine, the Reichsmarine, and the Kriegsmarine. Among these, three stand out: Gemzell's analysis of personal conflict and rivalry in the navy's strategic planning in the years 1888 to 1940; Herwig's study of the role of the United States in the Service's planning from 1889 to 1941; and the late Werner Bräckow's history of the naval engineer officer corps from 1849 until the early 1970s.[17] Finally, mention must be made of the two international conferences which took their inspiration either entirely or in large measure from the spate of research into German naval history. In April 1972, the Military Historical Research Office in Freiburg convened a conference at Kirchzarten in order to provide a broad spectrum for the recent *essais* into the Imperial Navy. Seven years later, the same institution was again instrumental in assembling a historical conference at Castle Büdingen designed to offer the latest insights into the history of the various German officer corps, both army and navy, of the last century.[18]

A glance at the notes of the present study will indicate my indebtedness to each of the above mentioned authors. In addition my sincerest thanks go to those on both sides of the Atlantic who helped me in so many ways with the research and writing of this manuscript. A very generous grant from the Deutscher Akademischer Austauschdienst (DAAD) enabled me to spend the academic year 1978–1979 at the Bundesarchiv-Militärarchiv in Freiburg, West Germany, where I was able to examine in detail the documents of the former Marinearchiv and the personal papers of a number of veterans of the navy. While there, I was assisted in innumerable ways by the personnel of the Militärarchiv, especially by Dr Friedrich Christian Stahl, Dr Hansjoseph Maierhöfer, Dr Volker Giessler, and the late Gert Sandhofer. Special thanks also go out to Albert Mahler and Ewald Wenzel of the *Benutzersaal* for their aid in deciphering the handwriting of those officers who apparently chose to compose their reports from the storm-tossed bridges of their ships, and to Frau Eleonore Müller of the published documents section of the Militärarchiv, whose unfailing patience and good humor did much to brighten many a winter day in Freiburg. In Kempten, Herr Helmut Fechter was gracious enough to share his memories of his father, Admiral (Ing.) Hans Fechter, and to treat my wife and me to an unsurpassed bit of "naval hospitality."

My debts of gratitude also extend to a number of people on this side of the Atlantic. The staffs of the Interlibrary Loan Departments of both Vanderbilt University and Georgia Southern College were diligent searchers for obscure volumes on German naval history. Becky Smith wrestled purposefully with my rather eccentric methods of typing when the manuscript was in its dissertation form. At Vanderbilt, Professors Charles Delzell, Samuel McSeveney, Emilio Willems, and the late Forrestt Miller read portions of the manuscript and offered valuable suggestions, as did Professor Paul G. Halpern of Florida State University. Dr Eric C. Rust of Baylor University took time from his own research on the German navy[19] to offer a very useful critique of this manuscript while it was in dissertation form. Dr Michael Moore of Georgia Southern College kindly offered stylistic suggestions for the latter portion of the manuscript, along with competition on the basketball court. I am indebted to all of these people. Those errors that remain are my own.

Finally, my deepest gratitude goes out to four people who have been with this project from the beginning. To Holger H. Herwig, I offer my sincerest thanks for the hours that he spent poring over one draft after another of this study. My feelings of guilt are assuaged only by the knowledge that he knows more than a little about pouring drafts. To my parents, I offer my appreciation for their understanding for the trials and tribulations of a professional student. My wife, Marti, has soldiered heroically through the demands that this manuscript has placed upon her—of breadwinner, tour guide, parent-in-chief, and, most recently, word processing mentor. This book is for her and for my grandparents.

Notes for Introduction

1 Albert Speer, *Spandauer Tagebücher* (Frankfurt, Berlin and Vienna, 1975), p. 507.
2 Karl Dönitz, *40 Fragen an Karl Dönitz* (Munich, 1979), p. 35.
3 See, for example, William A. Wiedersheim's otherwise useful "Officer Personnel Selection in the German Navy, 1925–1945," *United States Naval Institute Proceedings*, 73 (April 1947), pp. 445–449.
4 An exception to this are the reminiscences of Hitler's former naval adjutant, Karl-Jesko von Puttkamer, *Die unheimliche See: Hitler und die Kriegsmarine* (Vienna and Munich, 1952).
5 Bundesarchiv-Militärarchiv, Freiburg, West Germany, RM 6/104 "Die Entwicklung der Deutschen Marinepolitik 1933–1939."
6 Erich Raeder, *Mein Leben*, 2 vols, (Tübingen, 1956–1957); Karl Dönitz, *Zehn Jahre und zwanzig Tage* (Bonn, 1958). The similarity of the two memoirs is more than coincidental. Both were "ghost written" by Admiral (ret.) Erich Förste, who submitted the results of his endeavors for the admirals' approval.
7 See the foreword by Admiral (ret.) H. Kent Hewitt to Erich Raeder, *My Life* (Annapolis, Md, 1960). The English translation of Dönitz's reminiscences appeared the year before under the title *Memoirs: Ten Years and Twenty Days* (London, 1959).
8 F. H. Hinsley, *Hitler's Strategy* (Cambridge, 1951). The complete text of the two admirals' conferences with Hitler was reprinted earlier under the title *Fuehrer Conferences on Matters Dealing with the German Navy*, 7 vols (Washington, DC, 1947); also in abridged form in *Brasseys Naval Annual, 1948* (London, 1948), under the title "Fuehrer Conferences on Naval Affairs."
9 D. C. Watt, "Anglo-German Naval Negotiations on the Eve of the Second World War," *Journal of the Royal United Service Institution*, 103 (May and August 1958), pp. 201–207, 384–391. Watt presumably did not have access to the Marinearchiv for his earlier study, "The Anglo-German Naval Agreement of 1935: An Interim Judgment," *Journal of Modern History*, 28 (June 1956), pp. 155–175.
10 Carl-Axel Gemzell, *Raeder, Hitler und Skandinavien: Der Kampf für einen maritimen Operationsplan* (Lund, 1965).
11 Manfred Messerschmidt, *Die Wehrmacht im NS Staat: Zeit der Indoktrination* (Hamburg, 1969).
12 Michael Salewski, *Die deutsche Seekriegsleitung 1935–1945*, 3 vols (Munich, 1970–1975); and Michael Salewski, "Marineleitung und politische Führung 1931–1935," *Militärgeschichtliche Mitteilungen*, 2/1971, pp. 113–158.
13 Jost Dülffer, *Weimar, Hitler und die Marine: Reichspolitik und Flottenbau 1920–1939* (Düsseldorf, 1973).
14 Gerhard Schreiber, *Revisionismus und Weltmachtstreben: Marineführung und deutsch-italienische Beziehungen 1919–1944* (Stuttgart, 1978).
15 Holger H. Herwig, *The German Naval Officer Corps: A Social and Political History 1890–1918* (Oxford, 1973); Keith W. Bird, *Weimar, the German Naval Officer Corps and the Rise of National Socialism* (Amsterdam, 1977).

16 Jonathan Steinberg, *Yesterday's Deterrent: Tirpitz and the Birth of the German Battle Fleet* (London, 1965); Volker R. Berghahn, *Der Tirpitz-Plan: Genesis und Verfall einer innenpolitischen Krisenstrategie unter Wilhelm II* (Düsseldorf, 1971); Wilhelm Deist, *Flottenpolitik und Flottenpropaganda: Das Nachrichtenbureau des Reichsmarineamtes 1897–1914* (Stuttgart, 1976); Wilhelm Deist, "Die Politik der Seekriegsleitung und die Rebellion der Flotte Ende Oktober 1918," *Vierteljahrshefte für Zeitgeschichte*, 14 (October 1966), pp. 341–368; and Paul M. Kennedy, "Tirpitz, England and the Second Navy Law of 1900: A Strategical Critique," *Militärgeschichtliche Mitteilungen*, 2/1970, pp. 33–58. In contrast to the Wilhelmian period, the navy of the Weimar Republic has attracted little attention. However, Werner Rahn's *Reichsmarine und Landesverteidigung 1919–1928: Konzeption und Führung der Marine in der Weimarer Republik* (Munich, 1976), sets a standard for excellence that subsequent studies will be hard pressed to match.

17 Carl-Axel Gemzell, *Organization, Conflict and Innovation: A Study of German Naval Strategic Planning, 1888–1940* (Stockholm, 1973); Holger H. Herwig, *Politics of Frustration: The United States in German Naval Planning 1889–1941* (Boston, Mass., 1976); Werner Bräckow, *Die Geschichte des deutschen Marine-Ingenieuroffizierkorps* (Oldenburg and Hamburg, 1974).

18 Herbert Schottelius and Wilhelm Deist (eds), *Marine und Marinepolitik in kaiserlichen Deutschland, 1871–1914* (Düsseldorf, 1972); and Hans Hubert Hofmann (ed), *Das deutsche Offizierkorps 1860–1960* (Boppard, 1980).

19 See Eric Christian Rust, "Crew 34: German Naval Officers under and after Hitler" (PhD dissertation, University of Texas at Austin, 1987).

1

The Wilhelmian Legacy

The legacy of Imperial Germany was particularly strong within the navy after 1918. In contrast to the army, whose spokesmen could boast of a glorious history extending back to and beyond the baroque exploits of Friedrich Wilhelm, the Great Elector of Brandenburg-Prussia, champions of the navy had no similarly long tradition to serve their needs. Despite isolated attempts in the past to lay the basis for a navy—most notably by the Great Elector in the seventeenth century and by the ill-fated Frankfurt Assembly in 1848–1849—significant enthusiasm for a fleet remained subdued for the greater part of German history. The overwhelming attitude among monarchs and citizens toward the creation of a fleet in the period before Germany's imperial era in 1871 was best expressed by Friedrich II a century before: "Prussia is a continental power. It needs a good army but no fleet."[1]

Friedrich's admonition lost little of its relevance after Otto von Bismarck's unification of Germany under Prussian auspices to form the Second Reich. To be sure, Germany did eventually embark upon a modest program of naval expansion and colonial acquisition, but both Bismarck and the first German Kaiser, Wilhelm I, remained at best lukewarm advocates of a strong German fleet. In matters of budgetary expenditures and prestige of service, the navy continued to take a distant second place to the army. Entrance requirements into the naval officer corps remained relatively lax, perhaps in an effort to encourage lagging enlistment.[2] Even the enrollment into the navy of Wilhelm I's second oldest grandson, Prince Heinrich, could be interpreted as a symbolic gesture intended to bolster morale in a decidedly junior service.

With Wilhelm's death in 1888 and the untimely passing of his son, Friedrich III, that same year, the prospects for the young navy improved dramatically. The new Kaiser, Wilhelm II, was an enthusiast of German naval expansion, and his attitude awoke new hope within the navy that it would no longer be treated as a stepchild.[3] Wilhelm was not slow to satisfy this desire. Under his patronage, Germany embarked upon a naval program that soon dwarfed all previous German efforts at fleet construction. After Admiral Alfred Tirpitz's appointment to the influential position of state secretary of the Imperial Naval Office (Reichsmarineamt) in 1897, the pace of this already ambitious program

1

was increased still further.[4] Nor were the efforts of Wilhelm and his minions confined to matters of ship construction alone. Under Tirpitz's adept management, a News Bureau inundated the public with material stressing the need for a large navy.[5] Wilhelm demonstrated the new prestige that the Kaiserliche Marine enjoyed at court by the frequency and obvious pleasure with which he wore the uniform of a German admiral. Prince Heinrich's continued advancement to high positions of command and the enrollment of Wilhelm's own son, Prince Adalbert, in the navy at the age of 10 gave similar evidence of the increasingly valued position that the burgeoning officer corps enjoyed in the eyes of the Kaiser. And, lest the public get the impression that all this was empty symbolism, Wilhelm actively encouraged the self-esteem of the naval officers through his inventive rhetoric, which reached new heights in a speech to the officers of the Berlin garrison on January 1, 1900:

> And as My grandfather [did] for the Army, so I will, for My navy, carry on unerringly and in similar manner the work of reorganization so that it may also stand on an equality with My armed forces on land and so that through it the German Empire may also be in a position abroad to attain that place which it has not yet reached.[6]

This was heady stuff for the infant navy. Not surprisingly, the naval officer corps[7] reciprocated the feelings of it commander—despite an occasional uneasy feeling that the Supreme War Lord, as Wilhelm styled himself, was "a bit too much."[8] Like the army, the navy steeped itself in the hallowed tradition of service to God, king, and country. Indeed, given the navy's position as junior service, naval officers sought to surpass their terrestrial brothers-in-arms in their loyalty to the Crown. In the process, the navy frequently gave the bizarre appearance of being more Prussian than the Prussian army. Thus, although only a small minority of naval officers were members of the nobility, middle-class officers, who constituted the overwhelming majority, sought to emulate the behavior of the Junker-dominated Prussian army officer corps and "live nobly." The result was the development of a caste system identical to that of the army officer corps.[9]

This tendency was strengthened by a number of practices within the navy which effectively limited the pool from which the Service drew its officer candidates to a relatively small segment of German society. It also ensured that young officers were properly enculturated into naval routine. The relatively high cost of uniforms, books, and living expenses, which was borne by the officer candidate, automatically discouraged most members of the working class from applying to the midshipmen's training program. After the completion of midshipmen's training, candidates had to face election by the officer corps before they were admitted to the latter, which made almost certain that only those who subscribed to the conventions of the corps were accepted. Further promotion was based strictly on seniority, which encouraged orthodoxy rather than innovation.

The caste spirit intruded into the private life of the officer as well. The navy's insistence upon a *Vermögensnachweis*, a document proving access to a certain amount of money over and above the officer's regular salary for the support of a bride, served the expressed purpose of discouraging marriage before the officer reached the rank of Lieutenant. In addition, it ensured that most young officers learned the routine of service in the barracks and mess hall, without the distractions of the fairer sex and in the company of their peers and superiors. Nor was the long-suffering officer through with naval routine when he finally attained the coveted *Vermögensnachweis*, for he was required to submit a written sketch of the prospective bride and her parents for the consideration of his superiors. Final approval of the proposed marriage was a matter solely for the Kaiser, and it might hinge upon the social or political respectability of the bride-to-be.

The crowning glory in this system was provided by the "military courts of honor." Like so many other practices within the navy, the courts were borrowed from the army and were intended to consider offenses that were not specifically covered by the Articles of War. Elected by and composed of naval officers, these courts sat in judgment of officers whose behavior in the company of women, for example, might offend the unwritten rules of conduct subscribed to by nobles or would-be nobles. Likewise included in these unwritten laws was the necessity of obtaining "satisfaction" for any offense that might be offered by fellow officers or civilians. The result was an incitement to the *code duello* that would have gladdened the heart of the most reactionary nobleman. As the verdict from an honor court considering an altercation between an officer and a student expressed it in 1912:

> Officers [are] . . . constantly to make the preservation of the raised [status] of the officer class their own business. Anyone who starts trouble with an officer must feel that this is not child's play but a matter of risking one's life.[10]

Not every officer carried this institutionally prescribed chip on his shoulder, but there can be little doubt that the overall results of such a system of self-selection and caste-determined behavior were harmful to the navy. The urge to the gambling table or the incitement to the drinking bout, which largely stemmed from the mimetic impulse to live as nobles, were the least of the navy's problems, although both of these distractions could at times seriously impede the proper discharge of duty. The implications of the naval officers' "conscious adoption of the Prussian army officers' prejudiced outlook on life" were far more serious when it came to their relationship with German society as a whole.[11] Increasingly the corps turned inward, seeking answers to the great social and political questions of the day from its own narrow experience. In the process it became increasingly isolated from large segments of German society. In part, this was rendered unavoidable by larger political and diplomatic developments of the Wilhelmian

3

period. The adoption of Tirpitz's doctrine of the "risk fleet," for example, resulted in the concentration of the German fleet in a few key ports in order to menace Great Britain. This inadvertently ensured that social contacts for an officer and his family, if he were married, were generally restricted to a narrow circle of fellow officers and their families. In part, the naval officers' isolation from society was also caused by the shortsightedness of the German naval high command, which provided the officer candidate with a thorough training in matters of seamanship but which neglected to give him even the most basic introduction in political matters. In part, however, the isolation was self-willed as well, an expression of the caste spirit which shunned the company or advice of outsiders and which reveled in the self-appointed task of applying the standards of a "feudalized" officer corps to the twentieth century. These standards were not without their value, as the heroic sacrifices and the frequently chivalrous behavior of the naval officer corps would demonstrate in the Great War, but they carried with them potentially disastrous consequences as well. Among these was a decided tendency to mask political ignorance by a display of contempt for the entire parliamentary system or, to the extent that individual officers concerned themselves with politics at all, by a vehement aversion to political innovation as championed by the German Social Democratic Party. Xenophobia also made its presence felt, particularly when directed against Great Britain, whose naval tradition and officer corps attracted both the admiration and the envy of the German *Seeoffiziere*.[12] Finally, a mild but nevertheless distinct anti-Semitic bias was also present and expressed itself beneath the surface in officer elections and in the private correspondence of many members of the corps.[13]

It can be seen, then, that the caste spirit frequently complicated the officer corps' relationship with the public. It also assumed curious forms within the navy, most notably in the naval officers' relationship with two corps of specialists whose position fell between that of the executive officer (or *Seeoffizier*) and that of the ratings and noncommissioned officers. The first of these specialist groups comprised the naval engineers.[14] In the early days of the navy, more candidates for this group were generally drawn from a lower social stratum of German society, the lower middle class, than were candidates for the executive officer corps. Hence the engineers were generally viewed condescendingly by traditionalists as mechanics, tinkerers, and "greasers," not as leaders of men. Despite a gradual narrowing of the social gap between applicants for the engineer corps and those for the executive officer corps, and despite the increasing importance of technology in naval affairs, this view persisted well into the twentieth century. The naval engineers were relegated to a separate officer corps whose position was distinctly secondary to that of the executive officers. The most junior executive officer, for example, outranked the senior engineer officer aboard ship, and disciplinary power over engine-room personnel was assigned not to the Chief Engineer but to the First Officer, the second ranking officer after the ship's captain. Engineer officers were excluded from the executive

4

officers' mess when ashore and were not allowed a voice in the honor courts, even when a case concerned an engineer officer. Social contacts between wives of engineers and wives of executive officers were awkward and likewise discouraged. Perhaps most galling of all, the officer's sash, the outward symbol of military authority, was denied the engineer and reserved for the executive officer. The net result was a cleft between the two corps that was apparent to insiders and outsiders alike. One young engineer officer compared the relationship between engineer and executive officers to that between the officers of a modest line infantry regiment and the exclusively noble officers of an elite cavalry regiment. In both cases, a certain amount of snobbery was unmistakable, but in the army, at least, the officers of different regiments rarely saw each other in the course of duty. In the navy, by contrast, the two officer corps were assigned to the same garrisons or the same ships and were constantly interacting both on and off duty.[15]

Despite the dangers to leadership and morale posed by the spectacle of two potentially antagonistic officer corps, the navy moved with alarming slowness to bridge the gap between the two groups. This was doubtless due, in part, to the inertia evident in a military establishment at rest, but it was also due, in part, to the active resistance by the executive officers to concessions to their social inferiors. In 1912, one senior executive officer expressed his dismay at learning that brothers of engineer officers were now applying for candidacy in the executive officer corps and urged that this trend be arrested. Tirpitz, the guiding spirit within the navy between 1897 and 1916 and a late arrival on the social scene—his patent of nobility dated from 1900—likewise steadfastly opposed any substantive efforts to raise the professional and social status of the engineer corps. In the end, some palliatives were granted to the engineers, such as permission to wear the officer's sash in 1908 and the right of an engineer officer to replace the junior executive officer on honor courts in cases involving engineer officers, granted in 1909. By 1914, however, no satisfactory solution to the overall problem posed by the engineer officers had been attained. The engineers continued to feel slighted; the naval establishment continued to look upon them as technicians, not commanders.

The presence of a second corps of specialists, the deck officers, further complicated the navy's personnel policies.[16] This corps encompassed a number of positions such as boatswain, helmsman, master carpenter, and machinist and occupied an intermediary position between the executive officers and the petty officers. Although deck officer positions were not considered command functions, they nevertheless required considerable skill. In fact, in the days of sail the deck officer corps had enjoyed a degree of prestige exceeded only by that of the executive officer corps. As the role of technology, and with it the value of the engineer corps, increased, the relative importance of the duties performed by the deck officers diminished. This tendency was made clear at the turn of the century when, in 1899, the deck officers were reclassified and grouped with the noncommissioned officers and enlisted men for the purposes of ranking. In the years that followed, the deck officers sought to have their position as a separate officer corps reaffirmed. For a time the navy contemplated a number of plans to meet this end, including one that would have grouped the engineers and deck officers into a single corps just below the executive officers. This proposal was bitterly opposed by spokesmen for the engineers, who saw in this a diminution of their own hard-won position. In desperation, the deck officers turned to the aid of Reichstag deputies and pressure groups composed of retired deck officers.[17] To Tirpitz and other leading figures within the navy, this represented an attempt to bypass the chain of command, and their position hardened into one of no concessions. As in the case of the engineer corps, little had been done to pacify the deck officers by the outbreak of war in 1914.

The coming of the First World War provided an initial distraction from the internal problems of the navy. In the long run, however, the war exacerbated existing problems and shattered the precarious balance that had existed in the prewar period. In large measure, the peculiar course that the war at sea took was responsible for this. After a flurry of activity in 1914, highlighted by the escape of the *Goeben* and *Breslau* from overwhelming Anglo-French forces in the Mediterranean, by the exhilarating victory over the British at Coronel, and by the sobering defeats at the Falkland Islands and the Helgoland Bight, the war settled into a distant blockade of Germany by the British fleet. Outnumbered and without realistic chances of victory over the British Grand Fleet, the German High Sea Fleet was condemned to the dull routine of life in port. The sailor's monotonous existence was enlivened only by an occasional sortie of the fast Battle Cruiser Squadron or, even less frequently, by the entire fleet in the hope of catching a portion of the British fleet at sea and defeating it in detail. While the navy waited for this unlikely event to occur, Germany was slowly being starved to death by the blockade.

The effects of the enforced inaction varied. The executive officer corps found the course that the war took terribly frustrating. After years of increasing tension with Great Britain, the *Seeoffiziere* longed for a glorious decision to be won through the clash of battle squadrons on the high seas.[18] When the initial clashes at the Helgoland Bight in 1914 and the Dogger Bank in 1915 were resolved in favor of the British, the resultant recriminations within the top echelons of the German navy, aggravated by the divided command structure adopted before the war, did much to disturb relationships within the executive officer corps. Nor was the Kaiser immune from criticism in this matter; many naval officers were disappointed by his timid policy of withholding the surface fleet from major engagements. Later, after many within the navy came to see the submarine as the panacea for Germany's ills, the erstwhile special relationship between the Kaiser and the executive officer corps underwent further deterioration due to Wilhelm's continued support of the imperial chancellor, Theobald von Bethmann Hollweg, whose vacillating position regarding unrestricted submarine warfare made him a special target for the corps. No one found the situation more frustrating than Tirpitz, the spiritual father for many of the executive officers. When he resigned his position as head of the Naval Office in 1916, as a result of disagreement over naval policy with the Kaiser and the chancellor, and formed the ultranationalist Fatherland Party, his actions received the support of a majority of the executive officers.[19]

The situation was somewhat different within the engineer and deck officer corps. They, too, doubtless experienced the same frustrations felt by the executive officers in the face of the British blockade, but they had other unfinished business to worry about as well. During the initial phase of the war, both engineers and deck officers tended to relax their efforts to secure an improvement of their corporate status, but their demands were bound to re-emerge as the war dragged on. The engineer corps in particular appeared to have considerable leverage in its efforts for a merger with the executive officers or at least an equalization of the rights and privileges of the two corps, for during the war many of the engineers performed superlatively as technicians and as leaders of men.[20] In addition, the war-induced expansion of the U-boat force created an acute shortage of naval engineers, who were particularly needed to service the complicated and often cantankerous machinery aboard the early submarines. This notwithstanding, the naval hierarchy stood firm in the face of the demands of the engineer corps. The matter reached a head in July 1917, when Admiral Reinhard Scheer, chief of the High Sea Fleet, gave a conclusive rebuff to the aspirations of the engineer corps by ordering that the power to command, the final distinction between true officers and mere technicians in uniform, was the exclusive concern of the executive officers. There could be no merger. Nor could equal status between the two corps be granted. The engineers would have to remain content with their existing position.[21]

The deck officers fared little better in their endeavors to improve their status. Their continued reliance upon Reichstag deputies and pressure groups, which had originally manifested itself in the prewar period, did not endear the deck officers to the naval command. However, the corps did eventually gain a minor concession when the navy created a special rank of Deck Officer Lieutenant which was to be bestowed after twenty years of service and the deck officer's retirement from the navy. For a time, in the summer of 1918, the navy also contemplated reversing the decision grouping active deck officers with the ratings, and elevating them instead to a separate corps between the ratings and the engineer and executive officers. Changing attitudes within the high command and Germany's autumn crisis prevented the realization of this, the most important goal of the deck officers.[22]

Neither the engineers nor the deck officers, then, achieved measurable success in improving their status during the course of the war. Morale within the two corps suffered as a result, and their relationship with the executive officer corps not surprisingly deteriorated. By 1918 the situation had reached serious proportions. But by then, the navy faced an even more serious problem from another quarter which the divisions within the various officer corps had helped to create.

The great crisis of the navy concerned the enlisted men. Initially, their response to the coming of war was little different from that of their officers. As good patriots, for the most part, they were elated by the initial victories, saddened by the first defeats, and frustrated by the navy's inability to strike an effective blow at the distant British blockade. With regard to the enlisted men, however, the peculiar consequences that stemmed from waging war from home ports were especially harmful. Unlike the officers, who continued to have command functions to occupy their attention when the ships were in port and who had the pleasures of the officers' *Kasino* (mess) to distract them in their off-duty hours, the enlisted men could find little outside of the drudgery of routine service life to fill their days. Life on the "big ships" (*dicken Schiffe*), as the capital ships of the fleet were called, was uniformly dull, and wartime rationing soon reduced the seaman's daily fare to one of consistent monotony.[23] Nor did the situation improve when the enlisted men went ashore on liberty. Neither Wilhelmshaven, the main harbor for the High Sea Fleet when it operated in the North Sea, nor Kiel, the primary port for vessels in the Baltic, was the most exciting of places, even in the best of times. In addition, the navy feared ideological contamination of naval personnel by the local dock workers, a large number of whom were Socialists. Officers therefore sought to curtail contacts between ratings and workers by limiting shore leave to "safe" areas and by declaring bars that allowed Socialist meetings "off limits" to naval personnel.[24] With little to do and no place to go, the average sailor was condemned to a life of misery aboard ship.

The effects of these adverse conditions upon the seamen were not always predictable. Even though the chance of combat brought with it the prospect of a watery death, it at least offered relief from routine. Morale was seen to improve on those rare occasions when the fleet put out to sea. Significantly, morale and discipline remained highest among the crews of the submarines and minesweepers, vessels that remained active even when the large ships of the fleet were in port.[25] Despite very heavy losses to enemy action, the seaman in the submarine branch could feel that he was making a contribution to Germany's war effort. Here the relationship between enlisted man and officer also benefitted from the fact that, with the increasing emphasis on submarine warfare, the best junior officers volunteered for duty on the U-boats, where they could lead by example and not merely by the power of command.[26] Finally, the very intimacy between officer and crew necessitated by the cramped conditions aboard the small vessels meant that needless formality and outdated social pretensions were frequently forgotten in the interests of a smoothly running boat.[27]

It was different on the big ships. Shortly after the fleet resumed its station in port in the wake of the Battle of Jutland—or the Skagerrak, as the Germans preferred to call it—in 1916, morale declined once again. In part, this was doubtless due to the dawning realization among many that, whatever the tactical successes that had been won at Jutland, there was virtually no hope of defeating the British in a general fleet engagement.

8

Even among the enlisted men, many must have realized that the High Sea Fleet had been lucky to escape a severe mauling at Jutland and that another action on a similar scale was likely to be the German fleet's last. Thus, while subsequent sorties might bring temporary improvements in the morale of some sailors, among others there arose the distressing feeling that further effort and sacrifice on their part would not materially affect the outcome of the war. If the latter were to be won at all, it would be won with the submarine or with the might of the German army, not with the battle fleet.

The growing gap between officers and men on the big ships was likewise detrimental to morale. The executive officers continued to draw different, more varied rations than those provided the men, which caused considerable resentment within the fleet. In addition, the departure of the best junior officers to the submarine force meant that those who remained were generally the less able. This was particularly distressing, for the inexperienced junior officers, who were crucial to the maintenance of discipline, often covered their insecurity by an exaggerated display of caste pride or by an overly rigid insistence on the minutiae of military detail.[28] In the face of these problems—frustration resulting from Germany's desperate war situation, hunger resulting from war-induced rationing, and resentment resulting from continuing displays of arrogance—morale within the fleet sank to new levels as the war dragged on.

By the summer of 1917, the situation was serious. In June, a hunger strike protesting the wretched food and miserable living conditions broke out aboard the battleship *Prinzregent Luitpold* and soon spread to other vessels of the fleet. The strike assumed political overtones as representatives of the disgruntled sailors took up contacts with the Independent Social Democratic Party (USPD), whose members had split from the Majority Socialists (SPD) and were working for an immediate end to the war. As measure provoked countermeasure, the striking sailors and the representatives of the navy found themselves driven to extreme positions. On August 2, 1917, the navy played its trump card and arrested the leaders of the "mutiny." After a hasty court martial, five men were convicted of giving aid to a foreign power and of "treasonable incitement to rebellion." Anxious for "a few death sentences," Admiral Scheer confirmed the sentence of two men, Seaman Max Reichpietsch and Stoker Albin Köbis. Both men were executed on September 5, 1917.[29]

The navy was severely shaken by the events of the summer of 1917, and in the year that followed, the high command responded with a number of measures intended to bolster morale. Rations were improved temporarily, only to decline again.[30] In addition, the reassignment of part of the High Sea Fleet to the Baltic enabled the navy to carry out the highly publicized but relatively insignificant seizure of the islands of Moon, Oesel, and Dagö in the Gulf of Riga from the weaker Russians. Morale within the fleet temporarily rebounded at this success, but there was a limit to the number of islands that could be taken in this fashion, particularly after Russia, Germany's sole enemy in the Baltic, officially left the war in March 1918.[31]

A measure which promised more success was the navy's effort at "patriotic instruction." Selected speakers sought to school the enlisted men on the reasons why Germany was fighting the war and why continued vigilance on the part of the fleet was necessary. Initial efforts of this sort were made by speakers from the Fatherland Party and other super-patriotic organizations, but the results left much to be desired, for the war-weary crews were usually put off by the bravado of the civilian speakers. Later, the executive officers attempted to provide the requisite instruction, but they were handicapped by their ignorance of political matters, their inexperience at public speaking, and, in some cases, their apathy.[32] A typical case of attempted patriotic instruction involved daily readings from a biography of Friedrich II—hardly the most enthralling of topics for the average seaman—and one critic of such erudition termed the ordeal a "four to five o'clock love thy fatherland" course.[33] Despite isolated successes which, along with the more numerous failures, would provide ample food for thought for young officers in the postwar navy, the overall results were disappointing.

Other adjustments were outwardly more promising. In the late summer of 1918, the navy at last undertook the long-overdue consolidation of its many independent commands into a unified structure, the Seekriegsleitung, under the leadership of Scheer. The new office effectively removed Wilhelm II from active command, thereby illustrating how far the relationship between the Supreme War Lord and his officer corps had deteriorated since the halcyon days of 1900. The navy also announced the "Scheer Program," which was intended to produce submarines in unprecedented numbers and, in conscious imitation of the army's successful "Hindenburg Program," to redirect public attention to the importance of the navy. In truth, however, both of these efforts were palpable eleventh-hour measures. Neither could conceal that fact that, with the failure of the submarine offensive, Germany's last hope lay not at sea but with the armies on the Western Front. In March 1918 Germany's new masters, Field Marshal Paul von Hindenburg and General Erich Ludendorff, had launched a final, desperate offensive to defeat the British and French before the waxing strength of the Americans became decisive. When this push spent itself, and when the army at last began to retreat in July 1918, it was evident that Germany's bid had failed and that peace negotiations would have to be undertaken under conditions highly unfavorable for the fatherland. These were initiated in the fall of 1918 by the new chancellor, the liberal Prince Max of Baden, amid growing signs of collapse both at home and at the front. Indeed, so desperate was the Reich's situation that it was widely rumored that the army might attempt to soften the Allies' terms by offering major concessions at the expense of the navy.[34]

It was this frightening prospect—a peace bought by the surrender of the fleet—that apparently spurred at least two of the navy's spokesmen into action. On October 5, Captain William Michaelis, director of the

Navy's Central Office, proposed a final sortie into the North Sea by the fleet. Perhaps, he argued, a success against the British would bolster morale at home and enable the Reich to fight on until the Allies offered better terms. Admittedly, Michaelis continued, the odds were against the fleet, but in view of the catastrophe staring Germany in the face, he felt that the risks were worth taking.[35]

Michaelis was not the only one who favored last-minute heroics. The very next day, the chief of staff of the High Sea Fleet, Rear Admiral Adolf von Trotha, proposed a similar course of action to the one Michaelis had suggested. For the moment, he admitted, there were still some arguments in favor of withholding the fleet. A "fleet in being," he maintained, served as a "backbone" for the U-boats in the event that Germany continued unrestricted submarine warfare, for the mere existence of the capital ships protected the minesweepers which, in turn, kept the seaways open for the departure and return of the submarines. But under other circumstances it would be possible, indeed necessary, for the "big ships" to make one last sortie against the Allies. If the Anglo-American navies attempted to penetrate the Helgoland Bight, or if the Reich were compelled to abandon unrestricted submarine warfare as a precondition to armistice negotiations, then a general sortie by the surface vessels might be undertaken. It might also be possible, Trotha averred, for the capital ships to inflict more damage upon the British than the submarines could. But in the end, none of these considerations was paramount in Trotha's view. Far more important than the present military considerations were the long-term advantages to be derived from a climactic battle to the death on the high seas. As Trotha concluded:

[S]uch a battle constitutes the most important goal for the fleet, in order that this war does not end without the national force embodied in the fleet having its full effect.

Even if it is a fatal struggle in this war, a future German fleet will emerge from an honorable fight if the German nation remains true to itself. For a fleet shackled by a humiliating peace, the future is lost.[36]

Trotha submitted his plan to the Seekriegsleitung on October 8, along with a covering letter expressing his fear that the fleet might be delivered to the British without having struck a final blow. In response, Captain Magnus von Levetzow, chief of staff of the Seekriegsleitung, reassured Trotha that the fleet would never be surrendered as long as it could still fight. Levetzow approved contingency plans for a sortie into the Dover Straits. At the same time, he emphasized the immediate need to keep the fleet where it was in order to assure the continued prosecution of the submarine campaign. On October 20, this last obstacle to the active deployment of the surface fleet was removed when the Reich announced its willingness to terminate unrestricted submarine warfare. The Seekriegsleitung was ready with its justification for eleventh-hour heroics. In language bearing the unmistakable imprint of Trotha's suggestions of October 6, it argued:

> It is impossible for the fleet to remain inactive in the final battles that might precede an armistice. The fleet must be used. Even if it is unlikely that the course of events will be affected, from a moral standpoint it is a matter of the honor and existence of the navy that it did its utmost in the last battle.[37]

Once adopted, the notion of a fight to the finish obsessed the high command. In the face of pleas from Prince Max that the armed forces refrain from any provocative actions that might disturb negotiations with the Allies, the Seekriegsleitung gave its solemn promise of compliance—and then proceeded to complete its plans for a sortie.[38] The definitive orders were issued on October 24, with the envisioned action to take place on October 30. No effort was to be spared to make this a memorable occasion, and the naval high command, in the midst of what has been termed a "Thermopylae mentality," contemplated inviting the Kaiser to accompany the fleet on its death ride.[39] In the end, Wilhelm probably declined this honor; if the fleet were to put to sea, it would have to do so without the company of its Leonidas.

It soon became evident that the navy lacked the other requisite Spartans as well. As early as October 27, as rumors of the impending operation began to spread from the excited executive officers to the enlisted men, isolated cases of disobedience were reported aboard individual ships of the fleet. In spite of this ominous sign, the squadron commanders were summoned to Admiral Franz Ritter von Hipper's flagship on October 29 to receive their final briefing for the next day's operation. Shortly after their arrival, word followed that disorders had broken out on three of the five battleships of the Third Battle Squadron and that the sailors refused to take the ships out to sea. Faced with this disturbing news, Hipper, the new fleet chief, weighed the matter and finally announced that no sortie could be undertaken. The next day, in an apparent effort to halt the spreading disorder, he signed an address to the crews disclaiming any intention of undertaking offensive action and reassuring them of the peaceful intentions of the officers. Hipper also attempted to defuse the situation by dispersing the fleet among the ports of the North Sea and Baltic. This had the unintended effect of spreading the contagion. The vacillating behavior of the officers—here threatening to punish disobedience, there promising amelioration of grievances and a prompt end to the war—only exacerbated the situation.[40]

Worse was still to come. In the early November days that followed the dispersal of the fleet, the spirit of rebellion spread from ship to ship, from the fleet to the ports, and from the ports to the interior of the Reich. Everywhere sailors appeared at the forefront of what was by now a revolutionary tide engulfing Germany. The overwhelming majority of the executive officers chose the better part of valor and either disappeared from their commands or acquiesced in the new situation.[41]

The engineers likewise appear to have offered little opposition, but, curiously enough, some of the deck officers, with much less of a stake in the hitherto existing order than the other two groups, did try to resist the revolutionary sailors.[42] On November 9, Admiral Scheer informed his Kaiser that the navy could no longer be relied upon. Wilhelm replied that the Service had deserted him quite nicely and dismissed the admiral with the words: "I no longer have a navy."[43] That same day, the last Hohenzollern ruler left for Holland and for exile. Two days later, representatives of the German Reich, now an infant republic, signed the Armistice at Compiègne.

The events of late October and early November left champions of the navy stunned and humiliated. Admiral Scheer captured the mood of the executive officers best when he wrote: "A curse lies on the navy because out of its ranks revolution first spread over the land."[44] Others tried to exculpate the navy of responsibility for Germany's collapse. Some blamed the mutinies on the clever seduction of a few enlisted men by the Socialists or the Bolsheviks and alleged that the government's vacillating attitude toward the agitators had prevented the navy from proceeding against them. Grand Admiral Prince Heinrich blamed the débâcle on British bribery of the mutineers.[45] Perhaps the most imaginative explanation was that offered by a future commander-in-chief of the navy, then Captain Erich Raeder, who attributed the revolution to deserters, draftees, and reservists from the army. Admittedly, Raeder continued, a few sailors had deserted, but their appearance had attracted undue attention. In fact, many of the "sailors" were not really sailors at all, for other people, "frequently criminal elements," had donned naval uniforms "to gain acceptance into the revolutionary movement." Thus, Raeder concluded, the navy was really blameless in all that had happened.[46]

In truth, the explanation for the disorders within the fleet and within Germany in the fall of 1918 was somewhat more complex than the naval officers would allow. There were, indeed, contacts between enlisted men and representatives of the political left, but these appear to have played only an incidental role in the initial troubles that beset the fleet in late October.[47] Far more important was the general feeling of war-weariness that permeated virtually all segments of German society, the navy included, by 1918. Equally significant was the general air of expectancy, compounded by rumors of an impending armistice, which began to grip Germany with the appointment of Prince Max to the chancellorship. Together, the widespread war-weariness and the general anticipation of change made the situation in Germany a potentially explosive one by the fall of 1918. The disorders within the fleet merely triggered the explosion.

Yet why was it that the débâcle occurred first within the navy and not elsewhere? In part, one could argue that its was simply bad luck that the disorders should break out in late October, just after personnel changes associated with the creation of the Seekriegsleitung and the traditional biennial or triennial transfer of officers to new commands had left almost half of the big ships of the fleet with either new captains or new first officers.[48] On each of these ships, and particularly on those with both a new captain and a new first officer, the normal flow of orders and the smooth enforcement of discipline were bound to suffer until officers and men could become accustomed to one another. Had the initial disruptions occurred two months earlier or two months later, defenders of the navy could argue, they would have found virtually no support within the fleet and would have been swiftly mastered without further repercussions.

Such an explanation, however, neglects a number of factors. In the first place, the enlisted men's long-standing grievances concerning the deplorable food and the miserable living conditions had largely been allowed to go unanswered since the first danger signals had become evident in the summer of 1917. Likewise, the chasm that separated the executive officers from the rest of the navy remained unbridged. The executive officer corps continued in its splendid isolation unaware of and unconcerned with the problems of the engineers, the deck officers, or the ratings. It was precisely this isolation, reinforced by the presence of unfamiliar officers aboard ship owing to the fall transfers, which made it possible for rumors to circulate among the enlisted men that the new chancellor wanted peace but that the officers wanted war.[49] Apparent confirmation of these rumors was provided when news of the fleet sortie leaked out to the enlisted men in late October. Yet to the very end, an appreciation of the real state of affairs within the fleet evidently escaped the higher-placed executive officers. The problems of the rest of the navy appeared to be inconsequential to the canons of the corps. For men of the stamp of Scheer, Trotha, and Levetzow, orders were orders, to be issued and obeyed without question. It was a notion attractive in its simplicity, but one which neglected a fundamental consideration of leadership. As one of Trotha's subordinates, Lieutenant Commander Bogislav von Selchow, expressed it in the case of his superior, "the Chief of Staff thinks one just has to issue an order . . . . In truth, it always takes two to execute an order: namely, one to command—he is very important—and one to obey; he is important too."[50]

The events of late October and early November graphically demonstrated the accuracy of Selchow's observation. In the ensuing two and a half decades, under democratic republic and totalitarian dictatorship, Germany's naval officers would have ample time to consider how better to exercise the art of *Menschenführung* in the light of the Service's débâcle in the autumn of 1918. For the moment, however, it remained only for the *Marineoffiziere* to recognize the changed circumstances of navy and Reich. It was Wilhelm II, who had once styled himself the "Admiral of the Atlantic," who took the final, melancholy step toward facing the new reality. On November 28, 1918, the Kaiser released all his naval and military personnel from their oath of allegiance to the Crown.[51] With this act, the history of the Imperial Navy came officially to a close. What lay ahead for the

Service not even the most prescient of officers could have professed to know.

Notes for Chapter 1

1   Cited in Karl Erich Born, "Die Politischen Testamente Friedrichs des Grossen," in *Seemacht und Geschichte: Festschrift zum 80. Geburtstag von Friedrich Ruge* (Bonn–Bad Godesberg, 1975), p. 23.

2   Adolf von Trotha, who entered the navy in 1886, remembered that when one of his fellow applicants was unable to master even the very simple entrance examination, he was allowed to enter the navy on a trial basis. He never took the exam and eventually rose to the rank of captain. See Helmut Schubert, "Admiral Adolf von Trotha (1868–1940). Ein Versuch zur historisch-psychologischen Biographik" (PhD dissertation, University of Freiburg, 1976), p. 244.

3   Trotha, for example, expressed precisely this hope on Wilhelm's accession to the throne. Ibid., p. 93.

4   For Tirpitz's role in the construction of the fleet, see Volker R. Berghahn, *Der Tirpitz-Plan, Genesis und Verfall einer innenpolitischen Krisenstrategie unter Wilhelm II* (Düsseldorf, 1971), which modifies and in some cases supersedes Jonathan Steinberg's *Yesterday's Deterrent: Tirpitz and the Birth of the German Battle Fleet* (London, 1965). The German naval command structure in the Imperial period was complicated by the system of *Immediatstellungen* (literally, "immediate positions"), whereby heads of important naval offices were responsible directly and exclusively to the Kaiser. From 1899 until the outbreak of the First World War, the Imperial Naval Office was only one of eight such *Immediatstellungen*. Nevertheless, due to his personal influence over the Kaiser, his undeniable organizational ability, and the increasing esteem in which the German public held him, Tirpitz's position as state secretary of the Naval Office enabled him to play a far greater role in German naval affairs than the technical limits of the Naval Office would indicate. For this, see Holger H. Herwig, *The German Naval Officer Corps: A Social and Political History, 1890–1918* (Oxford, 1973), pp. 26–27.

5   For this, see Wilhelm Deist, *Flottenpolitik und Flottenpropaganda: Das Nachrichtenbureau des Reichsmarineamtes 1897–1914* (Stuttgart, 1976). Among those who gained useful experience at the Navy Bureau was the future commander of the navy, Erich Raeder.

6   "Die Ansprache Seiner Majestät des Kaisers an die Offiziere der Garnison Berlin am 1. Januar 1900," quoted in Herwig, *Naval Officer Corps*, p. 18.

7   As will be seen, the Imperial Navy included several corps of officers. The most important of these, from a numerical standpoint and from the standpoint of setting trends within the navy, was the *Seeoffizierkorps*. In keeping with the practice begun elsewhere for the Imperial period (see ibid., p. 68, n. 1), I have employed the term "executive officers" for *Seeoffiziere* of all ranks. For variety's sake I have also occasionally used the terms "the naval officer corps" or simply "the naval officers" to apply to the *Seeoffiziere*. Other corps such as the naval engineer officer corps or deck officers are referred to by their exact branch. The naval doctors and the naval infantry officers, who constituted separate officer corps, have largely been ignored in previous studies and, with isolated exceptions,

will not figure prominently in this study either. The naval doctors shared about the same prestige of service and presumably the same social outlook as the executive officers. See Erich Raeder, *Mein Leben*, 2 vols (Tübingen, 1956–1957), 1, pp. 176–177. The naval infantry officers also shared roughly the same rights and privileges that the executive officers enjoyed. See Werner Bräckow, *Die Geschichte des deutschen Marine-Ingenieuroffizierkorps* (Oldenburg and Hamburg, 1974), p. 110.

8   Schubert, "Adolf von Trotha," p. 142.

9   This and the following four paragraphs are based on Herwig, *Naval Officer Corps*, pp. 37–101.

10 Memorandum of station meeting, March 15, 1912, quoted in ibid., p. 87. It is worth noting, however, that in their one friendly fencing duel with their army counterparts, the naval officers came off a poor second best. Ibid., p. 86, n. 1. Friedrich Ruge, who entered the navy in 1914, remembers seeing a duel which, if typical, would explain why no rematches were scheduled. The participants were distinctly unskilled at their dangerous sport. Friedrich Ruge, *In vier Marinen* (Munich, 1979), p. 24.

11 The phrase is from Herwig, *Naval Officer Corps*, p. 72.

12 For this, see Paul M. Kennedy, *The Rise of the Anglo-German Antagonism 1860–1914* (London, 1980), especially pp. 313–314, 415–424; also Herwig, *Naval Officer Corps*, p. 92.

13 Herwig, *Naval Officer Corps*, pp. 95–98.

14 This and the following paragraph rely on ibid., pp. 102–133, 155–163 and Bräckow, *Marine-Ingenieuroffizierkorps, passim*. For one engineer officer's experiences from the late imperial period to the National Socialist era, see Helmut Fechter, "Admiral Hans Fechter," (Manuscript, Kempten, West Germany, 1979). Herr Fechter graciously permitted me to use his biographical sketch of his father in May, 1979, before it was added to the holdings of the Bundesarchiv-Militärarchiv in Freiburg.

15 Fechter, "Hans Fechter," p. 17.

16 For the history of the deck officers, see Bund der Deckoffiziere, *Deckoffiziere der Deutschen Marine; Ihre Geschichte 1848–1933* (Berlin, 1933); and briefly, but more critically, Herwig, *Naval Officer Corps*, pp. 134–153, 163–173.

17 The two most important organizations of this nature were the Committee of Seven (Siebener Ausschuss), founded in 1910, and the Union of Retired Deck Officers (Bund der Deckoffiziere a.D.), founded in 1912. Herwig, *Naval Officer Corps*, p. 142.

18 See Schubert, "Adolf von Trotha," p. 271.

19 For Tirpitz's actions and the executive officer corps' changing attitudes toward the Kaiser and Bethmann Hollweg, see Herwig, *Naval Officer Corps*, pp. 177–184; also Wilhelm Deist, "Die Politik der Seekriegsleitung und die Rebellion der Flotte Ende Oktober 1918," *Vierteljahrshefte für Zeitgeschichte*, 14 (October 1966), pp. 342–343.

20 Two engineer officers in particular distinguished themselves. Hans Fechter and a Marine-Ingenieur Rhinow were singled out for meritorious service aboard U-boats and awarded the Knight's Cross of the House of Hohenzollern with Swords. This was an exceedingly rare distinction for the two engineers. Their respective commanders, it should be added, were awarded the still higher *Pour le mérite* with Swords. Bräckow, *Marine-Ingenieuroffizierkorps*, p. 129.

21 Herwig, *Naval Officer Corps*, pp. 155–163.

22 Ibid., pp. 163–173.
23 For a telling account of the war as seen through the eyes of one enlisted man, see Daniel Horn (ed.), *War, Mutiny and Revolution in the German Navy: The World War I Diary of Seaman Richard Stumpf* (New Brunswick, NJ, 1967).
24 Herwig, *Naval Officer Corps*, pp. 93–94, 199–200.
25 See Richard Stumpf's entries in his diary in the wake of the Battle of the Skagerrak in Horn, *Richard Stumpf*, pp. 195, 204; also Daniel Horn, *The German Naval Mutinies of World War I* (New Brunswick, NJ, 1969), pp. 23, 31; also Raeder, *Mein Leben*, 1, p. 134.
26 Herwig, *Naval Officer Corps*, pp. 191–192.
27 Fechter, "Hans Fechter," p. 22. Ashore, the personal relations between Engineer Fechter and his commander, Lothar von Arnauld de la Perière, assumed a more formal level. Ibid., p. 23.
28 Herwig, *Naval Officer Corps*, pp. 191–192, 201.
29 A detailed account of the events of the summer of 1917 is given in Horn, *German Naval Mutinies*, pp. 94–168. For conflicting views of the disturbances, see Ulrich Czisnik, "Die Unruhen in der Marine 1917/18," *Marine-Rundschau*, 67 (1970), pp. 641–664; and Wilhelm Deist, "Die Unruhen in der Marine 1917/18," *Marine-Rundschau*, 68 (1971), pp. 325–343.
30 Horn, *German Naval Mutinies*, pp. 188, 195.
31 Herwig, *Naval Officer Corps*, pp. 224–226.
32 For the efforts of the army and the navy to implement "patriotic instruction," see Wilhelm Deist, *Militär und Innenpolitik im Weltkrieg*, 2 vols (Düsseldorf, 1970), 2, pp. 805–985, especially 911–918, 959–961; also Herwig, *Naval Officer Corps*, pp. 209–210; 224–227.
33 Ruge, *In vier Marinen*, pp. 71–72; Herwig, *Naval Officer Corps*, p. 210.
34 Deist, "Politik der Seekriegsleitung," pp. 343–345, 352.
35 Ibid., p. 353.
36 Ibid., pp. 352–353.
37 Ibid., pp. 353–355.
38 Ibid., p. 357. For the position of the government, see Prinz Max of Baden, *Erinnerungen und Dokumente* (Stuttgart, 1968), pp. 529–531.
39 The phrase "Thermopylae mentality" is from Gerhard Schreiber, "Zur Kontinuität des Gross- und Weltmachtstrebens der deutschen Marineführung," *Militärgeschictliche Mitteilungen*, 2/1979, p. 108. See also Deist, "Politik der Seekriegsleitung," pp. 360–361; also Herwig, *Naval Officer Corps*, pp. 247–250.
40 Deist, "Politik der Seekriegsleitung," pp. 361–366.
41 Horn, *German Naval Mutinies*, p. 245, lists only five executive officers who were killed in the wake of the November revolution.
42 Herwig, *Naval Officer Corps*, pp. 260–261.
43 Alfred Niemann, *Revolution von Oben—Umsturz von Unten: Entwicklung und Verlauf der Staatsumwälzung in Deutschland 1914–1918* (Berlin, 1927), p. 414; Reinhard Scheer, *Deutschlands Hochseeflotte im Weltkrieg* (Berlin, 1920), p. 499.
44 Scheer, *Hochseeflotte*, p. 499.
45 Schubert, "Adolf von Trotha," p. 219; Niemann, *Revolution von Oben*, pp. 386–387; Herwig, *Naval Officer Corps*, p. 259.
46 Raeder, *Mein Leben*, 1, pp. 150–151.
47 Deist, "Politik der Seekriegsleitung," pp. 362–363.

48 Deist indicates that in the three battleship squadrons and in the three reconnaissance groups, 48.4 per cent of the ships' captains and 45.4 per cent of the first officers had changed assignments between August and November 1918. Ibid., pp. 347–348.
49 Schubert, "Adolf von Trotha," p. 219.
50 Cited in Deist, "Politik der Seekriegsleitung," p. 365.
51 Herwig, *Naval Officer Corps*, p. 264.

2

The Weimar Legacy, 1918–28

The days that followed the Kaiser's abdication on November 9 were traumatic for Germany and the navy.[1] That same day Prince Max relinquished the office of Reich Chancellor to Friedrich Ebert, the parliamentary leader of the Majority Socialists (SPD). Control of the government was assumed by a committee of six Peoples' Commissars, which was headed by Ebert and which included three Majority Socialists and three Independent Socialists (USPD). Given Germany's state of military collapse, however, the government was powerless to implement its vision of a republic. It was in fact divided against itself, with the Majority Socialists pursuing a moderate pro-Western style parliamentary course, while the Independents favored a mixture of revisionist and revolutionary tactics that placed considerable emphasis on the workers' and soldiers' councils that were appearing throughout Germany and the front. To the left of both Socialist parties and outside the government were the Spartacists, who, it was feared, would attempt to emulate the Bolsheviks in Russia and launch a "second" revolution against the new Provisional Government. To the political right were the yet to be defined forces of the counterrevolution. While for the moment in disarray, they nevertheless might eventually be expected to try to undo the results of the November revolution and return Germany to a more authoritarian mode of government in the form of a royalist restoration or a military dictatorship. The prospect of civil war, then, loomed large, and each faction was busily recruiting armed support among the increasingly leaderless soldiers and sailors.

The navy stood in equally desperate straits. By the end of the first week of November, rebellious sailors had removed all but a few officers at Kiel from their commands. Elsewhere, officers remained in their positions only at the sufferance of their men. Effective command at the Naval Office in Berlin, at the various naval bases, and on most of the larger vessels of the fleet—in so far as authority could be said to exist at all—was being exercised by hastily formed councils of sailors.[2] To many observers, the wholesale abolition of the naval officer corps appeared to be the next order of the day.

Salvation from chaos for the Majority Socialists as well as the navy came from an unexpected source. Ordinarily, the army high command could have been expected to oppose all manifestations of revolution, but in these extraordinary times the army's spokesmen decided to close ranks with what they perceived to be the lesser evil, the Majority Socialists, in order to combat the greater threat from the extreme left. On the evening of November 10, scarcely twenty-four hours after Wilhelm II's abdication, General Wilhelm Groener, Ludendorff's successor as First Quartermaster-General, telephoned Ebert to inform him that the army was prepared to support the new government. In return, Groener demanded, the government was to aid the officer corps to maintain military discipline, to secure provisions for the army, and to keep the railways open to enable the troops to return from the front. Most importantly, Groener emphasized, the government was expected to combat any Bolshevik (that is, Spartacist) inspired uprisings. Within a matter of minutes, Ebert agreed to Groener's demands. In so doing he also paved the way for the eventual restoration of order within the navy, for the prestige of the new Socialist government could be expected to garner respect from the various sailors' councils. Even in the best of circumstances, however, it would be months before order could be restored completely.[3]

In the meantime, the navy endured further tribulations. On November 21, the "humiliating end" to the fleet that Admiral von Trotha had sought to prevent in late October became reality: the bulk of the High Sea Fleet was delivered to the British, pending the signing of a definitive peace treaty between Germany and the Allies. Admiral von Hipper expressed the somber mood of the officer corps that day when he sighed that his heart was breaking.[4] Shortly thereafter, both he and Scheer left the navy for ever. Their example was a compelling one, and many others soon joined the exodus from the corps. Some were unable to reconcile their royalist convictions with service in a republican navy. Others were discouraged by the dismal prospects of serving in a navy that would soon be reduced to minuscule importance.

Worse was still to come. Scarcely had the navy recovered from the surrender of the fleet when the activities of the Volksmarine Division underlined just how badly discipline had deteriorated. The Volksmarine Division had originally been recruited in early November from among sailors in Berlin and Cuxhaven to protect the Provisional Government.[5] The unit had promptly broken with the Majority Socialists and gradually drifted into the camp of the leftist opposition. Concurrently, the influence of the few moderate officers who had originally cast their lot with the division diminished. Throughout late November and early December, the situation in Berlin worsened as minor incidents between the sailors and government troops threatened to erupt into open conflict. On December 18, the tension increased as leaders of the Volksmarine Division and other soldiers' representatives passed a number of resolutions known as the Hamburg Provisions at the First Congress of Workers' and Soldiers' Councils. These provisions called for the abolition of rank insignia, the election of officers, and the vesting of supreme command of the armed forces in the Provisional

Government, but subject to the control of a central soldiers' council. Prodded by the army and the navy high command, Ebert managed to exempt the more important units of the armed forces, the navy included, from these resolutions, but this in no way eased the situation.[6]

On Christmas Eve, another incident led to a bloody clash between the Volksmarine Division and the army's Garde Kavallerie Schützen Division. To the surprise of many who had witnessed the sailors' decided lack of enthusiasm for fighting the British in October, the sailors defeated and disarmed their opponents.[7] The admirals, though, could take no solace in the belated fighting spirit of the men, for by now it was clear that the sailors were completely out of control. To many, indeed, it must have appeared as if the Volksmarine Division was about to initiate the dreaded "second" revolution. It was on this gloomy note that the momentous year 1918 ended.

The new year witnessed the navy at its nadir. In early January, Admiral Ernst Ritter von Mann, secretary of the Naval Office, joined the long list of officers who had left the navy by announcing his retirement on the grounds of "ill health."[8] It is more likely that he was simply exhausted by the current necessity of mediating between the demands of the sailors' councils and those of the increasingly frustrated officers. For those officers who did elect to stay on, however, the first faint signs of improvement in the navy's situation were becoming evident at the very hour of the Service's deepest discontent. Already, on December 27, two personalities who would contribute substantially to the navy's reconstruction, Gustav Noske and Adolf von Trotha, had arrived in Berlin on the same train.[9] Perhaps it was fitting that they came from Kiel, where, after all, the revolution had first spread from the fleet to the rest of Germany. Now it was also from Kiel that the nemesis of the revolution would come.

Noske was no stranger to the navy. In the decade preceding the German Revolution, he had acquired a reputation as the Social Democratic Party's leading expert on military and naval affairs; he was generally viewed as a moderate in naval circles. When the November unrest erupted in Kiel, he had been sent there by the government of Prince Max to try to stabilize the situation. Arriving too late to save the day for the chancellor or the princely houses of Germany, Noske eventually succeeded in restoring order in the city and in channeling the energy of the local workers' and sailors' councils along lines more acceptable to the cautious Majority Socialists. While in Kiel, Noske had also impressed a number of naval officers with his recognition of the need to restore military discipline.[10]

On December 28, the day after Noske's arrival in Berlin, the Independent Socialists left the Provisional Government in protest over Ebert's conciliatory policies toward the military. The next day, Noske became a member of the Cabinet with responsibility for military and naval matters. During the next year, as the Republic gradually put its affairs in order, he would become Provisional Reichswehr Minister and later the Republic's first regular Reichswehr Minister.

Among the first tasks facing Noske was the selection of a new head of the navy. After Mann's retirement from the Naval Office, rumors abounded that the more leftward leaning members of the Majority Socialists would force one of their candidates into the position. From the viewpoint of most active officers, these candidates, known collectively as the "three P's," Captain Eduard von Pustau, Captain Lothar Persius, and Lieutenant-Commander Hans Paasche, were the worst imaginable, for they had committed the unforgivable acts of leaving the Service and joining the political left. Paasche and Persius had gone so far as to embrace pacifism; Persius had compounded his error by writing "lurid exposés" of conditions within the Imperial Navy. To forestall the nomination of one of these men, Captain Erich Raeder, head of the Central Bureau of the Naval Office, visited Noske in January and stressed the desirability of having an active officer who enjoyed the confidence of the officer corps assume Mann's post. Raeder added that Adolf von Trotha, currently head of the Personnel Office and whom Noske knew from Kiel, was just such a man.[11] Although Trotha was known to be a monarchist and was doubly suspect to many because of the role he had played in the abortive plans for the fleet sortie the previous October, Noske was nevertheless receptive. He encouraged Raeder to discuss the matter with Ebert. The latter also promised to study the matter carefully, and while it is impossible to determine whether Raeder's intervention was decisive, the choice eventually fell upon Trotha.[12] To avoid needlessly antagonizing the sailors' councils, which continued to view former high-ranking imperial officers with great suspicion, it was decided to delay the announcement of Trotha's appointment until mid-March.[13] By then, if all went well, there would be no more councils to worry about. In the meantime, Noske would carry on alone.

Noske moved with characteristic energy in approaching the first of his tasks, the internal reconstruction of the navy. The sailors' councils were a prime target of his attention. In a series of power plays, he completed the process of emasculation that Ebert had initiated the previous December when he had exempted the navy from the Hamburg Provisions. On January 19, a government decree restored the exclusive command authority of officers in the army and navy; on February 2, the Central Committee, a steering organization for the larger "Council of 53," was disbanded. At about the same time, Noske, acting on the assumption that smaller bodies would be easier to control, informed the "Council of 53" that henceforth living allowances would be provided for only six representatives. Thereafter, the new council and its local counterparts were allowed to wither on the vine. Many of their functions were assumed by the new *Vertrauensleute* (ombudsmen). These were elected by the men and took part in the formulation of policies dealing with such matters as pay, food, clothing, and living conditions; their prerogatives did not, however, extend to purely military matters. While vestiges of the original councils lingered on until February 1920, when the Treasury stopped all support for them, the danger of a command system *à la russe* had long since disappeared.[14]

In March, further steps were taken toward the restoration of the navy. On March 26, Trotha's appointment as Chief of the Admiralty, as the head of the navy was now styled, at last became public. Two days later, Noske introduced the Provisional Navy Bill to the National Assembly. The bill vested supreme command in the hands of the Reich President, acting through the Reichswehr Minister and the Chief of the Admiralty. It stipulated that the navy was to be built on a democratic basis and composed of personnel from the old navy who had continued serving since the revolution as well as from qualified volunteers. It envisioned the immediate promotion of proven deck officers and noncommissioned officers to officer's rank, adding that in future the officer corps would be open to all members of the navy on the basis of ability and merit. Although the Bill was opposed by the Independent Socialists, who protested the continued presence of former imperial officers in a republican navy, it passed without undue difficulty the same day it was introduced and went into effect on April 16, 1919.[15] The Bill was of symbolic as well as practical importance. Following the elimination of the influence of the soldiers' councils, it offered more moderate critics reassuring evidence that the navy was indeed adapting itself to the changed political circumstances in Germany, and that the former exclusivity of the officer corps was about to disappear. To the officer corps, the Bill was just as significant, though for slightly different reasons. If diehards regretted concessions to the aspirations of the noncommissioned officers and the enlisted men, if they continued to doubt the wisdom of placing supreme command of the armed forces in the hands of an elected civilian, they could nevertheless be consoled that the legislators had concerned themselves with the navy at all. Indeed, this was perhaps the ultimate significance of the Provisional Navy Bill: it offered the first faint sign that republican Germany would have a navy, albeit a small one. Perhaps the experience gained at such effort and expense during the previous half century might yet be saved.

Unfortunately for advocates of German sea power, by the time the Provisional Navy Bill became law, the decision for or against a navy was no longer entirely in German hands. In May 1919, the Allies at last confronted the Reich with their demands concerning the armed forces. The clauses pertaining to the navy were severe.[16] Allied insistence that Germany assume full responsibility for the world war and deliver Wilhelm II and an as yet unspecified number of army and navy commanders for trial as war criminals offended the honor of the officer corps. Other restrictions threatened the professional interests of the corps, for the treaty limited the Service to a maximum strength of 13,500 noncommissioned officers and enlisted men and a mere 1,500 officers and deck officers. Conscription was forbidden. Volunteers had to enlist for twelve years in the case of the enlisted men and for twenty-five years in the case of officers, which effectively precluded the creation of a reserve.

Nor were the Allies generous in meeting the matériel needs of the navy. The treaty prohibited the possession of submarines and aircraft, and it limited the surface fleet to six small battleships, six cruisers, twelve destroyers, and twelve torpedo-boats.[17] Restrictions as to the maximum displacement for each class of vessel—which were far below the displacements of comparable vessels of other navies—further reduced the fleet's effectiveness. In spite of the severity of these stipulations, neither Noske nor Trotha could find an alternative to accepting them. On June 28, 1919, German representatives signed the Treaty of Versailles and thereby reduced their navy from second to eighth among the world's powers. It could easily have been worse. The Allies might have followed the example that they set for Germany's air force and abolished the navy altogether, or they might have assented to the Scheidemann Cabinet's suggestion that the Reich renounce its right to build the six battleships in return for more lenient terms for the army. As it was, the negotiations at Versailles left the Republic with a navy that would have done honor to almost any South American nation.[18]

The Treaty of Versailles was a bitter pill for Noske and Trotha to swallow. In the months that followed Versailles, however, the two men could at least console themselves that the formal restructuring of the navy was at last nearing completion. In August, the adoption and implementation of the Weimar Constitution promised to solidify the democratic basis that the Provisional Assembly had foreseen in March for the navy by requiring that all members of the armed forces take an oath to the new constitution.[19] In addition, the constitution broke new ground by abolishing military justice, which had been a source of some abuse in the imperial era, in all cases save in time of war and aboard ships at sea. The latter exception was inserted at the insistence of Trotha, who argued that a vessel's long absence from home port might make recourse to civilian courts difficult.[20] Although in other matters the constitution touched the navy only remotely, the relative ease with which its provisions were accepted suggested that the navy and the nation were coming into closer conformity.[21] Only Article 178, which added the unpleasant stipulation that the constitution could in no way alter the provisions of the Treaty of Versailles, reminded naval leaders of the Service's humiliations over the past year. In any case, whatever doubts may have existed concerning the wisdom of accepting either the Treaty of Versailles or the Weimar Constitution were largely forgotten in the fall as the navy entered a final round of administrative reorganization.

Unlike the changes of the spring and summer, which had been prompted in considerable measure by the demands of "outsiders"—the enlisted men, the noncommissioned officers, the new republican legislators, or the Allies—the autumn reforms were mostly the result of pressure from within the officer corps. In the course of the Great War, many engineer officers and not a few of the younger executive officers had recognized the danger that the navy's divided officer corps posed to the effective discharge of duty; in the year following Germany's collapse, a number of proposals suggesting a greater degree of unity among the various branches of the naval officer corps had been submitted to the high command. In October 1919, the navy finally addressed the longstanding grievances of the engineer officers and announced that henceforth all branches of the naval officer corps were equal to one another regardless of their particular duties or training. This measure also extended to such extra duty matters as the regulation of the officers' mess, where it decreed that officers were to share the same mess both aboard ship and ashore. It likewise removed an old bone of contention by providing that in the absence of the First Officer, who normally presided over the mess, presidency was to be exercised by the senior officer present, and not, as previously, by the senior executive officer. Further emphasis upon equality was provided by the adoption of a single uniform, whereby the individual officer was differentiated only by the insignia and the abbreviation of his particular branch.[22] Finally, the myriad of branches within the officer corps was reduced to four: executive officers, medical officers, engineers, and paymasters. The other officer corps (*Torpedoingenieur, Feuerwerksoffizier, Marineinfantrieoffizier,* and *Torpedo-Offizier des Torpedo- und des Minenwesens*) were abolished and their duties assigned either to retired officers who assumed the status of civil servants in the naval bureaucracy, or to technically competent executive officers.[23]

With the autumn reforms, the first phase of the postwar reorganization of the navy came to an end. Although many problems remained, important groundwork had nevertheless been laid. Together with the Military Code of March 23, 1921, the changes effected between February and October 1919 would form the basis of naval administration until the period 1933–1935.[24] If much had been conceded—to the navy's numerous republican critics, to the enlisted men, and to the noncommissioned officers and deck officers—much of the imperial legacy had been retained as well. With some major exceptions, naval regulations, drill, and procedures were taken over intact from the Imperial Navy. Much of the organizational basis of the old navy likewise survived the revolutionary disturbances under new names and was incorporated into the Republic's navy in a streamlined form.[25] Finally and most importantly, the ultimate meaning of the fleet as the embodiment of Germany's naval mission survived as well. Indeed, traditionalists within the Service could congratulate themselves on the fact that in Adolf von Trotha one of their own, a true disciple of Tirpitz, remained in direct command. For a force so badly compromised by the events of October and November 1918, that was no small accomplishment.

Yet the internal reconstruction of the navy was only part of Trotha's and Noske's task. A second challenge was to restore the image that the navy wished to present to the German public and the world. In one respect, this image had suffered far more during the revolutionary upheavals than outward appearances would indicate. Among many officers, the gnawing feeling remained that the navy was ultimately responsible for the miseries, both internal and external, that now beset Germany. Had its failures not unleashed the destructive genie of defeatism in the fall of 1918? Had this, in turn, not paved the way for military collapse and revolution in November? A number of accounts, then, remained to be settled before the honor of the navy could be restored.[26]

Perhaps the most vexing irritation was the continued internment of the German fleet at Scapa Flow.[27] Since late November 1918, about seventy vessels of the so-called Internment Force had languished in Scottish waters, awaiting final word from the Allies as to their ultimate disposition. Although the vessels retained German crews and were technically under German command, they were unarmed and for all practical purposes served as hostages to ensure that Germany would accept the Treaty of Versailles. Once this was done, the force would in all likelihood be distributed as war reparations among the Allies. The spectacle of the victors squabbling over this maritime bonanza promised to be one of the few grim amusements that defeated Germany could look forward to after the signing of the peace.

In the early summer of 1919, however, as the drama at Versailles reached its climax, Vice Admiral Ludwig von Reuter, commander of the Internment Force, solved the problem of the German fleet in his own way. On June 21, the Armistice between Germany and the Allies was scheduled to expire. Germany was to announce its acceptance of the Treaty of Versailles or face a resumption of the war. Rather than let his command fall into the hands of the enemy in the event of a resumption of hostilities, the German admiral ordered the scuttling of the fleet. This, the last act of the old navy, was carried out with grim efficiency on the morning of the scheduled deadline. In the largest mass scuttling in history, ten battleships, five battle cruisers, five light cruisers, and forty-six destroyers went to their graves in the icy waters of Scapa Flow.

The Allies were furious. For a while they threatened to try Reuter as a war criminal, and the British somewhat spitefully kept the admiral and his sailors in "internment" until January 1920. In addition, a special supplement to the Treaty of Versailles tightened the restrictions on the navy by requiring the Reich to surrender its five remaining modern light cruisers and four-fifths of all removable harbor facilities—approximately 400,000 tons of docks, tugs, dredges, and cranes.[28]

The German response to the sinkings was naturally somewhat different. For the public at large, the picture of the crafty Reuter cheating perfidious Albion of its ill-gotten gains at the very last moment proved irresistible. The officers and men of the Internment Force would eventually return to a hero's welcome. For the navy, the scuttling of the fleet had a more personal significance. At last the sailors had shown that they were prepared to obey orders again. At last the honor of the navy had been restored. Indeed, with a little imagination, the "deed at Scapa Flow" could be used to gloss over the Imperial Navy's failures in the First World War altogether. As Reuter expressed it in 1921:

Those [of the Internment Force] know that the sinking of the fleet represented only a part of their task. The other, greater one, the rebuilding of the fleet, still lies before them. Who can say whether it will be theirs to experience the first breath of spring of the third German fleet? Yet their duty has been fulfilled if they maintained the high esteem of the second German fleet, that splendid, young, strong fleet that at the Skagerrak gave the lie to the centuries-old motto "Britannia rules the waves."

It [this fleet] *was sunk undefeated in the harbor of Scapa Flow in a grave of its own choosing.*

God protect the third German fleet![29]

Thus the legend of the "undefeated navy" joined that of the army's "stab in the back" in the treasury of postwar German myths.

Scapa Flow contributed significantly to the restoration of the navy's self-esteem. On the other hand, it was equally obvious to many observers that an event of this sort was a luxury that few navies could enjoy more than once. It was, in the final analysis, an act of negation rather than creation. If the groundwork for the future German fleet were to be laid at this time, it would require a succession of positive achievements as well. Great naval traditions, after all, are not built on a history of successful scuttlings.

Fortunately for the navy, near the end of 1918, another means of vindication had been offered by the government's inability to restore order within Germany. Ironically, it was the Volksmarine Division's Christmas Eve victory over the Garde Kavallerie Schützen Division which first demonstrated this impotence; in the following weeks, the domestic situation worsened considerably. In Bavaria and in the Rhineland, separatist movements threatened the unity of the Reich. In the east, Polish insurgents attempted to expand the borders of the newly established Polish state at Germany's expense. Perhaps most frightening of all was the specter of Bolshevism, which assumed concrete form in the nation's capital in January 1919, with the first Spartacist insurrection. Without reliable forces of its own, the government found itself compelled to appeal to the army and navy for volunteer units (*Freikorps*) of professional soldiers. Again, the situation was not lacking in irony. The navy's great opportunity to redeem itself would come not on the high seas, but in the interior of Germany, far from the salt water of the North Sea.[30]

The navy was especially susceptible to the appeal of the *Freikorps*, and three naval brigades were eventually formed in response to the government's appeal.[31] Motives for joining varied greatly among individuals. Some merely wished to assure themselves a means of existence during what promised to be a lean period ahead. Others hoped through their service to the fatherland to help lay the basis for a new navy worthy of its predecessor. Convinced republicans joined the brigades in the belief that a swift restoration of order was necessary before the Republic could be securely established. Opponents of the Republic joined in the equally fervent belief that the restoration of order was necessary before the Republic could be destroyed.[32]

Initially, then, the naval brigades included volunteers from nearly every imaginable background. In time, however, the general range of *Freikorps* types narrowed considerably.[33] As if to make amends for having questioned naval orthodoxy during the Wilhelmian period, the deck officers and engineers sent a disproportionately large number of men to serve in the brigades. Officer candidates who had been too young to serve in the Great War but were now determined to prove their mettle against Germany's internal enemies also flocked to the colors of the *Freikorps*. Finally, the executive officers, particularly the younger ones, were strongly represented in the "field gray navy," as the Service's land formations were called, and they provided the stamp for at least two of the three naval brigades. Conscious, perhaps overly conscious, of their failure to contain the revolution in the past, these men were doubly determined to defeat it this time. One young officer, a Lieutenant Reinhardt, captured the mood in the brigades perfectly when he stated that his immediate wish was "to fight with a weapon in the hand for the tormented fatherland against the inner *Schweinhund*."[34]

Reinhardt and others like him got their wish in the spring of 1919. In March, the heirs of the Spartacists, the newly formed German Communist Party (KPD), attempted another revolt against the government in Berlin. Reinhardt had the satisfaction of participating in the defeat of the "worst enemy," the Volksmarine Division, which had been responsible for the "shameful acts" so deleterious to the navy's good name.[35] The action was marked by brutality on both sides, as neither the victorious government troops nor the vanquished revolutionaries gave much quarter to prisoners. In the ensuing months, the brigades participated in the overthrow of the short-lived Soviet Republic in Bavaria, in counterinsurgency operations against the Poles in Silesia, and in the suppression of strikes and the maintenance of order in various parts of Germany. In doing so, they built on the reputation for ferocity and ruthless efficiency that they had established in Berlin that March. By the fall of 1919, few traces of armed opposition to the government on the part of the radical left remained.[36]

In the meantime, however, both the composition and *mentalité* of the brigades were radically transformed as the scarcely concealed hostility toward the republic felt by many of the officers came to the surface. In the Second Naval Brigade, which eventually proved to be the most reactionary of the *Freikorps* units, the influence of its commander, Captain Hermann Ehrhardt, was decisive. Under his charismatic leadership and through the efforts of the officers—particularly the young leaders of the *Sturmkompanie* who idolized him—the Ehrhardt Brigade, as the unit came to be called, was politicized and converted into an anti-government force. Nor did the officers and men make any secret of their political sentiments. When the brigade left Berlin for Upper Silesia in August 1919, it did so not under the black, red, and gold flag of the new Republic, but under the black, white, and red colors of Hohenzollern Germany. When it returned in the fall, the troop train carrying the brigade was covered with swastikas, anti-Semitic slogans, and insults aimed at cabinet members.[37] It was about this time that one soldier asked Ehrhardt what seemed to many a long overdue question: "*Herr Kapitän*, when will we finally march on Berlin?"[38] With this question in mind, the brigade settled into winter quarters and awaited the coming of the new year and new opportunities.

The year 1920 opened with the tenuous alliance between the *Freikorps* and the Republic, now headed by Chancellor Gustav Bauer, a Social Democrat, showing increasing signs of strain. On January 10, the Reichstag ratified the Treaty of Versailles, thereby removing the last fading hopes among diehards that at least a portion of its military and naval clauses would remain a dead letter. One month later, in accordance with the treaty, the Allies published a list of "war criminals" to be turned over for trial by Allied courts. The list caused a particular uproar in the navy, for among the nearly 900 names were those of Tirpitz, Scheer, Trotha, several cruiser commanders and twenty-nine submarine commanders.[39] Although it remained to be seen whether the Bauer government would acquiesce in the Allied demands for the delivery of the accused, in the minds of many naval officers the government's mere consideration of such a measure was sufficient proof of its irremediable weakness. As Rear Admiral William Michaelis recalled: "The majority of the executive officers ... wanted first and foremost to topple the regime and put a rightist one in its place. In my view the time was not yet ripe."[40]

One man who apparently did think that the time was ripe for such action was Captain Ehrhardt. But then, he knew something that most naval officers did not. Since the previous July, a number of ardent nationalists, including Erich Ludendorff and Dr Wolfgang Kapp, a co-founder with Tirpitz of the old Fatherland Party, had been working toward the overthrow of the government. In October 1919, an organization known as the National Union had come into existence with this aim in mind.[41] Among the members of the National Union was General Walter Freiherr von Lüttwitz, commander of the military district that encompassed Berlin, and as such Ehrhardt's superior. Although considerable differences existed among the conspirators as to the exact nature and timing of the action to be taken against the government, they nevertheless hoped that the operation could unfold in April 1920.[42] Captain Ehrhardt's brigade was to play an important part in the planned coup, for, encamped at Döberitz, it constituted the strongest and most effective combat unit in the vicinity of Berlin.

Unfortunately for the conspirators, larger international developments were working against their endeavors. By the end of February, the Allies were demanding the dissolution of both the Second (Ehrhardt) and Third (Loewenfeld) Naval Brigades as part of the navy's scheduled reduction to the 15,000-man strength allotted it under the Treaty of Versailles. On February 29, after a sharp discussion with Lüttwitz, Noske scheduled their dissolution for March 10. In the next few days, however, Lüttwitz obstinately refused to carry out the order. Rumors of an impending *Putsch* began to spread through the capital. When the day for the scheduled dissolution of the brigades arrived, Noske opted for a different tack, proposing the withdrawal of the brigades from Lüttwitz's command and their placement under direct Admiralty control. Although Trotha was anxious to reassign the brigades' personnel to tasks related more directly to the navy's maritime mission, he nevertheless advised against the order on the grounds that it might precipitate the rumored *Putsch*. He suggested the gradual dissolution of the brigades through the phased reassignment of officers and men. Noske remained adamant, however, and ordered the immediate transfer of the brigades. Once again, Lüttwitz refused to obey the direct order and that same evening presented Reich President Ebert with a series of demands. The President was to dissolve the National Assembly, call new elections, and install new heads for the ministries of foreign affairs, economics, and finance. Ebert was also to name Lüttwitz supreme commander of the armed forces and withdraw the order dissolving the naval brigades. The President rejected the ultimatum, and Lüttwitz withdrew to consider his options. The next day, March 11, he was ordered on indefinite leave. He displayed as much fidelity to this order as he had shown those of the previous two weeks and instead went to Ehrhardt's camp to initiate the *Putsch*.[43]

March 12 was quiet, but rumors of an impending coup persisted in the capital. In spite of this, the Cabinet meeting that day was surprisingly passive. The only preventive step taken was to send Trotha to Döberitz to ascertain whether Ehrhardt's brigade was preparing for action. Trotha's subsequent behavior makes the wisdom of choosing the admiral for this task debatable. He telephoned Ehrhardt beforehand to announce his visit and upon his arrival confined his "inspection" to a conversation with Ehrhardt, wherein he posed his questions in such a way that the captain was able to avoid answering whether a *Putsch* was imminent. Trotha's companion on the trip, Lieutenant Commander Wilhelm Canaris, a veteran of the Loewenfeld Brigade, likewise took care not to find anything amiss. Upon his return to Berlin, Trotha informed Noske that everything was quiet at Döberitz, but added that since Ehrhardt's men were elite troops, this could change at any hour.[44]

Later that night, word reached Noske that Ehrhardt's men were indeed on the march. The harried Reichswehr Minister called a council of war to consider the government's options. Among others present were Trotha, General Walther Reinhardt, army commander, and General Hans von Seeckt, head of the Troop Department (Truppenamt), which was now serving as a camouflaged general staff. When Noske asked how soon the army could act against the rebels, he received from Seeckt the astonishing reply: "Troops do not fire upon troops."[45] Trotha was apparently no more encouraging. It became clear that if Noske were to put down the rebellion, he would have to do so through some means other than those of the regular armed forces. An emergency Cabinet meeting immediately recognized this fact. In the absence of any local military support, it was decided that the best course of action would be for the Cabinet and the Reich President to leave the capital and flee to what was hoped would be loyal troops at Dresden.[46] Trotha was excluded from this Cabinet session. It remains unclear whether this was because Noske suspected him of having intentionally misled him, or because by law the admiral had no vote in cabinet decisions.

Trotha awoke the next morning to news that the Cabinet had fled the city and that Ehrhardt's men were at the Brandenburg Gate. At noon, the new master of Berlin, General Lüttwitz, summoned Trotha and informed him that President Ebert was still in Berlin. Lüttwitz's group wanted to form a new Cabinet under the leadership of Dr Kapp, with Ebert's approval and with SPD participation. It was hoped that Trotha would support the new regime. The admiral consulted with his staff. They collectively decided to recognize the changed situation. Accordingly, Trotha announced to the navy that he had placed himself at the service of the new regime and that he expected the navy to follow suit. This had scarcely been done, when it became obvious to Trotha that Ebert was nowhere to be seen and that the expected popular approval for the new Kapp government had failed to materialize. Indeed, a massive general strike on the part of the workers throughout Germany was being organized by the legitimate government. It would soon bring the Kapp regime to its knees.[47]

In the meantime, Trotha apparently came to the conclusion that he had backed the wrong horse. He now began to work with moderates within the Kapp government as well as representatives of the legitimate government who had remained in Berlin to secure a "restructuring" of the old government without the necessity of its overthrow. By then, however, Trotha was hopelessly compromised. When the Kapp *Putsch* finally collapsed on March 17, there was no question of the admiral's readmission into the good graces of the Bauer government. It only remained to be seen to what degree his actions had damaged the interests of the navy.[48]

The immediate effects of Trotha's actions were most obvious at the navy's major ports, Wilhelmshaven and Kiel. During the *Putsch*, it soon became clear that at Wilhelmshaven the majority of the deck officers, noncommissioned officers, and enlisted men supported the legitimate government. Therefore, there could be no question of openly following Trotha's order to bring the naval base over to the side of the Kapp regime; the local station commander, Vice Admiral Andreas Michelsen, tried to ride out the storm by issuing a proclamation of neutrality. This was nevertheless interpreted by many as a covert decision in favor of the Kappists, and as the sentiments among the local population and the enlisted men shifted more and more in favor of the Bauer government, the impracticality of the admiral's position became apparent. A number of naval officers urged Michelsen to recognize this and to declare himself openly in favor of the constitutional regime. Michelsen countered with the imaginative response that some of the vessels of the fleet had already gone over to the Kappists, and that a declaration for the Bauer government would precipitate civil war. In the absence of any information to the contrary, the dissenting officers accepted this tale. The tense confrontation between officers

31

and men was allowed to continue. On March 16, representatives of the enlisted men's and noncommissioned officers' leagues (*Bünde*) tired of the suspense and arrested the officers of the naval station *en masse*. Some of the officers were handled roughly, but bloodshed was avoided. With Noske's blessing, overall command of the station was assumed by the president of the local branch of the Deckoffizierbund, the retired Chief Petty Officer Grünewald.[49]

Events took a more violent course at Kiel. More so than Wilhelmshaven, Kiel was known as a socialist city, and the local populace could be expected to support actively the Bauer government through strikes and armed force if necessary. The situation was further complicated because the naval garrison was divided in its political sentiments, with the enlisted personnel of the minesweeping forces generally favoring the political left, and a local detachment of the Loewenfeld Brigade, the Claassen Battalion, siding with their compatriots in the Ehrhardt Brigade. Both sides, therefore, had considerable armed support. For a while, the local station commander, Rear Admiral Magnus von Levetzow, followed the example set in Wilhelmshaven and proclaimed the navy's neutrality, arguing that the maintenance of law and order was of primary concern. As in Wilhelmshaven, this position was interpreted by representatives of the local government as a decision for the *Putschists*, and fighting soon ensued. Given the relative balance of forces, it readily became evident that with the Claassen Battalion, Levetzow had enough strength to hold only a portion of the city. An uneasy ceasefire, punctuated by sporadic outbursts of firing, soon settled over Kiel. For five days, this dangerous situation persisted. At one point, Levetzow's chief of staff, Captain Max Reymann, tried to convince the admiral of the futility of his position. Reymann urged that the navy accede to local sentiments in order to prevent further bloodshed. Levetzow refused, and instead relieved his assistant of his post.

The stalemate continued until March 17, when news of the collapse of the *Putsch* in Berlin reached Kiel. The next day, Levetzow obeyed an order to turn over his affairs to the commander of the Baltic Strike Force, Admiral Ernst Ewers, but on March 19 Levetzow reappeared before a company of the Claassen Battalion and announced his intention to resume command. He also ordered the arrest of Ewers. With some embarrassment, a number of officers took Levetzow aside and told him confidentially that the troops would no longer follow him and that they disapproved of his action. Levetzow thereupon agreed to release Ewers and promised "to go to his apartment and not to try anything else." Later that day, however, the admiral was on the loose again, making one last appeal to the Claassen Battalion to be allowed to retain command. A telephone call from Berlin finally convinced him that he had nothing more to do with command of the station. By then, however, the patience of the enlisted men was at an end. During the next four days, the officers were gradually removed from their commands and their places taken by deck officers and noncommissioned officers. The final repercussions of the *Putsch* were not over in Kiel until April 6, when Ewers was replaced by a former deck officer, a Lieutenant von Seidlitz. By then, the collapse of the officer corps was complete.[50]

The failure of the *Putsch* left the navy in a position of acute embarrassment. To be sure, a new acting head for the navy, William Michaelis, former chief of the Operations Department at the Admiralty, was immediately named to replace Trotha, but this could not disguise the Service's precarious situation. Confidence in the judgment of superiors had been shaken by the erratic behavior of such highly respected men as Trotha and Levetzow.[51] Trust between officers and men and the sense of discipline that stemmed from this had also been shattered in the tense encounters at Wilhelmshaven and Kiel. The rough treatment that some of the officers received at the hands of their men, and the spectacle of the deck officers and noncommissioned officers crowing that they could run the navy very well without the officers, made the situation even more difficult. For many officers, it was more than they could bear, and they joined their comrades who had left the Service after the First World War on the retirement list. Even for those who stayed, the navy's prospects appeared more dismal than ever. As one officer expressed it: "All the unending effort and care that had been spent in rebuilding the navy seemed in vain. It was November 1918 all over again."[52]

The Service's position vis-à-vis the Cabinet and the Reichstag also bore comparison with the navy's débâcle one and a half years before. After November 1918, however, the navy had at least been able to count on a small residue of goodwill to help it through the crisis, and it had succeeded in finding a strong spokesman for its needs in Gustav Noske. Now, Noske was being blamed for his failure to control the armed forces during the Kapp *Putsch*. He was soon replaced as Reichswehr Minister by Dr Otto Gessler. To the latter, it appeared that the navy had finally exhausted the patience of Germany's parliamentarians: "It had been the bearer of all mutinies, first in 1917, then in larger measure in 1918 and now again—this time with Admiral Trotha at the head—in 1920. First from the left, now from the right."[53] Confronted, then, with the apparent incorrigibility of the navy, some government leaders were willing to take the ultimate step: perhaps the navy ought to be abolished altogether.

The threat of abolition prompted desperate measures on the part of the navy's supporters. Reichstag representatives from Kiel and Wilhelmshaven were convinced of the irretrievable harm that their cities would suffer in the absence of naval bases and shipyards, and they carried their arguments to Gessler. Leaders within the Service lobbied energetically to impress influential members of the Cabinet with the merits of sea power.[54] Nor did the admirals neglect their powerful counterparts in the army. In April 1920, for example, one of the Service's most distinguished alumni, Reinhard Scheer, appealed to the new head of the army, Hans von Seeckt, to give his support in maintaining the navy. A fleet, he argued, was essential for Germany's long-term interests; once removed, it could be restored only with great difficulty. Seeckt's response was interesting. Perhaps enjoying the predicament of the army's great rival, he opined that the navy would have to start again from the beginning. Nevertheless, his overall response was positive, and he assured Scheer that he would do his utmost to preserve the navy.[55]

Whether it was due to the pressure of the representatives from Kiel and Wilhelmshaven, the persuasiveness of the admirals' arguments, or the support of Seeckt, the navy weathered the crisis. For a time, Ebert and Gessler continued to contemplate some sort of administrative merger of army and navy which would have undoubtedly written *finis* to the Reichsmarine's position as an independent entity within the armed forces, but by the late summer of 1920 they had evidently abandoned this idea.[56] In the end, Cabinet and Reichstag contented themselves with an investigatory commission, which eventually decided upon the dismissal of at least eighteen officers, including Trotha, Levetzow, and Michelsen. A number of others were sent on extended leaves or transferred to less sensitive positions.[57] As for the rest of the officers, Gessler hastened to reinvest them with the commands that had been wrested so rudely from them during the March disturbances.

Restoration to command promised to be a more difficult undertaking than might appear at first sight, for many of the deck officers and noncommissioned officers who had assumed positions of authority feared for their careers in the navy once they relinquished command. To facilitate the transfer of authority, therefore, Reichswehr Minister Gessler personally accompanied the new station commanders, Rear Admiral Hans Adolf Zenker and Captain Ernst Freiherr von Gagern, to their respective assignments at Wilhelmshaven and Kiel. On May 25 and 27, at special ceremonies timed to coincide with the fourth anniversary of the Battle of the Skagerrak, command of the navy's two most important bases was restored to the executive officer corps.[58] More than two months after the *Putsch*, conditions within the navy had apparently returned to normal. One lesson, however, would not be forgotten. The next time that the existing regime was threatened by a *coup d'état*, the navy would support the status quo.[59] There was to be no repetition of 1918 or 1920.

Nor were the admirals slow to draw two other lessons from the events of March 1920. The first of these concerned the Service's two remaining *Freikorps* units, the Ehrhardt and Loewenfeld Brigades. The Kapp *Putsch* made it evident that the *Marinebrigaden* now constituted a distinct liability for the future aspirations of the Reichsmarine. Not only did the *Landesknecht* mentality of the brigades' officers threaten the Service's relations with the Republic; their almost exclusive concentration on land warfare was an anomaly and ran the risk of deflecting the navy from its real task, the restoration of German sea power.[60] In the wake of the Kapp *Putsch*, therefore, the high command determined to regain control of the naval brigades and dissolve them.

The first steps toward this end were taken within a few weeks after the collapse of the *Putsch*. In April 1920, the Loewenfeld Brigade, which with the exception of the Claassen Battalion had remained relatively passive in Silesia during the March uprising, was reassigned to the Ruhr to combat a Communist insurrection that had been touched off there by the *Putsch*. This provided a convenient means of reintegrating politically suspect units into the armed forces of the Republic, and for a while it was thought that the government might also use the Ehrhardt Brigade in this manner. In the end, this step was apparently deemed too provocative to the workers who had helped save the Republic during the *Putsch*; the brigade went into camp instead. In May 1920, Ehrhardt left the navy and took an express train to Munich, where the particularist government of Bavaria offered protection against arrest.[61] In the fall, both the Loewenfeld and Ehrhardt Brigades were dissolved, and a large number of their former members were incorporated into the 15,000-man Reichsmarine.[62] Although many officers and men of the Loewenfeld Brigade were kept together and assigned as a unit to individual commands within the fleet, their reintegration into the navy progressed relatively smoothly. The only major repercussions from this occurred in 1922, when a number of staunch republicans questioned Loewenfeld's suitability, given his checkered career, to command the cruiser *Berlin* on an overseas goodwill mission for the Republic. Reichswehr Minister Gessler vigorously defended Loewenfeld's candidacy, and the captain received the command.[63]

The navy encountered greater difficulty with the former members of the Ehrhardt Brigade. Although many of its officers followed their commander's example and left the navy, those who stayed were determined to maintain contacts with their old comrades and to keep the Ehrhardt spirit alive.[64] These contacts became acutely embarrassing for the navy as Ehrhardt assumed ties with Adolf Hitler's fledgling National Socialist German Workers' Party (NSDAP) and as the terrorist activities of a secret successor organization to the brigade, *Organisation Consul*—which was responsible for the murders of the prominent republicans Matthias Erzberger and Walther Rathenau—became known to the public.[65] Problems also resulted at the Naval School at Flensburg-Mürwik, where the officer candidates who had participated in the *Freikorps* were sent to complete their interrupted education. There, the former members of the Ehrhardt Brigade acted as ringleaders in a series of antirepublican demonstrations that eventually resulted in the dismissal of twenty-seven of the 178 candidates.[66] Nevertheless, as the years progressed, the Ehrhardt spirit gradually subsided within the navy, a victim either of dismissals and defections, or, in isolated cases, increased maturity. When Ehrhardt participated in the Munich *Putsch* of November 1923, his actions provoked little response in the navy.

The summer and fall of 1920, then, witnessed energetic attempts by the navy to eliminate the disruptive influence of the *Marinebrigaden*. Concurrently, the Service took firm measures to apply a second purported lesson from the Kapp *Putsch*. On June 15, 1920, Reich President Ebert issued a decree to the navy, thanking those who had remained loyal to the government during the March crisis. He paid particular tribute to the deck officers and noncommissioned officers who had carried on in positions of authority during the regular officers' enforced absence from March until late May. This was to be the deck officers' last hurrah. Shortly after Ebert's message, the navy announced that, given the twelve-year service presently required for enlisted men, there was now time enough for each man to become a specialist and that there was consequently no longer a need for deck officers. An equally compelling but unacknowledged reason for this decision seems to have been the high command's desire to end the troublesome dichotomy between deck officer and officer that had plagued the navy for almost a quarter of a century. The Service had been considering such a measure even before the deck officers replaced the regular officers in the wake of the March uprising. The events of the Kapp *Putsch* apparently gave final proof of the irreconcilability of the two groups; in response, the navy simply stopped appointing deck officers. Along with some noncommissioned officers, a fortunate few were promoted to officer rank in the early days of the Republic. Attrition through retirement gradually accounted for the rest. Throughout the 1920s and early 1930s, the Deck Officer League actively campaigned for the reintroduction of its branch into the Service, but when the expansion of the navy came after 1933, the deck officers were conspicuous by their absence.[67]

With the resolution of the deck officer question and the integration of the *Freikorps* veterans, the pace of events in the navy slackened noticeably. In September 1920, Admiral Paul Behncke replaced Michaelis, who had been acting as head of the navy as a temporary replacement for Trotha. Under Behncke and his successor, Admiral Zenker, who would hold the office from 1924 to 1928, the navy was to enjoy almost eight years of comparative calm. If it enjoyed no stunning successes, neither did it suffer serious reverses. This was an accomplishment of sorts, for it gave the Service time to recover from six years of war and revolution. A sure sign that conditions were returning to normal appeared in 1922, when the navy for the first time felt sufficiently confident to send vessels on goodwill missions abroad.[68] In the mid-1920s, the navy would also receive its first modern vessels, and morale among both officers and men would improve accordingly.[69] While the navy concentrated on training and discipline, or so it was hoped, the all too numerous wounds of the recent past would be allowed to heal.

All of this boded well for the future. Unfortunately, although the high command made immense progress in resolving a number of the Service's internal problems, the navy's sensitive relationship with the nation's political representatives remained acute throughout the life of the Republic. Many republicans had always distrusted the naval officer corps as a matter of principle, viewing it as hopelessly reactionary; the Kapp *Putsch* seemed to confirm all their suspicions in this regard. Moreover, throughout the 1920s, many parliamentary representatives viewed the fleet as a needless extravagance whose expenses far outweighed the meager services that it could render in time of crisis. The officers, for their part, were apt to regard even the most well-intentioned of the Service's critics as meddlesome, ill-informed, and unable to keep secrets.[70] In the case of the Social Democratic Party and the German Communist Party, the officers' preconceptions were likely to be of an even more hostile nature. Mutual suspicions, therefore, characterized the navy's relationship with the political leaders of republican Germany. While these were at times masked by one side or the other, they never entirely disappeared.

This is not to say that sincere efforts were not made by men on both sides to bridge the gap separating the various factions. Immediately after the Kapp *Putsch*, for example, both the navy and the army took steps to depoliticize the armed forces by withdrawing the sailors' and soldiers' right to vote in elections and by prohibiting membership in political organizations during the period of active service.[71] In addition, the Reichswehr Minister from 1920 to 1928, Dr Gessler of the Democratic Party (DDP), won the respect of both Admirals Behncke and Zenker for his energetic defense of the navy before the Reichstag and for the free rein that he gave the admirals in running the Service.[72] In time, many naval officers also came to have a grudging respect for the President of the Republic, Friedrich Ebert. When the venerable Field Marshal Paul von Hindenburg succeeded Ebert as president in 1925, moreover, grudging respect gave way to open approval, at least as far as many officers were concerned.[73]

Yet even the most well-intentioned efforts on both sides were frequently interpreted in a hostile light by the other side. Republicans of all persuasions questioned the wisdom of withdrawing the vote from soldiers.[74] What better way, after all, was there to win a soldier for the Republic than by allowing him to participate in the electoral process? Others, including members of Gessler's own party, questioned the wisdom of giving the armed forces so much leeway in matters of planning, recruitment, and training. Many a Reichstag deputy must have yearned to see less of the good doctor and more of the admirals when it came to giving testimony before investigatory and budgetary committees.[75] Thus, despite a number of efforts to relieve the tension between the navy and the republican parties, the situation remained uncomfortable.

The Service's relationship with the Social Democratic Party (SPD) was particularly troubled. Like the other democratic parties, the SPD questioned the reasons for the disenfranchisement of Reichswehr personnel; more than the bourgeois parties, it suspected the policy that Dr Gessler took toward the armed forces. In addition, a number of incidents occurred throughout the 1920s that disturbed the party's relationship with the navy. In 1921, SPD deputies publicly questioned the suitability of the new cruiser (*Emden*) that the navy had requested to defend Germany's coast. They argued, among other things, that such a vessel was more suited for pleasure cruises abroad. That same year, the SPD succeeded in striking out appropriations for positions for three admirals, four captains, and three commanders. In subsequent years, party representatives would offer similar arguments that the navy was over staffed with high-ranking officers. Throughout the period under consideration, the SPD further lamented the navy's failure to recruit officer candidates from working-class families. The party was likewise disturbed by apparent traces of anti-republicanism within the corps. At times, the evidence for this could be relatively trivial, as when the SPD recoiled in horror upon learning that at the dedication of a new building for the Imperial Yacht Club, three cheers had been given for Wilhelm II, the club's founder. At other times, the navy's transgressions appeared more serious, as when in 1926 its shadowy contacts with Ehrhardt's Viking *Bund*, the successor to *Organisation Consul*, were revealed. Whatever the case, each new revelation, each new challenge, heightened the resentment that the navy felt for the Social Democrats. When, in the following year, the SPD voted against the budgetary appropriations for the construction of the navy's first *Panzerschiff* ("pocket" battleship), the act merely confirmed the admirals' suspicion concerning the lack of patriotism among the Socialists.[76]

The Service enjoyed an even stormier relationship with the German Communist Party (KPD). Whereas the Social Democrats were generally seen as poor patriots or hopeless idealists, the Communists were perceived in naval circles to be outright traitors who were actively seeking to subvert the navy. The KPD's Rote Frontkämpferbund (Red Veterans' League) included a naval auxiliary called the Rote Marine, which distributed propaganda leaflets to the sailors and which sought to recruit former naval personnel for the organization. The Rote Marine also staged a play commemorating the mutinies of 1917 and the martyrdom of Reichpietsch and Köbis; the naval high command thought it detected in this, and in Sergei Eisenstein's film *Potemkin*, a clever way of accentuating differences between officers and men. Another cause for concern was the similarity between the uniform of the Rote Marine and that of the navy, which left many outsiders with the impression that Reichsmarine sailors were regularly taking part in KPD demonstrations. Eventually, a series of lawsuits on the part of the navy forced the Rote Marine to alter the appearance of its uniform in order to prevent mistakes of this kind, but the high command remained suspicious. It continued, for example, to regard Germany's larger ports as particular havens for Communist agitators, and therefore welcomed the acquisition of smaller bases such as Stralsund and Pillau, where at least a portion of the navy could be insulated from evil influences.[77] Its fears of the Communists likewise carried over into the realm of foreign policy, where Zenker in particular proved skeptical of the political and military connections that the Foreign Office and the army were forging with the Soviet Union.[78] Even though by 1927 the KPD had apparently achieved little success in infiltrating the ranks of the navy, the admirals were nevertheless determined not to relax their vigilance.

Thus, the naval high command enjoyed only limited success in improving the Reichsmarine's relationship with the political leaders of the Republic. In another area, the internal consolidation of the navy, the admirals were considerably more successful during the period from late 1920 to 1928. Here, too, there was much work to be done. The many divisions within the Service—between officers and enlisted men, between executive and engineer officers, and, indeed, between spokesmen for the executive officer corps itself—had done much to hinder the effectiveness of the navy during the Great War and the revolutionary disturbances that followed. In view of this, naval reformers strove energetically to improve intra-service relations and thereby to lay a firm foundation for the future growth of the fleet. Although by no means all of their efforts were crowned with success, significant advances were made in the areas of discipline, morale, and intra-service harmony.

The era of Admirals Behncke and Zenker was especially important in reestablishing a healthy relationship between officers and enlisted men. Here, the peculiar circumstances of Germany's postwar navy proved to be both a benefit and a handicap to naval reformers. On the one hand, the small size of the Reichsmarine enabled recruiters to choose from among the very pick of Germany's patriotic young men in filling their ranks. In 1926, for example, there were 44,100 applications for a mere 635 positions among the enlisted men.[79] On the other hand, the twelve-year enlistment period posed particular problems to morale, for the chances of promotion in a service composed exclusively of long-term volunteers were minimal. As partial compensation, the navy took great care that the seamen were well provided for after the expiration of their enlistments by offering courses in business, administration, and management during the quieter winter months of active duty, and by assisting the enlisted men in finding employment in civilian life after they left the Service. Moreover, attempts to provide a reasonable amount of variety in day-to-day duties did much to improve morale among the enlisted men.[80] Nor did the changed attitudes of many of the officers toward their men pass entirely unnoticed. Throughout the 1920s, enterprising officers such as Karl Dönitz and Friedrich Ruge were drawing upon the lessons of the Great War and attempting, with success, to understand the problems of their men and to cope with them more effectively.[81] For the moment, at least, their endeavors were confined to their own small commands. But in the future, the experiences of these and other officers in providing effective leadership would be codified into training manuals for the entire officer corps.[82]

Relationships within the officer corps were changing as well. In April 1921, the first postwar class of officer candidates entered the navy, and for the first time engineer and executive officer candidates participated in the same primary training courses.[83] In addition, the postwar "Crews" at the Naval School generally numbered no more than a few dozen men, which meant that the younger officer candidates had much more contact with their counterparts in other branches of the Service than had previously been the case. Nor were the increasing contacts within the corps confined to the younger men alone. Officers of all branches now dined at the same mess, and on certain evenings of the year the entire officer corps of the Baltic or North Sea commands would assemble for a "Gentlemen's Evening" of skits, singing, and entertainment.[84] Officers were also likely to vacation at the same spots, perhaps one of the Reichswehr's reasonably priced resort hotels, and, beginning in 1924, selected executive officers for the first time joined their comrades in the engineer corps at the Technical University at Berlin-Charlottenburg for advanced study.[85] Finally, the navy's newly founded mutual aid society, the Naval Officers' League (Marine-Offizier-Verband, or MOV), likewise included members from all branches of the officer corps.[86]

It is clear that, as the 1920s wore on, the naval officers of every branch regarded themselves increasingly as members of a single corps. At the same time, however, a number of divisions persisted in spite of the increasing uniformity of the corps. The navy's paymasters, for example, resented that throughout the period 1920 to 1928, they were denied full officer status on the grounds that they were noncombatants. The engineers also continued to feel themselves second-class officers, a view that the attitudes of some executive officers did nothing to dispel. The crowning example of the residual prejudices against the engineers came in 1925, when the commander of the Naval School at Flensburg-Mürwik proposed that the navy eliminate common primary training for engineer and executive officer candidates:

> The prospective executive officer should be educated to a certain nobility of bearing [*Grosszügigkeit*] and above all to a leader personality, while with engineer candidates it is more a matter of creating someone good at small and limited things.

To many engineer officers, this appeared to be nothing less than an attempt to set the clock back thirty years. Fortunately for the solidarity of the corps, the new head of the navy, Admiral Zenker, rejected this return to Tirpitzian principles. Resolution of these lingering difficulties, however, would have to await Zenker's successor.[87]

In another area, that of naval history, the Tirpitzian legacy also proved to be a divisive influence within the corps.[88] In 1919, the former grand admiral published his memoirs, which were followed in the mid-1920s by a two-volume collection of documents from his tenure of office.[89] Along with a stinging criticism of Kaiser Wilhelm II and Chancellor Bethmann Hollweg, Tirpitz also singled out a number of Imperial Navy officers (most notably the retired Admirals G. A. von Müller, Henning von Holtzendorff, Hugo von Pohl, and Friedrich von Ingenohl) for their responsibility in "holding back" the High Sea Fleet at various times during the Great War. The offended officers countered with arguments of their own, and by the early 1920s, a fierce literary battle was raging among retired officers over the merits and demerits of Tirpitz's policies. Neither side was overly gentle in its choice of words, and the debate soon attracted the attention of the wider public and, not surprisingly, the active officer corps as well.

Unfortunately for the navy, the subject proved equally explosive for active officers. Although the high command would probably have preferred for the matter to go away—the spectacle of the former naval officers washing their dirty linen in public was, after all, distinctly embarrassing—personal ties with Tirpitz and his position as the architect of Germany's naval greatness eventually decided the question in favor of the grand admiral, at least as far as most of the higher-ranking active officers were concerned. As a result, the navy actively supported the Tirpitzian position, releasing archival material to his supporters and sending carefully prepared officers to discredit his critics at public forums. The navy's support did not stop here, however, and in the Service's multivolume history, *Der Krieg zur See*, Tirpitz's preference for the dreadnought and his doctrine of a decisive battle (*Entscheidungsschlacht*) on the high seas were emphasized at the expense of advocates of U-boat warfare (*Kleinkrieg*). In fact, the authors of this official history sometimes sought the advice of the master, sending Tirpitz prepublication proofs of their writings for his approval and revision.[90]

Yet, in spite of the navy's active support in this matter, the defenders of Tirpitz did not have it all their way. In 1926, Rear Admiral Wolfgang Wegener reissued a memorandum dating from the Great War in which he called into question many of Tirpitz's views, including his pet idea of a battle between the Thames and Helgoland.[91] Instead, Wegener suggested that the Reich ought to have seized bases in France and especially in Scandinavia, which would have enabled the navy to outflank Britain's favorable maritime geographical position and thereby to wage war upon the island nation's commerce. In the following years, Wegener's memorandum was circulated privately, initially among older officers, and then, with more success, among enthusiastic younger officers. The debate over Tirpitz therefore continued, until in 1927, the retired Grand Admiral Prince Heinrich felt compelled to call upon his brother officers, both active and inactive, to agree to a ceasefire.[92] By then, however, the navy was on the verge of a crisis of an entirely different nature.

The navy's new problem concerned neither the higher questions of politics, about which admirals and Reichstag representatives had bickered throughout the 1920s nor the questions of naval policy in the Great War, which so divided the corps internally. Instead, the issue involved a relatively trivial, and at times comical, matter of the Service's internal administration. In August 1927, the *Berliner Tageblatt*, a newspaper close to Reichswehr Minister Gessler's own Democratic Party, published a strange story that a certain Walter Lohmann, a captain in the Reichsmarine, had been channeling secret navy funds into a failing film company, Phoebus A.G., and that he had been supporting secret rearmament projects with other government funds.[93] At first, the Reichswehr Ministry denied the charges, but as other Democratic and Socialist newspapers picked up the story, it was announced that an investigation would be made. An audit revealed that Lohmann's business practices were, as one of Lohmann's brother officers rather delicately expressed it, "contrary to the basic principles for handling the budget."[94] Subsequent investigation revealed navy backing for a number of enterprises—sports clubs, shipping companies, the Phoebus film company, and a bacon-processing plant—whose contributions to the national defense were questionable at best.[95] Knowledge of the navy's secret rearmament projects, which largely revolved around submarine and torpedo-boat development by subsidized companies at home and abroad, never reached the general public. Nevertheless, the public and parliamentary outcry over Lohmann's cavalier dispensation of Reich funds rose to such a pitch that the navy was forced to initiate honor court proceedings against the unfortunate captain. The naval court acquitted Lohmann of the charge of personal dishonesty, but found him guilty of exceeding his authority. Lohmann's career was ruined, and he left the Service within a few months after the verdict.[96]

Had the matter ended here, the Lohmann Affair, as it came to be known, would have remained nothing more than an episode in the navy's administrative history. Unfortunately for the navy, a number of intriguing questions remained unanswered concerning the roles of Lohmann's superiors, Admiral Zenker and Reichswehr Minister Gessler, in the affair. Why had Lohmann not previously been audited? If Zenker and Gessler had known about the Lohmann-backed ventures, they were guilty of tolerating improper use of government funds in a number of highly suspect undertakings. If they had not known about the Lohmann schemes, they were guilty of an even greater sin, that of not knowing what was going on in their own household. Neither man had an answer to this dilemma. Gessler was the first to yield, announcing his resignation in January 1928. Zenker followed him into retirement a few months later. As at so many times before in the tumultuous decade since 1918, the navy was once more without a head.

Notes for Chapter 2

1　For a general history of the November revolution and its aftermath, see A. J. Ryder, *The German Revolution of 1918: A Study of German Socialism in War and Revolt* (Cambridge, 1967); also Gerhard A. Ritter and Susanne Miller (eds.), *Die deutsche Revolution 1918–1919* (Frankfurt and Hamburg, 1969).

2　Nominal control of the navy was exercised by the Naval Office, which received directions from a sailors' council, the Council of 53. For a description of conditions in Kiel and Wilhelmshaven, see Gustav Noske, *Von Kiel bis Kapp; Zur Geschichte der deutschen Revolution* (Berlin, 1920), pp. 13, 34, and *passim*.

3　For a general summary of the Ebert–Groener agreement, see Gordon A. Craig, *The Politics of the Prussian Army, 1640-1945*, rev. edn (New York, 1964), pp. 347–348. A more detailed treatment is in Wolfgang Sauer, "Das Bündis Ebert–Groener. Eine Studie über Notwendigkeit und Grenzen der militärischen Macht" (PhD dissertation, Free University of Berlin, 1957).

4　Holger H. Herwig, *Luxury Fleet: The Imperial German Navy, 1888–1918* (London, 1980), p. 254.

5　For the origin and history of the Volksmarine Division, see Kurt Wrobel, *Die Volksmarine Division* (Berlin, 1957); also Ulrich Kluge, *Soldatenräte und*

Revolution: Studien zur Militärpolitik in Deutschland 1918/19 (Göttingen, 1975), pp. 178–180, 260–264.

6   See Holger H. Herwig, "The First German Congress of Workers' and Sailors' Councils and the Problem of Military Reform," *Central European History*, 1 (June 1968), pp. 150–165.

7   Wrobel, *Volksmarine Division*, pp. 96–103.

8   Erich Raeder, *Mein Leben* 2 vols (Tübingen, 1956–1957), 1, pp. 156–157.

9   Noske, *Kiel bis Kapp*, p. 63.

10 For Noske's early career, see Ulrich Czisnik, *Gustav Noske: Ein sozialdemokratischer Staatsmann* (Zürich and Frankfurt, 1969); also Arthur H. Mills, "Bloodhound of the Revolution: Gustav Noske in German Politics 1918–1920" (Masters thesis, Vanderbilt University, 1973), pp. 7–30; as well as the autobiographical information furnished in Gustav Noske, *Erlebtes aus Aufstieg und Niedergang einer Demokratie* (Offenbach-Main, 1947). For the naval officers' esteem of Noske, see Raeder, *Mein Leben*, 1, pp. 154–155, and the sentiments of Magnus von Levetzow and a Commander Scheibe, which are cited in Friedrich Forstmeier, "Zur Rolle der Marine im Kapp Putsch," in *Seemacht und Geschichte: Festschrift zum 80. Geburtstag von Friedrich Ruge* (Bonn-Bad Godesberg, 1975), p. 53. Another author maintains that Noske came to occupy the role of "*Ersatzkaiser*" for Trotha, the future commander of the navy. Helmut Schubert, "Admiral Adolf von Trotha (1868–1940). Ein Versuch zur historischen-psychologischen Biographik" (PhD Dissertation, University of Freiburg, 1976), p. 245.

11 For an abbreviated list of Persius' writings, see István Déak, *Weimar Germany's Left-Wing Intellectuals: A Political History of the Weltbühne and Its Circle* (Berkeley, Calif., 1968), pp. 261–262. Paasche was later murdered by extreme nationalists; ibid., p. 64. For Raeder's actions during this period and his attitude toward the "three P's," see Raeder, *Mein Leben*, 1, pp. 158–159.

12 Noske, it turns out, put more faith in officers who openly admitted their monarchist prejudices but who were willing to serve the fatherland in its hour of need, than he did in latecomers to the republican cause. Schubert, "Adolf von Trotha," p. 244; also Gustav Adolf Caspar, *Die sozialdemokratische Partei und das deutsche Wehrproblem in den Jahren der Weimarer Republik* (Frankfurt, 1959), pp. 48–49.

13 Keith W. Bird, *Weimar, the German Naval Officer Corps and the Rise of National Socialism* (Amsterdam, 1977), pp. 40–42.

14 Kurt Stöckel, "Die Entwicklung der Reichsmarine nach dem Ersten Weltkrieg, 1919–1935: Äusserer Aufbau und innere Struktur" (PhD dissertation, Göttingen University, 1954), pp. 19, 21; Noske, *Kiel bis Kapp*, pp. 50–51; Bird, *Weimar*, p. 38, n. 143.

15 Bird, *Weimar*, pp. 56–58. For a summary of the Provisional Navy Bill, see Rudolf Absolon, *Die Wehrmacht im Dritten Reich*, 4 vols to date (Boppard am Rhein, 1969–), 1, pp. 23–24.

16 The relevant clauses of the treaty are given in Rolf Güth, *Die Marine des deutschen Reiches 1919–1939* (Frankfurt, 1972), pp. 25–29. For a history of the negotiations at Versailles, see H. W. V. Temperley (ed.), *A History of the Peace Conference of Paris* (London, 1920–1924).

17 With the exception of the submarines, the treaty made no mention of the smaller vessels of the fleet. At an Allied Ambassadorial Conference in March 1920, it was decided to allow the Reich to retain eighteen picket boats, thirty-eight minesweepers, and four artillery training

vessels. At the same time, the Allies conceded Germany the right to maintain an additional two battleships, two light cruisers, four destroyers, and four torpedo-boats as a reserve. Werner Rahn, *Reichsmarine und Landesverteidigung 1919–1928: Konzeption und Führung der Marine in der Weimarer Republik* (Munich, 1976), pp. 22–23.

18 Stöckel, "Entwicklung der Reichsmarine," p. 39; Rahn, *Reichsmarine*, pp. 24–25.

19 For the provisions of the Weimar Constitution, see Howard Lee McBain and Lindsay Rogers, *The New Constitutions of Europe* (Garden City, NY, 1923), pp. 176–212.

20 Stöckel, "Entwicklung der Reichsmarine," pp. 110–111.

21 There were some officers, however, who either took the oath to the Republic with reservations or else did not take it at all. Captain Hermann Ehrhardt, for example, had made earlier oaths to support the German socialist republic more palatable by defining socialism as work for all, law and order, and the absence of workers' and soldiers' councils. Bird, *Weimar*, p. 53. Later, Ehrhardt's officers systematically avoided giving the constitutionally required oath to their enlisted men. Gabriele Krüger, *Die Brigade Ehrhardt* (Hamburg, 1971), p. 50.

22 Werner Bräckow, *Die Geschichte des deutschen Marine-Ingenieuroffizierkorps* (Oldenburg and Hamburg, 1974), pp. 138–143. A naval engineer, for example, who had previously borne the title Chefingenieur was now designated Fregattenkapitän (I.). The insignia, which were worn on the sleeves of the uniform jacket and on the shoulder boards, consisted of a star for the executive officers, a gearwheel for the engineer officers, a caduceus for the medical officers, and an eagle for paymasters.

23 Ibid., p. 144; Raeder, *Mein Leben*, 1, pp. 174–178.

24 For a summary of the Military Code, see Güth, *Marine des deutschen Reiches*, pp. 49–51.

25 A major step in this regard had been taken in February 1919, when the old system of *Immediatstellungen* was eliminated and ultimate responsibility for both command and administrative decisions was placed in the hands of the Admiralty. Stöckel, "Entwicklung der Reichsmarine," p. 41.

26 For this, see Wilfried von Loewenfeld's sentiments, cited in Bird, *Weimar*, p. 51, n. 56.

27 For the experiences of the Internment Force, see Ludwig von Reuter, *Scapa Flow: Das Grab der deutschen Flotte*, 2nd edn, rev. (Leipzig, 1921), and Friedrich Ruge, *Scapa Flow 1919: The End of the German Fleet* (London, 1973).

28 Bird, *Weimar*, p. 64.

29 Reuter, *Scapa Flow*, pp. 94–95.

30 For a general history of the *Freikorps*, see Robert G. L. Waite, *Vanguard of Nazism: The Free Corps Movement in Postwar Germany, 1918–1923* (New York, 1969). For the navy's participation in the *Freikorps*, see Krüger, *Brigade Ehrhardt*; Bird, *Weimar*, pp. 44–125; and Forstmeier, "Marine im Kapp Putsch."

31 The brigades were given numerical designations, but they were more commonly known by the names of their commanders. The First Naval Brigade, or von Roden Brigade, was composed primarily of deck officers and noncommissioned officers; upon request, it was given a cadre of army officers for command purposes. A company of engineer officer cadets was later added to the brigade. Despite the fact that the brigade

was considered one of the best and most reliable units in government service, it was, with the exception of the engineer company, dissolved in May 1919. Raeder, *Mein Leben*, 1, pp. 155–156; Forstmeier, "Marine im Kapp Putsch," pp. 51–52; Stöckel, "Entwicklung der Reichsmarine," pp. 18-19, 170; Bird, *Weimar*, p. 46. The Second (Ehrhardt) and Third (Loewenfeld) Naval Brigades were formed in the winter and early spring of 1919. Their subsequent history will be outlined in this chapter.

32 Krüger, *Brigade Ehrhardt*, pp. 18, 23, 50; Bird, *Weimar*, p. 53.

33 One should perhaps distinguish between *Freikorps* "types" and *Freikorps* "tykes." For a time, recruitment lagged in some of the brigades due in part to the competition from the plethora of units that were springing up, and the navy resorted to the practice of enlisting 17-year-old boys without military experience. "Noske's children," as they were called, proved unsuitable, and the practice was discontinued. Krüger, *Brigade Ehrhardt*, p. 21.

34 Cited in Bird, *Weimar*, p. 50. For the composition of the *Freikorps*, see ibid., pp. 52–53; Krüger, *Brigade Ehrhardt*, pp. 36, 135, n. 13; Bräckow, *Marine-Ingenieuroffizierkorps*, pp. 134–135.

35 The sentiments were voiced by Reinhardt, cited in Bird, *Weimar*, p. 51.

36 Krüger, *Brigade Ehrhardt*, pp. 27–32; Bird, *Weimar*, pp. 46–52.

37 Krüger, *Brigade Ehrhardt*, pp. 32–36.

38 Quoted in Bird, *Weimar*, p. 55.

39 Ibid., pp. 65–66; Raeder, *Mein Leben*, 1, pp. 178–179; Noske, *Kiel bis Kapp*, p. 202.

40 Cited in Forstmeier, "Marine im Kapp Putsch," p. 54.

41 Johannes Erger, *Der Kapp-Lüttwitz Putsch: Ein Beitrag zur deutschen Innenpolitik 1919/20* (Düsseldorf, 1967), pp. 85–87. See also Heinz Hürten (ed.), *Zwischen Revolution und Kapp-Putsch: Militär und Innenpolitik 1918–1920* (Düsseldorf, 1977).

42 Erger, *Kapp Putsch*, pp. 97–107.

43 For Lüttwitz's actions, see Erger, *Kapp Putsch*, pp. 115–123; Bird, *Weimar*, p. 68. Lüttwitz's erratic behavior prompted Interior Minister Erich Koch-Weser to describe the general as "technically a Bonaparte, but psychologically a Hauptmann von Köpenick." Cited in Heinz Höhne, *Canaris: Patriot im Zwielicht* (Munich, 1976), p. 79.

44 Erger, *Kapp Putsch*, pp. 131–137; Krüger, *Brigade Ehrhardt*, p. 50; Höhne, *Canaris*, pp. 82–83.

45 Erger, *Kapp Putsch*, pp. 139–143. The quotation is from Friedrich von Rabenau, *Seeckt: Aus seinem Leben 1918–1936* (Leipzig, 1940), p. 221.

46 Erger, *Kapp Putsch*, pp. 143–149.

47 Forstmeier, "Marine im Kapp Putsch," p. 57.

48 Ibid., p. 58.

49 For the course of events in Wilhelmshaven, see ibid., pp. 59–65; Bird, *Weimar*, pp. 70–71.

50 For the events in Kiel, see Forstmeier, "Marine im Kapp Putsch," pp. 65–75; Bird, *Weimar*, pp. 71–77.

51 Forstmeier, "Marine im Kapp Putsch," pp. 63–64.

52 Cited in Stöckel, "Entwicklung der Reichsmarine," p. 116.

53 Otto Gessler, *Reichswehrpolitik in der Weimarer Zeit* (Stuttgart, 1958), p. 146.

54 Ibid., p. 147; Bird, *Weimar*, p. 90; Rahn, *Reichsmarine*, pp. 61–73.

55 Excerpts from Scheer's letter and Seeckt's reply are given in Rabenau, *Seeckt*, pp. 494–495.
56 Rahn, *Reichsmarine*, pp. 64–65, 72–73, 76–79.
57 Bird, *Weimar*, p. 102, n. 105.
58 Gessler, *Reichswehrpolitik*, pp. 147–149; Rahn, *Reichsmarine*, p. 63. Bird, *Weimar*, pp. 104–106, gives the dates as May 31 and June 1.
59 See Raeder, *Mein Leben*, 1, pp. 184–185.
60 In the fall of 1920, for example, twenty-one of the officers of the Ehrhardt Brigade informed the new head of the navy, Admiral Paul Behncke, that they wished to resign from the Service because they did not agree with the "redirection toward the water." Rahn, *Reichsmarine*, p. 92.
61 Stöckel, "Entwicklung der Reichsmarine," p. 114; Krüger, *Brigade Ehrhardt*, pp. 64–67.
62 Estimates of the total number of *Freikorps* veterans taken into the 15,000-man navy vary. One authority gives a total of 2,000 men for the two brigades together, while another suggests that 3,000 men were accepted from the Loewenfeld Brigade alone. Krüger, *Brigade Ehrhardt*, pp. 146–147.
63 Bird, *Weimar*, pp. 120–123.
64 Krüger, *Brigade Ehrhardt*, p. 70.
65 Ehrhardt's association with Hitler proved to be somewhat one-sided, for Hitler used the opportunity to win over many Ehrhardt men to his own cause. Krüger, *Brigade Ehrhardt*, pp. 68–131; also Andreas Werner, "SA und NSDAP. SA: 'Wehrverband,' 'Partietruppe' oder 'Revolutionsarmee'? Studien zur Geschichte der SA und der NSDAP, 1920–1933" (PhD dissertation, Erlangen/Nuremberg, 1964). For *Organisation Consul*, see Howard Stern, "The *Organisation Consul*," *Journal of Modern History*, 35 (March 1963), pp. 20–32.
66 Krüger, *Brigade Ehrhardt*, p. 70; Bird, *Weimar*, pp. 119–120.
67 For these developments, see Stöckel, "Entwicklung der Reichsmarine," pp. 98–99, also Appendix 7; Rahn, *Reichsmarine*, p. 59; Raeder, *Mein Leben*, 1, pp. 155–156. The number of deck officers in the Reichsmarine had dwindled from 601 in 1919 to a mere 37 by 1934.
68 A partial list of the navy's overseas cruises from 1922 to 1935 is given in Stöckel, "Entwicklung der Reichsmarine," Appendix 10.
69 Raeder, *Mein Leben*, 1, p. 248.
70 See Raeder's comments on politicians in *Mein Leben*, 1, p. 190; also Karl Dönitz, *Mein wechselvolles Leben* (Göttingen, 1968), p. 162.
71 Stöckel, "Entwicklung der Reichsmarine," p. 114.
72 Jost Dülffer, *Weimar, Hitler und die Marine: Reichspolitik und Flottenbau 1920–1939* (Düsseldorf, 1973), p. 63.
73 Bird, *Weimar*, pp. 146–147.
74 Caspar, *Partei und Wehrproblem*, p. 24.
75 Dülffer, *Hitler und die Marine*, p. 63.
76 For the Service's relationship with the SPD, see Caspar, *Partei und Wehrproblem*, especially pp. 24, 33–34, 50–54, 80–90; also Bird, *Weimar*, pp. 168–180. Caspar strongly emphasizes the SPD's rejection of the *Panzerschiff* appropriations as a factor in the armed forces' view that the party was unpatriotic. For the background to the *Panzerschiff* controversy and its impact on domestic politics, see Wolfgang Wacker, *Der Bau des Panzerschiffes "A" und der Reichstag* (Tübingen, 1959); also

Gert Sandhofer, "Das Panzerschiff 'A' und die Vorentwürfe von 1920 bis 1928," *Militärgeschichtliche Mitteilungen*, 1/1968, pp. 35–62.

77 For the high command's attitude toward the Communist Party, see Bird, *Weimar*, pp. 198–204; James M. Diehl, *Paramilitary Politics in Weimar Germany* (Bloomington, Ind., 1977), pp. 186–187, 352.

78 Dülffer, *Hitler und die Marine*, pp. 74–76. See also Gaines Post, Jr, *The Civil-Military Fabric of Weimar Foreign Policy* (Princeton, NJ, 1973).

79 Stöckel, "Entwicklung der Reichsmarine," pp. 94–95.

80 Ibid., p. 101; Friedrich Ruge, *In vier Marinen* (Munich, 1979), p. 71; Raeder, *Mein Leben*, 1, pp. 193–196.

81 Dönitz, *Wechselvolles Leben*, pp. 135–136, 166; Ruge, *In vier Marinen*, p. 72 and *passim*.

82 For the subsequent work by Ruge and Siegfried Sorge on the subject of *Menschenführung*, see below, Chapter 6.

83 Bräckow, *Marine-Ingenieuroffizierkorps*, p. 147.

84 Raeder, *Mein Leben*, 1, pp. 205–206; Ruge, *In vier Marinen*, p. 77.

85 Ruge, *In vier Marinen*, pp. 63, 80; Bräckow, *Marine-Ingenieuroffizierkorps*, p. 151.

86 The MOV was the successor to the Marine-Offizier-Hilfe (MOH), founded in December 1918 by Captain (ret.) Friedrich Freiherr von Bülow. Raeder, *Mein Leben*, 1, p. 180. The MOV rapidly became the most important organization outside the Service for naval officers, and, under its altered name, Marine-Offizier-Vereinigung, exists to this day. During the period under consideration, practically all active and retired officers belonged to the MOV.

87 Ibid., 1, pp. 177–178; Bräckow, *Marine-Ingenieuroffizierkorps*, pp. 137–159. For Raeder's efforts to deal with intra-service problems in the 1930s, see below, Chapter 5.

88 The subject of naval history was a matter of serious consideration for the Weimar navy, for, in a period of relative impotence, it provided the one means of preserving the lessons of sea power until the day when Germany would once again have a great navy. For this, see Keith W. Bird, "The Origins and Role of German Naval History in the Inter-War Period 1918–1939," *Naval War College Review*, 32 (March–April 1979), pp. 42–58. Also Edward Wegener, "Selbstverständnis und historisches Bewusstsein der deutschen Kriegsmarine," *Marine-Rundschau*, 67 (1970), pp. 322–324.

89 Alfred von Tirpitz, *Erinnerungen* (Leipzig, 1919); Alfred von Tirpitz, *Politische Dokumente*, 2 vols (Stuttgart and Berlin, 1924–1926).

90 Bird, "German Naval History," pp. 45–48.

91 For the history of the "Wegener thesis" to 1929, see Carl-Axel Gemzell, *Organization, Conflict, and Innovation: A Study of German Naval Strategic Planning, 1888–1940* (Stockholm, 1973), pp. 215–238, 266–271, 294–298, 319–345.

92 Bird, "German Naval History," p. 43.

93 For the Lohmann Affair, see Bird, *Weimar*, pp. 180–189; Dülffer, *Hitler und die Marine*, pp. 90–97; and a report from the year 1937 by a Captain Schüssler, reprinted in International Military Tribunal, *Trial of the Major War Criminals before the International Tribunal*, 42 vols (Nuremberg, 1947–1949), 34, pp. 552–565 (hereafter cited as IMT). Also, Höhne, *Canaris*, pp. 97–115.

94 Bird, *Weimar*, pp. 181–182; Raeder, *Mein Leben*, 1, p. 219.

95 Lohmann had some interesting ideas in this respect. The Phoebus company was to make defense-oriented films that would strengthen patriotism at home and allow German intelligence agents to operate under Phoebus covers abroad. The Berlin Bacon Company was intended to make money for other projects and also to support a fleet of fast bacon transports for delivery runs to England. In time of war the transports could serve as auxiliaries. Schüssler, "Kampf der Marine," in IMT, 34, pp. 560–564. Curiously enough, the bacon company was one of the few Lohmann enterprises to return a profit. Bird, *Weimar*, p. 185, n. 88.

96 Rahn, *Reichsmarine*, p. 288, n. 26.

3

The Navy in the Twilight of the Republic

The choice of a successor to Admiral Zenker loomed throughout the summer of 1928. Although the possibility of bringing Vice Admiral Konrad Mommsen out of retirement was considered in some circles, the most likely candidates for the position were the navy's three active vice admirals: Hermann Bauer, Hans Oldekop, and Erich Raeder. The dark horse among these was Raeder, the current head of the Baltic Naval Station, for he and Zenker were on poor terms. Raeder had repeatedly criticized what he perceived to be Zenker's preference for employing weak personalities on his staff at the Marineleitung in Berlin; he also felt that Zenker had not sufficiently protected the navy's interests against incursions by the army. Zenker, for his part, regarded Raeder's checkered political career as a distinct liability for a future chief of the navy. Raeder was under no illusion in this regard. Although he obviously viewed himself as the most qualified candidate for the position, he predicted that if Zenker had any role in the matter the choice would fall upon Bauer.[1]

The ultimate decision, however, rested not with Zenker but with the new Reichswehr Minister, Wilhelm Groener. Here Raeder enjoyed a far stronger position. Groener's naval adjutant at the time, Kurt Fricke, was a close associate of and former personal aide to Raeder. In addition, Raeder also enjoyed the strong support of the retired admiral, Magnus von Levetzow, and through him that of Friedrich Graf von der Schulenburg, an influential leader of the German National People's Party (DNVP).[2] Finally, Raeder had recently had an opportunity to impress the new Reichswehr Minister through his successful liquidation of the navy's interests in the politically suspect Imperial Yacht Club.[3] If Raeder could build on this favorable impression during the personal interview that Groener had scheduled for each of the three leading candidates, then perhaps the job would be his after all.

In early September, Groener summoned Raeder to Bad Kreuth in Bavaria. According to the admiral's perhaps overly dramatized reminiscences, the Reichswehr Minister questioned him for two days as to how he would run the navy if appointed its head. Raeder emphasized firm command from the top and insisted upon complete independence of the navy from the army in all matters. Although Groener was a dyed-in-the-wool army man—he had, after all succeeded Ludendorff as First Quartermaster General in 1918—Raeder's frankness appears to have made a favorable impression upon him. On September 15, Berlin newspapers announced the long-awaited resignation of Zenker and indicated that Raeder would probably be his successor.[4]

The announcement provoked an immediate storm of protest from moderate and leftist spokesmen, who were highly suspicious of Raeder's past connection with prominent opponents of the Republic. One newspaper saw the admiral as the real *spiritus rector* behind the navy's support of the Kapp *Putsch*, while another sought to connect him with *Organisation Consul* and its successors. Particularly disturbing were press allegations concerning Raeder's ties to the House of Hohenzollern. On three separate occasions during the past three years, it was charged, Raeder had presided over social events that had ended in royalist demonstrations for either Kaiser Wilhelm II or his brother, Grand Admiral Prince Heinrich.[5]

For a short while Raeder's position appeared precarious. The Reichswehr Ministry, however, was already taking steps to counter the accusations of the press. Under the leadership of Captain Friedrich Götting, the naval representative in the Wehrmachtabteilung (a joint army-navy agency for handling political problems that beset the Reichswehr), a careful defense was planned to refute many of the charges and to diminish the importance of others.[6] At the same time the text of a recent speech by Raeder was circulated among leading republicans such as Carl Severing and Hermann Müller to show that Raeder had indeed reconciled himself to the Republic.[7] Yet despite the favorable course that Götting's campaign was taking, Raeder's patience was beginning to wear thin. On September 24, he wrote Götting a stinging denunciation of his critics:

> I have educated the sailors and the officers of the Baltic station to be loyal to the constitution, so that they now hold uniformly the correct views. That was not the case at the outset. For the rest, I consider myself a prop of the republic a thousand times more valuable than all those noisy propagandists, who in reality only intend to make us loathe the Republic.[8]

In a sense the letter was superfluous. The same day a Marineleitung circular announced that Raeder was assuming immediate command of the navy. In the days that followed, the uproar in the press gradually began to subside. Nevertheless, the *8 Uhr Abandblatt* could not resist a parting shot: on September 29, two days before Raeder's promotion to full admiral and his formal assumption of command, the paper noted his professions of loyalty to the Republic under the headline "Admiral Raeder Is Even Enamored with the Republic."[9] Only those who did not know the navy's new leader could have missed the intended sarcasm.

Raeder brought over thirty years of professional experience to his new command in Berlin. Born in 1876 at Wandsbek near Hamburg, the future admiral was the son of Hans Raeder, a teacher of French and English at the local *Gymnasium*, and Gertraudt, the daughter of the court musician, Albert Hartman.[10] Raeder was reared in a style typical for the middle-class German youth of his day—one that he later characterized as Christian and God fearing, combining "discipline tempered with affection."[11] At school he proved to be a capable if not brilliant student, and for a time he contemplated a career as an army medical doctor. However, during his senior year in the *Gymnasium* at Grünberg, Silesia—where his family had moved when he was 13—he won a prize in a school contest. The reward was a book by Admiral Reinhold von Werner which among other things described the world-wide naval travels of Prince Heinrich of Prussia. For Raeder, who had previously shown no interest in a career at sea, the book came as a revelation. After reading and rereading it he decided to become a naval officer.

Raeder entered the Service in 1894. After completing his midshipman's training he occupied a number of positions which put him into close contact with some of the most influential figures of Wilhelmian Germany. In the late 1890s and again from 1901 until 1903, he served under Prince Heinrich, about whom he had read as a schoolboy. From the spring of 1906 until the fall of 1908 he was assigned to the Nachrichtenbureau in Berlin, where he learned Admiral von Tirpitz's techniques of influencing public opinion from the master himself. Finally, in the fall of 1910 he was assigned as navigation officer to the imperial yacht *Hohenzollern*. During the long summer cruises he gained a more personal acquaintance with Wilhelm II, for aboard the *Hohenzollern* the Kaiser often became his "real self—warm-hearted, quick of comprehension, interested in everything and eager to please others."[12]

The outbreak of the Great War found Raeder with the Scouting Forces of the High Sea Fleet. At the Battle of the Skagerrak (Jutland) he served under Vice Admiral Franz Hipper aboard the *Lützow*, and during the winter of 1917–1918 he assumed command of the new cruiser *Cöln*, one of only two sea commands that he would enjoy during his career. In early October 1918 Raeder was reassigned to Berlin as chief of the navy's Central Bureau. He witnessed most of the revolutionary disturbances of that memorable autumn from the capital. Moreover, he obtained a first-hand view of the navy's dire predicament on November 6, when he carried dispatches to Wilhelmshaven that indicated that army units would have to be sent to restore order in the port.

Raeder weathered the rest of the revolutionary storm without particular difficulty. During the early days of the Republic he appears to have had no qualms about serving Germany's new masters, and he continued to fulfill his duties at the Central Bureau. During the Kapp *Putsch*, however, his career nearly came to a premature end. Hearing of Captain Ehrhardt's action against the Bauer government, Raeder rushed back to Berlin from leave in Hamburg and, with Trotha and the rest of the Admiralty staff, placed himself at the service of the Kapp regime. In the aftermath of the *Putsch*, Raeder was discreetly transferred to the Naval Archives Section where he was safely out of the line of fire of outraged republicans. At the archives he wrote two of the navy's three volumes on cruiser operations in the Great War and acquired what proved to be a lifelong appreciation for the historical significance of the German fleet.[13] Moreover, although he would continue to differ with Tirpitz on certain elements of naval strategy, the prewar organization of the fleet in particular, Raeder developed an enduring reverence for the *Baumeister* of Germany's maritime greatness. By the summer of 1922 Raeder could once again leave the archives and assume supervision of the navy's training program. There he made substantial contributions to revitalizing courses for officers and enlisted men that had been neglected since the outbreak of the war in 1914. True to his own upbringing, the teacher's son insisted upon "firm but friendly discipline" for the seamen and a "modest but definite feeling of pride and self-respect" for the officers.[14] In late 1924 he assumed command of the Light Forces in the North Sea, but he was to enjoy this, the second of his two sea commands, for only a few months. On January 7, 1925, Raeder was assigned to command the Baltic Naval Station.

The new assignment represented perhaps the greatest challenge that Raeder had yet encountered in his career. Aside from the command of the navy itself, the post of chief of the Baltic Naval Station was the most politically sensitive in the Service. At station headquarters in Kiel, officers and men were under the constant supervision of the city's largely Socialist population, and the station commander had to be constantly aware of the impression that he and his men were making. Yet Raeder was showing signs of increasing political adaptability. Already in 1923 he had written his friend, Magnus von Levetzow, to express disapproval of General Ludendorff's participation in the Hitler *Putsch* in Bavaria. Constitutional revision by a rightist coalition, not conspiratorial activity, was the means to end Germany's present woes: Ludendorff ought to save himself in case he were once again needed against Germany's foreign enemies.[15] Moreover, as station chief, Raeder showed an ability to live and let live vis-à-vis the local SPD representatives. Although he occasionally gave private vent to his frustration over the "vile attacks of the left parties" on the armed forces, and although he more than once allowed a subordinate or former comrade to carry his adulation of the House of Hohenzollern beyond the boundaries of republican good taste, he was at least able to prevent serious friction between naval personnel and the local populace during the almost three years that he was station chief.[16] Perhaps the greatest testimony to his accomplishments in this regard was given in the fall of 1928 when Raeder left to assume command of the navy. From the Socialist chief of the Kiel police, Police President Dietrich, came the farewell message: "You have succeeded in getting in close touch with the working people .... We are sorry you are leaving."[17]

Many in Berlin were just as sorry to see the new admiral come to their city. As a result of the Lohmann affair and the recent revelations concerning his politically suspect past, Raeder assumed office amidst an atmosphere of widespread distrust toward the navy on the part of many government figures. Nor was resentment over Raeder's appointment limited entirely to civilian circles: Admiral Zenker apparently still begrudged him his nomination. The mood was icy, therefore, when the older man relinquished his office to his successor, with the two officers using the archaic third person singular (Excellency) as the mode of address.[18]

Nevertheless, Raeder was not the type of man to be daunted by adversity, and immediately after assuming office he sought to win over skeptical republicans. On October 4 Groener conducted a press conference on Raeder's behalf in which the Reichswehr Minister attempted to lay to rest persisting doubts concerning the admiral's loyalty to the Republic. At the same time, Raeder paid official visits to the more important members of the Hermann Müller Cabinet. Although Raeder was shocked to find his veracity questioned by the more skeptical Cabinet members, he overcame his discomfiture and countered their distrust with frankness. This technique was not without results, and the Socialist Minister of the Interior, Carl Severing, came away from his initial meeting with the impression that Raeder was a man who would tell the truth.[19]

Another opportunity for impressing the Cabinet came later in the month. On October 18 Groener summoned both Raeder and the head of the army, General Wilhelm Heye, to appear before the Cabinet to consider the final liquidation of the Lohmann affair. Many of the less important of the illegal rearmament programs had already been terminated, and, although the Reichstag would not be told, the Müller government had decided to assume direct responsibility for those that were to be continued. In return, the heads of the army and navy had to reveal to the Cabinet the exact nature of their secret projects and to promise to undertake no further steps in this direction without government approval. Once again Raeder made a strong impression. Although the admiral would continue to have some differences with the Socialists in the Cabinet, by the end of his first month in command he had made significant progress in solidifying his position with regard to the politicians.[20]

One potentially serious problem remained which, curiously enough, concerned Raeder's relationship with the man who had appointed him, Reichswehr Minister Groener. As a former army general Groener was quick to label himself as "no fleet enthusiast." The Imperial Navy, he maintained, had been a needless luxury which had drained funds from the army at a time when it could ill afford it. Raeder, for his part, tended to regard the Reichswehr Minister as yet another narrow-minded army officer who needed to be initiated into the mysteries of sea power.[21] It therefore remained to be seen whether Groener would energetically support Raeder's efforts to expand the fleet through an accelerated "pocket" battleship program. Were this not the case, then Raeder's tenure at the Marineleitung promised to be a short one.

When the clash came, however, it stemmed not from the larger questions of naval policy but from the day-to-day administration of the navy. Groener was determined to play a more active role than had his predecessor, Dr Gessler, in running the armed forces. Since his appointment the previous winter the new Reichswehr Minister had grown accustomed to taking matters up directly with army department heads, thereby bypassing General Heye. When Groener extended this practice to the navy, Raeder informed him that it directly contradicted the program that he had submitted to the Reichswehr Minister during their interview at Bad Kreuth the previous September. According to Raeder, the matter came to a head in December 1928 when the Reichswehr Minister publicly criticized his admiral for implementing a policy that was in fact Groener's own. Raeder blew up and threatened to resign, whereupon Groener apologized.[22] The confrontation evidently cleared the air, for the two men appear to have arrived at a *modus vivendi* shortly thereafter. Groener would respect Raeder's administrative prerogatives and pursue the "pocket" battleship program in so far as the Reich's limited resources would allow. Raeder, recognizing both the domestic and foreign opposition to rearmament, would accept a relatively slow tempo. In the meantime he would concentrate on stamping the navy with his own style until a time when there were enough ships to meet his expectations.

Raeder wasted no time in setting a new tone for the navy. Already on October 23, over a month before he and Groener thrashed out their compromise over the administration of the navy, an office circular had announced that the following guidelines would govern the future discharge of business at the Marineleitung:

- reduction of correspondence (too many and overly long reports)
- important reports from commanders and inspectors are to be sub-mitted to the chief of the navy
- reprimands at higher levels of command are to be carried out by the chief personally
- no reports to the [Reichswehr] Minister without prior notification
- chief decides whether he will take part in the report . . .
- once decisions are made by the chief they are to be supported by all officers
- no secret material [*G. Sachen*] unknown to the chief.[23]

The authoritarian tone of the circular was unmistakable, and it probably said more about the new commander than all of the press reports that had accompanied his appointment combined. Raeder, however, was just beginning. A week later another announcement informed the staff that henceforth there would be no discussion at joint meetings of department heads.[24] At the end of the month a number of older officers were placed on early retirement. Ostensibly the measure was part of an effort to bring younger men to positions of command, but among the victims of the "great seal hunt," as it was known to the junior officers, was the navy's leading maverick, Wilfried von Loewenfeld, the last of the *Freikorps* commanders.[25] Raeder was clearly taking no chances that his authority might be challenged by one of his more charismatic subordinates, and throughout Raeder's tenure of office one criticized the commander at one's peril.[26] Nor was the new head of the navy unaware of the change that he had wrought. Indeed, less than one month after his formal assumption of command, he wrote Levetzow that things were already changing in Berlin: "In contrast to the very weak attitude of my predecessor I have put a very tight rein on things for I noticed too much working at cross purposes. I hope it will work out well."[27]

A strong authoritarian tendency, then, characterized Raeder's leadership of the navy. Closely related to this was his pronounced emphasis upon tradition. One means of coupling the new Reichsmarine to the old navy was through the evocation of past glories, either through the yearly celebration of anniversaries such as the Battle of the Skagerrak and the scuttling of the fleet at Scapa Flow or by the christening of ships bearing the proud names of vessels or officers that had distinguished themselves in the Great War. Another manifestation of the strong traditionalist bent within the navy was Raeder's insistence that the naval uniform, the visible link with the past, be worn as frequently as possible.[28] Still another example in this regard was the navy's carefully maintained connection with former naval personnel, either on an individual basis or through veterans' groups.

The authoritarian and traditionalist impulses merged perhaps most closely in Raeder's own deep religiosity. During the last year of the First World War he had personally conducted religious ceremonies aboard the cruiser *Cöln*. Now, although the Weimar Constitution had made participation at religious observances a voluntary matter, he sought to encourage religious attitudes by example, by attending church as often as possible and by letting his officers know that church attendance on their part was desirable as well. Although a Protestant in an overwhelmingly Protestant navy, Raeder was also at pains to see that the Catholic minority within the navy felt that its spiritual needs were satisfied. Any divisive influence, after all, was taboo in the new navy, and its commander wanted to be certain that Germany's troublesome confessional question remained outside the Service.[29]

In many ways the authoritarian, traditionalist, and religious influences within the navy marked it off as a rather old-fashioned institution. In one respect, however, the navy was particularly modern. Raeder appreciated the value of good public relations. Indeed, given the widespread popular skepticism concerning the navy's past performance, its present usefulness, and Raeder's own suitability to command it, the concern assumed a position of virtual preeminence in the years 1928 to 1933. The period was seen as a preparatory phase, wherein the groundwork for a larger, stronger fleet, freed from the restrictions of Versailles, would be laid. It was clear that the navy would have to counter its unfavorable image with the broader public if it were to accomplish its task. Raeder later described his goal at this time as the creation of "one large 'navy family' throughout Germany."[30] In this mission Raeder was particularly well suited, for he had a highly successful model for popularizing the navy in the person of his mentor, Alfred von Tirpitz.

The master's influence was readily apparent in Raeder's dealings with what may be termed the more distant members of the German "naval family," the politicians and civilians. One tried and true method carried over by Raeder was the practice of influencing important Reichstag deputies by inviting them for short cruises when the navy was on maneuvers. Although the ships were still for the most part antiquated, the cruises nevertheless offered the opportunity to impress the laymen with the technical expertise and the strict discipline of the Service. The practice yielded substantial dividends when the naval budget came up for discussion in the Reichstag.[31] In addition, Raeder for a time sponsored a number of *Bierabende* to which influential leaders of Weimar Germany—politicians, businessmen, media personalities, and army officers—were invited to share the largesse of the navy and to imbibe the lessons of sea power. Unfortunately, by February 1930 depression-ridden Germany could no longer afford such measures, and the practice had to be terminated until better days.[32]

Another means of maintaining close ties with at least a portion of the public was through the various naval interest groups that existed in Weimar Germany. Here again Raeder showed himself to be a true *Tirpitzianer*. Already, as Inspector of Education he had been instrumental in founding the Skagerrak Club in Kiel to provide a forum for meetings between officers and civilians. Later, as commander of the Baltic Naval Station, the admiral with Frau Raeder had supervised the resurrection of the Naval Wives Society. As head of the navy Raeder's ability to foster these and similar activities increased significantly, and it was not long before he was warmly recommending to the naval personnel that they join the Naval League.[33]

If politicians and civilian enthusiasts represented the more distant "relatives" of Raeder's naval family, then the thousands of veterans of the Imperial and Republican navies formed the immediate kith and kin. Here Raeder's strong emphasis upon tradition reinforced his notion of *paterfamilias*, and he took special pains to uphold the ties between veterans and active service men. On one occasion he noticed that requests by former naval personnel were being answered in a curt, bureaucratic style. He "requested" that the practice cease and that in future all responses be phrased in a comradely fashion so as to emphasize the bond between those serving in the Reichsmarine and their predecessors. He made it a practice to invite all of the retired officers living in the immediate vicinity of Kiel and Wilhelmshaven when the navy held memorial services at its two main ports. Close ties between active and inactive officers were also fostered by their common membership in the League of Naval Officers (Marine Offizier Verband). Indeed, Raeder saw a particularly important role for the inactive members of this and other retired officer organizations as apostles of the gospel of navalism. As a Marineleitung circular of February 1932 put it while describing the prospect of lectures by a host of retired officers:

Few know more about the organization, the construction program and the wartime and peacetime activities of today's navy . . . . It is in the navy's own interest to foster the bonds between the active Wehrmacht with the veterans through such lectures.[34]

A final feature of Raeder's conception of the naval family was his dogged defense of his own spiritual father, Tirpitz. Although he was privately willing to acknowledge that Tirpitz had made some mistakes—particularly with regard to the divided command structure of the Imperial Navy—his own authoritarian and traditionalist proclivities prevented him from tolerating public criticism of the navy's patriarch. Moreover, by the time Raeder assumed command in 1928, the official naval history project, the overwhelming drift of which had been pro-Tirpitz, was approaching its tenth anniversary. Even the mildest criticism of Tirpitz would, in Raeder's view, compromise the admiral, his numerous protégés on the project (Raeder included) and, worst of all, the navy. Under Raeder, therefore, the official navy standpoint idolizing Tirpitz solidified. When Wolfgang Wegener's critical *Seestrategie des Weltkrieges* appeared in print in 1929, Raeder saw to it that the book's publisher, E. S. Mittler und Sohn, which did a significant business in official and unofficial naval literature, played down its advertisement. He also instructed Captain Otto Groos to discredit the book through lectures at the Marineleitung and at the bases at Kiel and Wilhelmshaven. Later, Raeder assured his friend Trotha, who was also a passionate devotee of Tirpitz, that no publications on the war at sea would be issued with which Trotha was not in agreement.[35]

Raeder's preferences in the depiction of the navy's past soon became common knowledge within the Service. When the retired admiral Kurt Assmann replaced Eberhard von Mantey as head of the naval archives, he found that Raeder was still primarily concerned that the navy's past be depicted in a favorable light and only secondarily with historical truth. The frustrated Assmann was eventually moved to remark: "I am convinced that it makes no difference to you Herr Admiral, what we write . . . . We must only write in such a way that you have peace from the old admirals." He was not far off the mark. As late as 1937, when the navy presumably had more important things to worry about than naval history, Raeder suppressed a study of the Admiralty Staff by Admiral (ret.) Gustav Bachmann on the grounds that "it is unconditionally necessary to hold back all publications contra Tirpitz."[36]

Such was the Raeder style. Some of its features, most notably its strong authoritarian tendency and its rigid control from the top, differed markedly from the practices of Raeder's predecessor at the Marineleitung. In other areas the two men's styles tended, to varying degrees, to merge. In one respect, however, the men were strikingly similar. Like Zenker, Raeder harbored a deep and abiding distrust of Communism. Moreover, Raeder was determined to make the struggle against Communism a primary feature of his tenure at the Marineleitung, and he was quick to reprimand those officers who did not share his enthusiasm for such a campaign.[37] The significance of this, the final feature of the Raeder style, was immense, for it strengthened the officer corps' already pronounced anti-Communist feelings. In addition, for reasons that will soon become evident, it goes far in explaining the Service's catastrophic misunderstanding of a similar totalitarian phenomenon, that of National Socialism. As such, Raeder's and the navy's attitude toward Communism during the last years of the Republic merits close attention.

As an active and widely traveled officer in the 1920s, Raeder had doubtless had a number of opportunities to witness the activities of the German Communist Party (KPD) before he assumed command of the navy. He nevertheless appears to have been somewhat surprised by the political storm that accompanied his appointment as head of the Marineleitung, and in a letter to Levetzow he placed the blame for the press attacks squarely on the shoulders of the navy's old bogeyman, the Communists.[38] Relations between the navy and the extreme left, which had never been cordial, were therefore poisoned from the very beginning of Raeder's command. Unfortunately a number of incidents, some major, some minor, served to accentuate the hostility between the Reichsmarine and the KPD throughout the remaining years of the Republic.

A foretaste of what was to come occurred as early as the first month of Raeder's command when authorities in Kiel uncovered evidence of a Communist attempt to infiltrate the navy. Throughout the following year efforts to follow up on this successful detection met with some isolated successes, but significant progress in the navy's struggle against Communist subversion foundered on a number of problems. There were legal objections to the dismissal of sailors who were merely suspected of being Communist agents and there were also government restrictions that limited the contribution that the Wehrmacht's own counterespionage agency, the *Abwehr*, could make in meeting internal subversion. Moreover, the navy encountered problems with local authorities. Some failed to take the problem of Communist infiltration of the armed forces seriously enough to suit naval officers. Others, particularly in the case of the Kiel police officials, were suspected of sympathizing with the would-be subverters of the Reichsmarine. As a result the eager anti-Communist campaign of the naval officers became an increasingly frustrating task. They found sufficient evidence to convince themselves that efforts at infiltration were indeed being made; they did not, however, apprehend enough suspects to feel that their countermeasures were having the desired effect.[39]

The situation was further exacerbated in the fall and winter of 1929–1930 by the so-called *Emden* affair.[40] On October 13, 1929, the cruiser *Emden*—at that time the showpiece of the navy—was homeward bound from a voyage around the world. When the ship put into Puerto Colombia, Colombia, some of the crewmen began a shipboard birthday celebration in the enlisted men's quarters. According to the navy's later account, in the course of the late afternoon and evening they became drunk on strong export beer and topped off the evening with a songfest. Unfortunately, their repertoire included a number of verses of the *Internationale*. Thus illuminated, two of the men borrowed a red handkerchief from a friend and hoisted it to the aftermast of the cruiser as a joke. It remained there until the next morning when it was noticed and removed.

There the affair ought to have ended. When the *Emden* reached Wilhelmshaven, however, the two culprits and the owner of the handkerchief were taken before a court martial. The two main offenders were sentenced to five weeks' imprisonment for singing a forbidden political song and for disorderly conduct. The handkerchief owner was acquitted. The navy nevertheless initiated dismissal proceedings against all three men.

It was at this point that the matter came to the attention of the press. On December 28 the *Welt Am Abend* published an account of the incident, and the next day the Communist *Rote Fahne* followed with its own version of the affair. Instead of attacking the severity of the punishment actually meted out—the offenses had, after all, been of a relatively trivial nature—the *Rote Fahne* chose to make a full-fledged mutiny out of the matter. Disgusted by the free and easy life style of the *Emden*'s officers and enraged by their own miserable existence aboard ship, the sailors, the *Rote Fahne* alleged, had rebelled, raised the red flag and forced the immediate return of the ship to Germany. The article concluded with the observation that the spirit of Reichpietsch and Köbis, of November 1918, was alive within the fleet.[41]

Subsequent articles embroidered upon the original story, and moderate and rightist newspapers eventually came to the point of asking themselves whether the authorities were trying to cover up something. A number of poorly conceived denials by the Reichswehr Ministry and the Marineleitung further contributed to the uneasy feeling that something was amiss in the fleet. By the end of February 1930 the affair had blown over, but not before the Reichsmarine had suffered acute embarrassment. Moreover, the incident left naval officers and Communists with their opinion of each other confirmed. To the officers it seemed that the Communists would stop at nothing to subvert the navy. To the Communists it appeared just as certain that the officers would stoop to any measure to maintain the reputation of the Service.[42]

The coming of the Great Depression further exacerbated relations between the Communists and the navy. The long lines of unemployed workers and the manifest inability of the reigning parties of the "Weimar coalition" to cope with Germany's economic crisis gave renewed hope to those within the KPD who were convinced that a proletarian revolution was just around the corner. At the same time the Communist Party's resounding electoral successes offered a clear indication that many Germans were joining the ranks of the KPD. In September 1930 the party gained over 1,300,000 more votes than it had in the previous national election (1928) and increased its Reichstag representation from 54 to 77 delegates. Two years later, in July 1932, it gained an additional 700,000 voters; its Reichstag representation rose to 89 deputies. And while the KPD's rival on the extreme right, the National Socialists, suffered a disheartening defeat when elections were held again the following November, the same could not be said for the Communists. KPD support rose by another 700,000 voters to an all-time peak of 5,980,239 and an even 100 representatives in the Reichstag. Clearly as late as November 1932 there was no indication that the red wave had crested.[43]

None of these developments was lost upon the leaders of the navy. Although active members of the Reichsmarine were partially shielded from the worst effects of Germany's economic crisis, fear of unemployment doubtless weighed heavily upon the minds of those about to leave the Service and made at least some of them more susceptible to the approaches of Communists who depicted a better life in the Soviet Union. KPD propagandists also sought to sow dissension in the ranks by contrasting the purportedly miserable life of the German sailor with his counterpart in the Red Navy, where there were supposed to be no differences between the living conditions of officers and men. One doubts whether these approaches had any significant effect on Reichsmarine personnel, but navy and Reichswehr Ministry officials were determined to maintain their guard. The Reichswehr Ministry adopted the practice of bestowing public praise upon sailors who contributed to the apprehension of civilian leaflet distributors. In addition, one eager officer pursued the feasibility of bringing Communists who had been caught attempting to subvert the navy in foreign ports back to Germany for prosecution.[44]

By the fall of 1931 the navy's concern with the threat of Communism had gone beyond the mere prevention of leaflet distribution and the like. Many officers feared that Germany's massive unemployment problem would soon create enough desperate men to allow a Communist uprising on the model of the Spartacist insurrections of 1919. The atmosphere was especially tense in Kiel, where rumors abounded of KPD black lists carrying the names of naval officers who were to be liquidated in the event of a *Putsch*.[45]

The commander of the Baltic Naval Station, Rear Admiral Gottfried Hansen, was determined to combat what he termed this "fear psychosis" on the part of his officers and men. Twice during the fall of 1931 he had his chief of staff, Fregattenkapitän Wilhelm Marschall, write the Reichswehr Ministry to call attention to the increased incidents of attempted subversion on the part of KPD agents. Marschall argued that the local criminal investigators could not devote enough attention to their work, and he therefore requested that a second inspector be sent who could work exclusively or primarily on the Communist problem.[46]

Hansen soon got into the act himself. On December 9 he issued an order wherein he complained about the unenthusiastic attitudes that officers were showing in the face of the Communist menace. What was worse, in some cases officers had even approved requests by fearful sailors that they be allowed to withhold their name or to transfer to another command after bringing testimony against Communists. Sailors had also been known to avoid returning home on leave for fear of the local KPD. Hansen reminded his officers that sailors could be issued firearms in those particular cases where their fears were legitimate. As for the rest, his solution was simple:

> I request that this weak, unmanly attitude on the part of our sailors, who ought to be the pick of our nation's youth and the defenders of

the fatherland, be fought with strictness on the one hand and with constant instruction and advice on the other. The advice ought not, however, to lead to subordinates refusing to report incidents out of fear of unpleasantness . . . . If the armed force of the state allows itself to be chased from the street by the terror of a minority then the firm bulwark of the state would be shaken and the KPD would have won a tremendous advantage.[47]

The tone of Hansen's order was, of course, music to Raeder's ears, for it was exactly what the commander of the navy had been preaching for years. Nevertheless, that Hansen had been forced to issue the order at all was an indication to Raeder that many were ignoring his own instructions to provide the sailors with the requisite instruction on the subject of Communism. Shortly after receiving a copy of Hansen's order, therefore, Raeder issued his own warning to the officer corps: "Superiors who do not recognize the great significance of this task and do not pursue it with the necessary zeal are not suitable for further service in the Wehrmacht."[48]

With Raeder's decree the battle began in earnest. In many respects, however, the struggle was a decidedly unequal one. Indeed, just how unequal was already becoming evident at the time that Raeder unleashed his December exhortation to battle, for by a stroke of good fortune the navy had obtained an inside view of its enemy's camp.

In the fall of 1931 the Hamburg police had confiscated a small hoard of papers from a local Communist named Friedrichs.[49] Friedrichs appears to have been primarily concerned with organizing KPD activities in the Reichsmarine, and the police dutifully delivered copies of the "Hamburg material," as it came to be known, to the navy. The reports contained therein offered a rare glimpse of the nature of Communist efforts to infiltrate the navy. In addition, the responses to the material by both the KPD and the Marineleitung provide considerable insight into the psyches of those two adversaries.

Part of the material was distinctly alarming to the navy, for Friedrichs spoke confidently of wide-ranging Communist plans to recruit sailors, organize cells, and publish illegal newspapers under the noses of the officers. In addition, one of Friedrichs' informants indicated that progress had already been made for the party had formed *Aktivgruppen* (groups of four or five men) aboard the battleship *Hessen* and at the naval establishment at Kiel-Wik. Two workers employed by the navy had been recruited elsewhere. Most alarming was a report dated June 3, 1931, which claimed that a giant cell of eighty-four sailors existed aboard the *Hessen*. This informant added that there had been a short work stoppage that spring in protest against poor food and harsh treatment by officers. Most sailors still stood outside the cell, but if things "blew up" they would come over to the party. One need not worry about the officers, the KPD informant argued, for they were even worse than their counterparts of the prewar era.

All of this must have been highly discomforting to the Marineleitung. On the other hand, the "Hamburg material" also indicated that the KPD was having problems of its own. Another report from the *Hessen*—presumably from a different informant—indicated that one *Aktivgruppe* had been completely useless and that preparatory work left much to be desired. Moreover, a report by a recently dismissed sailor provided an entirely different picture of life on the smaller vessels of the fleet.[50] There the men had little to complain about. They received as much as they wanted to eat, and living conditions, although close, were cheery enough. As to the great proletarian struggle, the men were completely indifferent, preferring card games, chess, food and drink, and, above all, women.[51] Proletarian literature was equally lacking, for the sailors preferred books about the Wild West or adventure novels like *U-Boot im Fegefeuer* (U-boat in Purgatory).[52] The men were for the most part convinced nationalists, and to the extent that they concerned themselves with politics at all, they supported the National Socialists, whose program many knew by heart. There were a few "comrades" around, but they were all very cautious. For all practical purposes the spirit of Reichpietsch and Köbis was dead and buried.

The "Hamburg material" thus presented a conflicting view of life in the navy. On the one hand it offered at least some evidence that conditions on the larger ships were conducive to the success of KPD efforts to infiltrate the Reichsmarine. On the other hand the picture aboard the smaller vessels was distinctly discouraging from the Communist viewpoint. Yet a number of qualifications are necessary to the assessment that the various reports gave of conditions within the navy. It must be remembered that recruits were carefully chosen volunteers who had to pass through a number of screening processes before they were admitted into the Service. Recruiters sought the most patriotic candidates, and although it was possible for agents to pose as convinced nationalists when entering, all but the most dedicated of revolutionaries would have balked at the navy's twelve-year service commitment. Isolated cases of successful recruitment of discontented sailors did occur, but the Marineleitung was on its guard and suspects were whisked out of the Service at a moment's notice. Nor should one make too much of the party's claims to have won over a sizeable portion of the crew of the *Hessen*. The report of a work stoppage there was doubtless encouraging to Friedrichs and company, but the officers aboard the ship appear not to have noticed the "revolt" at all.[53] Indeed, the more one analyses KPD reports emanating from the Reichsmarine the more one is struck by the contrast between the optimistic predictions and the meager results obtained by the party's agents. Perhaps Friedrichs' informants were trying to buoy up their own sagging spirits. Perhaps they were attempting to deceive their superiors (and employers) in the party. In either case it seems that the party would have been better served by the more sober analyses of the task that lay ahead, such as the one offered by the sailor from one of the small vessels of the fleet cited above. Instead, the party preferred to place its own interpretation upon the report. As a superior's jargon-ridden response expressed it:

Manifestly incorrect views and unpolitical consideration of the facts. So it appears in the heads of some sailors if they are not educated and cultivated. Actually there is neither contentment nor class harmony on the ships. Concrete proof [is] present that the tradition of Reichpietsch and Köbis is still alive.[54]

The KPD, it is clear, was unwilling to discontinue the struggle. The Marineleitung, for its part, was as determined as it had always been to eradicate all vestiges of Communist influence. For while the Hamburg documents showed the difficulty that the navy's adversaries were having in their efforts at infiltration, their occasional mentioning of cells and contacts proved too tantalizing for the navy's proven Communist hunters to ignore.[55]

Throughout the first months of 1932, therefore, the Marineleitung's energetic campaign continued. At times it must have appeared that the navy was singlehandedly carrying on the struggle. Law enforcement officers in the smaller garrison towns of Pillau and Swinemünde proved too disorganized or inexperienced to deal properly with Communist tactics, and the navy continued to harbor deep suspicions of the political sympathies of the police officials in Kiel. The Marineleitung also received the impression that its own officers were not sufficiently schooled in the methods of countering subversion. Familiarity with the Reichswehr Ministry's ordinances and procedures on the subject, for example, was lacking, and some officers were still not convinced of the seriousness of the problem. One Communist had slowly worked his way into an important civilian position at the naval hospital at Kiel-Wik and had been influencing sailors there for ten years without being noticed. The naval high command accordingly reemphasized the measures it had ordered the previous December: more instruction and advice for the sailors from the officers. Whoever was not up to the task was to be dismissed.[56]

Yet the situation was slowly evolving in the navy's favor. Gradually the combined measures of the police and naval officials—interception of mail, persistent shadowing of suspected seamen, veiled warnings to sailors who kept questionable company—began to have their effect. At Pillau in January 1932, the efforts of the police inspector who had just been sent there to supplement the hitherto ineffectual work of the local police uncovered the entire KPD organization in East Prussia. That same winter even Dietrich, the oft-maligned president of the Kiel police, showed signs of activity. In March the navy enjoyed perhaps its greatest success thus far, for with the cooperation of an enthusiastic new police inspector, Walther Schröder, it was able to break up an important Communist ring in Kiel and arrest its leader.[57]

Naval officers were ecstatic. In April Lieutenant Commander Topp, a staff officer at the Kiel Naval Station, wrote a colleague at the Reichswehr Ministry explaining just how much progress had been made. Topp was full of praise for Inspector Schröder and found him a definite improvement over his predecessor, Inspector Köhler. Unfortunately Schröder was still bound by the "silly" insistence of Police President Dietrich that

63

he also keep an eye on the activities of right-wing movements. Nevertheless, the recent elections for the Reich President, which pitted Hitler, Hindenburg, and the Communist candidate, Ernst Thälmann, against one another, had brought significant electoral losses to the Communists in Kiel, apparently in favor of the National Socialists. Topp hoped that the forthcoming elections for the state of Prussia would change matters even more in the navy's favor.[58]

By June the Marineleitung must have felt that at long last it was winning the struggle. Many of its own sailors who had fallen under suspicion had proven to be good patriots after all. Other names that were listed in confiscated reports, purportedly members of navy cells, were found to be fictitious. Best of all, both Wilhelmshaven and Kiel had now been quiet for several months. While this was no guarantee that the Communists were not merely regrouping their forces after their recent setbacks, it was still highly welcome news. Moreover, legal proceedings were underway against Police President Dietrich and Inspector Köhler, both of whom the navy had long suspected of covertly aiding the Communists, and their imminent transfer or dismissal seemed assured. In all probability responsibility for the continued struggle against the enemy would be assumed by the navy's new champion, the indefatigable Schröder, who just that month had journeyed to Berlin to press for more concerted efforts by the police in all of the coastal cities. While there, Schröder also made a request that was dear to the navy's heart, namely that his duties be restricted exclusively to the prevention of Communist subversion.[59]

Yet by midsummer of 1932, it was becoming increasingly unlikely that such a measure could be justified, for the Communist menace appeared to be evaporating before the navy's eyes. The few propaganda leaflets that turned up here and there bore all the marks of having been printed in Berlin or another city rather than in the navy's garrisons. More importantly, their content seemed to have altered as well. Earlier leaflets had addressed specific local grievances of the sailors, giving rise to the suspicion that the Communists did have informers inside the navy. The more recent ones, by contrast, addressed such general topics that it appeared that the KPD's sources within the Reichsmarine had all but dried up. Word reached police and naval investigators that differences over tactics had led to serious arguments within the local Communist Party organization at Kiel and even to some resignations. By September the other navy garrisons were also reporting a decrease in KPD activities. As far as could be ascertained—and it was always difficult to measure progress in the shadowy war against subversion—the navy had won the campaign of 1932 decisively. Whether new struggles would follow in the year ahead, however, remained an open question.[60]

The navy's response to the other totalitarian movement threatening Germany in the early 1930s, National Socialism, presents a marked contrast to its attitude toward Communism. Whereas the phenomenon of Communism weighed heavily upon the minds of the high command throughout the 1920s and early 1930s, the navy's leaders largely ignored the fledgling National Socialist German Workers' Party (NSDAP) during the first decade of its existence. To be sure, the navy did for a time maintain some loose connections with Hermann Ehrhardt's *Organisation Consul* and its successor formations, which in turn kept up a close liaison with the NSDAP. But direct contacts between the navy and the Party appear not to have existed. There were good reasons for this. Throughout the period prior to 1929, the NSDAP remained a marginal factor in the larger context of German politics. What influence it had was confined largely to Bavaria, and significant penetration by the Party into North Germany, where the navy's bases were and from whence the Service drew most of its recruits, was late in coming. The Party thus appeared to be of little concern to the Marineleitung, either as a potential ally or, even less likely, as a potential threat.[61]

The Great Depression changed this picture drastically. On the one hand it accentuated the navy's problems with the KPD, thus pointing out the need for additional support, both in the Reichstag and in the *Volk*, for what was perceived to be the life and death struggle of the Reichsmarine. On the other hand, through the polarization of the German electorate the depression seemed to offer up, *mutatis mutandis*, precisely this support in the form of an immensely strengthened movement from the right of Germany's political spectrum. As the NSDAP's electoral strength grew—from twelve Reichstag deputies in 1928 to 107 after the elections of September 1930—the Party became more and more an object worthy of the navy's attention.[62]

Upon examination by the navy, there was a considerable coincidence of interests between the Party and the Reichsmarine. Both institutions professed to seek a harmonious and nationalistic Germany that was free of class conflict. As such, both were highly antagonistic toward Marxists of all persuasions, particularly those in the KPD. Navy and Party likewise demanded revision of the Treaty of Versailles and German rearmament. Finally, in the realm of foreign policy, both navy and Party sought at least a temporary accommodation with the traditional makeweight in European politics, Great Britain.[63]

It was on this last question that the navy and the NSDAP began to part ways. Despite its setbacks in the Great War and the revolution, the navy continued to maintain that Germany's future lay on the water and hoped to obtain British acquiescence in German naval expansion through an adroit combination of alliance and security considerations (*Bündnis und Risikogedanken*).[64] In *Mein Kampf*, by contrast, Hitler argued that a policy of continental expansion alone held the key to Germany's future greatness. To win over Britain the Reich would temporarily have to renounce overseas colonies and sea power in order to establish a continental imperium.[65] To Raeder and to others within the Reichsmarine this was anathema. Unfortunately, Hitler's position showed little sign of changing in the years immediately following the publication of the National Socialist gospel. In 1928 party delegates did vote for the continuation of the navy's "pocket" battleship program, but this was more a symbolic gesture of Germany's right to rearm than an endorsement of German navalism. Hitler, for his part, cavalierly dismissed the Service's precious project with the words: "These are little ships [*Schiffchen*] with which we cannot command the seas."[66]

There was therefore good reason for the navy to be wary of the NSDAP. If Hitler's book and the pronouncements of his movement were to be taken seriously, then the National Socialists threatened the very existence of the navy. On the other hand the Party's pronounced nationalism and its strong emphasis upon the defense of the fatherland offered hope that it might eventually be useful to the navy. Much depended upon whether the leaders of National Socialism, particularly Hitler, could be won over to a more positive appreciation of German sea power.

The navy's treasury of retired officers offered one means of approaching the National Socialists. Unlike active officers, these men were not bound by the Reichswehr Ministry's strictures against "party political" activities; in fact, some of them had the leisure time to dabble in politics. Moreover, by the time the navy began to take the National Socialist movement seriously, the Marineleitung had a potential intermediary with the Party in the person of Magnus von Levetzow, who had resumed contact with the NSDAP in the fall of 1928 after a hiatus of four years. Levetzow was initially concerned with using the Party as a vehicle for bringing about the restoration of the exiled Kaiser, but he soon became an unofficial advisor to Hitler on naval matters as well. As such he occasionally passed official Reichsmarine material to Hitler with the knowledge of the Marineleitung, without, however, producing a noticeable alteration in the Party's attitude toward the navy. As time passed it became increasingly obvious that Levetzow was quite taken by Hitler. By November 1930, he was recommending *Mein Kampf* to his friends as "a pleasure to read," and by the following spring he was convinced that Hitler was the best man for the presidency of the Republic.[67] Nor was he reticent in expressing his increasingly favorable view of the Party's leader. In April 1932, he urged his comrades from the days of the Imperial Navy to vote for Hitler instead of Hindenburg in the forthcoming presidential election, and he closed his appeal with Admiral Scheer's command to the battle cruiser squadron at the Battle of the Skagerrak: "Full speed against the enemy [*Ran an den Feind*]."[68]

Other inactive officers drew similar conclusions. In the fall and winter of 1930 and 1931, retired Vice Admiral Paul Wülfing von Ditten, an ardent nationalist and president of the Kiel branch of the Vereinigte Vaterländische Verbände (an association of patriotic groups), on a number of occasions urged the Reichswehr Ministry to consider the futility of any struggle against National Socialist influence in the armed forces: "I in no way underestimate the dangers of this wild and seething movement, but I maintain that this nationalist impulse must be made useful for the fatherland and the Wehrmacht."[69] Others failed to see the dangers within the Party to which Wülfing alluded. In April 1932, Wilhelm Busse, a retired naval captain and member of the NSDAP, became president of Raeder's beloved Skagerrak Club. In November of the same year another retired officer, Captain Gustav von Stosch, first chairman of the League of Naval Officers (MOV), wrote Levetzow that his heart and convictions belonged entirely to the Hitler movement.[70] Whether the retired officers were having any impact on National Socialist views of the navy was unclear. What was clear was that National Socialism was having an effect upon them.

The example of the retired officers doubtless weighed heavily upon the minds of active officers. Curiously enough, however, it was not the older serving officers, who in many cases had been "crew comrades" of the inactive officers and who would presumably have been most apt to share their political views, who proved most susceptible to the appeal of National Socialism. Perhaps the repeated political embarrassments for the navy during the first decade of the Republic had bred a sense of caution into the more experienced officers. Perhaps they were uneasy with what one of their number termed the "psychosis" of Herr "Hittler" [sic] when it came to naval matters.[71] In any case, with a few exceptions, it was the younger naval officers who provided the initial converts to the cause of National Socialism.[72]

A number of explanations have been offered for the younger officers' enthusiasm for the Party. One factor may have been the improved chances for promotion if the National Socialists came to power and if the Service was able to convince them of the merits of naval expansion. Another consideration was doubtless the increasing economic plight of the younger officers. In March 1930, a Reichsmarine report found that while the circumstances of officers with the rank of lieutenant commander or above were generally satisfactory, the same could not be said for the navy's lieutenants. In addition, nearly all married personnel were encountering economic difficulties occasioned by high rents, frequent changes of assignments and the necessity of enrolling children in new schools. In short, the report concluded, the economic situation of almost all married men and younger officers was not healthy.[73]

Whatever the reasons for it, the increasing appeal of the Party revealed itself in various ways. As early as 1929 the head of the Ministeramt in the Reichswehr Ministry, Kurt von Schleicher, was alarmed at signs that the NSDAP was winning recruits among the workers and junior officers at the naval bases at Kiel and Wilhelmshaven. By 1930 even young officers who had the reputation of being democrats were defending the good intentions of their comrades who supported the National Socialists.[74] The next year evidence of party influence became so visible that KPD Reichstag deputies were compelled to abandon their aging hobby horse, the navy's supposedly scandalous treatment of the deck officers, and turn to the very real problem of National Socialist recruitment of naval personnel.[75]

By 1931, then, the problem had reached serious proportions. That fall the new commander of the Third Torpedo-Boat Flotilla, Leopold Bürkner, discovered that a large portion of his officers and men sympathized with the National Socialists.[76] Concurrently, naval investigators came across a published article that recounted a purported visit to the battleship *Hessen* by two Austrian party members. The report described crewmen reading the *Völkischer Beobachter* and singing the party anthem, the *Horst-Wessel-Lied*; it estimated that 90 per cent of the crew men supported the National Socialists. The commander of the ship, Captain Willy von Nordeck, might well have wondered whether this was the same *Hessen* that the Communists were citing as a model for their own infiltration techniques. Nevertheless, his decision to attach no importance to the report on the grounds that "it would only disturb the crew" would appear to have been somewhat shortsighted.[77]

Early in 1932 it became clear that the increasing penetration of the National Socialists into the Reichsmarine could no longer be ignored. Raeder nevertheless continued to pursue a cautious policy toward the Party. The Marineleitung did make what appears to have been a cautious overture to the National Socialists by permitting the Service's press representatives to distribute information on naval matters to party publications and by allowing the heads of the North Sea and Baltic Naval Stations to invite party editors to public relations activities sponsored by the navy. At the same time, however, the Marineleitung continued to frown upon too overt a courtship of the NSDAP. The openly pro-Hitler sermons of naval pastor Friedrich Ronneberger, for example, caused particular embarrassment to the navy and prompted some within the Marineleitung to demand his dismissal. In the end, Raeder opted for a personal letter to the pastor urging him to be more discreet in the future.[78]

Raeder proved to be a model of discretion in the spring of that year. In April Groener, who in 1931 had assumed the portfolio of Minister of the Interior in addition to that of Reichswehr Minister in the shaky cabinet of Heinrich Brüning, bowed to the urgings of the governments of the major German states and obtained the dissolution of the paramilitary organizations (primarily the SA or *Sturmabteilung*) of the National Socialists by presidential decree.[79] The reaction within right-wing circles was both immediate and predictable; it soon spread to a group of army officers headed by Groener's former protégé, Schleicher, who saw in the NSDAP a potential source for a renewed sense of German nationalism. Although Raeder also felt that Groener's measure was one-sided—the admiral favored the simultaneous prohibition of the *Reichsbanner*, a republican self-defense organization composed largely of SPD sympathizers—he loyally supported Groener in the ensuing crisis. When Schleicher sought to win Raeder over to a concerted effort to convince President Hindenburg, upon whose consent the continued existence of the Brüning Cabinet depended, to remove Groener from his position as Reichswehr Minister, Raeder dismissed the suggestion on the grounds that such activities did not appertain to the duties of the head of the navy. Although the storm over the SA prohibition did eventually compel Groener to resign as Reichswehr Minister in early May in a last-ditch effort to save the Brüning Cabinet, he expressly acknowledged the support of Raeder and his staff during the crisis and indirectly contrasted it with the behavior of army leaders.[80] It was clear that Raeder had learned at least one lesson from the 1920s: the head of the navy would support whatever government was in power.

At the same time, though, Raeder was careful not to alienate possible future governments. On May 13, the day after Groener's resignation, the admiral was surprised to read a Kiel newspaper report that he would assume the minister's vacant post. Raeder correctly surmised that this was a ploy by the wily Schleicher to tie him to Brüning's sinking ship, and he immediately instructed his chief of staff in Berlin, Rolf Carls, to publish a firm denial of the report. The rumor promptly disappeared. It nevertheless provided the National Socialists and the Marineleitung with an opportunity to feel one another out. On May 14 Levetzow wrote Raeder that he felt that his old comrade at arms would make an excellent Reichswehr Minister, and he assured him that he could count on the support of the NSDAP and other patriotic groups currently outside the government. Moreover, Levetzow exhorted, now was an excellent time "to harness this young, restless, and often impetuous and wild national strength" for the benefit of the navy. Raeder was not to be won over quite so quickly, however, and the following day he responded to Levetzow's veiled courtship with a suitably evasive reply: "If a strong Reich Cabinet appears possible I am conceivably prepared to enter it. I have, however, my own definite personal and professional demands, and these are by no means insignificant ones."[81]

Whether Levetzow passed the contents of Raeder's letter on to Hitler is uncertain. In any case the courtship of party and navy showed every sign of warming that month when Hitler ventured into Northwest Germany to rally support for the Party in the electoral campaign for the state of Oldenburg. On May 26 he spoke in Delmenhorst, a suburb of Wilhelmshaven, and received an invitation from Captain Franz Christoph von Schröder, the commander of the cruiser *Köln*, to visit the ship. Although Schröder was within his rights to ask anyone he pleased aboard, the invitation came as a disagreeable surprise to the older naval officers, who feared a political incident. The invitation as well as the timing of the *Köln*'s presence in Wilhelmshaven have occasioned speculation that the initiative for Schröder's action came from higher up. Both sides certainly behaved as if they were sounding each other out, and Hitler in particular gave every indication of anticipating some of the "personal and professional demands" that Raeder had mentioned to Levetzow in his letter of May 15. In the ship's guest book he expressed his desire to aid in the rebuilding of a fleet that was worthy of the Reich. Hitler privately repeated this promise, along with assurances that he would wipe out every instance of treason in the event that he became chancellor, to the officers of the *Köln*. Finally, in reference to the open secret concerning the Reichsmarine's rather blatant violation of the tonnage restrictions of the Treaty of Versailles in the case of the "pocket" battleship, he blustered: "If I say a ship is 10,000 tons, then it is 10,000 tons, no matter how big it actually is."[82]

This was indeed good news for the navy. For the first time since the publication of *Mein Kampf* the chief of the NSDAP gave a clear indication that the Party's position on the question of sea power had changed for the better. The National Socialists, for their part, were equally elated over Hitler's favorable reception aboard the *Köln*. Two days later Joseph Goebbels, the head of the Party's Reich Propaganda Leadership, visited the same ship and noted triumphantly in his diary:

> We visit the *Köln*. A marvel of technology. The Germans are not to be outdone. We tour the whole ship under the expert guidance of some officers. One is filled with pride and admiration.
> The navy is in fabulous form. Everyone, officers and men, completely with us. They read the *Völkischer Beobachter* and *Angriff*.

That night Goebbels accepted an invitation to dine aboard the battleship *Schlesien* and was equally impressed by conditions there: "The lieutenants are fine, tall boys, true pictures of soldierly manhood. All support us. . . . The navy is all right. A few officers accompany us to the meetings in mufti."[83]

Ultimately, jubilation over the favorable course of events in Wilhelmshaven proved to be premature. On May 30 Brüning submitted his and the Cabinet's resignation to the Reich President. Hindenburg, however, was still reluctant to entrust Germany's fortunes to the National Socialists, and the new chancellor turned out to be Franz von Papen, not Adolf Hitler.

Almost immediately a new note of caution entered into the Marineleitung's dealings with the Party. As Raeder wrote Levetzow on the morrow of Papen's appointment, it was now his wish that "*all* patriotically minded circles" would support the new government.[84] For the moment, at least, the National Socialists would once again recede to the back of Raeder's considerations.

The renewed sense of caution at the Marineleitung lasted throughout the summer. In early August the Reichswehr Minister in the Papen cabinet, the omnipresent Schleicher, found it necessary to warn both the army and the navy against National Socialist efforts to insinuate themselves into the armed forces. On August 10 Raeder's chief of staff, Carls, seconded Schleicher's efforts by reminding naval officers of the importance of maintaining the Service's above-party attitude "in spite of all understanding and sympathy for the patriotic and pro-military feelings of the nationalist oriented parties."[85]

Such admonitions increasingly fell upon deaf ears. Although the National Socialists received a major reverse on August 13 when Hindenburg refused Hitler's demand that he be named to head a government with emergency powers, many within the navy appeared not to notice this setback. Indeed, it was a visit to the Baltic resort of Heiligendamm and an enthusiastic reception aboard the battleship *Schlesien* that restored an exhausted Goebbels to his old fighting spirit: "All officers support us and are immeasurably sorry that it did not work out for us this time." Nor had the situation altered significantly by the fall of 1932, when Admiral Wilhelm Marschall, chief of the Baltic Naval Station, determined that the majority of his commanders were not sure of their men in the event of a National Socialist *Putsch*.[86]

In October, however, an event occurred which promised to reverse the favorable course that events were taking for the NSDAP within the navy. As Germany girded itself for new Reichstag elections on November 6—the fourth national election in less than a year—Hitler increasingly turned to violent attacks on the Papen government. On October 21 the *Völkischer Beobachter* published a lengthy critique of Papen's defense policies which included a blistering attack on the government's efforts to secure British and French permission to build battleships whose displacement would exceed the limitations imposed by the Treaty of Versailles. Battleship construction at this time, Hitler alleged, would only drive Britain into the camp of Germany's true enemies, Poland and the Soviet Union. What was more, the advisability of ever building battleships appeared highly questionable, for they were in reality just a "psychological reminiscence" of the Imperial era. For the foreseeable future, Hitler concluded, it would be far better for the Reich to devote its limited resources to strengthening the army and to leave the navy alone.[87]

Raeder's response was predictable. To Levetzow, who was now a National Socialist deputy in the Reichstag, he wrote indignantly:

> Hitler's contentions concerning rearmament a[nd] capital ships are among the silliest that he has come up with yet. How can the man disrupt foreign policy in so criminal a manner a[nd] jeopardize all the plans we have made, only to attack Papen . . . . What Hitler says about the Baltic and North Sea is really nonsense. If we were to follow him we would build a coastal defense force and would never be able to act against the French. Very soon our mission will once again be in the North Sea. One cannot remodel a navy overnight. He ought to leave negotiations with England to us a[nd] not act like a bull in a china shop. Aboard the *Cöln* he spoke quite differently.[88]

In the same letter Raeder also ventured the opinion that the young officers of the army and navy were now fully recovered from their infatuation with Hitler. Yet at the same time the admiral expressed the hope that the National Socialists would enter the government after the forthcoming election. Otherwise, he feared, the Party would fall under the influence of Gregor Strasser, who emphasized the socialist content of the party program at the expense of the nationalism that so clearly appealed to many within the navy. Thus while he was manifestly exasperated by Hitler's stubborn refusal to master the lessons that the Marineleitung had been seeking to impart for over a decade, Raeder still hoped that responsibility would sober the National Socialists and their enigmatic leader.

For a time, however, it appeared that the Party would never enjoy an opportunity to fulfill this hope. The November elections brought a serious setback for the NSDAP, whose representation in the Reichstag fell from 230 to 196 deputies.[89] The only consolation that many within the Party could take was that the slate of candidates supporting the government fared much worse, a clear indication that its days were numbered. In December the Papen government gave way to one headed by Schleicher, who at the last minute had managed to sever his ties with Papen in a manner suspiciously similar to the way in which he had turned on Groener the previous May. Unfortunately for Schleicher, Papen proved to be somewhat more vengeful than Groener had been. On January 4, 1933, he and Hitler met in Cologne to discuss the possibility of a coalition government headed by Hitler, with Papen as Vice Chancellor.[90] The spectacle of these two old enemies mending their political fences proved too much for Raeder. As he wrote Levetzow on January 7, the game of politics was becoming increasingly incomprehensible:

> May the new year finally bring a consolidation of the domestic situation! I no longer understand politics; I only see that the good of the fatherland plays almost no role in it, but only the ambitions of individuals or where possible money. The combination Papen–Hitler is completely inexplicable to me. When men fight in such a filthy manner they cannot later sit back down at the same table.[91]

Yet Hitler and Papen did sit at the same table. Indeed, on January 30 Hitler became the fifteenth and last chancellor of the Weimar Republic. Raeder was to be granted the domestic consolidation that he had wished for at the beginning of the new year. Whether it was exactly what he had in mind remained another question.

Notes for Chapter 3

1 Erich Raeder, *Mein Leben* (Tübingen, 1956–1957), 1, p. 220; Keith W. Bird, *Weimar, the German Naval Officer Corps and the Rise of National Socialism* (Amsterdam, 1977), pp. 206–207.

2 Jost Dülffer, *Weimar, Hitler und die Marine: Reichspolitik und Flottenbau 1920–1939* (Düsseldorf, 1973), pp. 106–107; Bird, *Weimar*, pp. 207–208.

3 For Raeder's role in withdrawing naval personnel from the Imperial Yacht Club and in founding the Naval Regatta Club (Marine Regatta Verein), see Bundesarchiv-Militärarchiv, Freiburg, West Germany (hereafter cited as BA-MA), RM 6/272 "RWM ML (FK Götting): Kaiserliche Jachtklub, 31. 8. 1926–15. 6. 1933."

4 Raeder, *Mein Leben*, 1, pp. 220–221.

5 Bird, *Weimar*, pp. 159, 209, 214–215; F. L. Carsten, *The Reichswehr and Politics 1918 to 1933* (Oxford, 1966), p. 288.

6 Bird, *Weimar*, pp. 211–217.

7 "Vortrag gehalten von Viceadmiral [*sic*] Raeder Dr. h.c. waehrend der Geschichtswoche in Kiel 23.I.28 und der Ratsstuhlstiftung in Stralsund am 8.II.1928," reprinted in International Military Tribunal, *Trial of the Major War Criminals before the International Tribunal*, 42 vols (Nuremberg, 1947–1949) (hereafter cited as IMT), 40, pp. 598–603.

8 Quoted in Carsten, *Reichswehr and Republic*, p. 288.

9 BA-MA, RM 8/50 MIB 2974, September 24, 1928; Bird, *Weimar*, p. 217.

10 Unless otherwise noted the following biographical information comes from Raeder's reminiscences in *Mein Leben*.

11 Ibid., 1, p. 16.

12 Ibid., 1, p. 64.

13 Germany, Marine-Archiv, *Der Kreuzerkrieg in den ausländischen Gewässern*, Vol. 1: *Das Kreuzergeschwader*, by Erich Raeder; Vol. 2: *Die Tätigkeit der Kleinenkreuzer "Emden," "Königsberg" und "Karlsruhe,"* by Erich Raeder; Vol. 3: *Die deutschen Hilfskreuzer*, by Eberhard von Mantey; 3 vols (Berlin, 1922–1937).

14 Raeder, *Mein Leben*, 1, p. 189.

15 Raeder to Levetzow, November 30, 1923, cited in Dülffer, *Hitler und die Marine*, pp. 102–103.

16 For the "vile attacks," see Raeder to Levetzow, January 5, 1927, cited in ibid., p. 104. For Raeder's problems with pro-Hohenzollern demonstrations see Bird, *Weimar*, pp. 159, 209, n. 24, 214–215; also Carsten, *Reichswehr and Politics*, p. 288.

17 Raeder, *Mein Leben*, 1, p. 221.

18 Ibid., p. 227. Carsten, *Reichswehr and Politics*, p. 288.

19 Raeder, *Mein Leben*, 1, pp. 227–228; Bird, *Weimar*, pp. 216-217. See also Severing's testimony on behalf of Raeder at the Nuremberg trials, IMT, 14, pp. 254–255.

20 Raeder, *Mein Leben*, 1, pp. 229–233; also Severing's testimony before the Nuremberg Tribunal, IMT, 14, p. 257.

21 Raeder, *Mein Leben*, 1, p. 228; Dülffer, *Hitler und die Marine*, pp. 109–110; Bird, *Weimar*, pp. 235–237.

22 Raeder, *Mein Leben*, 1, pp. 233–235; Bird, *Weimar*, p. 237.

23 BA-MA, RM 8/50 M 3292, October 23, 1928. See also BA-MA, RM 8/51 M 1338, July 10, 1929; M 1337, July 19, 1929.

24 BA-MA, RM 8/50 M III 3353, October 30, 1928.

25 Friedrich Ruge *In vier Marinen* (Munich, 1979), p. 82; Dülffer, *Hitler und die Marine*, p. 116.

26 BA-MA, N 172/41 Nachlass Boehm, "Meine Stellungnahme zu dem 'Erlass des Ob.d.M. zur Enthebung des Flottenchefs (Adm. Boehm) von seiner Stellung' vom 18. Okt. 1939 B. Nr. Chef MPA 14 265."

27 Raeder to Levetzow, October 30, 1928, cited in Dülffer, *Hitler und die Marine*, p. 116.

28 See, for instance, Raeder's grudging permission for officers stationed in Berlin to wear civilian clothes while off duty in BA-MA, RM 8/57 B. Nr. 1748 MZ, August 31, 1935. Younger officers liked to joke that Raeder did not even own a set of civilian clothes. Raeder, *Mein Leben*, 1, p. 206.

29 Ibid., pp. 138, 204. For Raeder's concern that confessional strife be prevented in the navy, see Siegfried Sorge, *Der Marineoffizier als Führer und Erzieher* (Berlin, 1937), a book which had the full approval of Raeder and which will be discussed in Chapter VI.

30 Raeder, *Mein Leben*, 1, p. 244.

31 Ibid., p. 245.

32 BA-MA, RM 8/50 M II 3435, November 8, 1928; M II 252, February 5, 1929; BA-MA, RM 8/51 M II 2028, November 21, 1929; BA-MA, RM 8/52, January 22, 1930; M II 222, February 10, 1930. Raeder clearly wanted to make sure that the navy's beer money was well spent, and he cautioned that "only those persons who have something to do with the naval budget

or are interested in it ought to be invited." BA-MA, RM 8/50 M II 3435, November 8, 1928.

33 Raeder, *Mein Leben*, 1, pp. 206–207; BA-MA, RM 8/53 A I c 5113, November 12, 1931.

34 BA-MA, RM 8/55 M 55, January 12, 1933; BA-MA, N 239/54 Nachlass Levetzow, "An den Vorsitzenden der Arbeitsgemeinschaft der Vereinigten Vaterländischen Verbände von Kiel und Umgebung," July 30, 1930. BA-MA, RM 8/54 M I B 320, March 12, 1932.

35 For the naval history project and Raeder's views on Tirpitz, see Keith W. Bird, "The Origins and Role of German Naval History in the Inter-War Period 1918–1939," *Naval War College Review*, 32 (March–April 1979), especially p. 50. For Raeder's hostility to Wegener, see Edward Wegener, "Selbstverständnis und historisches Bewusstsein der deutschen Kriegsmarine," *Marine-Rundschau*, 67 (1970), p. 324; Carl-Axel Gemzell, *Organization, Conflict, and Innovation: A Study of German Naval Strategic Planning, 1888–1940* (Stockholm, 1973), p. 349.

36 Bird, "German Naval History," pp. 49, 51.

37 Bird, *Weimar*, p. 237.

38 Cited in ibid.

39 Ibid., pp. 237–243.

40 The following two paragraphs are based on the official Reichswehr Ministry account of the *Emden* incident in BA-MA, RM 6/275 Der Reichswehrminister Nr. 241.30 W I b, January 23, 1930. Whether the matter took place exactly as described by the Reichswehr Ministry is uncertain. Nevertheless, the charges by the *Rote Fahne* and other newspapers which will be considered subsequently appear implausible given the prevailing conditions within the Reichsmarine.

41 *Die Rote Fahne* (Berlin), December 29, 1929.

42 For the Communist Party's exploitation of what it styled the "Potemkin Rebellion on the *Emden*," see the *Rote Fahne* editions of January 4, 10, 11, 15, 24, and 25, 1930. For the navy's embarrassment, see BA-MA, RM 6/279, "Schriftwechsel Amerikan. Marineattaché, Dezember 1928–März 1930."

43 The KPD's electoral successes are analyzed in Alfred Milatz, "Das Ende der Parteien im Spiegel der Wahlen 1930 bis 1933," in *Das Ende der Parteien 1933*, ed. Erich Matthias and Rudolf Morsey (Düsseldorf, 1960), pp. 747–748, 778–780, 786–787.

44 Examples of Communist *Bordzeitungen* (seamen's newspapers) are in BA-MA, RM 6/275. For the Reichswehr Ministry's efforts to counteract KPD subversion, see the Marineverordnungsblatt, 1930, 63/86; 139/159; 1931, 31/41; also BA-MA, RM 20/907, "Vorschläge für den Arbeitsplan der Flottenabteilung im Winterhalbjahr 1930/1931," September 29, 1930.

45 Ruge, *In vier Marinen*, p. 99.

46 BA-MA, RM 6/274 Marinestation der Ostsee A III 118 G.Kdos., December 9, 1931; Marinestation der Ostsee, October 23, 1931, November 6, 1931.

47 BA-MA, RM 6/274 Marinestation der Ostsee A III 118 G.Kdos., December 9, 1931.

48 BA-MA, RM 6/274 Chef der Marineleitung Entwurf Nr. /34 W I b, December 1931.

49 BA-MA RM 6/274 Beschlagnahmtes Material über K.P.D. Tätigkeit in der Marine, December 12, 1931.

50 Portions of the report are given in ibid. Lengthy excerpts are also given elsewhere in the same *Aktenband* under the title "Auszug aus einem

Bericht eines entlassenen Marinesoldaten," upon which the following description is based. Naval authorities assumed that the man was from a torpedo-boat.

51 As the sailor described the situation: "One saves for his girlfriend so that they can marry. Another has a girl in every city and has to write to all of them."

52 To this extent the sailors shared an interest with their future Supreme Commander, Adolf Hitler, who was an avid reader of the popular western and adventure novels of Karl May (1848–1912).

53 BA-MA, RM 6/274 Beschlagnahmtes Material über K.P.D. Tätigkeit in der Marine, December 12, 1931.

54 BA-MA, RM 6/274, "Stellungnahme der Bezirksleitung," in ibid.

55 See the remarks included by the Marineleitung in BA-MA, RM 6/274 Beschlagnahmtes Material über K.P.D. Tätigkeit in der Marine; also BA-MA, RM 6/275 Stichworte für Führerbesprechung bei Chef ML, January 11–13, 1931. From the content of the latter it is clear that it has been misdated and ought to read 1932 instead of 1931.

56 BA-MA, RM 6/275 Stichworte für Führerbesprechung bei Chef ML, January 11–13, 1931.

57 See the series of reports entitled "Vortrag bei Chef M.L.," January 21, April 23, and June 22, 1932, in BA-MA, RM 6/27; also RM 6/274 Marinestation der Ostsee B. Nr. Gkds. 66 A III, June 14, 1932.

58 BA-MA, RM 6/274 Marinestation der Ostsee, April 11, 1932.

59 BA-MA, RM 6/274 Marinestation der Ostsee B. Nr. Gkds. 66 A III, June 14, 1932; RM 6/27 "Vortrag bei Chef M.L.," June 22, 1932.

60 Ibid; RM 6/274 Police President in Kiel to Marinestation der Ostsee, September 7, 1932; RM 6/274 Vortrag, September 9, 1932.

61 Bird, *Weimar*, pp. 171–180; Gabriele Krüger, *Die Brigade Ehrhardt* (Hamburg, 1971), pp. 100–131; Walter Baum, "Marine, Nationalsozialismus und Widerstand," *Vierteljahrshefte für Zeitgeschichte*, 11 (January 1963), p. 43.

62 For the results of the September elections, see Milatz, "Wahlen 1930 bis 1933," p. 782.

63 Dülffer, *Hitler and die Marine*, pp. 201–203.

64 For the navy's plans in the late 1920s and early 1930s, see Gerhard Schreiber, "Zur Kontinuität des Gross- und Weltmachtstrebens der deutschen Marineführung," *Militärgeschichtliche Mitteilungen* 2/1979, pp. 114–120.

65 Adolf Hitler, *Mein Kampf* (Munich, 1940), pp. 151–156, 742, 753–755. Hitler also criticized the Imperial Navy's practice of building smaller ships with smaller guns than those of the British and the cautious deployment of the fleet during the Great War. Ibid., pp. 298–301.

66 See, for instance, Hitler's analysis of the "pocket" battleship question in his speech of October 10, 1928, excerpts of which are given in the *Völkischer Beobachter*, Munich edition, October 12, 1928. In an unpublished work from the same year, Hitler repeated his strictures against earlier naval policy and termed the present fleet "at most an object for enemy target practice." Adolf Hitler, *Hitlers Zweites Buch: Ein Dokument aus dem Jahr 1928*, edited and introduced by G. L. Weinberg (Stuttgart, 1961), pp. 100–102, 122, 147, 169–172. See also Dülffer, *Hitler und die Marine*, p. 215, n. 52.

67 For Levetzow's association with Hitler, see Holger H. Herwig, "From Kaiser to Führer: The Political Road of a German Admiral, 1923–1933," *Journal of Contemporary History*, 9 (April 1974), pp. 107–115. In July 1923

Levetzow had rejected Hitler as the answer to Germany's problem on the grounds that he lacked the "unfaltering sense of mission; he also lacks a leader." Ibid., pp. 107–108.

68 *Völkischer Beobachter*, Bavarian edition, April 2, 1932.
69 BA-MA, RM 6/25 Wülfing to Schleicher, January 22, 1931; Wülfing to Schleicher, February 16, 1931; Wülfing to Schleicher, March 8, 1931.
70 Bird, *Weimar*, pp. 283–284.
71 Quoted in Bird, "German Naval History," p. 46.
72 For the susceptibility of the younger officers, see BA-MA, N 316/68 Nachlass Weichhold, "Die deutsche Wehrmacht im nat. soz. Staat;" N 165/3 Nachlass Groos, "3. Buch: Unter der Diktatur;" also the recollections of Admiral Leopold Bürkner cited in Carsten, *Reichswehr and Politics*, p. 314; also Baum, "Marine und Widerstand," p. 43.
73 BA-MA, RM 23/1522 E I 315/30, "Tätigkeit der Marine im Jahre 1929."
74 Bird, *Weimar*, pp. 288–289.
75 BA-MA, RM 6/16, "Beschwerden und Anregungen die im Haushalts-ausschuss (Marine) vorgebracht wurden," March 11, 1931.
76 Carsten, *Reichswehr and Politics*, p. 314.
77 For the alleged visit, see BA-MA, RM 6/274, "Abschrift eines Ausschnittes aus der österreichischen Zeitung: 'Der Vormarsch.'" For Nordeck's response, see RM 6/274 B. Nr. G 867, December 15, 1931.
78 BA-MA, RM 6/27, "Vortrag bei Chef M.L.," February 29, 1932; RM 6/27, "Vortrag bei Chef M.L.," March 21, 1932.
79 For the "SA *Verbot*," see Thilo Vogelsang, *Reichswehr, Staat und NSDAP* (Stuttgart, 1962), which includes Groener's own account in Document Nr. 22, "Chronologische Darstellung der Vorkommnisse, die zu meinem Rücktritt als Reichswehr- und Reichsinnenminister geführt haben," pp. 449–457. For Raeder's description of the affair, see *Mein Leben*, 1, pp. 270–273, and BA-MA, RM 6/30, "Aufzeichnungen über SA Verbot und Begleitumstände." See also Karl Dietrich Bracher, *Die Auflösung der Weimarer Republik*, 3rd edn (Villingen, 1960), pp. 481–495.
80 Vogelsang, *Reichswehr und NSDAP*, Document 22, p. 456.
81 Raeder, *Mein Leben*, 1, pp. 271–272; also BA-MA, RM 6/30, "Aufzeichnung über SA Verbot und Begleitumstände," N 239/98 Nachlass Levetzow, Levetzow to Raeder, May 14, 1932; Raeder to Levetzow, May 15, 1932.
82 For Hitler's trip through Oldenburg and his reception by the navy, see Max Domarus (ed.), *Hitler, Reden und Proklamationen, 1932–1945*, 2 vols (Munich, 1965), 1, pp. 108–109; also Baum, "Marine und Widerstand," p. 43, and Dülffer, *Hitler und die Marine*, p. 222. Hitler's entry in the *Köln*'s guest book is reproduced in Werner Maser, *Hitlers Briefe und Notizen* (Düsseldorf, 1973), p. 116. Admiral Paul Zieb recounts Hitler's visit and his remark concerning *Panzerschiff* displacement in *Logistische Probleme der Kriegsmarine* (Neckargemünd, 1961), p. 140.
83 Joseph Goebbels, *Vom Kaiserhof zur Reichskanzlei*, 36th edn (Munich, 1942), entry for May 28, 1932.
84 Raeder to Levetzow, June 9, 1932, quoted in Dülffer, *Hitler und die Marine*, p. 130.
85 BA-MA, RM 20/891 Chef des Ministeramtes im Reichswehrministerium, August 5, 1932; RM 20/891 M2121/32 Gkds., August 10, 1932.
86 Goebbels, *Kaiserhof zur Reichskanzlei*, entry for August 17, 1932. Baum, "Marine und Widerstand," p. 44.
87 Dülffer, *Hitler und die Marine*, pp. 222–224.

88 BA-MA, N 239/98 Nachlass Levetzow, Raeder to Levetzow, October 23, 1932. The spelling of the cruiser *Köln*'s two predecessors from the Imperial Navy was *Cöln*. Despite his punctiliousness, Raeder sometimes lapsed into the earlier usage.

89 Milatz, "Wahlen 1930 bis 1933," p. 782.

90 The maneuverings of Papen, Schleicher and Hitler at the end of 1932 and the beginning of 1933 are recounted in Bracher, *Auflösung der Republik*, pp. 644–732; Vogelsang, *Reichswehr und NSDAP*, pp. 289–404; and, more briefly, in Carsten, *Reichswehr and Politics*, pp. 377–394.

91 BA-MA, N 239/98 Nachlass Levetzow, Raeder to Levetzow, January 7, 1933.

4

From the Machtergreifung *to the* Anglo-German Naval Agreement

Adolf Hitler assumed office on January 30, 1933. His appointment was met with a mixture of expectation and reservation in the Reichsmarine. On the one hand, many of the younger officers were convinced that the long-awaited beginning of the national renewal was at hand, and even though the requirement of strict political neutrality within the armed forces prevented public displays of support for the new regime, supporters in the navy could nevertheless take secret pleasure in the triumph of National Socialism. On the other hand, more experienced officers proved considerably more restrained. One old sea dog was disturbed simply because an Austrian now sat in the chancellery in Prussian Berlin.[1] Others had more substantial reasons for their caution: the navy had known too many disappointments in the recent past to embrace the new regime too openly. National Socialism, after all, might prove to be a flash in the pan, scarcely more substantial than the ill-fated National Union of Dr. Wolfgang Kapp thirteen years before. In addition, the navy knew far too little about the views of the Party. If the past pronouncements of its leader were any guide, it was definitely no friend of the Reichsmarine; one would have to ascertain the new chancellor's views on sea power before a serious commitment could be entertained.

The opportunity soon presented itself. On February 3, Hitler visited the home of army chief Kurt von Hammerstein-Equord for a birthday celebration in honor of Foreign Minister Konstantin von Neurath, a holdover from the previous cabinets of Papen and Schleicher.[2] Also present were Germany's leading military and naval figures. After dinner Hitler rose to address the audience. He began modestly enough, stating that it was a dream come true that he, a former corporal, might now address generals and admirals at the behest of Field Marshal von Hindenburg. He then proceeded to outline the future programs of the government. At home he promised the complete reordering of the political situation in Germany, the extermination of Marxism "root and branch," and the "strengthening of military mindedness through all possible means."[3] Abroad he envisioned revision of the Versailles *Diktat* and military equality with the Great Powers. Accordingly, the Wehrmacht would be strengthened by reintroducing conscription. But Hitler was not content to rest here. Perhaps he would use the resurgent Wehrmacht to gain overseas colonies or, preferably, to win contiguous territory (*Lebensraum*) in the east, which would then be ruthlessly Germanized. In either case, the Wehrmacht's future field of operations lay abroad, not at home, for Hitler had no intention of involving the armed forces in the domestic "consolidation" of the regime. The *Sturmabteilung* (SA) and the *Schutzstaffel* (SS) would see to that.

The admirals' response to the chancellor's lengthy monologue was mixed. Rear Admiral Otto Groos remembers that they remained skeptical; at least a few must have shared the predominant feeling among their army colleagues that talk was always bolder than action. Others, including Admirals Raeder and Conrad Albrecht, subsequently professed to have forgotten Hitler's more far-reaching goals entirely and to have remembered only his moving veneration for Hindenburg and the welcome news that the chancellor would keep the armed forces unsullied by the distasteful task of domestic consolidation (*Gleichschaltung*).[4] Yet at least one major aspect of Hitler's talk on February 3 ought to have given the admirals pause to think: the preference for *Lebensraum* before the acquisition of overseas colonies carried with it the disturbing implication that, for the foreseeable future, at least, the navy would occupy a distant second place in rebuilding the armed forces.[5]

This realization became clearer in the weeks that followed. Although Hitler indicated at a Cabinet meeting on February 8 that rearmament would be the first priority of the new regime, and although Raeder subsequently learned that the Reichsmarine would not be entirely neglected, the head of the navy soon received disturbing indications that the new chancellor was reverting to the deprecatory view of the navy that he had espoused before the *Machtergreifung*. On March 15, Hitler informed Reichswehr Minister Werner von Blomberg, an army general and one of the Führer's more enthusiastic admirers, that the army would indeed take priority in the initial stage of German rearmament. The navy was grudgingly willing to concede this for the short run, but the decision was nevertheless a disappointment to those in the Service who had hoped for more.[6]

Raeder moved energetically to correct this drift of affairs. On March 28, he met with Blomberg and expressed the view that the navy needed to set more ambitious goals for itself by upgrading the modest plans that it had promulgated. Blomberg was receptive, and he tentatively approved plans for larger warships for the fleet. Although Blomberg could as yet make no definite building commitment, Raeder nevertheless could be content with a modest first success with the Reichswehr Minister.[7]

The concessions that he made to the navy notwithstanding, Blomberg would remain in Raeder's view first and foremost an army man, a prisoner of the Prussian officers' continental conception of warfare.[8]

A more promising means of attending to the navy's needs perhaps lay in a direct appeal to the new chancellor. If Hitler could be won over to a more positive appreciation of the doctrine of sea power, then the navy would be freed of its historic dependence upon the army. Of paramount importance was that the navy show both its utility and its loyalty to the National Socialist state.[9]

Others had already urged this course of action, both before and after the *Machtergreifung*. On March 1, 1933, for example, the retired Captain von Stosch, who as chairman of the League of Naval Officers (Marine Offizier Verband) addressed both active and inactive officers, had urged his comrades to show their true colors: "Today it is no longer valid to vote for this or that party; today it is vote German or be un-German . . . . The hour has come to settle accounts with those who know no fatherland."[10]

Raeder was more restrained. Nevertheless, he played his own small role in the theatrically staged opening of the newly elected Reichstag on March 21, the so-called "Day of Potsdam," in a way that clearly showed that he knew which way the wind was blowing.[11] The fleet assembled at Kiel for the occasion, and there was a festive parade that included detachments from the navy, the police, the SA, and the strongly nationalist veterans' organization, the *Stahlhelm*, as well as deputations from the faculty and students of the university at Kiel. Elsewhere, Raeder saw to it that naval buildings were bedecked with the newly reinstated black, white, and red national flag, that Reichsmarine personnel had the day off if at all possible, and that both active and inactive officers were apprised that they were permitted to join the procession at Potsdam.[12] Raeder appeared immaculately clad in full dress uniform and watched solemnly while Hitler paid homage to Field Marshal von Hindenburg and to the Prussian traditions that the old man represented. The admiral could not have missed the vacant chair that the National Socialists had thoughtfully included as a reminder of Raeder's former war lord, the exiled Kaiser at Doorn. Nor could he have failed to notice the absence of Communist Reichstag deputies, many of whom now graced German prisons, or of the Social Democratic deputies, who were boycotting the ceremonies. Clearly Raeder, former imperial officer and inveterate enemy of Marxism, had to be impressed by what he saw.

On the other hand, eleven days later he must have been greatly disappointed when Hitler failed to attend the commissioning of the "pocket" battleship *Deutschland* and the launching of her sister ship, the *Admiral Scheer*. In his speech at the ceremonies, therefore, Raeder seemed all the more determined to remind the National Socialists that he was aware of the great debt that the nation owed the Party. Taking his cue from the date—April 1, the birthday of Otto von Bismarck—he expressed the hope that "the government of the National Revolution" would lead a "unified people, thoroughly imbued with the spirit of the great chancellor [Bismarck] to new heights." At the same time he counseled the assembled throng that only the support of the entire nation could guarantee success for the navy. Finally, lest the nation and its truant chancellor forget, Raeder pointed out that despite the powerful appearance of the trim new warships they were still a "silent, bitterly serious reminder for the German people" as they had been built under the restrictions of the Versailles *Diktat*. Thus Raeder made his profession of faith in the Party and at the same time staked a claim for the Reichsmarine: the navy thought much of the National Socialists, but it and the nation would expect still more from them in the future.[13]

Raeder was not disappointed. A few days later he had his first private meeting with Hitler on the state of the navy. Although what was said there remains a matter of some dispute, there can be no doubt that the two men got along better than Raeder had expected. Hitler showed himself to be surprisingly well-informed on naval matters, and Raeder was able to present his arguments both for the acceleration of naval construction plans and for the role that the navy might serve in fashioning new alliances (*Bündnisfähigkeit*). Although Raeder failed to convince Hitler of the validity of either of his two positions, he nevertheless came away from the meeting with something far more important: his visit established something of a precedent for direct access to the Reich Chancellor. In the future he would use this informal "*Immediatstellung*" in a manner strikingly similar to his old mentor Tirpitz.[14]

Initial contacts between Hitler and Raeder, then, offered the promise that the two men would be able to work together. It remained only for Raeder to cultivate the surprising interest that Hitler was now showing for sea power, and for the navy as a whole to reinforce the favorable impression that its chief was making on the chancellor. In this respect the navy's transformation had been unmistakable. Immediately after the *Machtergreifung* the Reichsmarine's relationship with party officials at the local level continued to reflect the political neutrality which, on the surface at least, had characterized the republican era. Like the army, the navy continued to forbid its officers and men to engage in political activity of any kind.[15] In addition, both services quickly reminded their civilian officials (*Beamten*), who fell into that twilight zone between military personnel and civilian employees, that they were not to wear their Service uniforms to political rallies. At times the navy's circumspection led to unpleasant encounters with local party stalwarts. Then Commander Friedrich Ruge, for example, remembers a goodwill visit to the small town of Wedel-Schulau on the Elbe, where the navy was feted with an evening of music and dancing. After midnight an SA detachment appeared uninvited and asked to join the festivities. They were allowed to do so, but only on the condition that they eschew politics altogether.[16]

The situation improved immensely in the spring and summer of 1933. In April, less than three months after the National Socialists had come to power, naval personnel were instructed to exchange salutes with police and *Landesjägerei* units, which now included a healthy number of SA bully boys.[17] Moreover, naval officers were at pains to show that, despite the continuing practical necessity of keeping the Party and the armed forces separate, the navy and the NSDAP had been working for a common cause all along. As one of them, Captain Karlgeorg Schuster, told a group of party and government officials in May, during the 1920s it had been the officers and men of the Reichsmarine who had held the line against the inner enemy—the "Marxist fungus" and the pacifists—until the National Socialist movement arrived on the scene to awaken the entire nation's will to freedom. Now the moment had arrived for founding a new Wehrmacht that was firmly rooted in that nation. Schuster urged his audience not to forget the navy at this critical moment, and he outlined the Marineleitung's by now familiar arguments for naval expansion. An enlarged fleet would enhance Germany's potential as an ally, protect German overseas interests, and provide a kernel for the even larger "world power fleet" (*Weltmachtsflotte*) that Germany would eventually build.[18]

Schuster then reminded his listeners that the NSDAP's support was crucial to this task. Only now, under the conditions created by the Party's triumph, could those forces within the navy, which for fourteen years had foundered on parliamentary divisiveness and the "infamous sabotage attempts of Social Democratic ideologues and pacifists," at last be liberated. Only now was love of country again in the ascendancy. Indeed, as Schuster concluded, only now could Party and navy "once again awaken and strengthen the *understanding*, the *love* of the sea and the will of the *nation* not to allow its life-lines, which lead over the *free* seas for a *free great* nation, to be severed."

Speeches such as Schuster's were not without their magic. Nor was it likely that the display of comradely ties between the Reichsmarine and the SA at the local "Hitler Day" at the "Marinestadt Kiel" on May 7 was lost upon the chancellor.[19] The clearest indication of the course that developments were taking for the navy, however, came in late May when Hitler returned to Kiel to pay his first official visit to the fleet. Although the occasion was marred by an untoward incident involving Hermann Göring—the corpulent Minister President of Prussia became seasick, and some junior officers had the temerity to joke about it—Hitler seems to have been impressed by the Reichsmarine. In a speech on May 22 he expressed Germany's pride in its bluejackets: "Although the fleet is small, all Germany looks upon it with joy. For it is the most visible representative of the German conception of honor and of German power abroad."[20]

The navy tried hard to reciprocate the praise that Hitler lavished upon it. At the ceremonies marking the Battle of the Skagerrak a week later, the chief of the Baltic Naval Station, Vice Admiral Conrad Albrecht, went out of his way to find a connection between the great naval engagement and the "National Revolution." Those who had died on May 31, 1916, he said, had not died in vain, for their sacrifice constituted the "iron bond" that cemented the new sense of community that Germany's leaders, Hindenburg and Hitler, had recently founded. In truth, Albrecht's apotheosis sounded a bit lame, but it was doubtless the thought that counted. With time and practice the admiral would get better.[21]

The feeling of euphoria within the navy lasted throughout the summer of 1933. By then the presence of the SA at naval functions, which had caused a stir the previous winter, passed unnoticed. Indeed, the SA now sometimes provided the music for such occasions, and the relationship between the navy, the Party, and the nation at large was so cordial that Commander Ruge could still remember it forty years later. The notion of *Volksgemeinschaft* (the community of the nation), he rather naively wrote, "was not merely a word then; it really existed, because people earnestly worked for better human relations. There were more songs sung than speeches given."[22]

Both the Reichswehr Ministry and the Marineleitung seemed determined to foster this feeling of unity with the nation. In June Blomberg enlisted the army and navy in the *Opfer der Arbeit*, a National Socialist-inspired relief measure, and he underlined the armed forces' support for the relief campaign by a ceremonial presentation of the Wehrmacht's total contribution. In August the Marineleitung urged its officers to turn out in large numbers for a "Peoples' Track Day" at which Blomberg would be present, presumably to impress the Reichswehr Minister and his master with the way the navy mingled with the new Germany. Similar considerations must have motivated the Marineleitung's liberal arrangements later that month for those of its officials and civilian employees (but not as yet its officers and enlisted men) who wanted to attend the Nuremberg Party Congress (*Reichsparteitag*) in September.[23]

Other measures soon followed. On August 28 Raeder instructed the Reichsmarine to answer the greeting "Heil Hitler" with the same words, arguing that the response had become common usage among the German people. Eight days later he ordered that naval personnel use the National Socialist or "German" salute in certain situations. Finally, in mid-September he urged the navy to pay greater attention to secrecy, among other reasons because carelessness might jeopardize the "great domestic work of the Führer."[24]

That same September the Reichsmarine held its annual fall maneuvers. As in years past the occasion provided the commander-in-chief of the navy with the opportunity to review the accomplishments of the preceding year in a concluding address to the officers of the fleet. Although Raeder did not ignore either technical or strategic considerations, the primary import of his message fell upon Germany's altered domestic situation. Recent developments, the admiral averred, had redeemed large segments of the population from their earlier anti-military sentiments and had opened the way for the navy to spread the doctrine of navalism to a broader public. What was more, the navy now had a powerful new ally in the person of Adolf Hitler. As Raeder triumphantly informed his officers:

> I can state with joy and satisfaction that the *Reichskanzler* himself continually mentions the necessity of building up the fleet and that he is deeply convinced of the great political significance of the navy, especially as a power and alliance factor in the politics of peace.[25]

Hitler had come a long way in the eyes of the navy since the previous fall when Raeder had characterized him as a bull in a china shop.[26] But by September 1933 the navy had come quite a way as well: just how far, would be fully illuminated in the months to come.

Perhaps to many this was not yet apparent. Indeed, in the months that followed Raeder's confident address to his officers the technical separation between Party and Wehrmacht continued undisturbed. In March 1934, for example, as the relationship between the SA and the armed forces was taking a turn for the worse, the Reichswehr Ministry broadened its definition of just what constituted a political body and prohibited rank and file membership in the National Socialist Motor Corps (NSKK), the motor auxiliary of the SA. In July Blomberg announced that the army's and the navy's *Landesschutzoffiziere* (retired officers who were secretly and quite illegally filling a number of vacant leadership positions in the Wehrmacht) must withdraw from active participation in any and all political activity, since they were regular officers for all practical purposes. Yet many of these efforts to keep the Wehrmacht unsullied by politics carried exceptions with them that inevitably encouraged the interaction of political and non-political activities. The Marineleitung, for example, followed up the Reichswehr Ministry's prohibition on membership in the NSKK with a reminder that this applied only to officers and enlisted men, not to Wehrmacht officials. Later the Reichswehr Ministry added that it would be inappropriate to conclude that the armed forces should stand aloof from the NSKK; on the contrary, it encouraged its personnel to cultivate close comradely ties with the NSKK and to use every opportunity to engage in common sporting activities with its members.[27]

Other measures were even less ambiguous. In February 1934 the party emblem, the swastika, was added to the uniforms of both army and navy. That same month, if not before, the Wehrmacht began to play the party anthem, the *Horst-Wessel-Lied*, in conjunction with the older *Deutschlandlied*.[28] Each of these measures would seem to indicate that army and navy leaders wished to prove a point—namely, that the Wehrmacht was as thoroughly National Socialist in its outlook as any party organization.

The armed forces' relationship with the Party was changing in other ways as well. In contrast to their practice with previous governments, the Reichswehr Ministry and Marineleitung now saw to it that the navy in general, and the officer corps in particular, received frequent opportunities to hear the great and the near great of the Third Reich. For the first time the Reichswehr Ministry made extensive use of loud-speakers and radios to carry Hitler's speeches to garrisons throughout Germany.[29] In addition, leading National Socialists were invited to address select groups of officers and officials. Judging from the demand for tickets, Propaganda Minister Joseph Goebbels was a speaker who rivaled the Reich Chancellor as an attraction; and on those occasions when the army took more than its share of admission tickets, Raeder had the speeches carried by loud-speaker to standing-room-only audiences in nearby buildings. Not all of the Party's speakers, however, exerted the same appeal as Hitler and Goebbels. When the armed forces failed to turn out in sufficient numbers for Frau Gertrude Scholtz-Klink, the leader of the League of National Socialist Women, Raeder found it necessary to remind his officers to make sure that tickets to future addresses were used by others in the event that "sickness" or "sudden official trips" prevented the original recipient from attending.[30]

Visits by influential leaders such as Goebbels were sponsored by the Reichswehr Ministry and were attended by army and naval personnel. The Marineleitung also invited National Socialism specialists to address its own series of "winter lectures," which were intended for the Marineleitung's staff alone. Here, too, the changed circumstances within the navy became evident. Before the *Machtergreifung* such talks had usually dealt with matters of specific interest to naval officers and officials—weapons systems, international maritime law, and disarmament questions. Now this largely technical material was supplemented by talks of a different sort: during the winter of 1933–1934 naval officers heard lectures on such ideologically tinged subjects as "The Work of the League for Germans Abroad," "National Socialist Economic Thought," and "The Third International and the Great War." The following winter they learned of "Race Hygiene in the Present" and "Leadership of Masses and Propaganda in War."[31] Here, Raeder did not have to worry about empty seats; attendance was obligatory for most Berlin-based officers and officials.

The increasing coincidence of navy and party views manifested itself in other ways as well. In June 1933, a postcard denouncing a certain Lieutenant Commander Carl Heinemann, a former deck officer, as a Socialist prompted the Baltic Naval Station to search police files to determine the political affiliation of Heinemann and other former deck officers. In November the North Sea Naval Station informed the Gestapo when a civilian official from the Auditing Office was heard to make such remarks as "Hitler has no following at all in the people" and "If I were a Frenchman, I would invade immediately." Apparently, the Gestapo saw less harm in the remarks than the station commander, for the official was soon released. Nevertheless, the Reichswehr Ministry strongly commended the navy's action in reporting the remarks and noted that if the offender had been a member of the Wehrmacht he would have been dismissed long ago.[32]

Similar attitudes characterized the navy's response to the reshuffling of its own civilian administrators as a result of the Civil Service Reconstruction Law.[33] Although some naval officers could and did intervene on behalf of their subordinates who were threatened by the loss of their jobs, the predominant mood would seem to have been set by Raeder. When a veteran of the Imperial Navy wrote him to ask for help in retaining his position in the local administration at Laboe, Raeder merely passed the letter on to the Inland Division of the Reichswehr Ministry. This department then curtly informed the applicant that Raeder regretted that it was a matter for the Prussian administration and that he could not intervene. Yet when the situation was reversed, the Marineleitung found that it could be quite helpful. When a civil engineer named Dekow asked for reinstatement at the "Deutsche Werke" in Kiel on the grounds that he had been dismissed in 1929 because he was a National Socialist, the Marineleitung declared itself willing to give the man special treatment provided that he was a particularly distinguished fighter for the NSDAP. Subsequent inquiries revealed that Dekow did indeed deserve special treatment.[34]

The Civil Service Reconstruction Law, then, affected those whose past political activities had failed to endear them to the National Socialists. It also incorporated important elements of the Party's racial theory, for Article 3 of the law stipulated that, with the exception of front line veterans and the fathers or sons of those who had fallen in the Great War, "non-Aryans" must leave government service.[35] Initially the measure was not applied to the Wehrmacht, but by mid-1933 Blomberg had voluntarily extended it to the Reichswehr Ministry's civilian officials. Moreover, in February 1934, he ordered verification of "Aryan" descent for officers, deck officers, noncommissioned officers, and enlisted men. Those who did not conform to the provisions of Article 3 were to leave the Wehrmacht as soon as possible.[36]

Blomberg's decree placed Raeder in an uncomfortable position. For one thing, the measure represented an unwelcome intrusion of the Reichswehr Ministry, and through it of the Party, into one of the navy's most jealously guarded prerogatives, that of personnel selection. For another, it promised to be a bothersome task at a time when the navy had more important concerns. According to the follow-up provisions of the Act, "non-Aryans" included all those who had a parent or grandparent who had been born a Jew.[37] The subsequent religious beliefs of the family and the current religious confession of the officer in question were immaterial. Thus, although there were apparently no practicing Jews in the Service, the navy would have to spend valuable time searching out its members' "Aryan" roots. These genealogical dabblings might reveal any number of officers and men who might or might not know that they were "non-Aryans."[38] Yet there was also one more reason why Blomberg's extension of the so-called "Aryan Paragraphs" to the armed forces must have given the head of the navy pause to think: whatever his other prejudices, Raeder was not an anti-Semite.[39]

The admiral, therefore, appears to have attempted to soft-pedal the whole issue. Like the army (and unlike Göring's Air Ministry), the navy took advantage of the exceptions granted under the Law and confined its genealogical investigations to those who did not qualify as "front line" veterans.[40] Perhaps it acted this way in the unlikely hope that none of those under scrutiny would turn out to be "non-Aryans." Nevertheless, two officers, four officer candidates, and a number of noncommissioned officers and ratings did prove to be "non-Aryans." These were dismissed from the Service with as little fanfare as possible. Judging from the letters of condolence that came to one of the cashiered officers, a number of colleagues saw the measure as unjust, and successful efforts were made by comrades within the navy at least to find them good positions in civilian life.[41] Yet others, such as Captain Hans-Georg von Friedeburg, a future commander-in-chief of the navy, were willing to accept the measure as "necessary . . . in order to act within the sense of our Führer."[42] For his part, Raeder seems to have been unwilling to undertake further measures to protect his subordinates. He refused to make any protest against the rising anti-Semitic tide out of fear that such a gesture would draw the navy into an area of domestic politics that he had assiduously sought to avoid. Doubtless out of embarrassment, he refused an audience with an officer who sought to discuss the reason for his dismissal. Finally, in May 1934, he also declined an opportunity to broaden the exceptions granted under the law to include participants in the Imperial Navy's colonial actions prior to the Great War on the grounds that no such cases involving individuals had yet arisen.[43] Like the good sailor that he was, Raeder was ultimately unwilling to rock the boat.

At least one reason for Raeder's inaction on the matter of the Aryan Paragraphs is not difficult to find. By the winter of 1933–1934 the armed forces as a whole were confronted with a problem that in the eyes of Wehrmacht leaders far overshadowed the question of racial origins. Since the previous fall the army's relationship with the NSDAP's most important paramilitary body, Ernst Röhm's *Sturmabteilung* (SA), had deteriorated rapidly. Now that the Party had seized power, now that a start had been made on purging Germany of its "antinational" elements, be they Socialist, Communist, or Jewish, the question concerning the future function of the SA within the National Socialist state was becoming acute. The SA felt that it had not made a revolution solely for the privilege of going into early retirement while other organizations took over the management of the state. In particular the SA had not sustained sacrifices so that the armed forces, which had watched passively while there had been hard work to do, could now continue as if nothing had changed. Yet this was precisely the way matters appeared, to the SA at least, by the end of 1933. While the Wehrmacht and a new generation of political functionaries within the Party decided the fate of Germany, the SA—the real maker of the National Revolution—was being relegated to the minor task of auxiliary police work.[44]

The SA, therefore, sought a continued active role in the National Socialist state. To many the best means of assuring this was through a merger of the SA and the army. The 100,000-man *Reichsheer* would provide the technical expertise; the SA with its two million men would provide the rank and file for a mass army.[45] In this way, or so the formula neatly read, a paramilitary body would become a military force.

Such a proposal was not new. In the days before the *Machtergreifung* it had been a major worry of the army, and as early as February 3, 1933, Hitler had assured the generals—ever jealous of their monopoly over national defense—that he had no intention of merging the two forces. But as the internal role of the *Sturmabteilung* dwindled into insignificance, there were disturbing signs that Röhm and his supporters were anxious to reverse the chancellor's decision against an SA based militia. The brown shirts appeared to be trying to use their immense numerical strength and their claim to ideological purity to wring concessions from the army. The latter resisted and attempted through various measures to display its loyalty to the chancellor and to the principles of National Socialism. The resulting confrontation was noticeable at the top, where army and SA leaders vied with one another for Hitler's support. It was even more apparent at the lower levels, where, either by accident or design, SA and army personnel came into open conflict.

Perhaps the navy could have stayed out of the matter altogether. There was a naval branch of the SA, but it was very small in relation to the rest of the *Sturmabteilung* and had until now spent its time agitating against leftists in the port cities or in organizing water sports.[46] Moreover, there could be no question of a serious rivalry between the navy and the Marine SA. The concept of an SA-based militia might be appropriate for the ground forces; the navy would always remain an elite branch whose training and skill in highly technical matters could never be replaced by the unruly men in brown shirts.

Yet by the winter of 1933–1934 the navy, too, was encountering increasing friction with the SA. At times this merely took the form of a noticeable coolness between the two organizations at official receptions.[47] At other times it manifested itself in public denunciations of the navy by the SA. In the worst instances naval personnel were beaten up by gangs of SA toughs.[48] Whatever the case, the *Sturmabteilung*'s and the Reichsmarine's perceptions of one another underwent a disturbing change. Despite its claim to be in the vanguard of the new Germany, the SA appeared to the navy as a disruptive, divisive force that was obviously unsuited to the orderly state of affairs that had supposedly existed since January 30, 1933. To the SA the navy appeared equally suspect. Its rank and file had been the bearers of the spirit of 1918, of revolt, of sailors' councils, and of the red terror. Its officers were hopelessly reactionary and were totally unable to adjust to the new *völkisch* state of Adolf Hitler.[49]

Such accusations touched a raw nerve within the navy, and the officer corps rallied with alacrity to defend the Service. Wherever possible, mis-understandings were handled at the local level through informal arrange-ments with SA leaders.[50] Unfortunately, many of Röhm's subordinates and not a few naval officers apparently went out of their way to see that relations between the two organizations deteriorated.[51] Moreover, the physical assaults on naval personnel seemed to defy a satisfactory solution. Officers were inclined—rightly so it would appear—to view these as attacks on the navy as a whole and were determined to make an example of any SA men who could be identified. Yet the Reichsmarine's efforts were often frustrated by conflicting evidence, by delays on the part of SA commanders and local officials, and, not least of all, by Reichswehr Minister von Blomberg's own unwillingness to press the issue with sufficient enthusiasm. The "Rubber Lion," as he was called, was placing his hope in Hitler, whose intervention alone would bring a solution to the overall problem between the armed forces and the SA.[52]

Blomberg's hope was well founded. By 1934 it was obvious that Hitler needed the officer corps far more than he needed the SA in the upcoming task of German rearmament. It was equally obvious that the Reichswehr Minister had proven to be a far more pliant subordinate than Röhm had been. Indeed, the prospect of a mass army under the leadership of Ernst Röhm must have been anything but attractive to Hitler, and on February 28, 1934, the Reich Chancellor once again rejected the idea of an SA militia.[53]

Hitler's decision appears to have made the SA more intransigent than ever, and as the stalemate between the army and the SA continued the navy found itself drawn increasingly into the conflict. Although Röhm made at least one attempt to separate the navy from the army by offering special concessions on the Marine SA and the Marine Hitler Jugend,[54] the *Sturmabteilung*'s relationship with the navy worsened. Throughout the spring of 1934 the Reichsmarine was the object of a vicious campaign of rumor-mongering which held the navy and the officer corps to be lukewarm toward National Socialism. Although the sources of such rumors were often difficult to determine, the most likely origin was the *Sturmabteilung*. By May even officers who had previously enjoyed reasonably good relations with Röhm's men were convinced of the seriousness of the threat to the armed forces.[55]

In June, as the overall crisis reached maturity and as rumors of an impending SA *Putsch* swept Germany, the navy was confronted with a number of alarming developments. At Kiel a Lieutenant Commander (ret.) Land, who was both a *Landesschutzoffizier* in the navy and a member of the Kiel SS, was told by his SS superiors that there would be a second revolution against the Wehrmacht. At Flensburg the local SA *Standarte* forced the cancellation of a memorial service by the Kyffhäuserbund (one of the largest veterans' organizations in Germany), and the SA seized the occasion to denounce the army, the navy, and the *Bund* as a pack of reactionaries. Elsewhere, while visiting the torpedo-boat *Albatross*, SA Brigade Leader Wilke had the audacity to call into question the Reichswehr Minister's loyalty to National Socialism. Later, at an officers' mess, Wilke extended his accusations to the Wehrmacht as a whole. Worst of all, on June 13, three Reichsmarine officers were physically assaulted and verbally abused by members of the Marine SA at Wilhelmshaven. The latter event seemed especially to point out the gravity of the situation. As far as can be determined, it was the first time that the Marine SA, as opposed to the regular SA, had turned on the navy. Moreover, it marked the first time that active Reichsmarine officers had been physically attacked.[56]

In a similar—though obviously less immediate—manner as the army, the navy appeared to be approaching a reckoning with the SA. Nevertheless, both the suddenness and the ruthlessness of Hitler's solution to the problem—the murder of Röhm and over fifty of his subordinates by SS execution squads on June 30 and the two days immediately following[57]—appear to have caught nearly everyone in the navy by surprise. Although there is one indication that Raeder may have known about Hitler's general intention as early as mid-June, the admiral was nevertheless away from Berlin at Hamburg for the launching of the *Graf Spee* during the so-called Night of the Long Knives.[58] Moreover, in contrast to the army, the navy took no unusual precautions in the event of an armed conflict with the SA. When news of an SA "revolt" reached far-away Königsberg, the commander of the naval units there had to make an independent decision to clear for action. It was only later that orders arrived confirming his decision.[59] As it turned out, the officer could have spared himself the trouble. Heinrich Himmler's SS was perfectly capable of restoring "order" in Germany without the aid of the Reichsmarine.

The Röhm affair brought an unexpectedly swift resolution to the navy's problems with the *Sturmabteilung*. Moreover, throughout the remainder of the summer, relations with other branches of the Party, which had also been somewhat strained during the SA crisis, seem to have improved. To be sure, there were still a few minor misunderstandings. In August the North Sea Naval Station became involved in a dispute with the *Nordwestdeutscher Freiheitskämpfer*, a periodical of the Hitler Youth, which had printed a story about an unnamed officer's wife who had supposedly behaved in an exceedingly haughty manner toward a group of girls in the Bund Deutscher Mädel.[60] In September a minor party functionary insulted a Reichsmarine sailor at the Nuremberg Party Rallies. Yet in contrast to earlier confrontations with the SA, both cases seemed more accidental than planned, and both were eventually resolved to the navy's satisfaction. These matters aside, by the late summer of 1934 it appeared that everything portended well for Raeder's continued determination—reinforced by the events of June 30—to keep the navy out of domestic politics.[61]

The renewed spirit of accommodation on the part of the NSDAP and the navy was most clearly shown in the question of a successor to the Reich President. On August 2 the aged and ailing Hindenburg died, and the government, with Reichswehr Minister von Blomberg's willing acquiescence, was already prepared with a law uniting the offices of Reich president and chancellor in the person of Adolf Hitler. That same day Blomberg ordered the soldiers and sailors of the Wehrmacht to swear an oath to Hitler, and the former corporal succeeded the field marshal as commander-in-chief of the armed forces.[62] The irregularity of the proceedings and the implications of the oath left at least a few army officers—most notably General Ludwig Beck—with an uneasy feeling.[63] Raeder, though, professed to have had no qualms about either, for he saw Hitler as the field marshal's "legal successor by universal interpretation."[64] Few naval officers appear to have differed with their admiral's opinion, and the administration of the oath in the Reichsmarine evidently proceeded without a hitch. By September 1934, when the armed forces participated at the Nuremberg Party Rallies for the first time, the relationship between the NSDAP and the Wehrmacht appears to have again reached a level unrivaled since the days of spring and summer 1933.

In truth, appearances were deceiving. By the fall of 1934 the Wehrmacht must have been encountering a collective feeling of *déjà vu*, for it was once again involved in a conflict that in its externals closely resembled the SA crisis of the past summer. This time, however, the adversary was not the motley brown shirts but rather the armed forces' erstwhile ally in the June crisis, Himmler's SS. Once again the primary issue was a party organization's objections to the army's "monopoly" over the territorial defense of the Reich.[65] Once again the navy's interests were only peripherally involved. On the surface, at least, the SS represented even less of a direct threat to the navy than the SA had. There was, for example, no "Marine SS." Yet for a variety of reasons, not the least of which were two troublesome legacies from the recent past, the navy was no more able to keep out of the present crisis than it had been in the case of the SA.

The first legacy, in fact, stemmed from the Röhm purge and concerned a certain Lieutenant Commander (ret.) Land, who, it will be remembered, was at one and the same time a Reichsmarine *Landesschutzoffizier* and a member of the Kiel SS.[66] On July 2, two days after the *Putsch* and eleven days after he had heard his SS commander denounce the Wehrmacht as being reactionary, Land sought to end his double status and submitted his resignation from the SS. Instead he was broken to the rank of private and expelled on the grounds that he had failed to respond to an SS alert on June 30. A few days later the local SS commander began to contemplate having Land punished more severely and perhaps even executed.

The Baltic Naval Station protested this action on July 13 and explained that Land's absence from the SS alert had been due to orders from his naval superiors. The SS withdrew the expulsion because of nonappearance, but renewed it immediately thereafter because of "undisciplined behavior" and "spreading of rumors." The SS subsequently accused Land of having offered the previous January to spy on the navy for the SS. Land was given no opportunity by the SS to respond to the charges that were being preferred against him.

The matter reached the Reichswehr Ministry in early August. Since most of the questions predated the Röhm purge—a matter that the Reichswehr Ministry was only too happy to forget—and since Blomberg was currently striving for good relations with the SS, the Reichswehr Minister sought to resolve the dispute through a letter to Himmler. The Reichsführer SS stood by the expulsion of Land. On October 16, therefore, Blomberg wrote Raeder and raised two vital questions. What was the state of the investigation concerning the allegations raised by the SS concerning Land's offer to spy for them? Was a person deemed unworthy of membership in the Party or one of its subordinate organizations to be allowed to remain in the Wehrmacht?[67]

Raeder's response was slow in coming, for Blomberg's first question obviously required an investigation and a hearing at a naval honor court. While these were set in motion the overall relationship between the SS and the Wehrmacht continued to deteriorate. The main reason for this undoubtedly was the campaign of vilification that the SS began against the army commander, General Werner Freiherr von Fritsch, in an effort to get this opponent of the SS's military ambitions removed from office.[68] To compound the issue, the navy found itself troubled with another bothersome legacy, this time from the late Weimar period, which further complicated its relationship with the SS and which quite possibly influenced Raeder's thinking on the case of the unfortunate Lieutenant Commander Land.

Curiously enough, the second legacy also involved a dishonorable discharge and a naval honor court. This time, however, the case involved not the expulsion of a Reichmarine officer from the SS but the reverse; or rather almost the reverse, for truth to tell the incident occurred before the officer in question found his way to Himmler's *Schutzstaffel*. In 1931, it seems, a certain lieutenant had been called before a naval honor court because he had broken off a relationship with a young woman in such a tactless way that she subsequently suffered a nervous breakdown. Rather than show any contrition before the court or concern for the woman, the officer had sought to put the blame for the matter on her. Since there was no room for such unchivalrous behavior in the puritanical navy of Erich Raeder (and since the girl's father was said to be a close friend of Raeder's), the young man had been dishonorably discharged. This was unfortunate for the navy, for by 1934 the officer in question, Reinhard Heydrich, had become the head of Himmler's powerful security service, the *Sicherheitsdienst* (SD). Heydrich was ambitious, capable, and unscrupulous, and he had not forgotten his humiliation at the hands of the navy.[69]

By 1934 the SD was rapidly consolidating its hold over Germany's non-military intelligence services. In April the Gestapo, which had formerly been under Göring, was placed under Himmler. To many observers it appeared only a matter of time until the former student of animal husbandry and his lieutenant, Heydrich, attempted to expand their power into the military's own sphere of influence. That same spring, therefore, the head of military intelligence (*Abwehr*), Captain Conrad Patzig, obtained an order from Hitler decreeing that military intelligence and counterespionage remained the exclusive function of the *Abwehr*. With that the battle between Patzig and Heydrich was joined, and throughout the summer both men sought to discredit the other. When at last Patzig convinced Blomberg to consult Himmler about replacing Heydrich, the Reichsführer SS bluntly refused. Blomberg took this as a personal setback which, in the face of his helplessness before Himmler, he blamed on Patzig. In October 1934, therefore, when the *Abwehr* carried secret aerial photography of the Maginot Line against Blomberg's expressed orders, a crisis became unavoidable. The Reichswehr Minister demanded Patzig's removal as *Abwehr* chief. Although Raeder thought highly of Patzig, he was unable to prevent the captain's dismissal.[70]

The question of a successor placed Raeder in a highly uncomfortable position. The admiral was determined that another naval officer should succeed Patzig as *Abwehrchef*, but when Patzig suggested Captain Wilhelm Canaris for the post Raeder answered: "Impossible! I cannot work with this man." Patzig responded that there was no other officer suitable for the position and that the only alternative was to return the post to the army. This was even less tolerable to the head of the navy. Canaris therefore got the job, but against Raeder's initial wishes. Furthermore, the admiral knew full well that the persons ultimately responsible for this unwelcome development were Heydrich and Himmler.[71]

The end of December 1934, therefore, found Raeder in a fighting mood. On December 29 he informed Blomberg of his position regarding the case of Lieutenant Commander Land. Although Raeder clearly did not want to take up the larger question that Blomberg had posed earlier as to whether those who were deemed unworthy to be in the Party were to be allowed to remain in the Wehrmacht, in this particular case the facts were so clear as to admit of only one solution. A naval honor court, Raeder announced, had acquitted Land of the charge of offering to spy for the SS. Moreover, the entire mode of handling the case by the SS contradicted the "simplest sense of justice." Even if Land had made the offer to spy, the admiral continued, the fact that the SS had waited from January until July to bring the accusation to the attention of the Reichsmarine did not reflect highly on the SS. Nor did Raeder see any reason to expel Land from the Wehrmacht. He opined that it was the SS's handling of the case that was intolerable, and he requested that Land be fully reinstated in the SS and then discharged, this time honorably. The admiral would then see to it that Land was transferred to another base to avoid further friction. More than that the exasperated navy chief was unwilling to do.[72]

Other naval officers shared Raeder's anger. Two days after the admiral's salvo at the SS, Captain Patzig went to Blomberg to take leave of his post. Patzig encouraged the Reichswehr Minister to take immediate steps to curb the excesses that were being committed in the name of National Socialism. In particular he singled out the SS as being a "pack of uprooted failures and criminals." Blomberg interrupted that the SS was an organization of the Führer, whereupon Patzig responded: "Then I regret that the Führer does not know what a pack of swine [*Sauhaufen*] he has under him." Not surprisingly, Patzig's interview came to a rather hasty conclusion.[73]

The naval command was obviously at the end of its patience. Furthermore, by the New Year the SS campaign against army commander Fritsch was also at its height, and both the Wehrmacht and the SS found it easy to suspect the other of harboring ideas of a *Putsch*. Blomberg, who had striven earnestly for better relations between the armed forces and the SS, was manifestly unable to reverse the deteriorating situation. The deadly confrontation of the previous June seemed destined to repeat itself, this time without a third force (such as the SS had been at the time of the Röhm purge) to prevent a direct clash between Wehrmacht and Party. Just how high tempers were running was indicated by a remark made that January by Blomberg's naval adjutant, Captain Hans-Georg von Friedeburg, an avid supporter of National Socialism, to Rear Admiral Hermann Boehm, who had just arrived in Berlin: "When one of us goes into an SS building, one does not know whether he will come out again."[74]

At this point Hitler decided to intervene in the crisis. The Führer called a meeting between the higher ranking officers of the Wehrmacht and leading figures of the Party at the State Opera House Unter den Linden on January 3, 1935. The day saw Hitler at his oratorical best. In a one and a half hour speech he professed his "unwavering determination" to lead Germany to new preeminence with the aid of the armed forces. The Wehrmacht and the Party, he maintained, constituted the basis of National Socialist Germany; mutual trust between the two organizations was therefore essential. According to Rear Admiral Boehm, Hitler illustrated the point most dramatically:

> Then perhaps someone comes from the Party and says to me "All well and good, my Führer, but General So and So speaks and works against you." Then I say "I do not believe it!" And if the man says "I bring you written proof, my Führer!" then I will tear the scrap of paper to bits, for my faith in the Wehrmacht is unshakable.

Boehm later recalled that the Führer had quietly added at the end of his speech: "And on the day that I lose this faith I must shoot myself."[75]

It was vintage Adolf Hitler and not without effect. Although both army and navy leaders continued to harbor a deep distrust of the SS, the crisis atmosphere disappeared; the officers of the Wehrmacht could look with gratitude at the Führer's statesmanlike intervention. Fritsch, whose reputation had been most damaged by the SS campaign that fall and winter, called Hitler's speech "a unique testimony to the loyalty of the army and its leader." Raeder, too, showed signs of willingness to forget the recent unpleasantness. He consoled Patzig by giving him command of one of the new "pocket" battleships. When the Reichswehr Ministry informed him that it was willing to let Land remain in the navy but that it was unwilling to reopen the matter of his dismissal from the SS, Raeder seemed content to let that matter drop as well.[76] Indeed, by early 1935, the Reichsmarine, the Wehrmacht, and the nation as a whole had far more important matters requiring their attention.

By the beginning of 1935 the Wehrmacht was completing the first stage of its illegal rearmament. On land the army stood ready to reveal its first overt expansion beyond the seven infantry and three cavalry divisions permitted under the Treaty of Versailles. Hermann Göring was likewise prepared to reveal the true nature of his Air Ministry, which had hitherto been rather thinly disguised as a Bureau for Civil Aviation. The navy, too, was ready to undertake measures that openly contravened the Versailles *Diktat*. It only remained to determine the right moment for announcing German rearmament to the waiting world. Already the announcement had been postponed to avoid complicating the plebiscite which was to decide whether the inhabitants of the Saarland wished to rejoin the

Reich. With the successful completion of the plebiscite on January 13, 1935, however, all obstacles to the revelation of Germany's renascent military strength seemed to have disappeared.[77]

The Luftwaffe's turn came first. On March 9, a Saturday, Hitler revealed that Germany once again possessed an air force. A week later, on March 16, he announced that Germany was reintroducing conscription and that the army now numbered thirty-six divisions.[78] Those experienced with Hitler's tactics of surprising especially the British Cabinet with weekend decisions might logically have expected a third announcement to appear the following Saturday concerning the navy. If so they were disappointed, for after his flurry of activity the Reich Chancellor appeared to have run out of surprises.

In fact, he and Raeder were jointly preparing perhaps the biggest surprise that National Socialist diplomacy had yet produced, for by the end of March 1935 the prospect of an agreement with Great Britain sanctioning German naval rearmament was becoming a very real possibility.[79] Such an idea, of course, was not new,[80] but it had foundered in the past on a number of obstacles. For one thing, it will be remembered that in the days before the *Machtergreifung* Hitler had often spoken of a renunciation (*Verzicht*) of German sea power and not of an expansion of the navy. For another, it was no small order to convince the British of the wisdom of any agreement that would allow the Reichsmarine to expand beyond the limits set by the Treaty of Versailles. The Imperial Navy had inspired justifiable fear in Britain in the period before and during the Great War, and Britain had been the power most responsible for the naval provisions of Versailles. Yet by the spring of 1935 some of the problems that had formerly stood in the way of an Anglo-German agreement in both Berlin and London had disappeared.

The first obstacle removed was Hitler's renunciation of sea power. From the autumn of 1933, when Raeder optimistically announced to his officers that the Reich Chancellor "continually" mentioned the necessity of building up the fleet, until the following summer, the admiral had spared no effort to keep Hitler's attention focused on the navy and to hammer home the advantages that an expanded fleet entailed for Germany. This was by no means an easy task, especially during the SA crisis of the spring and summer of 1934, but Raeder was persistent; he was also quite adept at tailoring his arguments to meet Hitler's own predilections. In June 1934, for example, while presenting an argument for German participation at the Naval Disarmament Conference scheduled for 1935, he elevated naval expansion to an "almost infallible" criterion for Germany's international standing, for "the measure of a nation's importance in the world [was] a measure of her power at sea."[81] Admiral von Tirpitz could hardly have put it better.

By the spring of 1934, at the latest, it would seem that Raeder's arguments were having an effect and that Hitler's ideas concerning the future of the fleet had undergone a change. To be sure, according to the Führer's new formula Germany would still have to make concessions to win Britain's favor, but Hitler's idea of a "renunciation" now entailed Germany's voluntary agreement to limit its navy to a size one-third that of the British fleet.[82] Given the minuscule size of the Reichsmarine at this time—one "pocket" battleship, three predreadnoughts, five light cruisers, and a handful of torpedo-boats of decidedly inferior quality—this involved not a limitation at all, but rather a three to fourfold expansion of the navy beyond its present strength.[83]

It remained to convince the British. Despite the difficulties involved, Hitler was undaunted, and from November 1934 until the following spring he wasted no opportunity to convince influential Britons of his peaceful intentions and of the possible services that a small but well-equipped German fleet could render the British Empire. Raeder appears to have been even more skeptical of the possibility of persuading the British, but he also did his utmost to bring them to the conference table. In November 1934 he hinted to the British naval attaché in Berlin that Germany would be interested in bilateral negotiations in the event that the Naval Disarmament Conference collapsed. Moreover, during the winter and spring of 1935 the Reichsmarine cautiously began to acquaint the Royal Navy with the modest expansion that it had already undertaken in order to render this surprise less unpleasant. That spring both Raeder and Hitler were able to report modest successes. On March 20, 1935, the German naval attaché in London, Captain Erwin Wassner, rendered his opinion that the Royal Navy no longer had any serious objections concerning the German proposals for the expansion of the fleet. Later that month, on March 26, Sir John Simon, the British Foreign Secretary, who was visiting Berlin for talks with Hitler, expressed his government's willingness to hold informal conversations on naval matters before the Naval Disarmament Conference. Although considerable differences remained between the British and the German positions, Hitler had taken the first crucial step in getting an agreement with Great Britain.[84]

One significant problem remained which, perhaps surprisingly, concerned the Reichsmarine's own objection to the projected agreement. In spite of the fact that Germany would be undertaking a tremendous expansion of its navy, a number of officers, Raeder included, were uncomfortable with the "modest" size of the projected fleet. Raeder had succeeded at an early date in persuading Hitler to raise the ratio from $33^1/_3$ per cent to 35 per cent of the British navy, allegedly for "practical reasons." A more likely explanation for the change was that 35 per cent was precisely the ratio that France, Germany's most likely enemy in the immediate future, enjoyed in capital ship tonnage vis-à-vis Great Britain by virtue of the Washington Naval Treaty of 1922. But even this figure was fraught with difficulty for German planners, for at the Second London Naval Conference in 1930 France had refused to be bound by the 35 per cent figure when it came to cruisers and lighter vessels, and had in fact subsequently built its total tonnage to a little over 50 per cent of the British. As a result, any agreement that limited Germany to 35 per cent would still leave the Reichsmarine considerably weaker than the French in certain ship categories.[85]

Navy objections to the projected agreement, then, were inevitable. As early as the spring of 1934, when the proposed ratio to be striven for with Britain was still a matter of debate, a navy study had found the tonnage envisioned for battleships according to the one-third ratio to be insufficient; its author withdrew his objections only in the belief that the agreement would be of a limited duration. At the same time the head of the Marinekommandoamt, Rear Admiral Groos, found the projected number of cruisers and destroyers to be inferior to the French and wrote: "Where is the parity with France then? A different ratio must be found for cruisers, destroyers, and U-boats." Raeder responded by allowing the Kommandoamt to study the possibility of a 50 per cent ratio as well.[86]

In January the idea of a treaty of short duration surfaced again on the grounds that the Reichsmarine could reach the strength of 35 per cent within five years. Later that month the navy began to entertain the hope that Japan's recent decision to repudiate the Washington Naval Treaty might be used as a pretext to obtain a higher ratio from the British. In April, after reading an article about French naval construction, Captain Otto Ciliax, Chief of Naval Operations, wrote: "One sees that we come up considerably short with 35% of the Eng[lish] tonnage." In the wake of such sentiments the new head of the Kommandoamt, Vice Admiral Günther Guse, even sought to use the unlikely argument that an increase in the navy beyond 35 per cent might be useful to the British as leverage against France.[87]

In late April Raeder brought the navy's concern to Hitler's attention. The chancellor would hear of no further increases in the proposed ratio, and the only thing Raeder received that spring was a new title, that of Oberbefehlshaber der Kriegsmarine.[88] When the German delegation under the newly appointed Special Ambassador Joachim von Ribbentrop left for London in early June it was pledged to the formula of 35 per cent, no more and no less.

The actual negotiations proved to be surprisingly simple, if somewhat embarrassing for the host country. Confronted with Ribbentrop's demand that the 35 per cent ratio was not negotiable and that it must be accepted before any further discussions were undertaken, the British were left with the choice either of agreeing or of watching the talks collapse almost before they had begun. After a hurried Cabinet meeting the British agreed to the main German demand on June 6. The next day the talks were recessed for a week-long break for Whitsuntide. During that time the British would inform the other naval powers of their intention to agree with the Germans' proposal. The latter would head home for further consultations with the Reich Chancellor.[89]

Ribbentrop's delegation returned to a Germany that was being inundated with naval propaganda. Already, on May 31, the public had been treated to elaborate celebrations marking the nineteenth anniversary of the Battle of the Skagerrak. The Whitsuntide break coincided with the navy's most ambitious public relations project since the days of Tirpitz, the initiation of an annual Navy Week modeled, appropriately enough, on a similar institution in the Royal Navy. Finally, at the conclusion of Navy Week there would come the famous Kiel Regatta, in which the Service's officers would play an important role as hosts, guides, and participants. As a result, the fatherland witnessed almost a month of frenetic activity calculated to whip up enthusiasm for Germany's claim for a navy suitable to its needs.[90]

The authorities spared no effort to make the ceremonies memorable. During May, sixty-three Imperial Navy banners were decorated with the *Frontkämpferkreuz*, and public thoroughfares throughout Germany had their names changed to honor the battles and heroes of the navy. The following month special excursions brought thousands of spectators to Navy Week in Kiel. A sailing competition was held for the coveted Hindenburg Memorial Cup, which the Kriegsmarine team won after three spirited races with officers from the Swedish, Danish, Dutch, and Polish navies. Another competition involved over 10,000 drawings and poems by German schoolchildren depicting German sea power. The lucky winners were to receive a trip on the "pocket" battleship *Deutschland*.[91]

Each of these measures, however, paled in comparison with the carefully orchestrated ceremonies that marked the official opening of Navy Week at the gigantic Nord Ostsee Halle in Kiel on June 11, 1935. That evening, beneath a huge eagle and swastika, a crowd of ten thousand saw a parade of historic flags, including those of the navies of Electoral Brandenburg and the Kingdom of Prussia. Then the lights dimmed, and a Kriegsmarine sailor recounted the engagements of the Great War. Afterwards a naval band played the moving song *Ich hatt' einen Kamaraden* while the men and women in the audience stood silently with their right arms raised in salute. The message was clear. The link between the past and the present, between the glorious royal and imperial navies and the new Kriegsmarine, was inseparable.[92]

When the lights came back on, the station chief, Vice Admiral Albrecht, gave the welcoming address. After pointing out Germany's unalterable claim to sea power and noting the service that National Socialism had rendered in uniting worker and sailor, he described the leader of the Movement himself: "He is for us soldiers the embodiment of the German front soldier, both yesterday and today. We seamen are thankful that he has understood the sea."[93] The address was followed by the *Deutschlandlied* and the *Horst-Wessel-Lied*. Then the navy gave an indication that it understood the Führer as well as he appeared to understand the sea, for the evening was topped off by a torchlight parade that rivaled the pyrotechnical displays seen at Nuremberg the previous September. Although Hitler was not present—he was in Bavaria convalescing from surgery on a vocal cord—there can be no doubt that he, too, got the navy's message.[94]

With the exhilaration of the naval spectacle safely behind them, Ribbentrop and the naval delegation returned to London on June 13.

Five days later, on June 18, the anniversary of the Anglo-Prussian victory over Napoleon I at Waterloo, an exchange of notes announced the Anglo-German Naval Agreement.[95] In all categories save one, Germany pledged to limit its naval construction to the 35 per cent ratio that Hitler had envisioned. A special clause allowed Germany to build up its submarine fleet to 45 per cent, with the additional right to expand the U-boat force to full parity with the British after giving due notice.[96] The ratios agreed to were to be permanent.

World-wide reaction to the agreement was mixed. While Denmark, Poland, and the Baltic states generally saw more positive than negative in the accord, two of Germany's more important neighbors were decidedly unreceptive to it. The French felt betrayed by their erstwhile ally, while the Soviet Union must surely have wondered what had motivated Britain to agree to such a massive increase in the size of the German surface fleet. The Italian and United States governments were outwardly unmoved by the German coup, but in private American diplomats also expressed their doubts concerning the wisdom of the British concessions. Indeed, of all the major naval powers, only Japan found cause for satisfaction in the agreement.[97]

In Germany, on the other hand, with the understandable exception of one important group, the naval convention was greeted with unrestrained enthusiasm. The diplomatic isolation in which Germany had found itself vis-à-vis the West since 1919 appeared to have been broken. A major portion of the Treaty of Versailles had been rendered null and void, and the Anglo-French-Italian "Stresa Front" of April 1935 had been undermined.[98] From the perspective of both the Wilhelmstrasse and the Reich Chancellery in Berlin, some sort of general Anglo-German accord seemed just around the corner. It is little wonder that a jubilant Hitler termed June 18, 1935, the happiest day of his life.[99]

The only discordant note was sounded from within the ranks of the naval officer corps. Hitler, for one, appeared to have anticipated this in June when he told the senior officer on the Ribbentrop delegation, Rear Admiral Karlgeorg Schuster, that he felt he would be criticized in some circles because he had not bargained for more, but that he knew from experience how much to demand. Nevertheless, veiled criticism was forthcoming from a number of officers. Some, such as Captain Karl Dönitz, were disappointed by the relatively small number of U-boats that the Kriegsmarine would build, even when the navy decided to achieve full parity with British submarine strength. Others were bothered by the modest size of the surface fleet. In July Vice Admiral Guse reported that a number of officers were asking whether the London accords really served the navy's best interests, and he cautiously added that "outside the navy" it was being said that the British had duped the Germans at London. Later, Captain Ciliax, while recognizing the political necessity of the agreement, complained that it meant that Germany would be dependent upon Britain on the world stage for the foreseeable future.[100]

Such criticism of the Führer's diplomatic coup was, of course, disturbing to Raeder, and during the summer of 1935 he had a guide drawn up to instruct officers how they ought to view the agreement. An early draft by Vice Admiral Guse described the Anglo-German pact in glowing terms:

> The Agreement is entirely satisfactory for years to come. Any substantially larger figure . . . could hardly be reached in the next decade. It will give us the opportunity of creating a modern fleet which is appropriately constituted and in accordance with our maritime needs.

In view of the permanent relationship envisioned in the agreement, the four words "for years to come" had a slightly incongruous ring to them, as if there would come a time when the ratio 35:100 would no longer be satisfactory to Germany. Consequently, the offending phrase was omitted in the final version. For the next few years, at least, Raeder would pay lip service to the permanency of the agreement.[101]

Erich Raeder could be well satisfied in the summer of 1935. Behind lay the days of indecision and doubt. In two short years he had bridged the gap between Republic and Third Reich. He had turned Hitler from a decrier of sea power into at least a lukewarm supporter. With but a few exceptions, the naval officer corps had been integrated into the National Socialist state: neither the SA crisis in the spring and summer of 1934 nor the subsequent challenge posed by SS claims to bear arms had disturbed the navy's relations with its Führer. On the diplomatic front the Anglo-German Naval Agreement had not only made manifest Hitler's interest in naval matters; it had also cooled relations between London and Paris and had given German naval expansion the official seal of approval by the British Cabinet and Admiralty. There no longer existed any need for deception or secrecy in German shipbuilding. Until at least the fall of 1942 the navy's shipyards would have to toil around the clock to reach the permitted strength of 35 per cent of the British surface fleet. Raeder, the former imperial naval officer and republican historian, must have felt in the summer of 1935 like his Kaiser had at the turn of the century, when Wilhelm II had depicted the future task in simple, direct terms: "Fleet, fleet, fleet."[102]

Notes for Chapter 4

1 Bundesarchiv-Militärarchiv, Freiburg, West Germany (hereafter cited as BA-MA), N 165/3 Nachlass Groos, "3. Buch: Unter der Diktatur;" Walter Baum, "Marine, Nationalsozialismus und Widerstand," *Vierteljahrshefte für Zeitgeschichte*, 11 (January 1963), p. 16.

2 A record of the meeting at Hammerstein's was retained by General a.D. Liebmann and is reprinted in Thilo Vogelsang, "Neue Dokumente zur Geschichte der Reichswehr 1930–1933," *Vierteljahrshefte für Zeitgeschichte*, 2, No. 4 (October 1954), pp. 434–435. Retrospective accounts by naval officers include those of Conrad Albrecht in BA-MA, RM 35 I/24, "Protokoll über die Befragung durch Oskar Richter, 20. Dez. 1959;" Otto Groos in BA-MA,

N 165/3 Nachlass Groos "3. Buch: Unter der Diktatur;" and Raeder's own account, which was written while in Russian captivity in August 1945, BA-MA, RM 6/104 "Die Entwicklung der Deutschen Marinepolitik 1933–1939," as well as *Mein Leben* (Tübingen, 1956–1957), 2, pp. 280–281. Raeder mistakenly gives the date as February 2.

3 This and the following from Vogelsang, "Neue Dokumente," pp. 434–435.

4 See BA-MA, N 165/3 Nachlass Groos, "3. Buch: Unter der Diktatur;" Raeder, *Mein Leben*, 2, pp. 106–107; BA-MA, RM 35 I/24, "Protokoll über die Befragung durch Oskar Richter, 20. Dez. 1959." For the army officers' response see Wolfgang Sauer, "Die Mobilmachung der Gewalt," in Karl Dietrich Bracher, Wolfgang Sauer, and Gerhard Schulz, *Die nationalsozialistische Machtergreifung*, 2nd edn (Cologne, 1962), p. 735.

5 Jost Dülffer, *Weimar, Hitler und die Marine: Reichspolitik und Flottenbau 1920–1939* (Düsseldorf, 1973), pp. 238–239.

6 Ibid., pp. 241–243.

7 Ibid., p. 244.

8 See Raeder's assessment of Blomberg in *Mein Leben*, 2, p. 108.

9 This is in a sense similar to the *"Loyalitätswettlauf"* (loyalty race) that the Wehrmacht as a whole was running with Ernst Röhm's SA. For this see Manfred Messerschmidt, *Die Wehrmacht im NS Staat: Zeit der Indoktrination* (Hamburg, 1969), pp. 23–24.

10 Cited in ibid., p. 37, n. 139.

11 For the "Day of Potsdam" see André François-Poncet, *The Fateful Years: Memoirs of a French Ambassador in Berlin* (New York, 1949), pp. 60–64; also Karl Dietrich Bracher, "Stufen der Machtergreifung," in Bracher, Sauer and Schulz, *Die nationalsozialistische Machtergreifung*, pp. 149–152. The ceremonies were important in establishing the style of the new National Socialist state. Two days later the Reichstag passed the Enabling Act that granted Hitler dictatorial power.

12 *Deutsche Allgemeine Zeitung*, March 22, 1933; BA-MA, RM 8/55 M III, March 18, 1933.

13 See the text of Raeder's speech in *Deutsche Allgemeine Zeitung*, April 2, 1933. Later that day Captain Hermann von Fischel, the commander of the newly commissioned *Deutschland*, gave a speech that conveyed a similar message to the National Socialists.

14 A copy of Raeder's notes for the meeting is reprinted in Michael Salewski, "Marineleitung und politische Führung 1931–1935," *Militärgeschichtliche Mitteilungen*, 2/1971, pp. 153–157. Both the date and the exact nature of the conversation are impossible to determine. For two plausible interpretations as to the course of the discussion see ibid., pp. 125–127; and Dülffer, *Hitler und die Marine*, pp. 244–247. Raeder's account (*Mein Leben*, 1, pp. 281–282, and 2, pp. 106–107) would seem to be faulty here, at least as far as many of the details are concerned.

15 See the excerpts from Reichswehr Minister von Blomberg's address to the naval garrison at Kiel wherein Blomberg emphasized that he and Hitler were in complete agreement concerning the necessity that the armed forces remain out of politics. *Deutsche Allgemeine Zeitung*, February 17, 1933.

16 BA-MA, RM 8/55 M I B, March 9, 1935; Friedrich Ruge, *In vier Marinen* (Munich, 1979), p. 108.

17 BA-MA, RM 8/55 Der Reichswehrminister Nr. 2330/33 W I b, April 18, 1933. *Landesjägerei* units were heavily armed police forces belonging to the various federal states of the Reich.

18 BA-MA, II M 58/3 Vortrag vor Führer der S.A., S.S., und des Stahlhelms sowie Vertretern der Reichs-Staats-pp Behörden in Kiel am 5. Mai 1933; see also notes for a speech of similar content by Schuster in BA-MA, II M 58/3 Stichworte für Vortrag vor SA-Führern an Bord Linienschiff "Schleswig-Holstein," February 7, 1934.

19 *Völkischer Beobachter*, North German edition, May 9, 1933.

20 *Völkischer Beobachter*, North German edition, May 24, 1933. Göring's seasickness prompted pranksters to draw up a bogus wireless message: "Neptune to Minister President Hermann Göring. Effective today you are appointed Reich Fish Feeder [*Reichsfischfuttermeister*] with the permission to wear a net shirt." Göring, who already had the reputation of being a title seeker, was enraged and demanded that the officers be punished. Their commander, Captain Wilhelm Canaris, refused to do anything more than issue a reprimand. Heinz Höhne, *Canaris: Patriot im Zwielicht* (Munich, 1976), pp. 136–137.

21 *Völkischer Beobachter*, North German edition, June 1, 1933.

22 Ruge, *In vier Marinen*, p. 115.

23 BA-MA, RM 8/55 Der Reichswehrminister Nr. 3567/33 W I c, June 16, 1933; B. Nr. A I b 3098, July 7, 1933; M I B, August 4, 1933; M I B, August 23, 1933.

24 BA-MA, RM 8/55 B. Nr. 1205 M I B, August 28, 1933; B. Nr. 1243 M I B, September 5, 1933; Keith W. Bird, *Weimar, The German Naval Officer Corps and the Rise of National Socialism* (Amsterdam, 1977), p. 293.

25 The text of Raeder's speech is given in BA-MA, RM 20/943 M L A Ia-II-27b.

26 See above, Chapter 3.

27 BA-MA, RM 8/56 Der Reichswehrminister Nr. 866/34 J I a, March 1, 1934; RM 20/910 Der Reichsverteidigungsminister Nr. 487/34 g Kdos., July 3, 1934; RM 8/56 M I B 527, April 10, 1934; Der Reichswehrminister Nr. 1480/34 J I a, April 17, 1934.

28 BA-MA, RM 8/56 M I B 242, February 19, 1934; M I B, February 22, 1934.

29 BA-MA, RM 8/55 Berlin, November 6, 1933; RM 8/56 M A Nr. 381/34 W I C, January 29, 1934. I have found no evidence that similar arrangements were made for previous chancellors.

30 BA-MA, RM 8/55 M III, November 25, 1933; RM 8/58 M Allg., November 10, 1936; Der Chef des Wehrmachtsamts, December 10, 1936; B. Nr. 3291 M Allg., December 16, 1936.

31 BA-MA, RM 8/55 Der Chef der Marineleitung A IV (I) c 4698, October 30, 1933; Der Chef der Marineleitung M I B 1793, December 27, 1933; RM 8/56 M I B, January 19, 1934; B Nr. A V c 6273, November 1, 1934; M Z 107, January 19, 1935.

32 BA-MA, RM 6/274 Nr. 196/33 g Kds W I b, June 13, 1933; RW 6/73 W II d, November 16, 1933.

33 The law was passed on April 7, 1933 and provided the basis for the removal of Jews and other "politically unreliable" persons from the civil service. In the words of Karl Dietrich Bracher: "It also opened the floodgates of petty, sordid careerist ambition, personal enmity, and profitable denunciation." *The German Dictatorship* (New York, 1970), p. 197.

34 BA-MA, RW 6/73 W I b, August 23, 1933; W I b, January 19, 1934; Der Reichswehrminister Nr. 224/33 W I b, January 23, 1934; W II d, August 14, 1933.

35 The term "front line veteran" was rather narrowly defined in the legislation that implemented the law. Initially the term included those who had participated in battles, skirmishes, and sieges of the world war and the subsequent engagements in the Baltic and Upper Silesia, as well as domestic engagements against Spartacists, separatists, and "enemies of the National Revolution." From this it was unclear whether many navy veterans were "front line veterans." The head of the Ministeramt, General von Reichenau, therefore suggested a modified form whereby naval *Frontkämpfer* were defined as "soldiers, officials or other crew members of a warship or auxiliary vessel if they were aboard during a naval action. Naval actions included battles, engagements, and operational missions and other recognized war activities such as mine sweeping and U-boat escort service." Messerschmidt, *Wehrmacht im NS Staat*, p. 41.

36 Klaus-Jürgen Müller, *Das Heer und Hitler: Armee und nationalsozialistisches Regime 1933–1940* (Stuttgart, 1969), pp. 78–82; Messerschmidt, *Wehrmacht im NS Staat*, pp. 43–45.

37 Messerschmidt, *Wehrmacht im NS Staat*, p. 41. A detailed discussion of the legal aspects of the National Socialist interpretation of the term *Jude* is beyond the scope of this study. Already during the Great War the German military had found its *Judenzählung* to be a difficult undertaking. Werner T. Angress, "Das deutsche Militär und die Juden im Ersten Weltkrieg," *Militärgeschichtliche Mitteilungen*, 1/1976, pp. 77–146.

38 Such things did happen. Perhaps the most celebrated case (although it occurred during the Weimar period) concerned the Second Chairman of the *Stahlhelm*, Theodor Düsterberg, who discovered very much to his dismay that one of his grandfathers had been Jewish. Volker R. Berghahn, *Der Stahlhelm: Bund der Frontsoldaten, 1918–1935* (Düsseldorf, 1966), pp. 239ff.

39 Raeder had personal reasons for disapproving of the Party's position concerning the Jews. His own son-in-law qualified as a "non-Aryan" and found it advisable to live abroad. BA-MA, RM 6/104 "Die Entwicklung der Deutschen Marinepolitik 1933–1939." With one significant exception, which will be dealt with in Chapter 6, Raeder appears to have eschewed Jew-baiting in his later addresses to the officer corps and in his private correspondence. Albert Speer, who subsequently had ample opportunity to know Raeder, confirms that the admiral was no anti-Semite. *Spandauer Tagebücher* (Frankfurt, Berlin and Vienna), p. 401.

40 Messerschmidt, *Wehrmacht im NS Staat*, p. 46.

41 BA-MA, RW 6/73 Reichswehrministerium Nr. J I a, June, 1934. Raeder makes much of the navy's taking care of its own. *Mein Leben*, 2, pp. 132–133. One officer attributed his new-found civilian position to the personal efforts of the then Captain Wilhelm Canaris and not to Raeder or the officer corps as a whole. Müller, *Heer und Hitler*, p. 82, n. 238 and p. 85.

42 Ibid., p. 82, n. 237.

43 Raeder, *Mein Leben*, 2, p. 133; Müller, *Heer und Hitler*, p. 82, n. 238; BA-MA, RW 6/73 Der Chef der Marineleitung B. Nr. A V w 2742, May 16, 1934.

44 For a dated but generally reliable analysis of the SA crisis see Hermann Mau, "Die 'Zweite Revolution'—Der 30. Juli 1934," in *Vierteljahrshefte für Zeitgeschichte*, 1, No. 2 (April 1953), pp. 119–137. For the army's role in the crisis see Müller, *Heer und Hitler*, pp. 88–133; also Heinrich Bennecke, *Die Reichswehr und der "Röhm Putsch"* (Munich, 1964).

45   The estimated strength of 2,000,000 men dates from the end of 1933.

46   A highly partisan history of one Marine SA unit up to 1934 is found in Bernd Ehrenreich, *Marine-SA: Das Buch einer Formation* (Hamburg, 1935). Ehrenreich gives the strength of the Marine SA in 1935 as 10,000 men. Ibid., p. 6.

47   See, for instance, BA-MA, RW 6/67 Teil 2 4654/34 J I b, June 1934; also Ruge, *In vier Marinen*, pp. 125, 134.

48   See the case of Chief Petty Officer Adam in BA-MA, RW 6/66; also the reports of Major Lindemann and Major a.D. von Sodenstern concerning an altercation on January 26, 1934, RW 6/67.

49   Examples of these mutually antagonistic attitudes can be found in BA-MA, RW 6/66 Commander Topp to Marinestation der Ostsee, Kiel, February 15, 1934; also RM 6/66 Verhandlung Kiel, January 2, 1934, wherein Chief Petty Officer Adam recounted SA accusations: "That is the navy of '18, those are Communists."

50   For an indication that this was the preferred course of action see BA-MA, RW 6/66 W II d. Vortrag of January 22, 1934.

51   A classic example of the unwillingness of both sides to compromise occurred in April, 1934, when the Lord Mayor of Kiel, an SA man named Walter Behrens, asked the citizens of Kiel to donate room and board to members of the SA as a birthday gift to the Führer. Behrens' proclamation stated that "the Reichsmarine city Kiel, from which the shame of the year 1918 was removed by the brown battalions of Adolf Hitler, will not want to hold back on this birthday gift to the Führer." The response of Vice Admiral Conrad Albrecht, Chief of the Baltic Naval Station, showed considerable irritation: "The Reichsmarine is of the opinion that the navy itself removed the shame of November 1918 from the city of Kiel. ... In Kiel ... a new navy has been created, which in discipline and ability can compare with any other navy, an accomplishment which the Führer has only recently rivaled with the SA." Subsequent exchanges took on a sharper tone. BA-MA, RW 6/67 Teil 1.

52   See for instance Blomberg's conciliatory letters to Röhm on the Adam case on January 18, January 25, March 9, and June 12, 1934 in BA-MA, RW 6/66.

53   Mau, "Der 30. Juli 1934," pp. 126–129; Müller, *Heer und Hitler*, pp. 98–100. Röhm privately denounced Hitler's decision as a "Versailles *Diktat*" and described the Führer as an "ignorant corporal." Ibid., p. 100, n. 72.

54   According to Rear Admiral Groos, the Marine SA and the Marine Hitler Jugend, which had previously enjoyed a fair amount of independence, were scheduled to be more closely integrated into their parent organizations. Groos met with Röhm, and the SA leader agreed to let the units keep their distinctive uniforms and allowed them to maintain independent brigades in the Hanse cities of Lübeck, Bremen, and Hamburg. In other areas of the Reich the two naval groups were to be joined organizationally with land formations, but they were also to keep their character as "special naval units." BA-MA, N 165/3 Nachlass Groos, "3. Buch: Unter der Diktatur."

55   BA-MA, RW 6/67 Teil 2 J I b, Vortrag of July 1934; Ruge, *In vier Marinen*, pp. 134–135; BA-MA, RW 6/67 Teil 1 Communications to A I, Berlin, June 11, 1934.

56 BA-MA, RW 6/67 Teil 2 J I b, Vortrag of August 9, 1934; RW 6/67 Teil 1, Wilhelmshaven, June 16, 1934; RW 6/67 Teil 1, Kommando Kreuzer "Leipzig" GP782, June 30, 1934; see also the report of the Kyffhäuserbund leader in Flensburg, Dr Reuther, to Wolf von Trotha, in BA-MA, RW 6/67 Teil 1, June 30, 1934.

57 Bennecke, *Reichswehr und Röhm Putsch*, pp. 87–88, lists eighty-three victims of the purge. In addition to members of the SA, the victims included a number of men who had crossed Hitler in the past, including Gregor Strasser, Gustav von Kahr, and two retired army generals, Kurt von Schleicher and Ferdinand von Bredow.

58 See BA-MA, N 165/3 Nachlass Groos, "3. Buch: Unter der Diktatur." Raeder's account of the events of June 30 is given in BA-MA, RM 6/104 "Die Entwicklung der Deutschen Marinepolitik 1933–1939"; also *Mein Leben*, 1, pp. 288–289.

59 Ruge, *In vier Marinen*, p. 139. For the army's preparations, especially in Bavaria, see Müller, *Heer und Hitler*, pp. 112–125.

60 See excerpts from the article entitled "Ich bin Offiziersfrau" included in BA-MA, RW 6/67 Teil 1. The author recommended that the lady be sent to a concentration camp as a cleaning woman to cure her of her arrogance.

61 BA-MA, RW 6/68 Teil 1 J I b, Vortrag of June 13, 1935; Raeder, *Mein Leben*, 1, p. 289.

62 Sir John W. Wheeler-Bennett argues that Blomberg promised his support for Hitler's succession to the presidency while the two men were aboard the *Deutschland* in April, 1934. *The Nemesis of Power: The German Army in Politics 1918–1945* (London, 1953), pp. 311–313. More recent studies do not mention this "Pact of the *Deutschland*." While the Führer's five-day voyage certainly afforded him ample opportunity to discuss important matters of state with his Reichswehr Minister, I can find no convincing evidence that such a pact was concluded. For this see Robert J. O'Neill, *The German Army and the Nazi Party, 1933–1939* (London, 1966), pp. 245–246. For a more recent view of the armed forces' role in the events of August 2, see Müller, *Heer und Hitler*, pp. 133–134.

63 Ludwig Beck, Chief of the General Staff, noted immediately after taking the oath that this was "the darkest day of his life." For his and other army officers' responses, see Müller, *Heer und Hitler*, pp. 136–137.

64 Raeder, *Mein Leben*, 1, p. 290. "Universal interpretation" clearly erred in this case, for the Law Concerning the Head of the German Reich violated, among other statutes, the National Socialists' own Enabling Act of March 24, 1933. Müller, *Heer und Hitler*, p. 133; Helmut Krausnick, "Vorgeschichte und Beginn des militärischen Widerstandes gegen Hitler," in *Vollmacht des Gewissens* (Frankfurt am Main, 1960), p. 236, n. 161.

65 On June 30, the same day as the Röhm Purge, Hitler decreed that the SS *Leibstandarte* would be equipped as a modern combat regiment. With that the military aspirations of the SS began to grow. For the subsequent tension between the SS and the army in 1934, see Müller, *Heer und Hitler*, pp. 147–166.

66 This and the following details are from BA-MA, RW 6/67 Teil 2 J I b, Vortrag of August 9, 1934.

67 BA-MA, RW 6/67 Teil 2 Der Reichswehrminister Nr. 799/34g J I b, August 11, 1934; Der Reichsführer SS III Nr. 6/393 Geheim, September 28, 1934; Der Reichswehrminister Nr. 1038/34g, October 16, 1934.

68 Müller, *Heer und Hitler*, p. 155.
69 Shlomo Aronson, *Reinhard Heydrich und die Frühgeschichte von Gestapo und SD* (Stuttgart, 1971), pp. 34–35, 260–261.
70 Ibid., *passim*, especially pp. 169–172, 187–190; Höhne, *Canaris*, pp. 161–163; Raeder, *Mein Leben*, 1, p. 117; Müller, *Heer und Hitler*, p. 161, n. 88.
71 Höhne, *Canaris*, p. 163.
72 BA-MA, RW 6/67 Teil 2 Chef der Marineleitung B. Nr. MPA 4180, December 29, 1934.
73 Krausnick, "Vorgeschichte des Widerstandes," pp. 249–250; Höhne, *Canaris*, p. 163.
74 Friedrich Hossbach, *Zwischen Wehrmacht und Hitler 1934–1938* (Göttingen, 1965), p. 61; Krausnick, "Vorgeschichte des Widerstandes," p. 256, n. 51.
75 Müller, *Heer und Hitler*, p. 159; Hermann Boehm, quoted in Krausnick, "Vorgeschichte des Widerstandes," p. 256; and BA-MA, N 328/53 Nachlass Förste, "Aus den persönlichen Erinnerungen Boehms." Hitler conveniently forgot this pledge during the "Fritsch–Blomberg crisis" of January 1938. For this see below, Chapter 7.
76 Müller, *Heer und Hitler*, p. 159; Raeder, *Mein Leben*, 1, p. 116; BA-MA, RW 6/67 Teil 2 Wehrmachtsamt Nr. 20/34g, January 19, 1935.
77 For a concise summary of the armed forces' rearmament see Wilhelm Deist, *The Wehrmacht and German Rearmament* (London, 1981), *passim*; also Wilhelm Deist, "Die Aufrüstung der Wehrmacht," in Deist *et al.*, *Das deutsche Reich und der Zweite Weltkrieg*, 10 vols (Stuttgart, 1979-), Vol. 1: *Ursachen und Voraussetzungen der deutschen Kriegspolitik*, pp. 371–532.
78 Nor was the navy unaffected by conscription: the Marineleitung foresaw the use of conscripts in the coastal artillery and in other land units as well as, for a limited period of time, aboard auxiliary vessels of the fleet. The main units of the fleet, however, were to be manned by long-term volunteers. See BA-MA, RM 20/909 "Beitrag für die grundsätzlichen Fragen zur Aufstellung einer Wehrordnung," Anlage zu A V a 712/34 Gkdos.
79 For the history of the Anglo-German Naval Agreement see Donald C. Watt, "The Anglo-German Naval Agreement of 1935: An Interim Judgment," *Journal of Modern History*, 28 (June 1956), pp. 155–175; Robert Ingrim, *Hitlers glücklichster Tag: London, am 18. Juni 1935* (Stuttgart, 1962); and Dülffer, *Hitler und die Marine*, pp. 279–354. The Royal Navy's attitude toward the negotiations is presented in Stephen Roskill, *Naval Policy Between the Wars*, Vol. 2: *The Period of Reluctant Rearmament 1930–1939* (Annapolis, Md, 1976), pp. 302–307. An overview of the negotiations is provided in Gerhard L. Weinberg, *The Foreign Policy of Hitler's Germany* (Chicago, 1970), 1, pp. 210–216.
80 In the late fall of 1933, for example, Raeder had sought to convince the British naval attaché of the use that Britain could make of a squadron of German capital ships against the United States! Dülffer, *Hitler und die Marine*, pp. 267–268.
81 This appeal was originally drawn up by Admiral von Freyberg. *Documents on German Foreign Policy* (hereafter cited as DGFP), C, Vol. 3, No. 25. Raeder used the memorandum at his meeting with Hitler on June 22, 1934. Salewski, "Marineleitung," p. 139.
82 The origins of the one-third ratio are obscure. Raeder says that the proposal came from Hitler at a meeting in the spring of 1933. *Mein Leben*, 1, pp. 282–283. Given the obstinacy with which Hitler defended the $33^{1/3}$ or 35 per cent ratios against all criticisms, this is highly likely.

However, the first mention of either of the two ratios within naval circles did not occur until the spring of 1934. Salewski, "Marineleitung," p. 133, n. 107; Dülffer, *Hitler und die Marine*, p. 279. It is possible that Raeder's memory was at fault concerning the date or that he and Hitler kept the figure to themselves for a year.

83 The reasons for the different estimates (three or fourfold) are as follows: during the 1920s and early 1930s the Reichsmarine had not built up to the maximum of 144,000 tons allowed under the Treaty of Versailles. Thus, while the 420,000 odd tons that the 35 per cent ratio eventually obtained for Germany represented a threefold increase in official tonnage, it represented a fourfold increase in actual tonnage. The list of vessels available to the Reichsmarine in the spring of 1934 is compiled from Erich Gröner, *Die deutschen Kriegsschiffe 1815–1945*, 2 vols (Munich, 1966).

84 See Dülffer, *Hitler und die Marine*, pp. 300–310, 319; *Documents on German Foreign Policy* (hereafter cited as DGFP), C, Vol. 3, No. 360; No. 555, pp. 1064–1073; also ibid.; C, Vol. 4, Nos 25, 52, 54, 58, 59.

85 Raeder, *Mein Leben*, 1, p. 282; Gerhard Schreiber, "Zur Kontinuität des Gross- und Weltmachtstrebens der deutschen Marineführung," *Militärgeschichtliche Mitteilungen*, 2/1979 pp. 116, 122–123; Dülffer, *Hitler und die Marine*, pp. 279–301, 342–345. Dülffer refers to the decision for 35 per cent instead of $33^1/3$ per cent as "a cosmetic correction."

86 Ibid., pp. 283–284; Salewski, "Marineleitung," p. 148.

87 Dülffer, *Hitler und die Marine*, pp. 311–312, 312, n. 49.

88 Ibid., p. 312. By the terms of the Military Code of May 21, 1935, the name of the armed forces was officially changed from Reichswehr to Wehrmacht. The latter designation had already enjoyed informal usage in armed forces circles for some time. By the same law the Reichsmarine became the Kriegsmarine, and the Chef der Marineleitung assumed the more imposing title of Oberbefehlshaber der Kriegsmarine.

89 For the course of the negotiations see DGFP, C, Vol. 4, Nos 131, 132, 135, 136, 137, 141, 148, 154, and 156. The view from the British side is given in Roskill, *Naval Policy*, 2, pp. 303–305.

90 *Völkischer Beobachter*, Munich edition, June 1, 12, 13, 14, 15, 16, 17, 1935. For the role of the navy during Kiel Week see Raeder *Mein Leben*, 1, pp. 209–210.

91 *Völkischer Beobachter*, Munich edition, June 8, 12, 17, 1935.

92 Ibid., June 13, 1935.

93 Ibid. Albrecht's statement was a pointed allusion to the opening line of Tirpitz's conclusion to his memories: "The German Nation did not understand the sea." *Erinnerungen* (Leipzig, 1919), p. 386. Surely Tirpitz, the master of what he had once termed "spiritual massage," would have been greatly impressed by the display of national enthusiasm that his erstwhile student, Raeder, paraded publicly for his Führer.

94 Max Domarus, *Hitler, Reden und Proklamationen, 1932–1945*, 2 vols (Munich, 1965), 1, p. 517.

95 For the text of the agreement see J. A. S. Grenville, *The Major International Treaties 1914–1973: A History and Guide with Texts* (New York, 1974), p. 168.

96 This was deemed necessary for two reasons. In contrast with its surface fleet, Britain's submarine force was relatively small, and a 35 per cent ratio would have given Germany very little tonnage to work with. In addition, Germany had already begun the construction of U-boats by

means of subassemblies and would soon pass the 35 per cent ratio in any case. The agreement merely provided a fig leaf for Germany's violation of the Treaty of Versailles. See DGFP, C, Vol. 4, No. 148; Weinberg, *Foreign Policy*, 1, p. 213.

97 Michael Salewski, *Die deutsche Seekriegsleitung 1935–1945*, 3 vols (Munich, 1970–1975), 1, pp. 17–18; Weinberg, *Foreign Policy*, 1, p. 214. Roskill, *Naval Policy*, 1, pp. 304–305, describes the American response as considerably more favorable.

98 On April 11, 1935, Britain, France, and Italy had issued a joint protest against Germany's announcement of rearmament at Stresa, Italy. The Italians were not slow to draw conclusions from what they perceived as Britain's display of weakness, and in the autumn they began the conquest of Ethiopia. For the effect of the Anglo-German accord on Italo-German relations, see Gerhard Schreiber, *Revisionismus und Weltmachtstreben: Marineführung und deutsch-italienische Beziehungen 1919–1944* (Stuttgart, 1978), pp. 82–83.

99 International Military Tribunal, *Trial of the Major War Criminals before the International Tribunal*, 42 vols (Nuremberg, 1947–1949) (hereafter cited as IMT), 14, p. 337.

100 Dülffer, *Hitler und die Marine*, pp. 331, 346–348; Dönitz's critique, written with the benefit of hindsight, is in *Zehn Jahre und zwanzig Tage* (Bonn, 1958), p. 15.

101 Dülffer, *Hitler und die Marine*, pp. 346–347, 347, n. 17. For two quite similar final versions of the guidelines see IMT, 41, pp. 3–5; and DGFP, C, Vol. 4, No. 275. See especially Donald C. Watt, "Anglo-German Naval Negotiations on the Eve of the Second World War," *Journal of the Royal United Service Institution*, vol. 103 (May and August, 1958), p. 202.

102 Holger H. Herwig, *Luxury Fleet: The German Imperial Navy, 1888–1918* (London, 1980), p. 19.

5

The Tirpitzian Legacy: Personnel Problems, 1933–8

The first half of 1935 had witnessed two significant changes for the navy. The more obvious of the two, the Anglo-German Naval Agreement, gave notice to the world that the Reich was determined to rejoin the ranks of the naval powers and laid the basic framework for this endeavor. In the years that followed the signing of the accord on June 18, the energies of the officer corps would increasingly be consumed by the Herculean task of building the fleet. If the burdens that the corps would have to bear appeared heavy, the ultimate rewards were undeniable, at least so far as the corps was concerned. Soon, the days of antiquated ships more suitable for a maritime museum than for a modern strike force would be gone for ever. Soon, the navy's technological curiosities, the "pocket" battleships, would yield pride of place to powerful new capital ships of the first order, ships that would bear the names of Gneisenau and Scharnhorst, of Bismarck and Tirpitz. When completed, the navy envisioned by Germany's leaders would be a modern, formidable weapon, capable of taking on any opponent with encouraging prospects of success. In this respect, June 18, 1935, marks a major turning point in the Service's history, for from the standpoint of matériel, there could be no comparison between the old Reichsmarine and the new Kriegsmarine of the Third Reich.

Nor could there be any comparison between the spiritual or intellectual outlook of the two German navies. Indeed, this, the second of the two changes made manifest by the spring and summer of 1935, was perhaps even more profound than the first. The old navy had been haunted by the past and tormented by the present. Its officers remembered the lost opportunities of the Great War, the mutinies of 1917 and 1918, and Germany's humiliation at Versailles. They knew firsthand both the Reichsmarine's military impotence and its disturbing isolation from large segments of German society. Although naval leaders might speak bravely of future glory, such words had a distinctly hollow ring to them in the bleak years of the 1920s. When the Weimar era came to a close in January 1933, the renewal for which the navy yearned had not arrived, and the advent of National Socialism offered precious little assurance that it was even near.

During the first two years that followed the *Machtergreifung*, the navy's prospects slowly began to change for the better. Nevertheless, many of its leaders, Raeder included, must have labored under the maddening suspicion that the right moment (and Movement) had come, but that the navy's efforts would somehow founder on the obduracy of Adolf Hitler. By early 1935, however, it appeared that Hitler had at last been won over to an appreciation of sea power that had escaped his predecessors at the Reich Chancellery. With this development, the change within the navy became quite perceptible. A succession of events—the restoration of Germany's military sovereignty in March, the symbolic change from Reichsmarine (with all the unpleasant memories that it conveyed from the early 1920s) to Kriegsmarine in May, the Anglo-German Naval Agreement, and the first Navy Week in June—seemed to herald the beginning of a new era for the Service. Its leaders might continue to pay lip service to the immediate past, rendering honor, for example, to the stalwart few of the Reichsmarine who had "held the line" during the republican period and thus laid the basis for the future. They might continue to evoke the experience of the past as lessons to be learned or, more significantly, mistakes to be avoided. On the whole, however, these cases represented the exception, not the rule. The new navy would look increasingly toward the future, not the past, confident of the support of Germany's Führer and secure in the knowledge that it had once again found its roots in the *Volk*.

The early months of 1935, then, mark a turning point in the history of the navy in a twofold sense. Yet as convenient as this period may be as a dividing line, it must not be allowed to obscure a number of continuities that also characterized the Service in this era. The officers of the Kriegsmarine may have been only too happy to regard the period of the Reichsmarine as a closed chapter in their history; they could not deny that its legacy would be with them for years to come. In this sense, at least, there were a number of problems that spanned the decade. The most obvious of these, of course, was the political relationship between the navy and the NSDAP, a matter which had its roots in the late Weimar period and which, as will be seen in succeeding chapters, would reveal its full complexity in the latter half of the 1930s. In addition, there were a number of problems associated with the expansion of the fleet which, while displaying many differences between the Reichsmarine and the Kriegsmarine, also revealed a number of connections between the two institutions. Many of these have been described elsewhere and are of only peripheral interest to a history of the officer corps.[1] Two issues—the navy's recruitment and training of the host of new officers to man the mammoth fleet of the future and its regulation of what might be termed intra-service relations within the corps—merit further attention here. Neither was totally divorced from the political developments of the day. Nevertheless, both for purposes of convenience and because the two problems straddled the decade, so to speak, it seems advisable to

110

treat them separately before resuming the primarily political narrative of the corps' experiences in the period 1935 to 1939.

Nowhere were the similarities and the differences between the old and the new navy more evident than in the recruitment and training of officers.[2] The officer corps of the Reichsmarine had been an elite in virtually every sense of the word. Beginning with his initial application for admission into the navy until his final promotion to the rank of lieutenant (junior grade), the prospective officer faced the most demanding criteria to determine if he were suited for a naval career. If the process was exceedingly time-consuming, it was thorough, and in those days when the navy was undisturbed by the demands of either a major naval building program or of war, it succeeded in producing officers of unquestionably high ability.

The selection process began early. A prospective officer was required to submit four references and an autobiographical sketch at least one year before he envisioned entering the navy.[3] In general, the Service demanded a school-leaving certificate (*Abitur*) from a recognized *Gymnasium*, although under pressure from republicans the navy made provisions in the early and mid-1920s, at least, for the admission of especially gifted men from the ranks.[4] The Inspection of Naval Training was able to reject a number of applicants at first reading, presumably on the basis of unsatisfactory grades, unenthusiastic references, or unconvincing reasons for desiring a career as a naval officer. In 1932, for example, only 641 out of 1,384 applicants survived the initial weeding-out process.[5] Those who passed the first cut were summoned to a Psychological Examining Station at either Kiel, Wilhelmshaven, or one of the seven military districts in Germany. There, the applicant underwent a grueling three-day examination under the supervision of a group of psychologists and naval officers. Some of the tests were of a fairly conventional nature, consisting of the usual physical, written, and oral examinations that might be expected of any military establishment, then or now. In addition, however, there existed a number of novel methods by which one attempted to gauge the applicant's fitness to serve in the navy. The psychologists analyzed a candidate's handwriting and reviewed films of his facial responses when under stress. Perhaps the most interesting examination was the so-called "test of courage" (*Mutprobe*), wherein each examinee was given a heavy metal bar and told to hold it as long as possible. An examiner would then send an electric charge through the bar and record the examinee's reaction. Some of the candidates immediately dropped the bar; others struggled doggedly to hold on, despite their rather scintillating discovery. Presumably, it was the latter type of young man whom the navy was after.[6]

Other examiners tested the applicant's coolness under pressure by giving him a complicated set of instructions and then observing how well he carried out his orders in the face of attempts to distract him. Further tests probed how well he got along with his fellow examinees and whether his natural leadership abilities came to the fore. One method of determining the latter was to present the candidate with a squad of (doubtless bemused) enlisted men and instruct him to deliver an impromptu lecture. The examining team would then observe how the applicant handled himself and how the enlisted men responded.

After the examination, the psychologists presented their findings to the Inspection of Naval Training. Although their report was not absolutely binding, it was decisive in most cases. Indeed, in 1938 the Inspection noted that a high percentage of those candidates admitted against the advice of the examining team eventually failed to make the grade.[7] In any case, the Inspection was quite selective in its final choice. Only a very small number of applicants—in 1931 just 58 out of 2,452, or 2.3 per cent—would be accepted into the officer training program.[8]

The cadets[9] came from every corner of Germany. As in the past, however, certain areas of the Reich were better represented in the corps than others. The birthplaces of those members of the Crew of 1932 who drowned in the *Niobe* disaster of July 1932, for example, reveal an overwhelmingly North German preponderance within the crew.[10] Of the thirty-six cadets who died, twenty-two had been born in Prussia, five in the Hanseatic cities (Hamburg, Bremen, or Lübeck), three in Wilhelmshaven, and one each in Mecklenburg, Brunswick, and Thuringia. Fully half of the crew members represented came from ports or from areas within 75 kilometers of the sea. Only two cadets came from south of the Main River, the traditional dividing line between northern and southern Germany.

A recent study of the much larger Crew of 1934 reveals a generally similar pattern of geographic origins as well as a wealth of information about the family backgrounds, childhood experiences, education, and age of the recruits.[11] Once again the overwhelming majority of the crew was from North Germany, with 51.8 per cent having birthplaces within 100 miles of the Baltic or North Seas. Only 9.1 per cent came from south of the Main, with most of the remainder coming from the densely populated Rhineland and Westphalia or from Thuringia and Saxony.[12] Twelve cadets, or 3.7 per cent of the crew, had birthplaces outside the old Reich, the sons of businessmen, soldiers, diplomats, or colonial officials.

The recruits of Crew 34 came overwhelmingly from the solid upper or middle class of German society. Although only sixteen cadets (5 per cent) came from noble families, upwards of 25 per cent were the scions of officers. In keeping with the navy's requirements since 1929, all of the initial members of the crew possessed the prerequisite for university admission, the *Abitur*. Average age upon entering the Service for Crew 34 was twenty years and two months.

Candidates accepted by the Reichsmarine reported for duty on April 1 of every year. The next four and a half years would make or break them as officers. For the first three months after enlistment, all members of the crew would undergo a grueling course in basic infantry training at the naval base at Stralsund.[13] Then, the cadets would be divided and introduced to the rudiments of their particular branch of the Service—either executive, engineer, paymaster, or medical officer corps. Henceforth, training would proceed in this manner, with general assignments involving the entire crew alternating with special courses for each particular branch of the corps.[14] In this way, the navy sought to foster crew unity and to avoid a repetition of the tensions, particularly evident between the executive and engineer officers, that had so poisoned the atmosphere of the Imperial Navy.

Most cadets were destined to enter the executive officer corps. Following the completion of their infantry training, executive officer candidates received three and a half months of training aboard a sailing ship.[15] They then rejoined the rest of the crew for fourteen months aboard a school cruiser. There, the cadets learned the duties of a common seaman, with changes in assignments taking place as often as possible in order to give the cadet the widest possible acquaintance with the workings of a modern warship.

The fourteen months aboard the school cruiser were the longest time that the crew would be together as a group. Most of the time was spent abroad, either on the open sea or in foreign ports. Besides fostering practical seamanship, the aim of the cruise was to awaken an interest in and an understanding of foreign cultures and to deepen the cadets' love of their own country.[16] In addition, however, the cruise served to cut off the cadet from the ties, loyalties, and prejudices that had existed in civilian life. Here, he was dependent upon his fellow crew mates for their friendship, for their technical skill, and, in the final analysis, for their mutual survival. Not surprisingly, it was the foreign cruise that saw the solidification of the phenomenon that experienced officers knew as *Crewgeist*. Here, bonds of friendship were formed that would last a lifetime.

At the conclusion of the training cruise, the executive officer candidates took the midshipmen's examination. They were then assigned a provisional ranking within the crew according to a formula that considered both the results of the exam and a subjective evaluation of each cadet's suitability as an officer (termed *Diensttüchtigkeit*) by his superiors.[17] Following this, the cadets were promoted to the rank of midshipman.

The executive officer candidates then underwent three more months of infantry training before they went to the Naval School at Flensburg-Mürwik for a year of academic training. Even here, the primary emphasis fell upon practical as opposed to theoretical skills. Mathematics and the natural sciences were taught, not for their own sake, but rather as the blocks upon which other courses deemed essential for the sea officer would build. These included navigation, seamanship, knowledge of regulations, and English. Courses of secondary importance included electrical engineering, mechanical engineering, and naval construction (all three of which would be the specialty of other branches within the corps or of the navy's *Beamten*), as well as gunnery, tactics, naval history, and athletics. The latter consisted of calisthenics, gymnastics, fencing, riding, and sailing. Dancing instruction could be assigned to those midshipmen endowed with two left feet. Spanish language courses were available for those with a particular aptitude for languages.[18]

The year at the Naval School concluded with the executive officers' examination. Six months of special instruction followed, with the candidates taking courses in gunnery, torpedo warfare, mine warfare, and the use of naval communications equipment. The midshipmen were then parceled out to the vessels of the fleet for another year of practical training. During this period, the cadets first performed the same duties as the noncommissioned officers, then gradually worked their way into the responsibilities of the junior officers. At the end of this year, the candidate was assigned another rating in *Diensttüchtigkeit*.[19]

One final hurdle remained. Near the end of the practical training with the fleet, the officers of each midshipman's ship (or flotilla in the case of the smaller vessels) would assemble for a secret election to determine whether the midshipman was unconditionally "worthy and suitable" for acceptance into the corps. Three results were possible. A majority vote against the candidate—apparently an exceedingly rare occurrence—virtually assured that he would serve out his enlistment as a rating or be retired from the Service altogether. If a minority of the votes were against him, it was still possible that he could be promoted into the corps. The ballots containing the written reasons for rejection would be passed along the chain of command, with each officer commenting on the validity of the objections in his turn. The final decision rested with the Reichswehr Minister, who could either invalidate the rejection, confirm it, or allow the candidate up to one year to make up the deficiencies that had prompted his original rejection. Finally, if the vote was unanimously in favor of the candidate, he would be given a final ranking in the crew based on the executive officers' examination and *Diensttüchtigkeit*.[20] He then issued a declaration that he had no outstanding financial debts and pledged to serve in the navy for a period of twenty-five years. On October 1, exactly four years and six months after entering the navy, he would be promoted to the rank of lieutenant (junior grade).[21]

The course of instruction for the engineers and paymasters followed a pattern generally similar to that of the executive officer candidates. Cadets of both branches underwent the same three-month infantry course as the executive officers. Then, while the sea cadets cut their teeth aboard a sailing vessel, the engineer candidates gained practical experience in a navy machine shop; prospective paymasters received an introduction to basic techniques of management. When the crew reassembled for the fourteen-month training cruise, the paymaster candidates would learn at least some of the same skills as their counterparts in the executive branch. The technological requirements of a modern warship were apparently too demanding to allow a similar arrangement for the engineer cadets, for during the training cruise they remained primarily in the engine room.[22]

Upon completion of the training cruise, the Crew divided once again. Engineer candidates partook of the same refresher infantry course that the executive candidates did, while paymaster cadets took more managerial courses.[23] Candidates of both branches then matriculated at the Naval School with the rest of the crew. They took some classes in common with the executive officer candidates, but in addition received still more instruction of a technological or business nature. Upon completion of the Naval School, the engineers were assigned another six months of duty at a navy machine shop, followed by a year of service with the fleet. Paymaster candidates spent their time at a Naval Intendancy and were with the fleet for only six months. Election and promotion to the rank of lieutenant (j.g.) followed the same pattern as that established for the executive officer candidates.[24]

With their promotion to the rank of lieutenant (j.g.), the young officers began their career in the Reichsmarine in earnest. But even then, the navy took care to allow the newest additions to the officer corps time to "season," for it was only after the expiration of another one to two years that the proud officers would be assigned positions of full responsibility as watch or division officers. Two years after receiving their commissions, the officers would be eligible for promotion to the rank of lieutenant. Those with the highest standing in the crew would be advanced first; the others might have to wait a year before becoming lieutenants. Henceforth, with but a very few exceptions,[25] all promotion would follow this pattern, by the slow, steady ladder of seniority (*Anciennität*).

Such were the training methods of the Reichsmarine during the last years of the Republic. The Service's program would appear to have been admirably suited to the needs of the Weimar navy. It placed a small, highly select body of students under the supervision of an equally select body of instructors. It gave candidates a thorough knowledge of the rudiments of their profession through that most effective of teachers, the school of practical experience. Above all, it allowed the candidates time to mature before thrusting them into positions of responsibility.

The expansion of the fleet would change all of this. Experienced officers who had formerly been available for training assignments would now be needed elsewhere, and the highly professional group of long-serving noncommissioned officers and enlisted men (which had doubtless facilitated many a raw lieutenant's transformation into a sea officer) would be diluted by volunteers and conscripts of far less experience. The corps of cadets would have to be expanded greatly, raising the question of whether the Service could retain the high standards of selection and training that it had enjoyed in the past. In short, the navy's training establishment would face challenges unknown since the days of Tirpitz. Whether the Service's time-honored methods of producing officers would be equal to the new task was at best uncertain.

The navy was not unaware of the problem. The Marineleitung, in fact, had begun to consider its increased officer requirements as early as the fall of 1932, when it had submitted a construction program (*Umbauplan*) to the then Reichswehr Minister, General Kurt von Schleicher.[26] Although the program was modest by the standards of the other naval powers, it was large for the Reichsmarine, envisioning a near doubling of the size of the officer corps from 1,100 to 2,000 men by the late 1930s.[27] Even before the National Socialist *Machtergreifung*, then, the navy had been confronted with the question of its future officer recruitment.

Initial assessments were not encouraging. On November 2, 1932, Rear Admiral Alfred Saalwächter, head of the navy department responsible for officer personnel planning (Marinewehrabteilung), reported that the shortage of officers was the most difficult aspect of the entire *Umbauplan*. The navy, in fact, was already seriously understaffed. Trenchant cuts in certain departments might produce fifty-eight officers for reassignment, but most of these would be swallowed up by the air arm that the Marineleitung hoped to establish or by the naval attaché service that had already been reintroduced at important embassies abroad. Other positions that had long gone unfilled would take up most of the remaining officers, with the net result that only eleven would be available to fill the eighteen positions created by the initial phase of the reconstruction program. This, moreover, was before the first keel had even been laid. In the coming years, the number of unfilled positions would increase, and Saalwächter could see no easing of the situation until the fall of 1938, when the large crew that the navy envisioned enrolling in April 1933 would be ready for front-line duty.[28]

Saalwächter offered no easy solutions in the interim. The navy might possibly extend the enlistments of active officers or curtail its policy of discharging mediocre ones. Both options carried with them natural disadvantages, and the admiral rejected them as practical solutions. He was also dubious as to the possibility of recalling those officers from the classes of 1916 and 1917, who had been reluctantly dismissed when the corps had been reduced in size in 1920. He noted that even the youngest of these men would be approaching his mid-thirties now and added: "They do not understand the conditions of the present navy and will hardly have the flexibility to adjust to the physical and mental demands that are placed upon a lieutenant. In any case, the best officers are no longer available." As a third possibility, the navy might consider training reserve officers for duty in the coastal artillery and antiaircraft units, but this would scarcely meet the need for experienced sea officers. Indeed, the more one looked at it, the more one became reconciled to waiting until the fall of 1938. Only then would a steady flow of officers be available.[29]

The report was pessimistic, to say the least. On November 7, however, the head of the Marineleitung's Flottenabteilung, Captain Günther Guse, addressed the problem in a slightly more encouraging tone. In particular, he failed to see the difficulties that the extension of enlistments or the retention of less gifted officers would entail. The earlier argument to the contrary, he was confident that there would be some suitable former officers "here and there" who could still meet the navy's requirements. Yet, beyond these two refinements, which promised to meet only a portion of the projected personnel requirements at best, his report had little to add.[30]

Neither analysis, then, offered a promising solution to the navy's problem. When Reichswehr Minister von Schleicher approved the overall outline of the rebuilding program on November 15, however, a resolution of the officer question became more pressing than ever.[31] By November 1932, the long-term future of any Reich Cabinet was exceedingly problematical, and it was important that the Marineleitung seize each and every opportunity the moment it was profferred. Otherwise, the navy might find itself a week later with a new Cabinet, a new Reichswehr Minister, and a collection of unredeemable promises.

Perhaps this consideration accounts for the new note of urgency that entered the Marineleitung's deliberations. In any case, on November 23, Guse submitted a new proposal which indicated that he had reexamined both Saalwächter's and his own earlier proposals and found them wanting. Measures such as the extension of enlistments, the reactivation of discharged officers, and the training of reserve officers were clearly necessary, he conceded, but they were palliatives at best. What was needed was a more comprehensive solution, even if this would take the navy "along hitherto unfamiliar paths."[32]

Some of Guse's proposals were indeed unorthodox, at least by the standards of the Weimar navy. Although the Marineleitung had occasionally admitted a few men from the ranks into the officer corps in the past, this had largely been an unwelcome and distinctly limited concession to republicans in the Reichstag who had hoped thereby to liberalize the corps. Now, the captain proposed the voluntary promotion of a fairly large number of qualified noncommissioned officers to officer rank. Although he added that the navy had not had great numerical success with similar measures in the past—due in no small measure to the resistance of traditionalists within the corps, he might have added—he suggested that the project be pushed a little more forcefully than had previously been anticipated.[33]

Another proposal involved enlisting merchant marine officers in the Reichsmarine, a practice that had occasionally been employed by the Imperial Navy. These men already had a thorough background in seamanship, and most if not all of them had trained on square-riggers quite similar to the ones that the navy used for its cadets. Guse was convinced that there were "completely qualified elements" among them. A trial group of a dozen or so merchant marine officers could be given infantry training that same winter of 1932–1933, and grouped with the Crew of 1931 the following spring. Thereafter, they would be treated exactly as regular members of the crew. If the experiment worked, it could be repeated again in 1934 with double the number of *Handlesmarineoffiziere*, and again in 1935, if need be. The navy would save many of the expenses of training these men, and it would get a substantial number of officers two years earlier than could otherwise be expected.[34]

One final possibility remained, which Guse was loath to consider: if the need for officers became sufficiently acute, the navy might be forced to shorten the training period for regular officer candidates.

For the moment, however, the author was confident that the other measures that he had outlined, both conventional and unconventional, would fill the Service's needs and that this, the least attractive of the possible solutions, could be avoided.[35]

Guse's study, then, presented the Marineleitung with a number of options. The navy's leaders, for their part, were not slow to respond to these suggestions, and on November 28, a circular announced the first definite personnel measures to result from the *Umbauplan*. It was a blend of the orthodox and the unorthodox, which went a long way toward meeting the navy's probable long-term goals. It also attempted to meet some of its short-term problems. Fifty more cadets would be added to the already large crew that was to be enrolled in April 1933, and one hundred additional cadets would be taken into the Crew of 1934. The influence of Guse's study was also evident, for the Marineleitung announced that twenty merchant marine officers would be enrolled in the Crew of 1931; they would be ready for front-line duty by the fall of 1935. The navy was also considering using long-term noncommissioned officers to fill officer assignments, but for the moment nothing was said about promoting them to officer rank.[36]

The decision of November 28 laid the basis for the first fairly large-scale expansion of the officer corps since the Great War. At the same time, though, there were apparently some within the Marineleitung who favored a more cautious policy in the area of officer recruitment. A number of officers, Raeder included, were deeply concerned about the possible adverse effects that an overly rapid expansion of the corps might have upon the internal solidarity, discipline, and professionalism of the corps. It was also highly questionable whether the Allies would accede to the cautious diplomatic efforts that Germany was making at Geneva for a modest expansion of its armed forces.[37] Finally, as has been indicated, the precarious state of the Reich government late in 1932 doubtless gave cause for concern, for it was highly unlikely that any Cabinet would last long enough to shepherd the *Umbauplan* and its attendant personnel increases through a divided Reichstag. Indeed, as if to prove the legitimacy of these fears, the Cabinet of Franz von Papen gave way to one headed by Schleicher on December 2. How long the general would last was anybody's guess, but in view of all of these considerations, many officers appear to have feared that the reconstruction plan would remain a dead letter and that the navy would be left with a surfeit of officer candidates if it pursued recruitment energetically.

It was to these advocates of caution that Saalwächter addressed himself in a new report on December 13, 1932. There, he reemphasized that the Reichsmarine was seriously understaffed, and added that if the navy waited for a "clarification of the situation," as some officers were apparently suggesting, then it might turn out that financial or political considerations would render the crucial increase in officer positions impossible. Saalwächter clearly wanted to take advantage of the favorable constellation offered by Schleicher's chancellorship while it lasted. He argued, therefore, that the Service proceed at full speed with recruitment. If any difficulties later appeared that might call for a termination of the program, then the navy would at least have done the best it could. Moreover, it was also possible that the gloomy scenarios envisioned by others within the corps would not occur. In all likelihood, he argued, Germany's rulers, whoever they might turn out to be, would simply accept the navy's *fait accompli* and allow the Service to keep its officer candidates.[38]

Saalwächter then buttressed his argument with a thinly veiled hypothetical case. If one branch of the armed forces proceeded energetically with officer recruitment while the other one held back, and the one that had begun was later "called down," it was still the "winner." There could be no question of the second branch later catching up. Yet this, Saalwächter maintained, was precisely what was happening in Germany. The army had already more than doubled its most recent class of officers from an average yearly intake of 160 to 340 for the class of 1932. In 1933, the army planned to enroll 500 cadets, and in each of the two following years the number was expected to rise to 600. The conclusion was clear: the army was already far ahead of the navy, and the latter would have to make up for lost ground. Even with the increases that the Reichsmarine was already projecting, the total number of officers would still be insufficient to meet the requirements of the *Umbauplan*. For the future, therefore, the order of the day could only be: "Enroll as many officers as possible as rapidly as possible so as to take advantage of the situation as long as it lasts."[39]

The admiral's eloquence was apparently not without effect. Although the Schleicher government fell in late January 1933—perhaps the "clarification of the situation" that Saalwächter had envisioned on December 13—the Marineleitung was prepared to submit the overall *Umbauplan* and its recruitment program to Schleicher's successor on February 2. That day, Hitler's representative at the Reichswehr Minister, General von Blomberg, was informed by the navy that it wanted to admit 120 cadets to the Crew of 1933 that April, and that it wanted to enroll 21 merchant marine officers and 7 certified civilian engineers in the older Crew of 1931. For 1934, the navy envisioned admitting 160 cadets into its regular program. The Marineleitung foresaw that this process of stepped-up recruitment would continue until the fall of 1945, by which time the Service's available personnel would presumably have caught up with the needs of an expanded fleet. Blomberg approved both the *Umbauplan* and its attendant personnel increases. With this measure, the first, modest steps toward the expansion of the navy were undertaken.[40]

The new Reichswehr Minister's approval offered the assurance that the navy would enjoy a steady flow of officers beginning in the fall of 1938. It did not, however, solve the problem of meeting the navy's current needs. Unfortunately, documents are lacking for the year following the interview with Blomberg, making it impossible to determine exactly what decisions were made concerning the Service's shortage of officers during the first year of the National Socialist dictatorship. Evidence from the beginning of 1934, however, indicates that the personnel shortage had in no way eased. Indeed, the situation may well have worsened. On January 25, 1934, for example, the Marineleitung announced that exceptions were being made to the basic demand that applicants for officer candidacy possess the *Abitur*. This was a likely indication that the navy planned to supplement the corps by promoting qualified noncommissioned officers.[41] In early February, another report called attention to nine unfilled positions and sought to find others that might be cut in order to fill them. Later that month, another study noted that unforeseen increases in the navy's personnel requirements had resulted from the commissioning of new vessels, from an increase in the complements of ships already in service, from increases in the size of training establishments, and from the compulsory transfer of naval personnel to the Air Ministry. The latter requirement was becoming a particular drain upon the navy's limited pool of officers, and by May 1, 1935, the Service would be forced to turn seventy-five veteran officers and sixteen officer candidates over to Hermann Göring's ministry.[42]

These were disturbing figures, indeed. Not only did they point to a worsening situation with regard to the navy's present officer strength; they also suggested that contrary to previous expectations, the flow of officers expected after the autumn of 1938 might be insufficient to meet the needs of the completed *Umbauplan*. On March 5, 1934, therefore, Raeder bowed to the obvious and took a step that had evidently been rejected a year and a half before and which many within the navy had long opposed: the corps would open its doors to a relatively large number of noncommissioned officers. Characteristically, Raeder presented the measure as a gesture of magnanimity. The promotions were to be as "recognition and appreciation of the noncommissioned officer corps' services in peace and war." Nominees would join the Crew of 1933 at the Naval School in the spring of 1935. Concessions would be made for those candidates who had not had the opportunity to complete their academic education. They would not be required to pass subjects that presupposed such an education, and they would be exempted from other courses entirely. Instead, the navy would emphasize the practical side of the officers' profession.[43]

Nevertheless, Raeder went out of his way to make sure that those noncommissioned officers so honored met the high canons of the corps. Nominees had to be the very best sailors, and promotion would not be merely a "reward for devotion to duty." If possible, the noncommissioned officers were to be unmarried. Bachelors, it was felt, could get along with the younger cadets more easily than married men, and wives were thought to be a distraction from total attention to the courses that the officer candidates would be taking.[44] Raeder was also at pains to see that each nominee was of strong moral fiber. Confidential enquiries were to be made as to his family on this regard as well. If the noncommissioned officer was married, it was important to make sure that the marriage had been entered into and was being conducted according to principles that corresponded to the elevated standards of the officer corps. Finally, both the nominee and his wife had to be "Aryan."[45] Assuming they met these requirements, the noncommissioned officers thus favored by the navy would be promoted to officer rank in the fall of 1937.

Meanwhile, the immediate shortage of officers continued unabated. Another half-hearted attempt to alleviate part of the difficulty came late in March 1934, when the Marineleitung announced that it intended to train 100 reserve officers in the coastal artillery detachments beginning the following December. Nevertheless, there were definite limits to what the navy expected from this project. The Marineleitung informed the *Sturmabteilung* (SA), which was assisting in the recruitment of university students for reserve officer training, that the navy had only a very restricted need for such students. Moreover, although the navy toyed with the idea of training a small number of executive and engineer reserve officers for duty aboard ship, it eventually rejected the idea. For the moment, at least, the use of reserve officers would apparently be confined to land assignments.[46]

In April, there was another disturbing indication of the unsatisfactory state of the Service's personnel situation when the Marineleitung was forced to extend the deadline for applications for the forthcoming Crew of 1935 by a month because not enough qualified men had applied. This measure brought only disappointing results, and in May, Raeder requested all officers, officials, and officer candidates to pass the word among their acquaintances that it was still possible to apply for admission. Raeder stressed that the recruitment was to go through private, not public channels. He added that he expected especial diligence from the younger officers and midshipmen, since they were the ones most likely to know suitable candidates. He closed with what was becoming the navy's new battle cry: "Recruitment must begin immediately."[47]

The recent developments were doubtless disturbing to the Marineleitung. Nevertheless, the perceptive observer might well have noted at least two important qualifications to the gloomy picture that the high command was painting vis-à-vis the personnel situation by the spring of 1934. It was quite possible that the perceived shortage of qualified applicants was more a consequence of the navy's own exaggerated expectations from the Weimar years, when recruiters could fill a limited number of slots from a plethora of applicants, rather than a lack of enthusiasm for a naval career on the part of Germany's youth. Moreover, there was a very strong likelihood that interest in the profession would increase once conscription was reintroduced at the end of 1934 or the beginning of 1935. It could be expected, after all, that many young Germans would prefer to be officers in the navy rather than privates in the army.

Yet, as much as the admirals might look forward to the resumption of conscription, it was evident that this represented no answer to the Service's immediate predicament—the crushing lack of experienced officers in the here and now. In late May 1934, therefore, the Marineleitung undertook yet another effort to master this increasingly difficult problem. Some of the solutions that it adopted were by now familiar. The navy would practice rigid personnel economy measures, eliminating superfluous positions here and there in order to free officers for more pressing assignments elsewhere. In addition, the Service would fill other positions, particularly staff and teaching assignments, with *Landesschutzoffiziere* ("L" officers), those "retired" officers who were now occupying "civilian" positions in the Reichsmarine.[48] Furthermore, thirty additional merchant marine officers would be enrolled, and still more noncommissioned officers would be admitted into the midshipmen's training program as well—assuming, of course, that the navy could still find suitable candidates from the ranks. Finally, the enlistments of some officers would be extended.[49]

Nevertheless, these measures could only partially alleviate the shortage of officers, and the Marineleitung was prepared to use other more drastic measures as well. Officers were instructed to scrutinize carefully the personnel demands of the Air Ministry, which was steadily sapping the navy of some of its best officers. In addition, the Service now planned to promote some of its few remaining deck officers and a number of long-term noncommissioned officers directly to officer rank, without their undergoing the customary midshipmen's training.[50]

These ameliorative measures, however, paled in comparison with new decisions that the Marineleitung now announced. On May 18, 1934, Raeder swallowed a very bitter pill and ordered that the midshipmen for the Crew of 1932 were to be promoted to the rank of lieutenant (j.g.) in December 1935, instead of October 1936.[51] Although no mention was made of future crews, it was unlikely that this departure from the navy's rigid four and a half year training schedule could be reversed, once it was established. At the same time, it became evident that the training of future crews would be curtailed in other ways as well. The Crew of 1935 would be the largest yet assembled, and there would not be room aboard the sailing ship *Gorch Fock* for the construction engineers (who, though technically *Beamten*, were now training with the fleet) or for the medical officer candidates. Moreover, although the Reichsmarine was now using two light cruisers for its overseas training voyages instead of one, it would still be impossible for the cadets of the recently reconstituted ordnance branch to ship out with the rest of the Crew.[52] Although the technical training of all these cadets could largely be made up elsewhere—and one questions, incidentally, just how much the professional expertise of a medical officer suffered from his neglected training aboard a windjammer—the crew solidarity and *mentalité* which the Marineleitung so cherished were bound to suffer as the officer candidates were strewn to the four winds.

The curtailments in the training programs in May 1934 were an indication of a personnel crisis of the first order. Indeed, one final ameliorant provides perhaps the most convincing proof of the seriousness of the situation. That same month Raeder, who, like Tirpitz, put so much store in the material expansion of the fleet, announced that he was prepared to take some of the navy's vessels out of service temporarily in order to free their complements for more essential assignments. In addition, he was willing to delay the commissioning of other vessels for up to six months or longer for lack of a full crew complement. Only the "pocket" battleships were to be immune from this consideration. Their construction and deployment were to proceed on schedule.[53]

It was anticipated that the measures undertaken in May 1934 would eventually give the navy a breathing space. In September of that year, Raeder once again took note of present personnel shortages, but hoped for a real increase in the supply of officers in the fall of 1935. The commander-in-chief of the navy was, in fact, sufficiently confident that a resolution of the Service's personnel problems was at hand, that he ruled out one solution to the officer problem which some had apparently suggested, namely, a resurrection of the deck officer corps. As he told his officers:

> The deck officer corps is dissolved and will remain dissolved. The uncomfortable military relationship between the noncommissioned officer of over 18 years of service and the young lieutenant may not recur. As will be known, I have brought about the dissolution of the Deck Officer League. On the other hand, I will promote those tried and true deck officers of the Reichsmarine who are of officer material to officer rank. With that, I see the question of the deck officer as ended once and for all.[54]

Yet, by December 1934, it was again clear that the shortfall in officers would last at least until October 1937, when the Crew of 1934 was due to be promoted to the rank of lieutenant (j.g.) a full year ahead of schedule. In the meantime, the navy would simply have to rely on still more "L" officers to fill its ranks.[55] It was becoming an increasingly familiar pattern: the older officers would be retained beyond their prime, and the young midshipmen would be hurried into front-line positions before they were ready.

Not surprisingly, the navy encountered difficulties with both groups. Many of the "L" officers had been out of the navy for over fifteen years. Although this was not necessarily all to their or the Service's disadvantage—they brought useful connections with German industrialists, financiers, and party leaders when they returned to the navy—there was no denying that they lacked experience with a modern navy.[56] Nor was their reintegration into the Service entirely free of problems. In a circular dated January 14, 1936, Raeder stated that some of the *Ergänzungsoffiziere* (as the *Landesschutzoffiziere* had been designated after March 5, 1935) had failed to meet the expectations that the Service had placed upon them. Although censure of subordinates was certainly not foreign to Raeder's practices, such an open admission of problems within the corps was rare indeed. Moreover, there are indications that some regular officers did not sufficiently appreciate the services being rendered by the "E" officers, and that some of the latter did not understand the natural limits that were placed upon their employment in the new navy. Not a few of the "E" officers, it seems, aspired to more exciting commands than the training and staff positions to which they were usually assigned. In both cases, Raeder was compelled to intervene and to appeal for mutual understanding on the part of the two groups. To the regular officers, he stressed the valuable contributions that the "E" officers were making in rebuilding the fleet. To the "E" officers, he expressed his appreciation for a job well done, but he reemphasized as well that some positions would remain the private preserve of the regular officers.[57]

The problem with the midshipmen was equally vexing. By the spring of 1935, it was obvious that the curtailments in the length of officer training that the Service had adopted the previous May as a temporary measure were now becoming permanent. A report dated April 8, 1935, indicated that the Crew of 1936 would be the largest by far of all the midshipmen's classes yet seen, numbering 725 cadets in all.[58] Moreover, the Marineleitung reserved the right to add still more executive and engineer officer candidates to the crew, if need be. The Service's training facilities were likewise being pressed to the limit. The navy's one sailing vessel was now inadequate even for the executive officer candidates, and the Marineleitung was weighing the possibility of chartering additional vessels until two more sailing ships, the *Horst Wessel* and the *Albert Leo Schlageter*, would be ready. The school cruisers were equally overburdened. In 1936, the report continued, they would be able to accommodate only the 280 executive officer and engineer candidates. The rest of the crew would have to train ashore or aboard the navy's ancient predreadnoughts, the *Schlesien* and the *Schleswig-Holstein*.[59]

In the face of such difficulties, the quality of officer training was bound to suffer. Yet, in the years that followed, the navy found it impossible to reverse this unfavorable trend. The demand for new officers placed recruiters under intense pressure to come up with a larger number of suitable candidates, with the result that much of the Service's earlier selectivity disappeared. In 1933, for example, only 6.5 per cent of the total number of applicants for the engineer officer training program had been accepted. By 1939, the figure would soar to 34.3 per cent. Moreover, those who were now enrolled into the Service's training program were not as carefully screened as in earlier days, for the navy had been unable to expand sufficiently its staff of psychologists to examine thoroughly each applicant.[60]

Nor were these the only problems that plagued the Kriegsmarine in the latter half of the 1930s. Once admitted, the large number of new cadets appears to have overwhelmed the navy's training establishment completely.[61] Further, in the face of the Kriegsmarine's seemingly insatiable appetite for young officers, the high command had no choice but to curtail still further the time devoted to their education. By the end of the 1930s, the training period allotted officer candidates had been reduced from the normal four and a half years to a bare two years and four months in some cases; midshipmen who had previously been instructed in all four of the weapons courses (*Waffenlehrgänge*) were now restricted to only one. Nor was the situation likely to improve in the foreseeable future. So crucial, in fact, had the demand for officers become, that the navy had been compelled to enroll an entire second Crew for the year 1937, which entered the Service that October.[62]

The navy had clearly reached its limits in so far as training officers was concerned. As a report drawn up for Raeder in the winter of 1937/38 indicated, the dearth of officers had manifested itself time and again during the preceding year, and the situation could be expected to deteriorate still further in the future. Officers of intermediate rank—lieutenant commanders and commanders who had been part of the minuscule crews of the Weimar navy, for example—were in particularly short supply. This was especially unfortunate, for it was men from these grades who served as division officers, company commanders, and company officers, and who were thus "the most important carriers of discipline." The navy could see no easy solution to its problems. It would hardly be possible to recall still more inactive officers to duty, for anyone worth his salt had presumably been recalled to duty long ago. The navy had also been forced to give up promoting noncommissioned officers to "E" officer rank due to "questions of principle." Further increases in the corps would have to come from the regular midshipmen's crews alone. About the only thing that could be done in the meantime was to check rigorously every department's new request for officers so as to achieve maximum efficiency in their assignment. In principle, there would be no increase in the size of the rear echelons; additional officers would go to "the front."[63]

Thus, the officer situation appeared as discouraging at the beginning of 1938 as it had over five years before, when the problem had first come to the navy's attention. Then as now, the navy's leaders eventually fell back upon personnel economy measures as short-term responses to their problem. Then as now, they were compelled to await an influx of junior officers at some time in the future as the long-term solution. Unfortunately for the navy, the situations of 1932 and 1938 were different in one crucial respect: in 1932 war was a possibility, to be sure, but it was by no means probable, if only because the Reich's leaders at the time were aware of Germany's military impotence. By 1938, however, Adolf Hitler was increasingly leaning toward war as a solution to Germany's problems, both real and imagined.[64] Although the navy had undoubtedly made progress in the six years that separated the two periods, it was as yet utterly unprepared for such an eventuality. This was just as true from the standpoint of personnel as it was from the standpoint of matériel.

There were a number of reasons for this. In part, the navy was simply the victim of circumstances beyond its control. During the mid-1930s, for example, many of its officers were siphoned off by the renascent Luftwaffe, and in 1937 its training schedules were disrupted by the deployment of a substantial portion of the fleet off the coast of Spain, where the Kriegsmarine was directed to assist Generalissimo Francisco Franco's Nationalists in their struggle against the Spanish republic. Another factor was the widespread delay in the navy's shipbuilding program, which left many ship's cadres with little to do but to wait for their vessels to be commissioned while other important positions remained unfilled. Yet the most important reason for the Service's personnel crisis would seem to be that the Kriegsmarine had simply outgrown the framework of the *Umbauplan* of November 1932. Personnel decisions that had appeared quite adequate when the fleet had existed only on paper, were now totally inadequate. In the past, Raeder had frequently argued that it was impossible to build a fleet overnight. By the end of the 1930s, he was discovering, if he did not already know it, that this lesson applied as well to officers and men as it did to ships.[65]

The expansion of the fleet, then, brought nearly insuperable difficulties for the officer corps in the area of recruitment and training. Its effects, however, were not limited to these two matters alone. Another area of concern was the potentially disruptive effect that the flood of new faces would have on the homogeneity and internal solidarity of the corps. By 1935, it was clear that many of the young men who would soon be entering the corps would be from backgrounds that were quite different from the majority of the older officers in the navy.[66] Others, after a few years in the Hitler Youth, would doubtless bring with them potentially disturbing ideas about the role of politics in an officer corps that still clung proudly to the fiction that it was above politics. By the mid-1930s, then, it was already obvious that the tight "naval family" that Raeder had sought to foster in the Weimar era would be an increasingly threatened institution in the future. If the Service was to retain its cohesion, the veteran officers would have to meet the influx of younger officers as a bloc. Only in this way could the corps retain its values and traditions in the hectic days that undoubtedly lay ahead.

In respect to cohesion, at least, the navy was in a decidedly better position than it had been in the matter of officer recruitment and training, for considerable progress had been made in intra-service relations since the Great War. The legal equality (*Gleichberechtigung*) of the various branches of the officer corps had been established as early as 1919.[67] In the dozen or so years that had followed, the atmosphere within the corps had improved noticeably as naval reformers moved to implement this decision and as a new generation of officers who shared many of the same experiences from basic training, the overseas cruise, and the Naval School moved into positions of responsibility. By the 1930s, many of the divisions that had once characterized the navy were indeed long gone, remembered, if at all, only as historical curiosities.

Nevertheless, a few inequalities, a few residual tensions between the Service's different categories of officers, persisted. To the executive officers, this continued disparity between principle and practice was perhaps less obvious than it was to some of the other officers. The former were a comfortable majority within the Weimar navy, their status as officers had not been questioned since the revolutionary days of 1918 and 1919, and their senior representatives constituted the overwhelming majority of the *Admiralität*.[68] In view of the foregoing, it is neither surprising that they set the overall style for the Weimar navy, nor that some of their number took the preeminence of their branch for granted. Representatives of the other branches adopted a decidedly different view. Many of their spokesmen had painful memories from the Imperial Navy, which had denied their character as naval officers, and they were often quick to point out the differences that remained within the corps. If, as will be seen, some of their grievances verged on the trivial, others were of a more serious nature; together, they threatened to disrupt the solidarity of the corps at a time when it would be increasingly vulnerable to pressures from without. It is not surprising, therefore, that the mid-1930s witnessed renewed efforts on the part of the navy to remove divisions within the old officer corps before the flood of new recruits arrived on the scene.

Some problems were removed with little or no difficulty. The navy's paymasters, for example, had long suffered from their rather cumbersome dual position as Reich officials (*Beamten*) and officers. Militarily, they were under the jurisdiction of the navy, but in a number of other functions they were responsible to the Finance and Interior Ministries, with the net result that their character as true naval officers was sometimes denied both within and without the Service. In addition, their role as officials and the fiction that they were noncombatants, carried with them significant financial disadvantages when their income was compared with officers of equivalent rank in the other branches. During the early 1920s, the navy had sought to confirm the paymasters' role as full-fledged officers, but this endeavor was blocked by the Finance Ministry, presumably because of budgetary considerations. With increased funds going to the armed forces after the *Machtergreifung*, however, this objection became increasingly irrelevant. In 1934, Raeder managed to secure Finance Minister Lutz Graf Schwerin von Krosigk's agreement to an alteration of the paymasters' status, and on February 26, 1935, Raeder decreed that the paymasters would be redesignated as administrative officers as of April 1. With this announcement, the place of the administrative officers as members in good standing within the corps appeared secure.[69]

The integration of other groups into the *Seeoffizierkorps* proved to be considerably more difficult. Members of the two new ordnance branches—one each for surface and underwater weapons—apparently found the Service's subtle discrimination in favor of the executive officers to be particularly vexing. By September 1939, for example, over 37 per cent of the ordnance officers of Crew 34 had left the Kriegsmarine, many for more promising careers in the army or the Luftwaffe. Those who remained often felt that they were not considered full-fledged officers, unless, of course, an executive officer suddenly needed their expertise.[70]

Yet the grievances of the administrative and ordnance officers notwithstanding, it was the engineers who were apparently the most vocal in their dissatisfaction with the high command's apparent favoritism toward the executive officers. A number of factors account for this. The administrative and ordnance officers remained a very small minority within the overall corps, and their proper sphere of influence was fairly easily delineated by their professional duties. Accordingly, they posed little threat to the preeminence of the executive officers. The engineers, on the other hand, were a more significant minority, with an influential group of "alumni," and their function within the navy was assuming added importance with the increasing technological complexity of the navy's new warships. Nor was the proper boundary between the responsibilities of the engineer and those of the executive officer as easily drawn as it had been in the case of the other specialists. Discipline of engine room personnel and the direction of damage control, for example, two traditional prerogatives of the executive officers, remained bones of contention throughout the 1920s and 1930s.[71] Finally, there was one other significant difference between the other specialists' relationship with the executive officers and that of the engineers. The other specialists' spokesmen seem to have been relatively passive and content to let the Marineleitung take the initiative in bettering their lot. The engineers, by contrast, were prepared to take active steps to further their cause.[72] In this respect, the legacy of the Imperial Navy appeared to be a particularly fateful influence, for the examples of Tirpitz, Müller, and Scheer seemed to tell the engineers that, if they did not take up their own cause, no one else would.

The engineers' grievances encompassed a plethora of items. Among the more serious was the problem posed by the executive officers' virtual monopoly over the more important commands within the navy. Although the engineers were willing to concede the necessity of this for shipboard commands, they failed to see compelling reasons why important shore-based assignments could not be entrusted to an engineer officer now and then. Nor were they unaware of the practical effects of the navy's policy in this matter. Because nearly all of the senior positions within the navy went to executive officers, there were few assignments available for engineers above that of Chief Engineer. As a result, engineer officers were generally retired at a considerably earlier age than were their counterparts among the executive officers.[73]

Other sources of discontent were equally vexing, but somewhat more difficult to define. In part because of the absence of higher-ranking representatives at the command level, the engineer officers felt that the Marineleitung did not attach sufficient weight to their fund of practical experience when it came to designing new vessels or improving old ones.[74] As a result, they continued to regard themselves as stepchildren within the navy, an impression that some of the executive officers, with their view that the engineers were something less than "real" officers, were only too willing to share. Nor was this all. Engineer officers continued to find what they considered to be unjustifiable differences in the training furnished the cadets of the two branches at the Naval School.[75] Moreover, off-duty contacts between engineers, executive officers, and their respective families often remained at a very formal level, to the extent that they existed at all.[76]

These grievances were not unknown to the navy's leaders. Throughout the late 1920s and early 1930s, officers from both executive and engineer branches had made a number of proposals to alleviate the engineers' dissatisfaction. Most notable among these was the proposed creation of an Inspection of Ships' Machinery (*Schiffsmaschineninspektion*), which would embrace all matters relating to propulsion and power plants aboard ship. Not only would this create a powerful new channel for bringing the engineers' practical experience to the attention of the Marineleitung, but it would also eventually provide a number of staff assignments for engineer officers beyond the position of chief engineer. In principle, at least, the Marineleitung professed to agree with such proposals, but it contended that at present the limited budget and the tight personnel situation of the Weimar navy did not allow the formation of such an inspection.[77]

As had been the case with the paymasters, the *Machtergreifung* greatly altered the situation. On the one hand, the naval budget increased dramatically, thus removing the Marineleitung's objection that financial considerations precluded the formation of an Inspection of Ships' Machinery. On the other hand, the projected expansion of the fleet promised to overburden the navy's sole engineer admiral, the Staff Engineer at the Marineleitung. As the navy was finding out, in fact, he was already completely engaged by the duties surrounding the commissioning and maintenance of the handful of cruisers and torpedo boats that had been approved during the Weimar years, and it was obvious that when full-scale rearmament got underway, he would simply be overwhelmed. Accordingly, when the senior engineer officers approached Raeder with the support of a number of prominent executive officers in 1934, the head of the navy at last gave way. On September 23, 1934, Raeder approved the formation of the new inspection, which was to take place on October 1, 1935.[78]

The creation of the Inspection of Ships' Machinery was a milestone for the engineer officers, and it ought to have done much to foster a spirit of comradeship within the officer corps as a whole. Enthusiasm on the part of the engineers, however, was almost immediately dampened by a new development, for at the same time that Raeder was removing one of their sources of discontentment, he appeared to be erecting another that struck at the very principle of equality between the various branches of the corps. The result was an imbroglio that for a time threatened to destroy the bridges that had been painstakingly built between the engineer and executive officers in the years since the Great War.

It was widely known within the officer corps that the Service's regulations were being rewritten in order to take into account the myriad changes in procedure and protocol that had occurred in recent years. Among other revisions that were rumored to be in the offing was one involving the public honors that were to be rendered the navy's flag officers. In the past, this category had included all officers with the rank of rear admiral or higher. Now, word had it that the new regulations envisioned limiting the definition of flag officer to active executive officers. To the engineers, who now numbered two rear admirals among their ranks, it appeared as if Berlin were giving them an intentional snub.[79]

It was the younger officers, who had entered the Service under the presupposition that the technical equality of all officers was understood, who were the most incensed over the proposed new measure. Yet, to the newly appointed Inspector of Ships' Machinery, Rear Admiral Hans Fechter, fell the unenviable task of approaching Raeder in an attempt to head off the impending storm. Sometime during the winter of 1935/6, he broached the subject with the head of the navy in the course of a private conversation and asked Raeder whether he intended to implement the measure that was being envisioned. Raeder replied that he had planned to do so, but that the final wording had not yet been determined. Raeder then took the offensive and complained bitterly about certain engineer officers who had not met his expectations, and about the dissatisfaction that appeared to be prevalent among the engineers in general. Nevertheless, he praised Fechter personally and requested him to reassure his fellow engineers of the commander-in-chief's continued esteem for their branch of the navy at their next important assembly, a continuing education course (*Weiterbildungslehrgang*) that was to take place that January. Fechter, knowing Raeder's extreme dislike of attempts to pressure him from below, was doubtless satisfied that he had made his point, and he left it to the navy's chief to draw the proper conclusions. In any case, the interview ended on a friendly note.[80]

There the affair might have ended. Unfortunately, for some time after the interview with Fechter rumors continued to drift back to the high command in Berlin of the engineers' continuing dissatisfaction.[81] This time, it was Raeder's turn to be incensed, and he determined that it was time to have a word with his unruly and ungrateful subordinates. Accordingly, Raeder, not Fechter, ultimately gave the main address at the *Weiterbildungslehrgang* at Kiel. Because of the date—January 27, 1936—what followed entered the annals of the engineer corps as the "Kaiser's Birthday Speech," a designation by no means inappropriate. In less than an hour, Raeder displayed an ability to arouse an audience that rivaled that of the former Supreme War Lord. The effect, however, was not quite what he had intended.[82]

Raeder began by expressing his disappointment that relatively unimportant matters were distracting the engineers at a time when all of their attention ought to be concentrated on the navy's immediate task, the construction of the fleet. He also conveyed his irritation that confidential matters, whose final nature had not even been determined, had found their way from Berlin to the "front" and were apparently being bandied about in the open. This contradicted his expressed orders, and he pointedly reminded his audience that there was no such thing as a "private information network" for engineer officers in his navy. At the same time, Raeder expressed his regret that thoughtless remarks by a few executive officers had caused dismay, and he reemphasized the complete equality of all branches of the officer corps. Finally, he reminded the engineers that they were indispensable to the navy and reassured them of his continued esteem and that of the rest of the high command.

Unfortunately, Raeder was not content to let it rest there. Not only was the overall tone of the address more than a little condescending—that of a schoolmaster talking to naughty and somewhat slow-to-learn children—it was meanspirited as well. As he had done in his earlier discussion with Fechter, Raeder singled out the failures of a few unnamed engineers in what appears to have been an attempt to elicit a collective *mea culpa* from the entire corps. Moreover, Raeder inflated completely out of proportion the relatively mild dissatisfaction thus far manifested by his subordinates and compared it with the spirit of 1919. Such discontent, he continued, had no place in a navy built upon the *Führerprinzip*, for it was a "revolutionary manifestation." Superior officers were to spare no effort to extirpate it from the navy. Those not up to the task were not fit to remain in the Service.

These remarks alone would probably have sufficed to engender animosity among the audience. Raeder's clumsy handling of two crucial matters, however, virtually guaranteed that his address would cause an uproar. In seeking to delineate the proper fields of activity for the engineers from those of the other officers, he reminded his listeners that they were engineers (*Betriebsingenieure*) first and officers second. The use of the word *Betriebsingenieure* carried with it unpleasant connotations, especially for the older officers within the audience, for this was precisely the term that had been used to reject their claim to full officer status during the imperial period. Raeder might just as well have called the engineers "tinkerers" and been done with it. Moreover, given the already heated atmosphere, many listeners must have taken the formula "engineers first . . . officers second" as yet another contradiction of the spirit of equality that the head of the navy professed.[83]

Raeder's attempt to alleviate what he took to be another cause of the engineers' discontent—the Service's arrangements for defending the honor of the flag in war and peace—proved to be equally disastrous. The command of a ship, he patiently explained, devolved upon the senior executive officer present; therefore, "this *Seeoffiziere* alone was responsible for the honor of the flag." Although Raeder almost immediately went on to detail those rare instances when an officer from another branch might assume command (when all of the executive officers had been rendered *hors de combat*),[84] it is unlikely that many within the audience caught this distinction, for they were doubtless befuddled by their commander's enunciation, from out of the blue, of the executive officers' prerogatives in this matter. Was the admiral trying to exalt the position of the executive officers over the rest of the corps? Was he implying a lack of honor on the part of the engineers? And why had not Raeder taken up the real cause of their discontent, the navy's failure to render public honors to the engineers' two flag officers? Once again, the engineers had apparent confirmation of the head of the navy's seemingly incurable prejudice against them.[85]

131

Far from easing the discontent within the engineer corps, then, the "Kaiser's Birthday Speech" contributed to an immediate deterioration in relations between the high command and the engineers. A number of engineer officers submitted their resignations in the wake of the address, and for a time Fechter considered tendering his as well. In the end, cooler heads prevailed. Fechter thought the matter over and concluded that nothing would be gained by resigning; his successor might indeed prove to be more pliant in Raeder's hands than was necessary. Moreover, other officers might look upon his resignation as a capitulation, and Fechter accordingly remained at his post. As for the other disgruntled engineers, they, too, remained in the Service after a number of executive officers privately let it be known to them that they disapproved of Raeder's remarks.[86]

Thus, the short-term repercussions of the address of January 27, 1936, proved to be surprisingly muted. More surprisingly still, the long-term effects were even salutary, for Raeder's salvo seems to have cleared the air. Like his discontented subordinates among the engineers, the commander-in-chief of the navy seems to have become more sober upon reflection. In truth, he probably had even less of a choice than they did. If he pursued his threat to dismiss the dissenters from the corps, he would only exacerbate the alarming shortage of officers that the navy was already feeling. If the engineers resigned on their own initiative, the same result would ensue. In either case, the good of the navy, Raeder's primary concern then as always, would suffer. In the end, the admiral let the matter rest where it lay.

After a period of sulking on both sides, therefore, the relationship between the engineers and the high command underwent a gradual improvement. As has been suggested, one factor involved here was doubtless the recognition on both sides that the navy's best interests could only be harmed by a continuation of the dispute. At the same time, however, it is impossible to ignore the host of new positions at the navy's shipyards, arsenals, and staff offices, some of which at least had previously been reserved for executive officers, that began to be assigned to engineers in the wake of the January address.[87] Almost certainly, many of these would have come the way of the engineers as rearmament entered full swing, but it is difficult not to conclude that Raeder, once he was assured of his ultimate authority within the navy, conceded at least some of these positions as a means of defusing what had by now become a highly disagreeable situation to him.

Nor was the Raeder touch entirely lacking from the ultimate solution to the flag officer question. For a while, the whole issue was downplayed by engineer and executive officers alike, but in March 1938, Raeder was invited to a rally in the Harz mountains for the National Socialist Motor Corps (NSKK). Instead of going himself, he sent Fechter, now a vice admiral, as his deputy. Since there was a possibility that the Kriegsmarine's representative might be slighted unless he were accorded flag-officer status, Raeder relented and took the appropriate steps to uphold the Service's honor. Fechter's automobile proudly flew the flag of a vice admiral as it embarked for the Harz.[88]

Thus, as the 1930s wore on, most of the original reasons for the engineers' discontent tended to disappear. Along with that of the rest of the officer corps, their attention was increasingly absorbed by the gigantic task of constructing and training the fleet. Some small degree of tension between engineers and executive officers and between the engineers and the high command persisted up to and through the Second World War, but matters never assumed the serious proportions that they had reached that day in Kiel on January 27, 1936. In this respect, at least, the later history of the Kriegsmarine was distinctly different from that of its imperial predecessor.

Notes for Chapter 5

1 For the overall history of the expansion of the navy, see Jost Dülffer, *Weimar, Hitler und die Marine: Reichspolitik und Flottenbau 1920–1939* (Düsseldorf, 1973); for the strategic implications of expansion, see Michael Salewski, *Die deutsche Seekriegsleitung, 1935–1945*, 3 vols (Munich, 1970–1975), 1, *passim*.

2 There is no comprehensive account of the navy's training program during the interwar period. The following analysis, therefore, is an *essai* in the strictest sense. Three works, however, proved useful in reconstructing the Service's training routine. Although primarily concerned with the Imperial Navy, Karl Peter, "Seeoffizieranwärter-Ausbildung in Preussen/Deutschland, 1848–1945" (Manuscript, Militärgeschichtliches Forschungsamt, Freiburg, West Germany, n.d.), has statistical information on length of training and the size of certain crews. Eric Christian Rust, "Crew 34: German Naval Officers under and after Hitler" (PhD dissertation, University of Texas at Austin, 1987), provides a thorough analysis of the experiences of one crew during the mid-1930s. Heinz Schaeffer, *U-977: 66 Tage unter Wasser* (Wiesbaden, 1950), contains interesting descriptions of training methods during the late 1930s.

3 Bundesarchiv-Militärarchiv, Freiburg, West Germany (hereafter cited as BA-MA), RM D4 67a, "Seeoffizier-Ergänzungsbestimmung vom 24. Juli 1926. Neudruck 1931." One authority suggests that navy connections were important in the Weimar period: "With such a wide selection . . . it is not surprising that personal connections tipped the scales when all other qualifications were equal. Recommendations from active or inactive members of the navy were commonplace and were given consideration where possible, especially since the navy alone determined the choice." Jost Dülffer, "Die Reichs- und Kriegsmarine 1918–1939," in *Handbuch zur deutschen Militärgeschichte*, 5 vols (Munich, 1964–1979), p. 371.

4 BA-MA, RM D4 M. DV. Nr. 67a "Seeoffizier-Ergänzungsbestimmungen vom 24. Juli 1926. Neudruck 1931." For the efforts of republicans to recruit more officers from the ranks, see Keith W. Bird, *Weimar, The German Naval Officer Corps and the Rise of National Socialism* (Amsterdam, 1977), pp. 150–151, and Gustav Adolf Caspar, *Die sozialdemokratische Partei und das deutsche Wehrproblem in den Jahren der Weimarer Republik* (Frankfurt, 1959), pp. 51–55.

5 Dülffer, "Reichs- und Kriegsmarine," p. 371.

6 For the examination, see William A. Wiedersheim's rather lively "Officer Personnel Selection in the German Navy, 1925–1945," *United States Naval Institute Proceedings*, 73 (April 1947), pp. 445–449, which is based on interviews with captured German naval personnel. His account is confirmed by an examination schedule of 1932 in BA-MA, RM 20/314, "Psychologische Prüfstelle III Aktz B 28610, Prüfplan für die Offizier-Anwärter-Prüfungen. Prüfungsausschuss C. Anl. la." Word about the tests appears to have slipped out to many of the applicants so that they were not entirely surprised by the horrors that the navy had in store for them. Schaeffer, *U-977*, p. 24.

7 BA-MA, RM D4 67n, "Ergänzungsbestimmungen für die Offizierslaufbahnen in der Kriegsmarine vom 30. September 1938," Anlage 2 zu #8. The results of the psychological examination remained confidential so that candidates who were admitted in spite of having failed it were not prejudiced in their efforts to become officers.

8 BA-MA, RM 6/235, "Die Tätigkeit der Reichsmarine im Jahre 1931." The navy was almost equally selective in its choice of enlisted men. In the same year, 41,966 men applied for these positions; a mere 1,253 (or slightly less than 3 per cent) were accepted.

9 The navy recognized differences between officer candidates, cadets, and ensigns that were based on the trainees' progress within the program. For purposes of convenience and for the sake of variety, I shall use the three terms and the overall designation of midshipman interchangeably.

10 The *Niobe*, the Reichsmarine's sail training ship, capsized and sank in a storm on July 26, taking with her a total of sixty-nine victims, including over half of the executive and medical officer cadets of the Crew of 1932. For the names and birthplaces of the deceased, see BA-MA, RM D1/1932 Marineverordnungsblatt, 63. Jahrgang, Heft 22, Berlin, August 15, 1932. Information is lacking for the paymasters and engineer cadets among the crew, who were not assigned duty aboard the navy's sailing vessels and were not aboard the *Niobe* when she went down. There is no reason to suspect that the pattern for the small number of paymaster candidates would have differed significantly from their counterparts in the executive and medical officer branches. The geographical distribution of the engineer candidates, on the other hand, probably did vary somewhat from the rest of the crew. A later analysis of applicants from the engineer branch of the Kriegsmarine revealed that these young men tended to come from the industrialized areas of the Reich—the Ruhr, the Rhineland, Saxony, Silesia, and the city of Berlin. See the study composed by Engineering Commander Otto König, "Erziehung des Ingenieuroffiziers und des Offizier-Nachwuchses unter Berücksichtigung des Reserve-Offizier-Nachwuchses und der Kriegsoffizieranwärter," June 23, 1942, in BA-MA, Nachlass Bräckow, N 582/3, p. 17.

11 This and the following paragraph are based on Rust, "Crew 34," pp. 34–86.

12 These figures are especially interesting when compared with findings for the Crew of 1907 in Holger H. Herwig, *The German Naval Officer Corps: A Social and Political History, 1890–1918* (Oxford, 1973), p. 41. Although Herwig's study was concerned only with executive officers, it reveals a pattern quite similar to that of the Crew of 1934. In 1907, 65.9 per cent of the crew came from Prussia and 12.6 from south of the Main. In 1934, 57.3 per cent of the crew had been born in Prussia, 61.2 per cent had grown

up there, and, as indicated, only 9.1 per cent had birthplaces south of the Main. Geographically speaking, the naval officer corps was certainly not the "melting pot" of Germany that some of its spokesmen have claimed it to be.

13 BA-MA, RM D4 M DV. Nr. 67a, "Seeoffizier-Ergänzungsbestimmungen vom 24. Juli 1926. Neudruck 1931." For a description of the course from a slightly later period, see Schaeffer, *U-977*, pp. 26–34.

14 The medical officer candidates provided the sole exception. They underwent the same three-month infantry course that their fellow crew members did and then shipped out with the executive officer candidates aboard the sailing ship in order to learn the living conditions of the average sailor. After that, however, they returned to study medicine at their respective universities or, from 1934 on, at the Militärärztliche Akademie in Berlin. Henceforth, their direct association with their crew mates would be limited to the summer vacations, when they would again ship out with the fleet to gain practical experience. For information on the medical officers, see Werner Bauer, *Geschichte des Marinesanitätswesens bis 1945* (Berlin, 1958).

15 BA-MA, RM D4 M. Dv. Nr 67h, "Vorschrift für die Ausbildung der Freiwilligen bzw. Kadetten der Seeoffizier- Ingenieuroffizier- Sanitäts-offizier- und Zahlmeisterlaufbahnen der Reichsmarine," Berlin, 1930. After the *Niobe* disaster, voices were raised calling for an end to the navy's use of sailing vessels for cadet training. The navy resisted these demands on the ground that the executive officers needed to know "pure" seamanship before they were schooled in the more modern techniques of warfare. A public subscription was held to secure funds for a new sailing ship, which was commissioned in 1933 under the name *Gorch Fock*.

16 Ibid.

17 Ibid. *Diensttüchtigkeit* was defined as the "sum of character and intellectual ability, talent for the profession, leadership, devotion to duty, and performance."

18 BA-MA, RM D4 M. Dv. Nr. 67f, "Dienstvorschrift für die Marineschule Flensburg-Mürwik," Berlin 1930. The Naval School, the Service's equivalent of Annapolis, was housed in the old Imperial Naval School. It was bedecked with trophies, war memorabilia, and battle flags, some of which were so old that in 1940 one irreverent young cadet noticed that it literally "stank" of tradition. Schaeffer, *U-977*, p. 50.

19 BA-MA, RM D4 M. Dv. Nr. 67a, "Seeoffizier-Ergänzungbestimmungen vom 24. Juli 1926. Neudruck 1931;" BA-MA, RM D4 M. Dv. Nr. 67i, "Vorschrift für die Ausbildung der Fähnriche auf den Sonderlehrgängen und im praktischen Dienst an Bord der Schiffe," April 21, 1931.

20 Ibid. Recent research indicates that the election was largely a formality by the 1930s. Although thirty-three members (10.3 per cent) of Crew 34 had left the Service by the time their crew mates were commissioned as lieutenants (j.g.), their decision to leave was evidently either voluntary or else occurred before the election. Fifteen cadets of Crew 34, however, did have their commissions delayed, which meant automatic relegation to the bottom of the seniority list. Rust, "Crew 34," pp. 126, 148–149, 161.

21 BA-MA, RM D4 M. Dv. Nr. 67a, "Seeoffizier-Ergänzungsbestimmungen vom 24. Juli 1926. Neudruck 1931." The time allotted to training amounted to fifty-three and one-half months. Approximately two weeks of leave brought the total time spent as a midshipman to an even fifty-four months.

22 BA-MA, RM D4 M. Dv. Nr. 67h, "Vorschrift für die Ausbildung der Seeoffizier- Ingenieuroffizier- Sanitätsoffizier- und Zahlmeisterlaufbahnen der Reichsmarine." Whether the practice of training the paymaster candidates in executive officer duties was continued in later crews is uncertain.

23 BA-MA, RM D4 M. Dv. Nr. 67i, "Vorschrift für die Ausbildung der Fähnriche auf den Sonderlehrgängen und im praktischen Dienst an Bord der Schiffe," Berlin 1931.

24 BA-MA, RM D4 M. Dv. Nr. 67f, "Dienstvorschrift für die Marineschule Flensburg-Mürwik," Berlin 1930. BA-MA, RM D4 M. Dv. Nr. 67i, "Vorschrift für die Ausbildung der Fähnriche auf den Sonderlehrgängen und im praktischen Dienst an Bord der Schiffe," Berlin 1931.

25 Werner Bräckow, *Die Geschichte des deutschen Marine-Ingenieuroffizierkorps* (Oldenburg and Hamburg, 1974), p. 190. In 1942, the navy began to promote a few especially capable officers ahead of their crew mates. Hans Black, "Die Grundzüge der Beförderungsordnungen," in Gerhard Papke *et al.*, *Untersuchungen zur Geschichte des Offizierkorps: Anciennität und Beförderung nach Leistung* (Stuttgart, 1962), pp. 146–147. Among the first officers to be so honored was Raeder's eventual successor, Karl Dönitz. For this, see Gert Sandhofer, "Dokumente zum militärischen Werdegang des Grossadmirals Dönitz," *Militärgeschichtliche Mitteilungen*, 1/1967, pp. 59–81.

26 The *Umbauplan* foresaw a fleet of six *Panzerschiffe*, six cruisers, six half-flotillas of destroyers or large torpedo-boats, three half-flotillas of minesweepers, three half-flotillas of smaller torpedo-boats (*Schnellboote*), one sail cruiser, and numerous auxiliary vessels. If possible, the Service also hoped to build a submarine force of sixteen U-boats and a naval air arm of one carrier and nine squadrons of aircraft. BA-MA, RM 20/877 A I 518/33, February 2, 1933; also Erich Raeder, *Mein Leben*, 2 vols (Tübingen, 1956–1957), 1, pp. 273–274.

27 BA-MA, RM 20/877 A I 518/33, "Niederschrift über den Vortrag des Chefs des Marine-Kommandoamtes beim Reichswehrminister am 2. Februar 33." The discrepancy between the 1,500 officers permitted by the Treaty of Versailles and the 1,100 officers actually carried on the rolls is explained by budgetary considerations and by the residual presence of the deck officers, who counted against the 1,500 limit but who were listed as noncommissioned officers in the Reichsmarine's Rangliste.

28 BA-MA, RM 20/877 A I u 2417 Pl, November 2, 1932. Why the Kommandoamt foresaw the fall of 1938 as the time when the shortage would ease remains unclear. By then, the cadets of 1933 would, under normal circumstances, already have been promoted to the rank of lieutenant (j.g.) in the fall of 1937, but they would still need another two years of "seasoning" before they were ready for assignment as watch and division officers in the fall of 1939. Perhaps the Kommandoamt was already considering shortening the period of practical experience that followed promotion to lieutenant (j.g.) from two years to one.

29 Ibid.

30 BA-MA, RM 20/877 A II m 2981/32 Pl, November 7, 1932.

31 For the date of Schleicher's approval, see Raeder, *Mein Leben*, 1, p. 273.

32 BA-MA, RM 20/877 Neu A II 20231/32, "Gedanken zum Umbau der Reichsmarine," November 23, 1932.

33 Ibid.

34 Ibid.

35   Ibid.
36   BA-MA, RM 20/877 A I u/A III 20270/32, November 28, 1932. Among the first merchant marine officers to be enrolled was the future U-boat ace, Günther Prien. Prien's autobiography, *Mein Weg nach Scapa Flow* (Berlin, 1940), was published during the Second World War as a popular morale booster and sheds little light on his experiences as a midshipman in the Reichsmarine.
37   For Germany's efforts in this regard, see Dülffer, *Hitler und die Marine*, pp. 254–256.
38   BA-MA, RM 20/877, "Überlegungen über Offiziersvermehrung beim Umbau," which bears the date December 13, 1932 at the end.
39   Ibid.
40   BA-MA, RM 20/877 A I 517/33, "Vortragsnotiz zum Vortrag beim R.W.M. am 2. 2. 33;" A I 518/33, "Niederschrift über den Vortrag des Chefs des Marine-Kommandoamtes beim Reichswehrminister am 2. Februar 33." See also Dülffer, *Hitler und die Marine*, p. 239. Both Crew 33 and Crew 34 would eventually exceed the size the navy had foreseen for them. Crew 33 numbered 149 rather than 120 cadets, whereas Crew 34 boasted 318 members—almost twice the number envisioned in the original *Umbauplan*. See the figures in Rust, "Crew 34," p. 37.
41   BA-MA, RM 20/874 Stellungnahme zum Vorgang: Chef d. HL. Nr. 91/34 P.A., January 25, 1934. In addition, having left home around the age of 16, few of the merchant marine officers that were being added to the crews possessed the *Abitur*. Rust, "Crew 34," pp. 52–53, 127–128.
42   BA-MA, RM 20/909 B. Nr. A V a 274/34, February 6, 1934; Anlage zu B. Nr. A V a 498/34 "Unterrichtung über die Personallage, im besonderen zum Herbst 1935;" BA-MA, RM 20/874, Document without any heading, archivist's page 58. The same document adds that by October 1, 1936, the navy would have given another 103 officers and officer candidates to the Air Ministry.
43   BA-MA, RM 20/909 B. Nr. A V c 799/34, March 5, 1934.
44   The navy eventually had to revise this policy when not enough single candidates could be found. Of the twenty-five noncommissioned officers who were enrolled as executive officer cadets in May 1934 and who were still in the program the following October, fourteen were married. BA-MA, RM 20/874, "Nachweisung der am 1. Oktober 1934 vorhandenen Seeoffizieranwärter."
45   BA-MA, RM 20/909 B. Nr. A V c 799/34, March 5, 1934.
46   BA-MA, RM 20/909 B. Nr. A V a 1096/34, March 26, 1934; B. Nr. A V w 1572/34, April 30, 1934.
47   BA-MA, RM 20/910 B. Nr. A V c 1725/34, May 8, 1934.
48   For the "L" officers, see above, Chapter 4.
49   BA-MA, RM 20/874 B. Nr. A V 2108/34, May 31, 1934.
50   Ibid.
51   Ibid. Peter, "Seeoffizieranwärter-Ausbildung 1848–1945," p. 110, gives the actual date of promotion as January 1, 1936, and indicates that the Crew of 1931 also received early promotion.
52   BA-MA, RM 20/874 B. Nr. A V 2108/34, May 31, 1934. The ordnance officers (*Waffenoffiziere*) had been reintroduced in 1934 and were largely assigned to naval arsenals. They were occasionally given shipboard assignments as well. For the *Waffenoffiziere*, see Bräckow, *Marine-Ingenieuroffizierkorps*, p. 228; also Raeder, *Mein Leben*, 1, p. 178.

53 BA-MA, RM 20/874 B. Nr. A V 2108/34, May 31, 1934.

54 BA-MA, RM 20/870 A 3612/34, "Beitrag für die Ansprache des Chef Mar. Ltg. am 21. September 1934."

55 BA-MA, RW 6/151 B. Nr. A V a 4796/34, December 3, 1943.

56 For the "L" officers' connections with civilian circles, see BA-MA, RM 20/874 B. Nr. MPA 351, January 14, 1936; also Michael Salewski, "Das Offizierkorps der Reichs- und Kriegsmarine," in *Das deutsche Offizierkorps, 1860–1960*, ed. Hanns Hubert Hofmann (Boppard am Rhein, 1980), p. 216.

57 BA-MA, RM 20/874 B. Nr. MPA 351, January 14, 1936. For the redesignation of the "L" officers, see Rudolf Absolon, *Die Wehrmacht im Dritten Reich*, 4 vols (Boppard am Rhein, 1969–) 2, pp. 57–58.

58 BA-MA, RM 20/874 B. Nr. A V c 286, April 8, 1935. The crew would include 345 cadets of the "S" and "F" branches, who were being trained for the Luftwaffe.

59 Ibid. The *Gorch Fock* had room for only 198 cadets out of the 220 executive officer candidates scheduled to enter the Crew of 1936. Erich Gröner, *Die deutschen Kriegsschiffe 1815–1945*, 2 vols (Munich, 1966), 2, p. 628. The *Horst Wessel* and the *Albert Leo Schlageter* were commissioned on September 16, 1936, and February 10, 1938, respectively, and alleviated the navy's shortage of square-riggers. Dülffer, *Hitler und die Marine*, p. 585.

60 BA-MA, N 582/3 Nachlass Bräckow, "Erziehung des jungen Offiziers ...", p. 18; Wiedersheim, "Officer Personnel Selection," p. 449.

61 Material on this aspect of the training program is, admittedly, scarce. If the experiences of the Militärärztliche Akademie and its naval successor, the Marineärztliche Akademie, are any indications of the difficulties faced by the navy as a whole, the effect of the greatly increased number of cadets was well nigh catastrophic. See the report of Flottenarzt A. Evers in BA-MA, III M 5 "Denkschrift der Marineärztlichen Akademie," Kiel, January 28, 1941.

62 Peter, "Seeoffizieranwärter-Ausbildung," p. 110; BA-MA, M 1528/Akte Geh I a, "Ausbildungsübersicht über die Jahrgänge 1933–1940."

63 BA-MA, RM 6/54, "Unterlagen zur Rede Anfang 1938." The "questions of principle" that Raeder mentioned in his speech may well have concerned the acute shortage of NCOs that the Service was experiencing concurrently with its dearth of officers. The Kriegsmarine's leaders may have simply preferred to keep some NCOs in positions where they were sure that they could render valuable service rather than tie them up in a lengthy training course that many might eventually fail. For the shortage of noncommissioned officers, see BA-MA, RM 6/54, "Unterlagen zur Rede Anfang 1938" and the earlier analysis in BA-MA, RM 20/909 Anlage zu B. Nr. A V 498/34, "Unterrichtung über die Personallage, im besonderen zum Herbst 1935."

64 On November 5, 1937, Hitler had informed the leaders of the Wehrmacht and the Foreign Minister, Neurath, that the problem of *Lebensraum* could be solved by force alone. For Raeder's reaction to this news, see below, Chapter 7.

65 BA-MA, RM 6/54, "Unterlagen zur Rede Anfang 1938;" also Raeder's "Erster Vortrag beim Führer," reprinted in Michael Salewski, "Marineleitung und politische Führung 1931–1935," *Militärgeschichtliche Mitteilungen*, 2/1971, p. 154.

66 In 1933, to take the example of the engineers, the navy had admitted no applicants from the families of workers, artisans, or the middle and lower officialdom. By 1939, applicants from these groups numbered 40 per cent of the total candidates admitted. BA-MA, N 582/3 Nachlass Bräckow, "Erziehung des jungen Offiziers . . . ," p. 19.

67 Bräckow, *Marine-Ingenieuroffizierkorps*, p. 140.

68 At the end of 1935, there were twenty-two admirals, vice admirals, and rear admirals among the executive officers. Absolon, *Wehrmacht im Dritten Reich*, 4, p. 229. By contrast, there were then only three officers of admiral rank among the other branches: the head of the medical officers, the Staff Engineer at the Marineleitung, and the recently created Inspector of Ships' Machinery. Helmut Fechter, "Admiral Hans Fechter" (Manuscript, Kempten, 1979), p. 47.

69 Fritz Brennecke, "Marine Zahlmeister, 1867–1967," *MOV-Nachrichten*, 16 (1967), pp. 273–274; Raeder, *Mein Leben*, 1, pp. 177–178; BA-MA, N 328/53 Nachlass Förste, Friedrich Hüffmeier to Förste, May 10, 1956.

70 Rust, "Crew 34," pp. 148, 164.

71 Bräckow, *Marine-Ingenieuroffizierkorps*, pp. 139–141, 168–175. See also Friedrich Forstmeier, "Stellung und Disziplinarbefugnisse des Ersten Offiziers an Bord von Kriegsschiffen der deutschen Marine, 1847–1945," *Marine-Rundschau*, 66 (1969), pp. 34–50.

72 This contrast was carried over into the postwar literature of the administrative and engineer officers as well. Compare, for example, Brennecke's favorable treatment of Raeder with Bräckow's essentially negative evaluation of the Grand Admiral.

73 Bräckow, *Marine-Ingenieuroffizierkorps*, pp. 153, 182, 207, 209; Fechter, "Hans Fechter," p. 41.

74 Bräckow, *Marine-Ingenieuroffizierkorps*, pp. 177, 178, 209.

75 BA-MA, N 582/2 Nachlass Bräckow, "Ansprache K. Adm. Ing. Berndt," 1931.

76 BA-MA, N 582/3 Nachlass Bräckow, "Gedanken über die Ingoffizierlaufbahn," Kiel, 1935/1936.

77 For the early efforts to secure an Inspection of Ships' Machinery, see Bräckow, *Marine-Ingenieuroffizierkorps*, pp. 154–156, 176–181, 208–212; also Fechter, "Hans Fechter," p. 38.

78 Among the executive officers who played an important role in this development were the commander of the fleet, Richard Foerster, and his chief of staff, Rolf Carls. Bräckow, *Marine-Ingenieuroffizierkorps*, pp. 206–207, 212–213, 344–346; Fechter, "Hans Fechter," pp. 42–45.

79 Bräckow, *Marine-Ingenieuroffizierkorps*, p. 229; Fechter, "Hans Fechter," pp. 46–47.

80 Bräckow, *Marine-Ingenieuroffizierkorps*, p. 229; Fechter, "Hans Fechter," p. 47.

81 Ibid., p. 49.

82 The text of the speech is reprinted in Bräckow, *Marine-Ingenieuroffizierkorps*, pp. 346–355. Analyses of the speech are given in ibid., pp. 229–231; and Fechter, "Hans Fechter," pp. 47–49.

83 Bräckow, *Marine-Ingenieuroffizierkorps*, p. 230.

84 Ibid., pp. 352–353. See also Siegfried Sorge's review of Bräckow, which contends that Raeder intended no slight to the engineers and that he wished merely to demonstrate the indivisibility of command. As Sorge argues: "Raeder's mistake was that he did not foresee the possibility of

his being misunderstood in the tense psychological situation." *Marineforum*, 50 (1975), pp. 94–97.

85 Bräckow, *Marine-Ingenieuroffizierkorps*, p. 230.
86 Ibid., p. 231; Fechter, "Hans Fechter," p. 49.
87 Bräckow, *Marine-Ingenieuroffizierkorps*, p. 232. For the engineers' "penetration" of important positions within the corps, see ibid., pp. 232–238.
88 Fechter, "Hans Fechter," pp. 52–53.

6

Accommodation: Service–Party Relations after the Gleichschaltung

The years that immediately followed the Anglo-German Naval Agreement of June 1935 brought immense challenges to the navy vis-à-vis the recruitment and training of its officer corps. But these were not the only problems that the Kriegsmarine faced during the period, for coupled with them were additional pressing matters that absorbed the attention of the Service's leaders. In this respect, the years 1935–1939 stood in sharp contrast to the roughly fifteen years that had preceded them. Then, virtually all of the admirals' attention had been centered upon a single problem, that of winning the Reich's political leaders over to an appreciation of the necessity of a strong navy. Now, that goal seemed to have been achieved, but in its place there appeared a variety of new challenges that collectively were more formidable than the old one. Having obtained Adolf Hitler's basic agreement to build a surface battle fleet, Raeder now had to supervise a building program which, in its intensity at least, was the most ambitious that Germany had ever undertaken.[1] To do this would require a continued ability to navigate between the demands of the Party, the War Ministry, and the other two branches of the Wehrmacht. At the same time, Raeder and his advisors would have to work closely with other representatives of the Reich—especially the Wilhelmstrasse—to see that the growing power of the navy served as an asset and not, as in the case of Tirpitz, as a liability in the foreign policy of the fatherland. Finally, and perhaps most importantly, having at last gained Hitler's attention, Raeder would now have to make doubly sure that he kept it. All of this was a tall order, even for a man of Raeder's energy. Indeed, there must have been times in the late 1930s when the admiral yearned for the simpler days of the Weimar navy. The Reichsmarine had been small, to be sure, but it had been manageable. There had been a singular sense of purpose in the minds of virtually all the officers, and there had been a shared conviction that time was ultimately on the side of the navy. Now, the very growth of the fleet threatened to overwhelm its creator, and Raeder often found that the demands of the new navy left his subordinates working at cross-purposes. Above all else, however, loomed the nagging feeling that time was working against the navy.

The most obvious problem, of course, concerned the construction of the fleet.[2] In the seventeen years that separated the end of the Great War from the Anglo–German Naval Agreement of 1935, a number of developments had occurred within the German shipbuilding industry that were distinctly unfavorable for a rapid expansion of the navy. Germany's capacity for naval construction had been reduced drastically as a result of the compulsory delivery to the Allies of four-fifths of its movable dockyard equipment after the scuttling of the High Sea Fleet at Scapa Flow in 1919. After a brief recovery in the 1920s, fueled largely by the expansion of the merchant marine, the industry had been hit hard by the general constriction in world trade during the Great Depression. Smaller contractors had been forced to shut down, and the larger yards had cut back on their shipbuilding capacity. At the same time, laborers had either retired or drifted into other lines of work. Now, with the resumption of an ambitious naval building program, there was an alarming dearth of experienced workers and raw materials, and the navy stood in sharp competition for them with the expanding army and air force.

Nor was this all. Despite the navy's best efforts to keep abreast of technological developments, most notably by subsidizing submarine construction abroad, Germany's naval designers had fallen behind in a number of areas.[3] It had been almost twenty years since a German yard had completed a warship larger than a *Panzerschiff*, and roughly an equal period of time since a foundry had produced a gun of battleship caliber. The skills that it took to construct a modern navy could not be relearned overnight. As a result, even though the Kriegsmarine theoretically had the capacity to undertake the first phase of naval expansion after 1935, it soon fell behind on its building schedule. By December 1937, the navy was anticipating delays of anywhere from three to twenty-two months in the completion of individual warships, with the average delay per vessel amounting to just over one year. The Service was going to be hard pressed to reach the strength of 35 per cent of the British navy by the target date of 1942.[4]

The construction program, then, proved to be a major headache for the naval high command. Another potentially troublesome area was the Service's changing relationship with the Party. Both the Party and the navy had displayed a certain tentativeness toward one another in the years immediately following the National Socialist takeover. Although each hoped to use the other for its short-term advantages, neither was completely certain that its long-term interests were tied to the other. Indeed, a number of unpleasant incidents between naval personnel and party functionaries—most notably representatives of the SA and the SS—had further clouded the relationship. Yet by the summer of 1935, the situation had changed considerably. The SA had been emasculated in June 1934, and Hitler had subsequently made a moving appeal for cooperation between the Wehrmacht and the SS. What was more, he now appeared to have committed himself to the idea of a strong fleet. The navy, for its part, could be reasonably certain by the summer of 1935 that National Socialism was here to stay. It is not surprising, therefore, that the rather cautious approaches that had characterized the first two years following the *Machtergreifung* now gave way to attempts to find a closer, more permanent relationship between Party and Service.

This first became evident in the spring of 1935 with the publication of a new Military Code regulating the duties and obligations of Germany's male citizens in the Wehrmacht. Previously, the Reich government had seen fit to manage Party and Wehrmacht relations on an *ad hoc* basis, and the old Military Code of March 23, 1921, had remained technically in effect. The reintroduction of conscription in March 1935, however, fundamentally altered the citizen's role in national defense, and on May 21 a new code was announced to the public. The Party's influence was evident in a number of areas, most notably in the provision under Article 15, Paragraph 1, that "Aryan" descent was a precondition for active service.[5] In one respect, though, the code appeared to remain faithful to its imperial and republican predecessors: Article 26 forbade soldiers from participating in political activities. Moreover, their membership in the NSDAP—by now the only legal party in Germany—or in any of its auxiliary organizations was to become dormant during their period of active duty.[6]

Article 26 thus appeared to uphold the inviolability of the armed forces at a time when virtually every other institution within the Reich had succumbed to the mastery of the Party. In truth, however, it soon became obvious that General von Blomberg, the newly redesignated War Minister, was willing to allow a number of exceptions to Article 26 that would, in all likelihood, soften the general prohibition on political activity espoused there. To be sure, on June 21, 1935, he clarified the question of membership in the Party's auxiliary organizations, which were not listed in the Military Code, and forbade all active duty Wehrmacht personnel from membership in the SA, the SS, the NSKK, the Hitler Youth, the National Socialist League of Students, and, for the sake of the Wehrmacht's female employees, the National Socialist League of Women. At the same time, a seemingly innocuous provision encouraged members of the armed forces to continue their contributions to the National Socialist Peoples' Welfare and gave them permission to attend activities of the party-sponsored "Strength through Joy" program. These were admittedly small deviations from the Military Code's apparent attempt to keep the Wehrmacht free from political influence. Nevertheless, in an era in which virtually every aspect of German life was becoming politicized, they point out the obvious difficulty of insulating the armed forces from society at large.[7]

Nor did Blomberg's measures stop at these relatively minor exceptions to the spirit of Article 26. One day after his general prohibition against membership in the Party's auxiliary organizations, he seemed to backtrack when he informed the armed forces' commanders that it was "self-evident" that the Wehrmacht pledged itself to the National Socialist view of the state. It was therefore necessary that reserve officers be chosen according to this principle and that only those who were "inwardly and outwardly" in support of the National Socialist state were to be selected for such positions. Later that summer, Blomberg showed another sign of relaxing the prohibition on political influence within the Wehrmacht. Although membership in the Party continued to be forbidden for the Wehrmacht's soldiers and sailors, officials and civilian employees were permitted to remain in the Party.[8]

The naval high command dutifully passed each of these measures on to the Kriegsmarine. Moreover, it undertook steps of its own which indicated that it, too, was altering its earlier stand on the matter of the Service's relationship with the Party. On July 22, 1935, in a likely sign that the Service was now interested in discovering some early ties with the Movement, the navy's Central Office asked all Berlin departments to report any naval personnel who were members of the National Socialist "Blood Order" honoring veterans of the *Putsch* of November 1923. In August, the high command announced that commemorative wreaths for funerals and other public occasions would henceforth bear the swastika insignia in addition to the national colors that they already carried. Two months later, the navy informed its non-salaried employees that they, in contrast to the *Beamten* and salaried employees, would be allowed to retain positions of leadership within the SA, the SS, and the NSKK. Finally, in November 1935, the naval high command decreed that its personnel respond to greetings of "Heil Hitler" in a similar manner.[9]

Clearly, then, the War Ministry and the naval high command were pursuing parallel courses in the matter of party political influence within the armed forces. In succeeding months, the two commands showed that they could work together smoothly to bring about a closer union of Party and Wehrmacht. A good case in point concerned the War Ministry's announcement on November 4, 1935, that it intended to introduce "national political education" at the officer schools and academies of all three branches of the armed forces. The navy high command was receptive to the idea and added that this instruction might also be given to those officers who would be shipping out on overseas training cruises, so that they could better represent the Third Reich to foreigners and Germans living abroad. At the same time, the navy pointed out the practical difficulties of finding capable instructors at the local level and suggested that this might be better handled by the War Ministry. Another, more serious problem concerned the lack of time available for instruction, for the Naval School was already scheduled to reduce its classes to a mere six and one-half months' duration. Nevertheless, the navy was confident that it could achieve the main aim of the political instruction, which it defined as "acquainting the officer or ensign with the intellectual content of National Socialism and with the most important dates of the Movement, so as to give him a better insight . . . into this matter than that of his subordinates."[10]

The exact allocation of time for instruction proved to be the most troublesome question. The War Ministry felt two hours per week would be necessary for the course; the navy thought two hours per month should suffice. Blomberg might well have concluded for a moment that the Kriegsmarine was taking this project too lightly, but if so, he was swiftly set right in his ideas. As a second report from the navy made clear, the Kriegsmarine thought so much of "national political education" that it had already incorporated it into its course on *Dienstkenntnis* at the Naval School, apparently without having informed the War Ministry accordingly. As proof, the report cited past directives from the Inspector of Naval Education and appended a reading list that would have done honor to the military section of any smaller National Socialist library.[11] This seemed to carry the day, for the War Ministry soon adopted a compromise solution that incorporated many of the navy's suggestions. According to Blomberg's decree of January 30, 1936, "national political education" would be given at least two hours a month at the Wehrmacht's schools, but an additional proviso stated that, when possible, every other possibility, including speeches by "outside personalities," was to be used to supplement this instruction.[12]

The War Ministry and the naval high command were not the only agencies that swiftly forgot the Military Code's separation of Party and Wehrmacht. Local commanders also made decisions which brought their garrisons into close and comradely ties with the Party or its auxiliary organizations. This, in turn, invariably blurred the differences between what was political and what was not. To recount more than a few instances in which the barriers between Party and navy were relaxed at the local level would involve needless detail and more than a little repetition. Instead, the experiences of a single command in the year 1936, in this case the naval base at Flensburg-Mürwik, will perhaps suffice to indicate the slow, almost imperceptible nature of the accommodation between Party and Kriegsmarine.

The commander of the base at Flensburg-Mürwik for the first part of 1936 was Wolf von Trotha, a man who had encountered difficulty with the Party in the past, and who probably had less reason than most officers to harbor illusions about the nature of the NSDAP.[13] Nevertheless, until his departure from Flensburg in the fall of 1936, Trotha promoted closer contacts between the naval garrison and local party organizations in a number of ways. Throughout the winter of 1935–1936, for example, he warmly recommended that the garrison attend plays, lectures, and films that hammered home with varying degrees of subtlety positions that were espoused either by the Party alone or by the War Ministry acting in conjunction with the Party.[14] In February, Trotha urged his subordinates to turn up in large numbers for an exhibition sponsored by the local branch of the party-controlled German Labor Front (DAF), celebrating the Reich's maritime industry; in March, he directed the attention of the garrison toward an exhibition entitled *"Volk und Rasse"* at the German Hygiene Museum at Flensburg. In April, the sailors were "requested" to turn out *en masse* for the Führer's birthday, while the cadets at the

Naval School were ordered to appear at the celebration. Trotha capped the first part of the year 1936 by "expressly recommending" a visit in May to the "Culture Day of the Hitler Youth."[15]

The flurry of party-sponsored or party-related activities at Flensburg subsided somewhat that summer.[16] When Trotha turned over his command to Captain Hubert Schmundt on October 1, 1936, however, the recommendations resumed at full force. During the month of October alone, Schmundt directed or recommended that the officer corps or the garrison as a whole appear at three activities closely linked to the Party. On October 4, a delegation of officers was commanded to attend a local party-sponsored celebration, while the rest of the garrison crowded around the Deutsches Haus at Schmundt's request to hear a broadcast of Hitler's speech from the Bückeberg marking the harvest festival. On October 12, Schmundt recommended attendance at the National Socialist Cultural Association for a series of readings by the president of the Reich Chamber of Authors [*Reichsschrifttumskammer*]. Finally, lest the spouses of naval officers feel neglected, on October 19 Schmundt recommended a large turnout by husband and wife for the enthralling exhibition of the *Reichsluftschutzbund*, Ortsgruppe Flensburg, entitled "The Woman and Civil Air Defense."[17]

Such was the case of the garrison at Flensburg-Mürwik in the year 1936. Similar encounters between Kriegsmarine personnel and party organizations undoubtedly occurred any number of times at the navy's other bases in the period leading up to the war. Individually, they admittedly did not amount to very much: collectively, they represented a reorientation of the attitude of the Kriegsmarine toward political activities in general and toward the NSDAP in particular. Previously, in the Weimar era and even in the early days of the National Socialist dictatorship, local commanders would doubtless have thought twice before suggesting, much less ordering, attendance at an activity sponsored by a political party, no matter how innocuous the event or how tenuous the connection with politics. Now, "suggestions" to attend this or that activity came almost automatically, and political influence followed as a matter of course.

Yet the change was only partially the responsibility of the navy's commanders. By the middle to late 1930s, German society had changed so drastically that it scarcely resembled the conditions of the late Weimar period, when the notion of a nonpolitical Reichswehr still had some validity. Now, the influence of the Party was omnipresent, and virtually every activity in Germany, whether it was an exhibition on maritime commerce or a literary round table, carried with it political significance. Indeed, the only conceivable means of insulating the Service from party influence would have been to seal it off completely and to confine the sailors to base quarters permanently.

Raeder, for one, was unwilling to consider this alternative. In essence, such a policy would have represented a throwback to the days of the Imperial Navy, when the officers had whiled away their time at the *Kasinos* and the men had languished in their rusting vessels as part of a plan to protect the navy from the wicked influences that supposedly lurked outside the gates. The results had been disastrous, beginning with the isolation of the officer corps (but not the majority of the enlisted men) from large segments of German society, and ending with mutiny and revolution. Now, after fifteen years of bemoaning the Service's isolation, Raeder was not about to divorce it from society once again at precisely the moment when the breakthrough to the nation seemed assured. Indeed, by the summer of 1936, it appeared that the Kriegsmarine was striving harder than ever to maintain and extend its contacts with the Party and the *Volk*.

Nowhere was this more evident than in the navy's ambitious celebration of the twentieth anniversary of the Battle of the Skagerrak at the end of May 1936. Throughout the week leading up to the event, special excursion trains brought about 25,000 veterans of the Imperial Navy and the Reichsmarine to the city of Kiel. On Thursday, May 28, Hitler arrived to a tumultuous welcome by the citizens and garrison of the famous "*Marinestadt.*" For the next three days, thousands of spectators jammed the banks of the Kieler Bucht to watch the fleet or to catch a glimpse of the Führer. Few could have been disappointed, for they were treated to a display of pomp and power that completely overshadowed the festivities of Navy Week the year before. On Thursday, Hitler boarded the "pocket" battleship *Graf Spee* and looked on while the recently commissioned vessel performed a series of complicated maneuvers in the company of three half-flotillas of torpedo-boats. That evening, he witnessed night exercises by torpedo-boats from the deck of the *Köln*. The next day, virtually the entire fleet assembled in the bay for a stately review. In the van were the navy's three "pocket" battleships, their crews lining the starboard sides of the vessels in white dress uniforms. Close behind were four light cruisers, followed by a host of auxiliary vessels, torpedo-boats, and tenders. At the end of the parade came the newly commissioned U-boats, with the larger submarines *U-25* and *U-26* at the fore and the smaller boats of the "U-Flottille Weddingen" bringing up the rear.[18]

The review offered a convincing preview of the naval power that the Reich would enjoy in the years to come. Perhaps the most impressive display, however, occurred the next day, May 30, when the navy dedicated a gigantic monument to its fallen comrades of the Great War at the small Kiel suburb of Laboe.[19] There, before an audience of 50,000, Hitler received a delegation from the National Socialist Naval League and then listened intently as a succession of speakers discoursed upon the meaning of the Navy Memorial and the heroic accomplishments that it commemorated.

Raeder reserved the keynote address for himself. The Navy Memorial, the admiral proclaimed, was an eternal reminder that nothing could shake the Reich's military and naval spirit. He found it especially appropriate that the leader of the reborn Wehrmacht was present to witness the dedication of the memorial, and he took Hitler's forthcoming presentation of a laurel wreath as a symbol of the Kriegsmarine's

147

unshakable loyalty and its willingness to emulate the sacrifices of the fallen. Raeder then recalled the grim days that had followed the Battle of the Skagerrak, when Germany and the navy had been threatened by the forces of revolution. Fortunately, there had followed the "redemption" of the navy at Scapa Flow, which had, in turn, expressed the entire nation's "inflexible will to live."

Raeder then turned to more recent history. If the navy's deed at Scapa Flow had proved its spiritual health, it was the NSDAP and its leader who had given the Service the opportunity to build once again on its heroic past. Indeed, Raeder's gratitude threatened to overflow in the excitement: "My Führer. You have led us and the entire German nation out of the dark into the dawn of a bright new future. May the blessings of the Almighty accompany you and the nation on the steep, difficult ascent upon which you will lead us."

Raeder's apotheosis was followed by a number of stately hymns. Then, a steady drum roll sounded as a solemn procession bore a collection of the Imperial Navy's battle-scarred banners into the memorial's dedication hall. At precisely twelve noon, Hitler placed a wreath—the only one of the day—at the memorial, amid absolute silence. He left without saying a word. Onlookers could well have imagined that he was too overcome with emotion to speak.

After the touching display of Saturday morning, the remaining ceremonies were something of an anticlimax. Indeed, Hitler did not even stay for the subsequent addresses that evening at a massive gathering in the Nord-Ostsee-Halle; by the next day, when memorial services were held throughout northern Germany to commemorate the actual anniversary of the Skagerrak, Hitler was already back in Berlin. The reasons for this rather hasty departure remain unclear. Perhaps Hitler had planned to make his exit from Kiel on Saturday afternoon all along. Perhaps his departure was occasioned by the untimely death of the retired General Karl Litzmann, an early convert to National Socialism. Or perhaps the Führer, the would-be artist, was displeased by the aesthetic merits of the Navy Memorial—the stark brick tower which he later termed "an unparalleled piece of *Kitsch*"—or by reports of discourtesy shown by individual naval officers toward a high-ranking party official.[20] Whatever the reason, and whatever the transgressions the navy might have committed in the realm of architectural taste or etiquette, Raeder still had good cause for satisfaction. Hitler had come to Kiel and seen the navy. His blessings, if not those of the Almighty, seemed assured.

The Kriegsmarine remained in the limelight throughout the remainder of the summer of 1936. On June 11, Hitler paid the navy a return visit, this time to the North Sea Station at Wilhelmshaven. The next day, the cruiser *Karlsruhe* returned from a successful eight-month training cruise and was greeted at Kiel by the Baltic Station Commander, Vice Admiral Albrecht, and the Deputy Gauleiter, Walter Behrens; both men appeared to have forgotten their differences from two years before.[21] A day later, yet another indication of the close unity between Party and Kriegsmarine was provided at the launching of the Service's newest training vessel, the *Horst Wessel*. Although this time Hitler stayed away from the festivities at Hamburg, his deputy, Rudolf Hess, attended in the company of Admirals Otto Schultze, Alfred Saalwächter, and Max Bastian. Hess's christening speech nicely summed up the new times: Just as the navy's first sail cruiser, the *Gorch Fock*, had carried the name of the navy's poet and warrior, so the second one, the *Horst Wessel*, carried the name of the Movement's poet and warrior.[22] Hess's message, like Raeder's two weeks earlier, could not have been clearer. The Party and armed forces—in this case the navy—represented the twin pillars of the National Socialist state.

The summer of 1936, then, saw the courtship between Party and navy reach a new level of intensity. In the years that followed, both NSDAP and Wehrmacht leaders appeared determined to strengthen in every way possible the ties uniting the two institutions. In January 1937, the first of the National Political Instruction Courses established by Blomberg the previous year was held in Berlin for selected officers of all three branches of the Wehrmacht. Twenty-seven Kriegsmarine officers attended, most of whom were directly involved in the training of the Service's enlisted men or its growing corps of ensigns and junior officers. The list of speakers amounted to a virtual "Who's Who" of the Third Reich. Alfred Rosenberg gave the opening address, which was entitled "The Ideological Basis of the Third Reich." During the next eight days, the audience was treated to eighteen additional lectures that included talks by Rudolf Hess on "The Nature and Goals of the NSDAP," by Dr Wilhelm Frick on the "Structure and Building of the Third Reich," by Dr Joseph Goebbels on "The Basis of National Socialist Propaganda," and by Dr Walter Frank on the "History of the NSDAP from 1919 to 1933." Sandwiched in between were visits to the leading laboratories and "think tanks" of the New Order, including the euphemistically styled Reich Committee for National Health, the Reich Academy for National Planning and Geographic Research, and the headquarters of Reinhard Heydrich's *Sicherheitsdienst* (SD). The intent of these visits and lectures was clear: the participants were to return to their respective schools and academies to propagate the Party's message in all three branches of the Wehrmacht.[23]

The National Political Instruction Course apparently met the expectations that the Party and the Wehrmacht leadership had placed on it. Two years later, a similar course was held at the party retreat at Bad Tölz in the Bavarian Alps for about 180 officers, including eighteen from the Kriegsmarine, who had particularly distinguished themselves in conveying National Socialist ideology to the troops. Once again, the NSDAP sent many of its best and brightest speakers to acquaint the officers with the Party's message, and the participants were again treated to afternoon excursions to see its teachings being translated into reality. In addition, the Party sponsored a display of the most important books on National Socialism, which did a brisk business during the week and which resulted in "an unusually large number of orders" from the officers.[24]

Unfortunately, there is no record of the feelings of the Kriegsmarine participants concerning the overall value of the course, but if they were anything like the reaction of their army colleagues, they were extremely favorable. Admittedly, some officers appear initially to have been troubled by the campaign that the Party was now conducting against the Church, while others were palpably disturbed that some party members still doubted or professed to doubt the sincerity of the officer corps' devotion to the cause of National Socialism. But the reassuring words of Reich Leader Rosenberg on the matter of church participation seemed to have assuaged their fears concerning the first matter, and the enthusiastic participation of the officers in the present course gave lie to the second. Indeed, as one officer put it, interest in some of the topics was so intense that discussions often lasted well into the night; another suggested that it would be good if an officer from every battalion could attend such a course in the future. Nor was there any doubt that the Party was pursuing the proper course in sponsoring this instruction in political education. An army captain (Mecke) maintained that the courses showed that most young officers were particularly well suited for reinforcing the impact of National Socialist ideology among the troops, while a major (Klar) added that company commanders could best fulfill this task because of the trust that their subordinates placed in them.[25] By the winter and spring of 1939, therefore, the National Political Instruction that Blomberg had introduced three years earlier was definitely bearing fruit.

Not all of the initiatives for the political education of the naval officer corps, however, stemmed from the Party or the Wehrmacht leadership. By 1937, at least two naval writers were also addressing this question, either directly or indirectly. The more influential of the two was Commander Siegfried Sorge, whose work was entitled *Der Marineoffizier als Führer und Erzieher*.[26] Its origins revealed a great deal about the times in which the navy was living. In 1932, Commander Friedrich Ruge had published an article in the influential *Marine-Rundschau* dealing with the qualities of leadership in a naval officer, and it was well received within the Service.[27] As a result, Raeder announced a literary competition within the Reichsmarine for a more detailed treatment of the question. Sorge's entry was the winner, and with good reason. His work incorporated a number of insights from psychology and sociology, which gave it a distinctly "modern" flavor (to the somewhat tradition-bound officers of the navy, in any case). It presented a wealth of information with apt examples from the history of Prussia and Germany, dealt gently but openly with the failings of the navy in the Great War, and offered a number of suggestions for better performance in the future. There was only one thing lacking: Sorge's original draft, which was completed in 1932 or 1933, contained no mention of National Socialism.[28]

Perhaps it was this omission that accounted for the failure of the book to be published until 1937. By then, the author had added what one sympathetic observer has rather delicately termed "a few positive utterances concerning National Socialist programs."[29] In truth, this would seem to be something of an understatement, for the personal example of the Führer now joined and in many cases overshadowed the earlier ones of Julius Caesar, Frederick the Great, and, predictably enough, Alfred von Tirpitz, which Sorge had cited as models for the young officers of the Kriegsmarine. Indeed, the humble veteran of the trenches, Adolf Hitler, frequently became the link between the soldierly virtues of the past and the National Socialist ones of the present. In analyzing the *Führerprinzip*, for example, Sorge noted that this "leader principle" was deeply rooted in soldierly thought, but he argued that it was Hitler who most clearly embodied it to the German nation. In similar fashion, he used Hitler's elegant formulations from *Mein Kampf* to emphasize the joy one should feel in assuming responsibility (*Verantwortungsfreudigkeit*). And when Sorge wished to impress upon aspiring officers the necessity of good physical training, both for them and their subordinates, another passage from Hitler's book provided the starting point.[30] In short, "positive utterances" concerning the Führer and National Socialism abounded in Sorge's work.

Certain features of the Party's ideology, however, received special attention at Sorge's hands. His message concerning the relationship of officer and wife, for example, had a distinctly National Socialist flavor. The future bride was to be a shining example of German womanhood in the way she led her life, fulfilled her duties, and ran the house. As the future mother of his children, it was important that the officer's wife come from a "hereditarily sound family." It was equally essential that the young officer be able to take up these questions with his subordinates so that he could show them "the old German respect for the pure wife and mother, the guardian of the customs of *Volk* and Race, and the eternal 'mother of the nation.' " In this respect, Sorge perceived the navy to be in a particularly advantageous position, for its overseas voyages had shown the extremes within the world, ranging from the Orient, where women served as beasts of burden, to "other lands" (France or the United States?), where they were spoiled pleasure objects. Fortunately, in Germany they were neither of these, but rather comrades and helpers of men.[31]

Sorge also had interesting things to say about how the young officer ought to lead his unit. Once again, he found the teachings of the Führer to be especially relevant. With a firm appreciation of Hitler's ability as a speaker, he noted that, in addressing crowds or groups of soldiers, the firm assertion and the quick, decisive slogan worked far more effectively than the literal truth or the long debate. Citing from *Mein Kampf* again, Sorge added that "the psyche of the broad masses is not responsive to anything halfhearted or weak," and noted approvingly that the Führer was a master of winning over others through the power of his appearance or the force of his words. Officers were advised not only to hear his speeches, but to immerse themselves in Hitler's book so as to learn the art of directing the masses.[32]

This was particularly relevant for the navy, for Sorge conceded that there had been times near the end of the last war and during the revolutionary disturbances which followed it when the art of mass psychology had not been handled properly by naval officers. He then cited the examples of Fritz Witschetzky, former gunnery officer from the auxiliary cruiser *Wolf* in the First World War, of Ferdinand Magellan, and of Julius Caesar, each of whom had defused unrest among their subordinates by a good understanding of psychology. But here, too, it was a more recent example that seemed to catch Sorge's admiring gaze: "It is impossible not to think of the Führer Adolf Hitler in describing these scenes, for he also nipped a serious mutiny in the bud through the swift intervention of his mighty personality alone, without having to wait for the arrival of the approaching troops." Admittedly, Sorge went on to say, not everyone could be a Magellan, a Caesar, or a Hitler, but one could still learn an important lesson from these masters: only fearless determination and clear dedication transformed men into leaders.[33]

Perhaps the most striking aspect of Sorge's work was the closeness with which his view of recent developments in German history coincided with the Party's teachings. Permeating his work was an overwhelming concern for the unity of the Reich. At one point in the book, he referred to an "era of individualism and the tendencies toward dissolution" that had characterized the recent past; elsewhere, he wrote of the worst "hereditary failure" of the Germans, their tendency toward disunity and discord. In yet another passage, Sorge spoke of the great social question that had arisen through the alienation of the workers from the rest of the *Volk* and of the wrong turn that they had made toward Marxism under the leadership of Jews. Now, however, the Reich was at last on the road toward realizing true national unity, and Sorge did not doubt that the explanation for this rebirth was the inspired leadership of Hitler.[34]

To be sure, much remained to be accomplished. According to Sorge, the present generation's task was to solve the "social question" by winning the workers back to a true German Socialism that was untainted by "Jewish materialism" or by "Marxist agitation." But in a curious way, the very magnitude of the task and the long-overdue recognition of the dangers of disunity could now be expected to facilitate Hitler's mission. As Sorge expressed it: "There is no better means [than this recognition] of making the Germans energetic and thankful followers of the Führer and of helping them understand that the Führer also had to use a heavy hand and sometimes must continue to do so in order to accomplish his fantastic aim."[35]

Siegfried Sorge was not the only one within the Service to put his thoughts on the new state of affairs to paper. In the fall of 1937, a Commander Kreysing published an article in the *Marine-Rundschau* entitled "Der Offizier im nationalsozialistischen Staat." In a number of ways, Kreysing went considerably beyond Sorge in embracing the teachings of the Party. The question of race had admittedly played a significant role in Sorge's analysis of the ideal officer, but for Kreysing it was the *alpha* and *omega* of the National Revolution. As he somewhat redundantly stated it:

National Socialism is the application of a healthy understanding of mankind to all aspects of life. The racially-formed community of the *Volk* is the central problem of this Revolution, and race is at the center of life in the *völkisch* state . . . . Race is therefore the essential principle of life, the essential maxim of life, and the eternal principle of work.[36]

This realization led Kreysing into some interesting conclusions with regard to the military. Precisely because earlier generations of Germans had failed to appreciate the essential unity of the *Volk*, they had also failed in their efforts to form a true "community of arms" (*Wehrgemeinschaft*) that was essential to the defense of the Reich. To be sure, there had been universal conscription in both Prussia and Germany, but the benefits that ought to have arisen from this had been thwarted by the special position that the officer corps had enjoyed within the armed forces. Thus, the officer corps could and did make enormous sacrifices on the field of battle in the Great War, but it had been unable to make itself into the guardian of a nationally rooted will to arms. Fortunately, this picture had recently changed, for Adolf Hitler's triumph had at last made *Volk* and State synonymous. The officer, conscious of the benefits that resulted from this unity, must accept the new order without question and "immerse himself in the depths of National Socialist ideology."[37]

Thus, both Sorge and Kreysing planted the navy squarely in the National Socialist camp. It is, of course, impossible to determine precisely how much influence these and other works[38] exerted upon the officers of the Kriegsmarine. Coinciding as their message did with many of the lessons that were currently being taught in the Hitler Youth and the Reich Labor Service (RAD), through which the young men of Germany were now passing, it is likely that their impact was extensive. And there is considerable evidence that one work, Sorge's *Marineoffizier*, exerted a particularly strong influence over the Service's new generation of junior officers. Already on September 7, 1936, Raeder had ordered that all officers of the rank of lieutenant commander or below were to possess the book when it was ready. He further recommended that older officers obtain a copy and study Sorge's work. Apparently, the officer corps took Raeder at his word, for the book eventually went through five editions and became the unofficial "bible" of the naval officer. Many veterans of the Kriegsmarine still remembered it fondly a good thirty years after the end of the Second World War. Indeed, for many, the author had ceased even to require a first name and had become known simply as *"the* Sorge."[39]

The speeches of Raeder, the addresses by the party leaders at the National Political Instruction courses, and the works by Sorge and Kreysing stressed one theme in common. They all pointed to the benefits that National Socialism had allegedly brought to the Reich, the Wehrmacht and the navy. Yet, by the summer of 1936, thoughtful observers within the Service might well have asked themselves whether the increasingly close relationship with the Party was fully beneficial for the navy. To be sure, the alliance was bringing its rewards. The Kriegsmarine was in the midst of a building program that was the envy of most navies around the world, and if the throngs which turned out for the dedication of the Navy Memorial were any indication of public sentiment, the Service was enjoying a popularity such as it had seldom, if ever, seen. The navy apparently had the Party and its Führer to thank for both of these developments. Yet, as those who had dealt with the National Socialists in the past knew, the Party rarely did anything for free, and by 1936 at the latest, the more percipient naval officers must have had the vague but uncomfortable feeling that the Service was now beginning to pay for past favors.

To be sure, much of the navy's routine appeared unchanged, for even in the engrossing whirlwind of National Socialism, Raeder could bury himself in a host of trivial bureaucratic decisions in order to maintain the "naval style" that he desired. In June 1935, when War Minister von Blomberg requested that Wehrmacht officers confine the carrying of briefcases to and from work to a minimum so as to avoid the suggestion of a bureaucratized officer corps, Raeder leapt upon the order with such alacrity that he specified that Blomberg's injunction be repeated after every spring and fall transfer of personnel to assure that newly posted officers would not commit this breach of etiquette. The admiral likewise forbade the use of monocles and ruled that officers eschew raincoats, except on days when rain was almost certain, as these greatly detracted from the smartness of the dark blue uniform. Indeed, much like his erstwhile Supreme War Lord, Wilhelm II, Raeder could carry his concern for decorum to ridiculous extremes. Thus, in 1935, when he witnessed an officer smoking a pipe while driving a car, he described it as a "military impossibility" and insisted that this "deplorable state of affairs" cease. Similarly, in February 1939 he enjoined officers in uniform from dancing the "Lambeth Walk," which was then the rage of Europe.[40] Apparently, the revolutionary social dynamism of the National Socialist Movement had not yet reached the admiral's inner sanctum.

Yet, in the meantime, the forces of National Socialism were transforming Germany root and branch, and the navy could scarcely hope to remain unaffected for long. Indeed, by the middle to late 1930s, signs of change were virtually everywhere. One disturbing feature of the new order of things was the way in which party organizations seemed to renew their efforts to intrude themselves into the affairs of the armed forces. Previously, the primary threat to the independence of the Wehrmacht had appeared to be the demands of the Party's two paramilitary organizations, the SA and the SS, for an extensive and ultimately dominant role in the Reich's military affairs. By 1935, the first of these organizations had been vanquished and the second seemed to have been channeled, if only temporarily, into a more useful direction as an unofficial "fourth branch" of the armed forces.[41] But in their place there appeared a number of other party organizations which aimed not at a direct military role, but rather an administrative one within the affairs of the Wehrmacht. At this level, the generals and admirals were doubly disadvantaged. On the one hand, the individual demands of the Party now appeared more restrained than those of the paramilitary bodies had been and hence were more difficult to refuse. On the other hand, their proposals did not directly affect the Wehrmacht's coveted "weapons monopoly" and were, in fact, occasionally useful. And yet, collectively these intrusions by the Party would ultimately circumscribe the Wehrmacht leadership's freedom of action just as surely as the earlier demands of the SA would have.

The efforts of the leader of the German Labor Front (DAF), Robert Ley, are a good case in point. Throughout the latter half of the 1930s, Ley tirelessly sought to broaden the powers of the DAF Abteilung Wehrmacht, which had been set up to deal with the labor management relations of the armed forces' civilian employees. In 1936, he attempted to secure a greater role for the "*Kraft durch Freude*" (KdF) program in the recreational activities of the officers and men. Here, the War Ministry was on particularly vulnerable ground, for it doubtlessly recognized the need for a sound recreational program for the new conscripts and yet it understandably wanted to pour its funds into other areas more directly related to rearmament, namely weapons and equipment. Thus, Ley was eventually able to cajole War Minister von Blomberg into an agreement whereby the KdF assumed much of the responsibility in recreational activities. Although Ley pledged that the KdF would abstain from politics in the "Wehrmacht homes" that it established for the off-duty use of the troops, he quickly seemed to forget this promise, and the War Ministry at one time threatened to cancel the agreement, to no apparent avail.[42]

Nor was Ley the only one of Hitler's paladins to seek to expand his power at the expense of the Wehrmacht. In August 1935, the Party Commission for the Protection of National Socialist Literature obtained a voice in the censorship of military publications that dealt with the Movement. The following winter, Alfred Rosenberg attempted to secure control over the handling of ideological questions within the armed forces and was eventually rewarded with a rather vague right of codetermination in this area. Finally, in 1938, Goebbels' Propaganda Ministry secured the right to appoint the reporters, broadcasters, and cameramen of the army's newly formed propaganda companies. When the Kriegsmarine established similar units in the summer of 1939, this arrangement was extended to the navy as well.[43]

The naval high command's response to these developments is rather curious. As far as can be determined, neither Raeder nor any of his immediate subordinates uttered a word of protest. Admittedly, the incursion by the Party concerned the collective interests of all three branches of the armed forces, and primary responsibility for dealing with them fell therefore to the War Ministry, not to the naval high command. Nevertheless, concessions to the Party or government in these areas would invariably limit the Kriegsmarine's administrative freedom of action as well, and it is thus somewhat surprising that Raeder, who had doggedly defended the independence of the navy against all comers in the past, appeared to be so little concerned. Perhaps he hoped to use his influence with the Führer for other, more pressing matters, or perhaps he was simply tiring of the long struggle he had waged on behalf of the navy's independence. In any case, he would find that party functionaries rarely relinquished positions of power once they had attained them.

Another unwelcome sign of the change by the latter half of the 1930s concerned the exercise of the Christian religion within the Service. Raeder showed considerably more energy in this area in defending the navy's prerogatives against encroachments by the Party. He was aided here by the personal predilections of the Führer, for, in contrast with his obsession with the "Jewish question," Hitler initially had shown relatively little interest in the concerns of the Christian Church. To be sure, there were some firebrands within the Party who urged a complete break with the Church, and others—the so-called "German Christians"—who called for a "second German Reformation" to purge the Church of its "Jewish legacy" (including the Old Testament and the supposed adulteration of Christ's message introduced by the "Rabbi Paul"!), but neither of these groups included Hitler. The Führer tended to regard the Church as an anachronism that would either linger on harmlessly among the superstitious or else would wither away completely once National Socialism had reached maturity. In the meantime, as the rather bland commitment to "positive Christianity" in Point 24 of the Party Program and in the Reich's Concordat with the Vatican on July 20, 1933, indicated, Hitler was perfectly willing to live in peace with both the Catholic and the Protestant denominations—provided they gave him a free hand in secular matters.[44]

Initially, therefore, there was little cause for a change within the navy's established religious practices. Soldiers and sailors already enjoyed the right to attend or refuse to attend religious services as they saw fit, and in the absence of any new initiatives from the Reich government, both Blomberg and Raeder were content to leave matters essentially as they were. Moreover, when Hitler once again made a public commitment to "positive Christianity" in the course of a speech on August 17, 1934, and promised to protect the rights of the two great confessions in Germany, Raeder even seized upon his words to make a modest statement for Christianity. In the wake of the Führer's pronouncement, the admiral asserted, the numerous contradictory utterings by other party leaders on the subject of religion were of no consequence. Naval personnel who were contemplating leaving the Church (as many in the Party were currently doing), were therefore advised that the navy's religious regulations were official regulations and that a renunciation of the Church for the purpose of making an impression on outsiders would not be tolerated. Nor were religious questions to be discussed with outsiders. In particular, Raeder forbade any contact with the so-called

"German Faith Movement," a rather bizarre assortment of free thinkers, mystics, atheists, and pagans that Reinhard Heydrich was currently seeking to exploit in the interests of the anticlerical movement within the Party.[45]

Thus, Raeder espoused religious orthodoxy within the navy, using the example of Adolf Hitler, of all people. In time, the admiral was to discover that the Führer's religious convictions constituted a very slender reed upon which to lean. By 1935, the religious situation in Germany had worsened considerably. The government's attempts to secure a pliant clergy had proven only partially successful, and a minority within both Catholic and Protestant denominations, appalled at the Party's brutal tactics in secular matters and its clumsy handling of ecclesiastical affairs, was coming into increasing conflict with Reich officials. Among Catholics, this opposition initially took the form of individual acts of defiance; it would culminate in the issuance of the Papal Encyclical "*Mit brennender Sorge*" by Pope Pius XI in March 1937.[46] Among Protestants, opposition to the regime manifested itself in the formation of what came to be known as the Confessing Church under the leadership of the former U-boat commander, the Reverend Martin Niemöller. Party leaders such as Goebbels, Rosenberg, and Baldur von Schirach responded by urging their Führer to undertake more extreme measures against the Church. Hitler refused, for tactical reasons, to be drawn into the conflict. Nevertheless, from 1935 on, he allowed his henchmen increasingly free reign to pursue their semiofficial campaigns of terror and intimidation against the Church.

These developments boded ill for the religious peace within the armed forces. Especially after the introduction of conscription in March 1935, it became obvious that the Wehrmacht would soon be flooded with nearly every type of believer (Jews excepted) and nonbeliever imaginable. Perhaps for this reason Raeder found it expedient to withdraw the navy from the relatively exposed position that he had staked out for it in the wake of Hitler's speech the previous summer. On July 19, 1935, the naval high command announced that any discussion of religious questions and, above all, any proselytization by naval personnel for a particular denomination were forbidden. Participation at meetings which were aimed at proselytization or which in any way exacerbated the church conflict was likewise prohibited.[47]

It was clear that Raeder hoped to ride out the impending storm on the matter of religion by a policy of strict neutrality. Nevertheless, it soon became equally clear that the Reich government, while paying lip service to this neutrality, was in fact determined to reduce the influence of religion within the armed forces to the barest possible minimum. In 1935, for example, both the army and the navy were enjoined from providing honor companies for religious processions and from beflagging their buildings on religious holidays. In 1937, Blomberg ended the practice of using civilian clergymen at the smaller bases and restricted the official Wehrmacht pastors, who were counted among armed forces personnel, to the larger garrisons of the army and the navy. In May 1938, the War Ministry ordered that soldiers and sailors who went to church on their own volition were not to form groups on the way to or from the service or at the service itself. Finally, in March 1939, a new decree required Wehrmacht pastors to submit speeches or sermons intended for civilian audiences to their immediate superiors before delivering them.[48]

In this manner, the Party sought to strip the armed forces of the privileges that they had hitherto enjoyed in the exercise of religion. Raeder, it should be pointed out, was unwilling to yield the field entirely to the anticlericals. While there appears to be no written evidence to support his contention that the navy simply disregarded the instructions of the War Ministry when these prejudiced the ministry of the Church, there are indications that the navy did employ a number of stratagems to soften the impact of the government's measures in this regard. When soldiers and sailors complained that they had been ordered to take part at Wehrmacht functions that included religious ceremonies, the navy succeeded in establishing a difference between "Military Celebrations with Religious Dedications" (to which Wehrmacht personnel could be commanded) and "Religious Ceremonies" (to which they could not).[49] When the War Ministry forbade any cooperation with confessional organizations, Raeder appears to have made sure that the navy defined the term "confessional organization" narrowly enough to free the Service to continue working with as many organizations as possible. Finally, and perhaps most importantly, the navy managed to retain control over the nomination of pastors within the Service and was thus able to maintain a measure of independence from both the War Ministry and the government as a whole.[50]

Yet none of these successes, guarded as they were, was achieved without making compromises. In return for the right to continue religious services within the navy, Raeder evidently renounced almost all interest in the larger, wider questions of the Church in Germany. Although some pastors of the Confessing Church may have been allowed to serve in the Kriegsmarine,[51] Raeder seems to have regarded the movement as a whole as a misdirected effort. When Niemöller was arrested by the Gestapo, the admiral at first showed a somewhat tentative interest in the case of his former brother-in-arms, but quickly decided to leave the matter to others when he discovered that the pastor had offended Hitler.[52] Indeed, Raeder could never accept the activist role that the Confessing Church embodied, and he tended toward a more traditionally Lutheran view that accepted the secular powers as they existed. As he informed a certain Chaplain Hölzer when he entered the navy in 1937: "It will not be your duty to wage a religious or political battle in the navy or to go expressly into an analysis of the intellectual currents that National Socialism has aroused. As chaplain, you are to preach Christ earnestly and without compromise. Never cease to do that."[53] In short, naval pastors could perform the rituals of Christianity, but they could not apply its teachings to the burning issues of twentieth-century Germany.

Both the Party's penetration into the administrative affairs of the navy and its interference with the exercise of the Christian religion offered thoughtful observers cause for concern. Another disturbing indication of the way in which the Service was paying the price for its alliance with the Party could be gauged from its increasingly vocal acceptance of the Party's teachings on race. Admittedly, some officers remained immune to the racial diatribes of the Party or else managed to stand party doctrine on its head. In 1935, for example, when Fregattenkapitän Karl Dönitz commanded the *Emden* on the last overseas cruise that he would enjoy before assuming command of the U-boat force, he concluded that the racial mixing between the natives and the French colonists in the Seychelle Islands had produced a "refinement of the races," particularly with regard to the women. But other observers were less charitable toward the refining process that Dönitz professed to see, and by the mid-1930s voices in prominent naval circles were echoing the party line on the question of race. In January 1936, the *MOV-Nachrichten* noted with palpable satisfaction the impression that the racially pure crews of the navy had made abroad, and it quoted an enthusiastic report from one German living overseas that many of the natives now regretted that the maintenance of racial purity was no longer possible where they lived.[54] Later that year, the same periodical also made a number of appeals in the form of articles or favorable book reviews urging the white race to awaken to the challenge posed by the "coloreds" of the world.[55]

In matters of race, however, the attention of the navy was not directed exclusively toward the outside world. From 1935 onwards, there were growing indications that the party attitude toward "non-Aryans" at home was becoming that of the Wehrmacht as well. Although the Military Code of May 21, 1935, continued to see certain exceptions to the measures it announced, it decreed "Aryan" descent a precondition for active duty in the armed forces and forbade marriages between Wehrmacht personnel and "non-Aryans." In this manner, the Wehrmacht leadership anticipated the notorious Nuremberg Laws of September 1935, which prohibited marriages between Germans and Jews and which reserved the rights of Reich citizenship solely for "Aryans."[56] War Minister von Blomberg took another step in the Party's direction in July 1935, by announcing to armed forces commanders that it was not desirable for Wehrmacht personnel to buy from "non-Aryan" shops. The navy sent this order along to its garrisons five days later without additional comment. Toward the end of 1935, in the wake of increased anti-Semitic agitation associated with the Nuremberg Laws, the War Ministry announced that all officers and officials who had not yet produced proof of "Aryan" descent would have to do so now, or else leave the armed forces. This time, the navy waited two weeks to issue the order; it cannot be determined whether the delay was occasioned by the forlorn hope that the disagreeable problem would go away, or by simple bureaucratic laziness.[57]

By the end of 1935, therefore, the War Ministry was hardening its stand against the Jews. Many officers in the Kriegsmarine were inwardly troubled by this development, and there are indications that some officers, both young and old, continued to remember fondly the past contributions that Jews had made to the navy—in spite of the Party's attempt to discredit their overall role in German history.[58] Other officers suffered the persecution of their erstwhile comrades in silence, perhaps waiting for an opportune moment to make their misgivings known to the head of the navy. Yet, if the report of one officer is any indication of the sentiments within the corps, some of the naval officers swallowed completely the party line concerning the alleged "Jewish threat." In December 1935, a Captain Lohmann returned from a semiofficial trip to South Africa filled with notions that sounded remarkably similar to those that were being broadcast within Germany by the Propaganda Ministry. Lohmann reported that there were said to be more Jews in Johannesburg—80,000 in all—than in any city of the world save New York, and that their monetary contribution to the Zionist cause was second only to that of the New Yorkers.[59] The South African radio, Lohmann continued, was entirely in Jewish hands. The pernicious influence of the Jews, however, did not stop there. Samuel Untermeyer, the president of the World Sectarian Anti-Nazi Council (which Lohmann simply termed the "Jewish Boycott Movement"), was reputed to have set up an office in Johannesburg, and it was also reported that Jews and Communists were seeking to propagandize among the blacks of South Africa, presumably in an attempt to incite them against the local "Aryan" minority.[60] Yet, if all this sounded daunting to Lohmann or his audience, there was a silver lining to the cloud that the captain had conjured. Precisely because of the large Jewish role in South Africa, Lohmann continued, a strong anti-Semitism was also present there.

Thus, opinion toward the Jews would seem to have been divided within the officer corps. In the face of this, many officers may well have looked toward their commander-in-chief for some indication as to the course that they ought to take with regard to the "Jewish question." Unfortunately, by the middle to late 1930s Raeder would appear to have been just as confused on this matter as his subordinates. He continued to retain some especially fortunate officers of "non-Aryan" background within the Service either by making use of exceptions granted by the War Ministry,[61] or by evoking his rival Hermann Göring's celebrated maxim: "I decide who is a Jew." In addition, he continued to intervene privately for friends and acquaintances who had fallen victim to the anti-Semitic legislation enacted by the Reich government. Finally, when indignation among some of the most prominent leaders of the officer corps—men such as Foerster, Patzig, Lütjens, and Dönitz—threatened to erupt after the infamous *Reichs-Kristallnacht* in November 1938, Raeder brought their protestations to Hitler's attention.[62]

Yet, beyond these by no means insignificant measures Raeder could not or would not go. By his own account, he feared drawing the navy into what he called the "crossfire of domestic politics." On the one occasion when he did express his misgivings to Hitler in the wake of *Kristallnacht*, he allowed his protest to be deflected by the Führer's patently absurd explanation that the excesses of the regime were occurring against his will and without his knowledge.[63] As a result, whatever palliatives Raeder chose to apply remained of a distinctly limited nature and were confined to a private group of subordinates and acquaintances. Nor did Raeder's official actions always reinforce the moderating influence that he allegedly sought to exert upon Hitler and other party leaders behind the scenes. To the end of his tenure, the naval command continued to pass the anti-Semitic measures of the Party and the *Wehrmachtführung* on to the fleet with precious little in the way of comment or delay that might have discreetly informed the rank and file of the Service as to what their admiral actually thought about the "Jewish question." Indeed, when the occasion warranted, Raeder found that he could parrot the language of the Reich Chancellery and Propaganda Ministry to perfection. In a Memorial Day speech of March 12, 1939, he publicly embraced the ideology of the Party once again and enthusiastically seconded "the clear and merciless declaration of war against the Bolsheviks and international Jewry, whose destructive drive we have felt in abundance within our own body politic."[64] It was small wonder, therefore, that Hitler had little difficulty in rebuffing the admiral on those occasions when Raeder's conscience stirred him to action.

Notes to Chapter 6

1 As Raeder noted in the spring of 1938, the most tonnage that had ever been under construction at any one time during the Wilhelmian era had been 200,000t, whereas the Kriegsmarine was now struggling with a burden of 520,000t. Jost Dülffer, *Weimar, Hitler und die Marine: Reichspolitik und Flottenbau 1920–1939* (Düsseldorf, 1973), pp. 457–458.
2 There is no comprehensive account of the physical rebuilding of the navy in the 1930s. Dülffer's *Hitler und die Marine*, however, contains useful information and provides the basis for the following analysis of the navy's problems.
3 For a contemporary account of the navy's surreptitious efforts to continue development of submarine technology, see the report of 1937 by a Captain Schüssler, "Der Kampf der Marine gegen Versailles," in International Military Tribunal, *Trial of the Major War Criminals before the International Tribunal*, 42 vols (Nuremberg, 1947–1949) (hereafter cited as IMT), 34, pp. 552–565.
4 Dülffer, *Hitler und die Marine*, pp. 428–434, 568–569.
5 The text of the Military Code is provided in Rudolf Absolon, *Die Wehrmacht im Dritten Reich*, 4 vols (Boppard am Rhein, 1969–), 3, pp. 342–378. "Non-Aryans" were defined as those who had a parent or a grandparent who was a "non-Aryan" and in particular a Jew. Article 15, Paragraph 2, of the code foresaw certain exceptions to the general prohibition against "non-Aryans," which accounts for the otherwise superfluous stipulation in Paragraph 3 that only "Aryans"

could occupy positions of command. Paragraph 4 prohibited marriages between "Aryan" members of the Wehrmacht and "non-Aryans," whereas Paragraph 5 foresaw the possibility of special duty for "non-Aryans" in the event of war.

6 Article 26, Paragraphs 1 and 2. Other relevant portions of Article 26 included the stipulation that soldiers had to obtain permission from their superiors before becoming members of any organization, both within and without the Wehrmacht, and the provision that allowed the War Minister to include Wehrmacht officials and employees under the restrictions announced in Paragraphs 1 and 2. As will be seen, Blomberg made only sparing use of the latter provision.

7 Bundesarchiv-Militärarchiv, Freiburg, West Germany (hereafter cited as BA-MA), RM 8/57 Nr. 3239/35 J I a, June 21, 1935. See the differing interpretations placed upon these measures in Robert J. O'Neill, *The German Army and the Nazi Party, 1933–1939* (London, 1966), p. 69, and Manfred Messerschmidt, *Die Wehrmacht im NS Staat: Zeit der Indoktrination* (Hamburg, 1969), p. 94.

8 BA-MA, RW 4/841 Nr. 1390/35 Geh. L II d, July 22, 1935; BA-MA, RM 8/57 Der Reichskriegsminister und Oberfehlshaber der Wehrmacht, September 10, 1935. Membership in the SA, the SS, the NSKK, and the Hitler Youth continued to be prohibited. Blomberg also reminded his subordinates that they were still bound by his earlier injunction to treat Wehrmacht information as confidential.

9 See BA-MA, RM 8/57 B. Nr. MZ 1393, July 9, 1935; B. Nr. 1989 MZ, October 1, 1935; B. Nr. 1476 MZ, July 22, 1935; B. Nr. 1625 MZ I, August 30, 1935; B. Nr. 13971 C I, October 23, 1935; B. Nr. 2510 M Allg., November 30, 1935.

10 BA-MA, RW 6/160 Nr. 5848/35 J IV b, November 4, 1935; B. Nr. 8462 A V c, November 23, 1935.

11 BA-MA, RW 6/160 B. Nr. 9643/35 A V c, January 9, 1935; also Abschrift zur B. Nr. 9643/35 A V c. Among the works cited were three decrees by Blomberg or Raeder which drew the attention of the cadets to important statements by Hitler on various aspects of National Socialism; two works by Adolf von Trotha, who by 1935 had become a relatively important figure in the Party; Hermann Foertsch's *Der Offizier in der neuen Wehrmacht* (Berlin, 1935); and Hitler's *Mein Kampf*. In addition, the list indicated that the work of Commander Siegfried Sorge, which will be analyzed later in this chapter, was being used in manuscript form for the edification of the midshipmen.

12 BA-MA, RW 6/160 Nr. 5848/35 J IV b, Entwurf, January 30, 1936.

13 For Trotha's problems with the National Socialist editor of the *Flensburger Nachrichten* prior to June 30, 1934, see BA-MA, RW 6/67 Teil 1.

14 BA-MA, M 80 [E]. The films included *Stander Z vor, Einer zuviel an Bord*, and *Auf grosser Fahrt*. Lectures included one on the "The Meaning of Reich Labor Service." The production with the greatest ideological content might well have been a play performed by the Niederdeutsche Bühne, Flensburg, entitled *Der Etappen Hase*, (very loosely, "The Trench Rabbit"), a story from the Great War which depicted the resentment of the "front soldier" toward the "jackasses in the rear echelons."

15 BA-MA, M 80 [E], Standorttagesbefehl Nr. 8, Flensburg-Mürwik, March 13, 1936; B. Nr. 617 March 13, 1936; B. Nr. 904, April 17, 1936; Standorttagesbefehl Nr. 28, May 15, 1936.

16 One possible explanation for this may have been the navy's ambitious ceremonies at Kiel marking the twentieth anniversary of the Battle of the Skagerrak that May (see below), and the Olympic Games, which took place in Berlin and Kiel that August. Both of these events were heavily laden with party propaganda, and the local party stalwarts in the backwaters of Flensburg may well have been unable or unwilling to compete with these larger attractions.

17 BA-MA, M 80 [E], B. Nr. 2442, Flensburg-Mürwik, October 3, 1936; Standorttagesbefehl Nr. 62, October 12, 1936; Standorttagesbefehl Nr. 63, October 16, 1936.

18 *Völkischer Beobachter*, Munich edition, May 29, 30, 1936. Another account of the festivities is given by Rear Admiral (E) Malerholz in *MOV–Nachrichten* 18, No. 12 (June 15, 1936), pp. 204–208.

19 For the ceremonies and Raeder's address, see the *Völkischer Beobachter*, Munich edition, May 31/June 1, 1936; also BA-MA, RM 8/58, "Rede des Oberbefehlshabers der Kriegsmarine anlässlich des Staatsaktes in Laboe am 30. 5. 1936."

20 *Völkischer Beobachter*, Munich edition, May 31/June 1, 1936. For Litzmann's death and Hitler's remarks on the merits of the memorial, see Max Domarus, *Hitler, Reden und Proklamationen, 1932–1945*, 2 vols (Munich, 1965), 1, p. 624. For reports that a party official had not been properly greeted during the festivities, see BA-MA, RM 8/58 B. Nr. 1226 M II, June 4, 1936.

21 *Völkischer Beobachter*, Munich edition, June 12, 13, 1936. For Albrecht's and Behrens' difficulties in 1934, see above, Chapter 4, n. 51.

22 *Völkischer Beobachter*, Munich edition, June 15, 1936.

23 A list of the naval officers, who ranged in rank from lieutenant commander to captain, is provided in BA-MA, RW 6/161. The program for the course is given in BA-MA, RM 8/59 OKM B. Nr. 314 A V c, January 14, 1937.

24 BA-MA, RW 6/165 J (II), "Sonderlehrgang für Schulung in national-sozialistischer Weltanschauung im Reichslager der NSDAP zu Bad Tölz vom 27. 1.–4. 2. 1939;" OKM B. Nr. 15524 M Wehr I c, January 16, 1939; BA-MA, Nordseestations Tagesbefehl Nr. 21 Ziffer III, January 26, 1939.

25 The responses by army officers are given in BA-MA, RW 6/165, "Erfahrungsbericht über den Offz. Lehrgang v. 27. 1.–4. 2. 1939 im Reichslager der NSDAP, Bad Tölz."

26 Siegfried Sorge, *Der Marineoffizier als Führer und Erzieher* (Berlin, 1937).

27 Friedrich Ruge, "Ausbildung zum Seeoffizier," *Marine-Rundschau*, 37 (1932), pp. 101–110.

28 For the background to Sorge's book, see Dieter Stockfisch, "Der Marineoffizier als Führer und Erzieher: Gedanken zu einem Offizier-handbuch aus der Kriegsmarine," *Marineforum*, 50 (1975), pp. 156–157.

29 Ibid.

30 Sorge, *Marineoffizier als Führer und Erzieher*, pp. 15, 79–80.

31 Ibid., pp. 22–23, 126–127.

32 Ibid., pp. 61–62. Sorge likewise advised officers to use *Mein Kampf* and the collection of Hitler's speeches published by the Eher-Verlag when selecting material for lectures to enlisted men. Ibid., p. 146.

33 Ibid., pp. 62–67.

34 Ibid., pp. 70, 127, 145.

35 Ibid., pp. 117, 130.
36 Cited in Messerschmidt, *Wehrmacht im NS Staat*, p. 162.
37 Ibid., p. 163.
38 Mention must be made in passing of two other naval histories: Captain Hellmuth Heye, *Die Deutsche Kriegsmarine: Aufgaben und Aufbau* (Berlin, 1939), and Lieutenant Commander Friedrich Giese, *Von Scapa Flow zur Kriegsmarine Grossdeutschlands* (Berlin, 1939). Although Heye was by no means enamored with all aspects of National Socialism (see below, Chapter 7), both he and Giese adopted Raeder's by now familiar litany of Scapa Flow, naval rebirth, and *Freikorps* experience, and dovetailed these with the later triumph of National Socialism. For those who remembered the mutual suspicions of the Party's and the navy's leaders in the period before the *Machtergreifung*, this must have seemed a considerable literary achievement.
39 BA-MA, RM 8/59 B. Nr. 865 M Allg., March 25, 1937, which reminded the Berlin departments of Raeder's order of September 7, 1936; Stockfisch, "Gedanken zu einem Offizierhandbuch," p. 157.
40 BA-MA, RM 8/57 B. Nr. MZ 1292, June 26, 1935; Werner Bräckow, *Die Geschichte des deutschen Marine-Ingenieuroffizierkorps* (Oldenburg and Hamburg, 1974), pp. 231, 353; BA-MA, RM 8/59 OKM circular, May 3, 1937; BA-MA, RM 8/57 B. Nr. 2529 M II, December 3, 1935; BA-MA, RM 8/61 B. Nr. 594 M, February 28, 1939.
41 At the same time, however, a certain aloofness on the part of the War Ministry and the naval high command toward the Party's paramilitary units remained evident. On March 1, 1938, for example, the navy's Berlin office informed its officers that attendance at a lecture by SS Oberführer Ing. Rudolf Jung was not desired because he "pursued goals which contradicted those of the Oberkommando der Wehrmacht." BA-MA, RM 8/60 B. Nr. 605 M Allg., March 1, 1938. See also BA-MA, RM 8/60 B. Nr. 605 II M Allg., March 4, 1938, for a similar prohibition of attendance at a lecture by an SA Standartenführer Krebs.
42 Messerschmidt, *Wehrmacht im NS Staat*, pp. 108–110.
43 Ibid., pp. 62–63, 151. For the propaganda companies, see below, Chapter 8.
44 For an analysis of party and church relations, see John S. Conway, *The Nazi Persecution of the Churches, 1933–1945* (New York, 1968). Messerschmidt, *Wehrmacht im NS Staat*, pp. 171–199, has useful information on the role of religion in the relationship between the armed forces and the Party. For the "German Christians," see Kurt Meier, *Die Deutschen Christen: Das Bild einer Bewegung im Kirchenkampf des Dritten Reiches* (Halle, Saale, 1964).
45 Erich Raeder, *Mein Leben*, 2 vols (Tübingen, 1956–1957), 2, pp. 144–145. See also BA-MA, RM 20/870 II Ftge. Einschreiben, "An den Konteradmiral und Chef der Marinestation der Nordsee, Herrn Otto Schultze, Wilhelmshaven." A brief analysis of the "German Faith Movement" is provided in Hans Buchheim, *Glaubenskrise im Dritten Reich: Drei Kapitel Nationalsozialistischer Religionspolitik* (Stuttgart, 1953), pp. 157–204.
46 The text of the encyclical is given in *The Persecution of the Catholic Church in the Third Reich: Facts and Documents, translated from the German* (London, 1940), pp. 523–537.
47 BA-MA, RM 8/57 B. Nr. 1615 MZ, August 16, 1935, which passes B. Nr. 4797 A V c, July 19, 1935 on to the Berlin offices of the navy.

48 Messerschmidt, *Wehrmacht im NS Staat*, pp. 189–190, 198.
49 Raeder, *Mein Leben*, 2, p. 147; BA-MA, RW 6/128 Kommando der Marinestation der Nordsee, Buch Nr. P 3808 P I, March 9, 1938; OKW Nr. 651/38geh. J (Ic), March 29, 1938; OKM B. Nr. 3935 M Wehr II b, July 15, 1938; OKW Az 31811 J (Ic) 615/38 geh., July 1938.
50 BA-MA, RM 91/7 OKW B. Nr. I p J (Ic), July 1, 1939; OKM B. Nr. 1937g. M Wehr II b 1939, July 8, 1939. Raeder, *Mein Leben*, 2, p. 145.
51 Messerschmidt, *Wehrmacht im NS Staat*, pp. 189–190.
52 Raeder, *Mein Leben*, 2, pp. 141–142. When the admiral was asked to intervene on behalf of Niemöller by members of the Reichsbund der deutschen evangelischen Pfarrervereine, he answered: "Due to considerations of principle, I regret that I am unable to take up the matter of Pastor Niemöller, since I can only disapprove of his behavior, which has damaged the Evangelical Church severely." Cited in Friedrich Zipfel, *Kirchenkampf in Deutschland, 1933–1945: Religionsverfolgung und Selbstbehauptung der Kirche in der Nationalsozialistischen Zeit* (Berlin, 1965), p. 103, n. 130.
53 Raeder, *Mein Leben*, 2, p. 144.
54 Marinestabszahlmeister a.D. Fritz Brennecke, "Die Reichsmarine im Jahre 1935," *MOV-Nachrichten*, 18, No. 2 (January 15, 1936), p. 11.
55 See Captain (ret.) Paul Ebert, "Seefahrt, Lebensraum, and Rasse," *MOV-Nachrichten*, 18, No. 21 (November 1, 1936), pp. 349–353; also the review of Friedrich Burgdörfer's *Völker am Abgrund* in ibid., p. 360; also the review of Paul Bang's *Die farbige Gefahr* in *MOV-Nachrichten*, 20, No. 19 (October 1, 1938), p. 312.
56 The text of the Nuremberg Laws is given in Kurt Meier, *Kirche und Judentum: Die Haltung der evangelischen Kirche zur Judenpolitik des Dritten Reiches* (Göttingen, 1966), pp. 66–67.
57 BA-MA, RM 8/57 Der Reichskriegsminister und Oberbefehlshaber der Wehrmacht, July 15, 1935; B. Nr. 1449 M Z I, July 20, 1935; Nr. 6553/35 J I c, November 27, 1935; B. Nr. 2580 M Allg., December 11, 1935.
58 See the notes that Eberhard Weichold took during a lecture by Admiral (ret.) Eberhard von Mantey at the Marineakademie on November 5, 1936, concerning Admiral Felix Bendemann of the Imperial Navy, in BA-MA, N 316/61 Nachlass Weichold, "Aufzeichnungen aus Vorträgen über das Offizierkorps der Kaiserlichen Marine von Admiral a.D. von Mantey."
59 BA-MA, RM 6/235, "Auszug aus dem Bericht des Kapitän zur See Lohmann über seine Berufsbelehrungsreise um Africa vom 14. 8.–18. 12. 1935." This was not the same Lohmann of the "Lohmann Affair" of 1927–1928.
60 Samuel Untermeyer (1858–1940) was the first president of the World Sectarian Anti-Nazi Council. Founded in Amsterdam in 1934, the council hoped to secure a change in German policy toward the Jews and other minorities by organizing a world-wide boycott of German goods.
61 Raeder, *Mein Leben*, 2, p. 132; Friedrich Ruge, "Erich Raeder zum hundersten Geburtstag: Seeoffizier—Oberbefehlshaber—Mensch," *Marineforum*, 51 (1976), p. 91; BA-MA, N 172/31 Nachlass Boehm. Draft of a letter to the *Frankfurter Allgemeine Zeitung*, 1961.
62 Raeder, *Mein Leben*, 2, pp. 133, 338–339; Ruge, "Erich Raeder," p. 91.
63 See Raeder, *Mein Leben*, 2, pp. 133–134.
64 Excerpts from Raeder's address are reprinted in IMT, 34, pp. 310–312.

7

Changing Times: From the Anglo-German Naval Agreement to the Outbreak of War, June 1935–September 1939

The Party's intrusions into the administrative prerogatives of the War Ministry and the Kriegsmarine, its increasingly visible campaign against the Christian Church in Germany, and its vehement stand against the Jews were all disturbing signs of the direction that developments were taking for the navy by the end of the 1930s. Overshadowing all other matters during this period, however, was the increasingly ominous nature of National Socialist foreign policy.[1] As Hitler continued to proceed from one astonishing triumph to another, a coalition of anxious European states began to take shape that was increasingly concerned about the rising power and bellicosity of the Reich. At the head of this coalition was Great Britain, a timid and sometimes unwilling leader, but nevertheless the one power that the Kriegsmarine, in its present state of unreadiness, was totally unprepared to fight. The primary question on the minds of Raeder and the other leaders of the navy in the latter half of the 1930s, therefore, was whether the protective mantle offered by the Anglo-German Naval Agreement since the summer of 1935 would last until the navy was sufficiently strong to challenge Britain with reasonable prospects of success, or whether the Kriegsmarine, like the Imperial Navy before it, would be drawn into war before it was ready.

At first, it appeared as if developments would favor the navy. Although some technical difficulties arose over implementing the agreement of June 1935, these were overcome in a matter of weeks through firm but friendly bargaining by both sides. A new problem emerged when French objections to German participation (and the Kriegsmarine's own reservations concerning the advisability of entering into multilateral limitations on armaments) necessitated the Reich's absence from the

166

London Naval Conference the following winter. This potentially explosive situation was defused through an arrangement whereby British representatives kept the German naval attaché in London informed of all deliberations. Although the results of the conference were exceedingly meager in any case, Germany privately assured Britain that it would abide by the one significant decision that had been reached, an agreement to institute a "building holiday" for the next few years on the construction of heavy cruisers.[2] Nor were these the only indications of a continuing spirit of cooperation between the navies of the British Empire and the Third Reich. On November 23, 1936, Germany signed the so-called London Protocol, which bound the signatory states to respect "Prize Law" in waging submarine warfare. This measure promised to restrict considerably the effectiveness of the U-boat as a strategic weapon, and it did much to allay the fears of a British public that remembered the Imperial Navy's submarine campaign during the Great War.[3] Finally, on July 17, 1937, Germany and Britain signed another Naval Agreement that pledged the two nations to exchange technical information as to the size of their respective building programs. Although one German officer later asserted that the only practical effect of the agreement was that each side obtained the other's information more swiftly and at less expense than with traditional methods of espionage, that the two nations could continue to negotiate in an amicable fashion offered at least a modicum of hope for the future.[4]

This notwithstanding, a number of developments were occurring beneath the surface that would eventually undermine the fragile understanding between the two navies. Some of these were admittedly beyond the purview of either Service,[5] while others stemmed from the curious dual role that the Royal Navy continued to play privately in the minds of many German naval officers both as a model and potential ally, and as a potential enemy.[6] Yet, the most important factor by far in the eventual deterioration of the relationship between the two navies was without question the new turn in foreign policy taken by Hitler.

Hitler had spent the first two years after his assumption of power working for a special relationship with Britain that would allow him to realize his plans to acquire *Lebensraum* on the European continent while concurrently allowing Britain a free hand in the overseas world. By 1935, with the signing of the Anglo-German Naval Agreement, he clearly believed that he was well on the way to attaining such an accommodation. But after June 1935, it became increasingly obvious that Anglo-German relations were headed toward a dead end. Having made what they considered to be a concession in allowing the Reich to rearm beyond the limits of the Treaty of Versailles, British diplomats now sought to draw Germany back into the framework of the League of Nations. Hitler, by contrast, was convinced that Germany had made the major sacrifice by limiting its naval construction to a fraction of that of the British, and he now sought repayment in the form of British acquiescence in his plans on the Continent. Both sides were disappointed in their expectations. After a period of waiting, Hitler decided to try a different tack. A series of unilateral actions on the part of Germany would strengthen the Reich's position and emphasize its immense value as an ally.[7] At the same time, these measures would allow Hitler to test the mettle of British statesmen. Being the reasonable, kindred race that they were, the British would surely recognize the folly of opposing Germany and join it instead.

The first step to implement Hitler's overall "program" occurred on March 7, 1936, when German troops reoccupied the previously demilitarized Rhineland.[8] The British did not energetically oppose this measure, but neither did they display any indication that they had grasped the wisdom of Hitler's position. In the next few months, therefore, Hitler seized other opportunities to demonstrate the Reich's newly found freedom of action. That spring, he took firm control of the previously neglected colonial movement within Germany, thereby permitting him to emphasize or deemphasize the Reich's unresolved demand for colonies as the occasion warranted. In this way, he hoped to put pressure on the British and thus to wring concessions from them.[9] In July 1936, Germany came out openly on the side of the insurgent armies of Generalissimo Francisco Franco in Spain. That fall, the Reich arrived at a loose agreement with Italy—the basis for the famous "Rome–Berlin Axis"—and secured Japanese acceptance of the Anti-Comintern Pact. Nominally, neither of these most recent measures greatly concerned Great Britain, but privately, Hitler's message to London appeared clear. Britain could either join the coalition of states that was materializing under German leadership or it could oppose it. In the world struggle that must inevitably come there could be no middle ground.[10]

Naval considerations also played a role in this new policy of exerting pressure upon Great Britain. In May 1936, less than three months after the conclusion of the London Naval Conference, Germany threatened to renege on its promise to abide by the "building holiday" on heavy cruisers by announcing its intention to build two more vessels of this type in addition to the three that were already under construction. Ever dependent upon the security of its sea communications, Britain reacted with considerably more alarm than it had displayed in the case of the Rhineland. Hitler appears to have concluded that this was not the best way to win over the British and, in November 1936, he and Raeder arrived at a cosmetic solution whereby the two new ships were announced as light cruisers and then built surreptitiously as heavy ones. Since it was unlikely that British naval observers would long be deceived by this measure, Germany informed them that it might be necessary to upgrade the armament of the vessels at a later date.[11]

By the time the navy extricated itself from this imbroglio, another potential area of conflict had emerged in the form of the Reich's intervention in favor of Franco's forces in Spain.[12] Here, too, the navy's role was important, for not only did the Kriegsmarine take responsibility for chartering the freighters that carried the flow of military supplies and "advisors" to Spain, but its warships provided their sea escort until they reached the security of Nationalist-controlled waters. In August 1936—the same month that the first of these transports left Germany for Spain—the Reich announced its intention to join the British-sponsored Non-Intervention Committee, whose aim was to stop foreign supplies from reaching either side in the Spanish conflict. For the next two and one-half years, the Reich publicly supported the fiction of nonintervention, while privately helping the Nationalists to victory. The low point in this international farce occurred between April and June 1937, when Germany sent warships to participate in an international naval patrol sponsored by the Non-Intervention Committee. In the Mediterranean Sea, German and Italian patrols searched diligently for vessels bound for Republican ports, while in the Atlantic, Kriegsmarine warships helped their own freighters, now disguised under Panamanian registry, elude Anglo-French patrols and reach Nationalist ports.[13] Although the British government was willing to tolerate this state of affairs, the charade evidently became too much for Hitler, the acknowledged master of deception, and on June 23, after incidents with Republican air and naval forces involving the *Deutschland* and the *Leipzig*, Germany withdrew from the international naval patrol.[14] German warships would remain assigned to Spanish waters until 1939, however. Although the relationship between the Kriegsmarine and the Royal Navy does not appear to have suffered as greatly as that between the British and Italian navies (the latter of whose submarines were responsible for sinking a number of British merchantmen on the high seas), the potential for conflict had always been there. Reflective British officers, moreover, might well have regretted this tailor-made opportunity for the Kriegsmarine to gain tactical and logistical experience under near battle conditions far from home.

Both the issue of the new heavy cruisers and the question of the Kriegsmarine's involvement in Spain demonstrated the fragility of the Service's relationship with the Royal Navy. Yet, despite these forewarnings of trouble, naval officers were reluctant to draw the conclusion that Britain might head the list of possible opponents in a war in the immediate future. Throughout the mid-1930s, the navy's *Kriegsspiele* (war games), which usually endeavored to consider theoretical conflicts with the most likely enemies of the Reich, foresaw a two-front war with France and the Soviet Union and posited British neutrality. The Service's Provisional Battle Instructions, issued in May 1936, stated flatly that the high command could issue no directives as to how any future war with Britain ought to be fought because the navy's position in such a confrontation would be hopeless. In the fall of that year, Fregattenkapitän Hellmuth Heye, the First Operations Officer at the Seekriegsleitung (as the navy's command center in Berlin was now termed), reiterated this position when he concluded that British neutrality was essential to any chance of success by the navy.[15]

By the following spring, this picture was changing. To be sure, the navy still fervently desired British neutrality in the event of war on the

Continent, but many officers were becoming increasingly resentful of the price that the Kriegsmarine appeared to be paying to assure this neutrality. The lapsing on January 1, 1937, of the qualitative restrictions of the Washington Naval Treaty, which had established the initial system of ratios among the Powers, left Germany as the only nation still bound by a percentage system; many officers deplored what they considered to be a British yoke. Moreover, difficulties in projecting British naval strength three to four years in advance led to problems in establishing the Service's own building program, which was directly dependent upon that of the Royal Navy. This, in turn, fostered a suspicion on the part of Raeder that the British were intentionally underestimating their naval construction in order to reduce the size of the Kriegsmarine.[16] For his part, the navy's commander-in-chief inadvertently strengthened British suspicions when he pressed for the fastest possible tempo in expanding the navy. Such measures may well have been directed against powers other than Britain—in February 1937, for example, Raeder argued that the fleet might be decisive in a war against France and Russia and asked the Führer for greater priority for the navy in the field of armaments[17]—but British observers must nevertheless have wondered whether Hitler and Raeder intended to stop when they reached that magical figure of 35 per cent of the Royal Navy.

By the spring of 1937, then, naval considerations were contributing to the gradual deterioration of Anglo-German relations. In March, the Kommandoamt produced a study of future German shipbuilding programs that seemed to presuppose a period of continued peace lasting until 1942, if not longer, but by May, the assessment was decidedly more pessimistic. France and Russia remained the most likely opponents, but in a new study aimed at assisting the high command in drawing up revised Battle Instructions, Fregattenkapitän Heye now saw fit to include England as a potential opponent for the first time. Heye, as he had the year before, once again pointed out that the navy had no chance in a war with Britain. The only solution that he could propose was for Germany to form an alliance with one of the larger continental powers, either France or Russia. Yet these were precisely the Reich's most likely opponents in any future war. Heye therefore avoided making a hard choice and simply placed the matter in the hands of the political leadership: "Although the soldier is not excused from the duty of confronting the existing political situation and the possibilities of conflict that emerge from it, he must demand that the politician create favorable conditions for battle." Herewith, the navy had squared the circle and returned to the indecision of 1914.[18]

Heye's study evoked considerable interest among the navy's leaders. Otto Schultze, chief of the North Sea Station, was appalled by the prospect of a war against Britain, and he cautioned that it was "dangerous even to speak of this possibility in an official memorandum." Like Heye, he felt that the political leadership would have to be informed of this fact. Conrad Albrecht, chief of the Baltic Station, was equally pessimistic, and he drew an additional conclusion that Heye had perhaps

170

realized but had been reluctant to state. It was true, Albrecht wrote, that the coalition of France and Russia was the maximum combination of powers that Germany could hope to defeat, but this was no longer the most likely scenario, for, in all probability, Britain would enter any war against the Reich. But two of Raeder's leading lieutenants either failed to grasp the immensity of the change wrought by the addition of Great Britain to the list of possible enemies, or else seized the opportunity to revive the earlier demands of Wolfgang Wegener that Germany counter hostile British moves by expanding into Scandinavia. Fleet chief Rolf Carls noted that if England joined the opposition, all previous restraints that the Reich had exercised with regard to Denmark were removed. Wilhelm Marschall, head of the Operations Department, was of the opinion that Danish neutrality was preferable to occupation, but he added that if the high command did decide to take Denmark, it should throw in Norway for good measure.[19]

Thus, the navy was considering the possibility of war with Britain even as its representatives signed the Second Anglo–German Naval Agreement on July 17, 1937. Raeder and his advisors nevertheless continued to hope that this eventuality would not materialize until the navy was fully prepared. In the meantime, it was important that the Kriegsmarine continue its rearmament so as to be ready for the two-front war with France and Russia, which remained the official dogma of most naval planners. For a variety of reasons, though, the navy's building program continued to lag behind schedule. Both raw materials and workers were in short supply, and the slipways for two of the battleships that the Kriegsmarine hoped to complete by 1944 did not even exist. In 1938, moreover, the navy would be able to launch only one cruiser and one aircraft carrier instead of the two battleships, two cruisers, and two carriers that it had originally planned. As it now stood, the Kriegsmarine's position was a desperate one, and on October 25 Raeder appealed to Blomberg for a decision by the Führer that might give the navy a higher priority in the nation's rearmament scheme.[20]

Hitler was evidently receptive to Raeder's suggestion. On the after-noon of November 5, 1937, he convened a meeting of his closest military and diplomatic advisors—Blomberg, Fritsch, Göring, Neurath, and Raeder—to discuss the problem.[21] Before turning to the ostensible reason for the meeting, however, the Führer addressed the larger questions of diplomacy that were on his mind. He explained that the essence of the Reich's foreign policy must be to preserve and to enlarge the *Volksmasse*. Since this could be attained neither by a policy of autarky nor by dependence upon foreign trade, the acquisition of *Lebensraum* in the east was essential to any future policy. This would not necessarily be an easy task, for the "attacker" would always come upon a "possessor." In addition, he stated, Germany would have to reckon with two "hate-inspired antagonists," Britain and France, which could be expected to oppose the expansion of the Reich. But, at the moment, a number of factors were working in Germany's favor. Britain was already facing problems with its empire. France would probably encounter domestic unrest in the not too distant future. Moreover, Germany presently enjoyed an advantage in military preparedness, thanks to the rearmament program that the National Socialists had pursued since 1933, and it would be a number of years before the Western democracies could catch up in this field. It was therefore Hitler's unalterable decision that Germany solve the question of *Lebensraum* by the years 1943–45 at the latest, before its relative advantage over France and Britain disappeared.

What sort of a solution did Hitler have in mind? The first step was to be the seizure of Austria and Czechoslovakia at the earliest possible moment, before 1943–45, if opportunities presented themselves. The Führer was convinced that swiftness on the part of the Reich and divisions within the camp of the Great Powers would prevent their intervention on behalf of either of the threatened states. Moreover, he seemed confident that the army and air force, both of which he deemed ready for action, would suffice for the short, localized wars that he envisioned against Germany's weaker neighbors.

Hitler was less specific about what was to follow the incorporation of Austria and Czechoslovakia into the Reich. One thing, however, was certain: by 1943–45, all three branches of the armed forces would have to be prepared for a lengthy war, for by then, the Führer intended to embark on a solution to the problem of *Lebensraum* that would last "for one or two generations." For the moment, Hitler declined to mention the new targets of German aggression by name, but in view of his repeated pronouncements from the mid-1920s on, he could have intended only one course of action: a war of expansion against the Soviet Union or Poland or the two states in combination. If the Western powers were foolish enough to try to intervene, then Germany's land, air, and naval forces (the last of which would have been greatly expanded by 1943) would fend them off until the great work of conquest had been completed in the east. By then, the Greater German Reich would presumably possess a sufficiently large land mass to be invulnerable to any and all attempts at a maritime blockade, the likes of which had brought Imperial Germany to its knees in the Great War. In the distant future, it might prove necessary to undertake additional territorial expansion overseas—the world power phase of the Hitlerian scheme—but for the moment, on November 5, 1937, the Führer was content to leave this final task to future generations of Germans.

It is possible (and indeed likely) that Hitler's advisors remained unaware of the ultimate extent of his plans for continental and overseas expansion. In any case, most members of Hitler's audience on November 5 were not nearly as confident as their Führer and, indeed, even professed to see difficulties with the initial phase of German expansion, which, according to Hitler's calculations, ought to have been the one least fraught with danger. Foreign Minister von Neurath remained skeptical concerning the likelihood of an Anglo-French war with Italy, upon which Hitler placed many of his hopes for Western nonintervention in a German-Czech war; Generals von Blomberg and von Fritsch stated that even if a Mediterranean war did ensue, it could not be expected to draw off many French troops. Both generals emphasized repeatedly that Britain and France must not be allowed to appear as the common enemies of the Reich. And while Göring attempted to make a bold show by attacking the opinions of the generals, he, too, betrayed perhaps a touch of timidity when he suggested that if war in the east was likely, then the Reich ought to consider liquidating its commitments in Spain beforehand.

Of all the participants, Raeder alone had nothing to say. Many years later, he explained this silence by recounting that he had been forewarned by Göring that Hitler was merely trying to spur the army generals on to greater diligence in their rearmament program; consequently, he concluded that the Führer's warlike pronouncements were intended only for show. Leaving aside the question of why Raeder would have believed anything that Göring told him—the navy and the air force were currently vying for control over the naval air arm—a more likely explanation for the admiral's reticence was his desire to save his thunder for the second part of the conference, when the all-important question of the navy's rearmament program was to be taken up. If so, Raeder was not disappointed. That afternoon, Hitler decided that the navy would receive a substantially increased quota of steel and that additional allocations would go to the Krupp concern to enable it to build a large mill at Salzgitter, which would further increase the navy's future steel supply.[22]

Hitler's decision in favor of an expanded naval building program doubtless gave Raeder cause for satisfaction with his performance at the Reich Chancellery that November afternoon.[23] But the admiral had even greater reason to congratulate himself on his silence two months later, when Blomberg and Fritsch, the two men who had objected most strenuously to Hitler's immediate timetable on November 5, were removed from their positions. Although Blomberg's resignation was occasioned largely by factors other than his reluctance to implement the Führer's plans,[24] there can be little doubt that Fritsch's lack of enthusiasm for what Hitler had to say was instrumental in setting off the bizarre chain of events that led to his departure in January 1938. When the Gestapo reopened a highly suspect charge that Fritsch was a homosexual, Hitler, who just three years before had piously declared that his faith in the Wehrmacht leadership was unshakable, now reversed his position and announced that he would personally assume the overall functions of the War Minister. Wilhelm Keitel, a man whom Blomberg had once rather condescendingly described as "the man who runs my office," would assist the Führer with the paper work, while Walter von Brauchitsch would be the new head of the army. In a single stroke, Hitler had arrogated to himself the prerogatives that had been his in theory, if not in fact, since the death of Hindenburg.[25]

This sordid interlude seems to have caused Raeder only a minimum of concern. To be sure, his sense of fair play prompted him to support energetically Fritsch's efforts to prove himself innocent of the charge that had been leveled against him, but until this had happened, there could be no question in Raeder's mind of the general's remaining in office. By the time the charges had been refuted, Hitler's *coup de main* was an accomplished fact. Fritsch was left with no choice but to retire to the dreary plains of Ülzen and to await a new assignment, one that never came.[26] As for the Führer's decision to assume *de facto* control of the armed forces, Raeder may actually have welcomed it. Although the admiral did for a time apparently nourish hopes that a separate Naval Ministry might result from the crisis, he quickly returned to reality when this proved impossible. Raeder entertained no illusions about the advisability of becoming War Minister. By 1938, he was sufficiently confident of his own relationship with Hitler that he welcomed the Führer's decision to take personal command of the armed forces as the most viable alternative to the candidacy of the admiral's powerful rival at the Air Ministry, Hermann Göring.[27]

Thus, the navy evidently weathered the shake-up at the beginning of 1938 completely unscathed. Yet, in due time, Raeder would have good reason to regret that he had not done more to dampen Hitler's enthusiasm for an aggressive foreign policy when the opportunity had presented itself on November 5. With the cautious Blomberg and Fritsch now on the sidelines, the future direction of the Reich depended increasingly upon the intuitive "genius" of the Führer. If he were wrong in his assessment of the West, and a general European war broke out before the Kriegsmarine's building program was completed, then both the Reich and the navy would suffer.

At first, the course of events seemed to prove the validity of Hitler's assumptions. Britain and France scarcely stirred when Germany annexed Austria in March 1938.[28] Nevertheless, there were signs that Raeder and other leaders of the Kriegsmarine recognized the increasing likelihood of war with the Western Powers at some future date. At the conclusion of a *Kriegsspiel* at the beginning of April, the navy's commander-in-chief told a wider circle of officers for the first time that British participation alongside France in the event of war was now considered likely. Later that month, the Seekriegsleitung's specialist on naval conferences was instructed to work out a schedule indicating when the growth of the fleet would so far surpass the 35 per cent limit envisioned by the Agreement of June 18, 1935, that the British would have to be informed.[29] After this time, the likelihood of hostilities with Britain would be increased considerably.

Both of these measures were indications of a worsening relationship between Germany and Great Britain. Raeder nevertheless continued to operate under the assumption that war with the West would come only in 1944, or later, if it came at all. A new development threatened to bring about an immediate war in May 1938, however, when the government of Czechoslovakia, acting in response to rumors of German mobilization, ordered a partial mobilization of its own forces.[30] Both the French and the British governments warned Berlin of the serious consequences of any aggressive move against the Czechs by the Germans. In the face of this unexpected display of resolution, Hitler decided to back down temporarily, but at the same time he determined that he would crush Czechoslovakia at the earliest possible moment. This time, the Führer appeared to be somewhat less certain that the Western Powers would stay out and, on May 24, he informed the navy of measures that he felt ought to be taken in the wake of the new situation. The U-boat building program was to be accelerated, and the completion deadlines of the battleships "F" and "G" (the future *Bismarck* and *Tirpitz*) were to be advanced to the spring of 1940, half a year earlier than had previously been anticipated. At the same time, Hitler decided that the *Scharnhorst* and the *Gneisenau* would be upgunned from an armament of nine eleven-inch guns to one of six fifteen-inch guns, thus making them more worthy adversaries in the event of war. But Hitler did not stop at these measures. That same day, he also ordered the navy to investigate the possibility of constructing six new slipways that would provide the ships for another great burst of naval construction, designed to carry the Kriegsmarine well into the mid-1940s.[31]

Hitler's announcement of his intentions on May 24 must have come as bittersweet news to the navy's representatives. On the one hand, the Führer's desire to accelerate the current building program and to allocate resources for a second round of capital ship construction offered convincing proof that the navy was about to receive its due. On the other hand, the new urgency that was now visible in Hitler's actions must have left many officers with the uneasy feeling that the added priority the navy was about to receive had come too late to make a difference. It was all well and good to make grandiose plans for a future battle fleet (and few of the admirals had not done the same thing in their private flights of fancy), but the new slipways would merely be so much wasted effort if war came before the ships were substantially completed.[32] And although international anxiety over the unresolved question of Czechoslovakia subsided somewhat after the May crisis, the danger of an immediate war continued throughout the summer of 1938. In view of this, a few officers within the Kriegsmarine began to question the wisdom of the course that Germany appeared to be pursuing under Hitler's leadership and to consider ways that the dangerous direction of German foreign policy might be reversed.

The two most significant proposals along these lines came from within the offices of the Seekriegsleitung. Sometime in the early summer of 1938, Admiral Günther Guse, Raeder's current Chief of Staff and Head of the Kommandoamt, instructed Fregattenkapitän Hellmuth Heye of the Operationsabteilung to draw up an analysis of the Czechoslovakian question.[33] The resulting study was remarkable in a number of ways. Although he sought to buttress some of his arguments with quotations from *Mein Kampf*, Heye's aim was not to justify the policies of the National Socialist regime but rather to secure a change in them. And although Heye, like so many Germans, appeared to regard a weakening of Czechoslovakia as essential to the security of the Reich, he was nevertheless convinced that Hitler's present course of action would ultimately prove disastrous for the fatherland. The Party's brutal measures against the Jews and against the Churches had cost Germany the support of thinking men everywhere, and German bellicosity was inspiring such fear among the nations of the world that the Reich was dangerously isolated. If Germany attacked Czechoslovakia under these circumstances, there was a very real danger that Britain and France—and perhaps Russia and the United States—would seize the opportunity to solve the "German question" once and for all. What was needed, Heye argued, was a return to law at home through the strengthening of the authority of the State at the expense of the Party. Abroad, Germany would have to acquire strong allies and well-intentioned neutrals. Then, and only then, could the question of Czechoslovakia be resolved under conditions that were considerably more auspicious than those of the present.

Heye's analysis neglected to delineate exactly how this reversal of policy ought to be accomplished. Guse, on the other hand, made a proposal which, while admittedly not the most promising or original, at least offered a beginning. There is strong evidence that by the summer of 1938, Guse was in contact with his army counterpart, General Ludwig Beck, chief of the General Staff, who was then trying to convince his own superior, Brauchitsch, of the dangerous direction in which the Reich appeared to be headed. Like Beck, Guse apparently concluded that the only way to secure a change in German foreign policy was to convince the commanders of the Wehrmacht to undertake a collective protest that would deter Hitler from his present course. Guse already knew that he was slated for a transfer to a quieter assignment in the fall, but he made one last attempt to exert his influence over Raeder before events removed him from daily contact with his commander-in-chief. On July 17 he submitted a memorandum to the head of the navy which clearly outlined the dangers Germany now faced. It was impossible, he argued, to surprise the Czechs with a lightning campaign, and few officers thought that a German–Czech war could be localized. In any future conflict, Germany would be weaker than the coalition of powers arrayed against it. Defeat would jeopardize all that Hitler had thus far accomplished. Under these circumstances, he continued, the Führer's advisors continued to be bound by their duty to obey him, but they also had a duty "to intervene with all the force at their disposal to prevent a development that threatens the existence of the Reich." Although Guse entertained strong doubts as to whether Göring, the second-ranking National Socialist, would be party to this measure, he was convinced that Raeder and Brauchitsch could and should act alone. His memorandum made no mention of what ought to be done if Hitler refused to rethink his policies. Guse presumably felt that a display of resolution by the two commanders would be sufficient, or else was reluctant to consider other alternatives until this one had been attempted.[34]

Unfortunately, Guse's proposal fell on deaf ears. No matter how innocuously they might be phrased, collective protestations to the Führer were definitely not Raeder's style, and the head of the navy was not about to risk the Service's recent gains for anything as problematical as the measures Guse proposed. Instead, the admiral adhered to his earlier decision to transfer Guse, and he sent Heye back to his planning desk. The two subordinates evidently concluded that there was no hope of getting Raeder to act independently and quietly dropped their plans to secure a change in German foreign policy from within.[35] General Beck apparently drew similar conclusions concerning Raeder. For the moment, he and his army colleagues were likewise stymied by Brauchitsch's reluctance to act against Hitler, but, in contrast to their counterparts in the navy, they did not give up all hope of acting in the future. The next time the army planned a *Putsch*, however, it would do so alone.[36]

Raeder, then, would have nothing to do with the efforts of Guse and Heye to avert the impending crisis in foreign policy. By the early autumn of 1938, relations with France and Britain had deteriorated to the point that war over the fate of Czechoslovakia seemed inevitable, and it must have appeared to observers both within and without the navy as nothing less than a miracle when Hitler was able to secure the peaceful annexation of the Sudetenland by Germany at Munich that September.[37] But once again, as after the *Anschluss* with Austria the previous spring, many must have suspected that this latest triumph merely postponed the ultimate reckoning with the West. Apparent confirmation of this fear was soon forthcoming, for on October 21 Hitler issued a secret directive to the Wehrmacht high command instructing it to prepare for the occupation of the remainder of Czechoslovakia in the spring.[38] Few aside from the Führer could have doubted the serious repercussions that this move was likely to have upon relations with Britain and France.

The navy was not slow to draw the necessary conclusions from these latest developments. Already in the late summer of 1938, Heye had drafted a new plan on Raeder's instruction which surveyed the measures to be taken in the event of war with Britain. Earlier studies had presupposed that the Reich would eventually build up a sufficiently large force of battleships to enable the navy to break any British blockade and to allow Germany to maintain seaborne communications with the outside world. Heye abandoned this hope as illusory: due to Britain's "favorable geographic situation," Germany could never hope to defeat the British battle fleet, even if the Kriegsmarine constructed a fleet of battleships that was equal to, or even slightly larger than, that of the Royal Navy. Instead, Heye proposed a campaign against British commerce on the high seas. Battleships would continue to play a modest role in Heye's plan, but the brunt of any future action would be borne by raiders that were far more dangerous to British maritime commerce than a fleet of dreadnoughts. For the new type of warfare, Heye envisioned a large force of improved *Panzerschiffe*, light cruisers, and U-boats.[39]

The fleet that Heye proposed had one decided advantage over those of earlier planners: it could be constructed in a considerably shorter period of time than a traditional fleet of battleships. Given the existing state of international tension by the autumn of 1938, this was by no means an unimportant consideration, and it was perhaps for this reason that Heye defended his concept so tenaciously that September and October, when a special naval planning board met to reevaluate the Service's building program for yet another time. Although Heye was the junior officer on the panel, his arguments were apparently persuasive. The board's final report refused to abandon plans for an extensive battleship fleet, but it did make provisions for a modest *Panzerschiff* program as well. And when Raeder met with leading members of his staff on October 31 to consider this plan, he came out even more forcefully in favor of a new emphasis on *Panzerschiffe*. Indeed, in a reversal of form that must have surprised those who thought they knew the admiral's preferences, Raeder, the naval traditionalist *par excellence*, indicated that he was now contemplating the possible postponement of battleship construction for quite some time so that four *Panzerschiffe* could be ready by 1943.[40]

The next day, Raeder met with Hitler to secure the Führer's agreement with the proposed change in emphasis. Although there is no direct record of what transpired, it is clear from subsequent directives that Hitler insisted that the navy adhere to the existing schedule which he had set for it the previous May. To be sure, Hitler added that other types of vessels, including *Panzerschiffe* and U-boats, were to receive priority as well, but given the navy's well-nigh hopeless situation with regard to laborers and raw materials, this decision meant that neither the battleships nor the lighter vessels would receive their due and that the Kriegsmarine's construction program would fall squarely between two stools. In earlier times, Raeder might have protested more energetically against Hitler's potentially disruptive decision, but much had changed since those days when the admiral had been the tutor and the Führer the pupil. Indeed, by the fall of 1938, there were clear indications that Hitler was thoroughly dissatisfied with the snaillike pace of the navy's construction program, and he apparently threatened to turn over some of the navy's tasks in a future war to the ever-ready arms of the Luftwaffe. Under these circumstances, Raeder seems to have swallowed whatever reservations he might have had concerning the Führer's decision and determined to make the most he could of the situation.[41]

Still, some of Raeder's advisors evidently hoped that Hitler would reconsider his decision. In a memorandum dated November 17, 1938, Heye, Kurt Fricke, and Rolf Junge considered a new building program that would give priority to *Panzerschiffe*, light cruisers, and U-boats and postpone the completion of the battle fleet until sometime between 1945 and 1948. But if Raeder entertained any idea that Hitler would tolerate such a departure from his decision of November 1, he was swiftly disabused of this notion. At the end of November, the Führer seized upon a routine briefing by Raeder to criticize virtually everything the navy had accomplished or was planning. The exact cause for Hitler's tirade is uncertain. In all likelihood, he was merely giving his admiral a none-too-subtle warning that he expected the navy to adhere to the timetable that he had set for it and that the battle fleet would have to be ready for action by 1944. Raeder bristled under this unprecedented criticism of his leadership and threatened to resign, but he then allowed himself to be cajoled into staying on with almost indecent ease. His decision would have fateful consequences, for henceforth it would be Hitler and not Raeder who increasingly determined the extent and nature of the shipbuilding program.[42]

Throughout the month of December 1938, the navy considered a number of proposals which might fulfill the dual priorities of battleship and *Panzerschiff* construction that Hitler had selected on November 1. On December 9, Raeder endorsed a plan which foresaw the completion by 1943 of four battleships and four improved *Panzerschiffe* which would join the four battleships and three older *Panzerschiffe* that the navy already had in commission or on order; in 1945, an additional two battleships and four more *Panzerschiffe* would be added to the fleet. This was admittedly not the exact program that Hitler appeared to desire—that is, all six new battleships by 1943—but it represented the maximum that the navy felt it could achieve. Indeed, as a succession of studies during the next two weeks made clear, even this slightly more modest schedule could be fulfilled only if a number of conditions were met. The expansion of the submarine and light cruiser forces would have to be delayed, and merchant marine construction would have to be curtailed considerably. In addition, the Kriegsmarine would have to be assured that it would get the necessary workers for the increased responsibilities it would be facing.[43]

On January 4, 1939, Raeder conveyed this assessment to Hitler through General Keitel and requested that raw material deliveries for the Kriegsmarine take precedence over all other projects of the Wehrmacht and the German export industry. Otherwise, he added pointedly, there would be a delay in the time by which the navy "would be sufficiently strong and ready [to act] against big sea powers." Two weeks later, the admiral personally presented to the Führer the new program, which was now designated as the "Z Plan."[44] When Raeder again pointed out the difficulties involved in completing the six battleships by 1945, Hitler chided him and remarked: "If I can build the Third Reich in six years, then the navy can surely build these six ships in six years." Nevertheless, Hitler evidently saw the validity of Raeder's argument for additional men and material. On January 27, he acceded to Raeder's request of January 4, and gave the navy priority over the needs of the other branches of the armed forces and the export industry.[45] When completed, the "Z fleet" would consist of 10 battleships, 4 aircraft carriers, 15 *Panzerschiffe*, 5 heavy cruisers, 44 smaller cruisers, 68 destroyers, and 249 U-boats.[46] With such a fleet, the navy's planners saw a very good chance of defeating the British in a war.[47] All that the Kriegsmarine needed now was time.

Yet, by the early months of 1939, time was precisely the commodity in shortest supply, and the navy bore at least a portion of the responsibility for this development. For, even as the Service's planners thrashed out a building program which presupposed a continuing development under peacetime conditions, its leaders were pursuing a short-term policy which rendered the maintenance of this peace less and less likely.

Already in December, German naval representatives had announced to the British the Reich's intention to expand its U-boat fleet to parity with that of the Royal Navy's submarine force and to arm the cruisers "K" and "L" with eight-inch guns. Although neither measure was a violation of the agreement of June 18, 1935, the German decision, coming as it did when Anglo-German relations were already strained, was a disturbing sign that the days of the Naval Agreement might well be numbered. Indeed, had the British known what was going on in Berlin, they would have been even more alarmed. By February 1939, Raeder was collecting reasons that would justify the termination of the agreement.[48] For the moment, the admiral was content to bide his time, but by the beginning of March, it was clear that there was no conceivable way the battle fleet envisioned under the "Z Plan" could be reconciled with the 35 per cent limitation that the navy had professed to recognize since 1935.[49] In the eyes of many officers, the time had now come to make a clean break with the British no matter what the repercussions of such a move might be. As a naval memorandum expressed it on April 4, the one thing that the Seekriegsleitung feared was that the British might somehow seize "a new opportunity . . . to show themselves generous and breathe new life into the treaty."[50]

The admirals probably need not have worried about this possibility, for Hitler was already in the process of making his own break with the British. On March 15, he had occupied "rump" Czechoslovakia in clear violation of the Munich Agreement. Eight days later, Lithuania yielded to German pressure and returned to the Reich the Memelland, which it had seized in 1923. By now, any illusions that Hitler's desire for territorial expansion was sated had disappeared, and on the last day of March, the British Prime Minister, Neville Chamberlain, announced his government's willingness to support the independence of Poland, the next likely target on Hitler's list, with all the means at Britain's disposal.[51]

Hitler was furious over the news of this development, and that same day he promised to brew the British a "devil's drink" that they would not soon forget. He was not long in revealing what he had in mind. The next day, he journeyed to Wilhelmshaven for the launching of the navy's newest battleship. The name had already been chosen, but under the circumstances, the symbolism could not have been more appropriate. Not only was the vessel named after Britain's old adversary, Alfred von Tirpitz; Raeder was promoted to the rank of Grand Admiral as well. But Hitler was not content to let the matter rest here, for that evening he delivered a lengthy denunciation of what he professed to see as a British policy of encirclement, and openly threatened to repudiate the Anglo-German Naval Agreement of 1935. This time he was as good as his word. During the last week of April, representatives from the navy and the Foreign Office worked on a draft note for the British, and on April 28, Hitler announced the abrogation of both the Polish-German Nonaggression Pact of 1934 and the Anglo-German Naval Agreement.[52]

After this, the pace of events quickened measurably. In early May, the navy issued Battle Instructions which stated flatly that "the Kriegsmarine must be aware that today we are already in a prewar situation and that the conflict between the ... nations has already begun, even if the guns have not yet commenced firing."[53] Later that month, on May 23, Hitler stated the case even more clearly when he informed Raeder, Brauchitsch, Göring, and eleven other leading officers of the Wehrmacht that war with Poland was inevitable. Although Hitler was concerned that there would be "no simultaneous conflict with the Western Powers," his assessment nonetheless displayed considerable uncertainty over whether Britain and France would stay out of a conflict. In fact, more of the session seems to have been spent making plans for waging war against Britain than it was making plans against Poland. Yet, according to Raeder, when he approached the Führer after the meeting to express his alarm at the possibility of war, Hitler's uncertainty evaporated. The Führer reassured his admiral that he had matters well in hand and that there would be no war with Britain over the Polish Corridor. In view of the uncertainty that he had just displayed before the larger audience, Hitler's renewed assurance must have sounded more than a trifle suspect, but Raeder professed to have believed him. Indeed, he somewhat incredibly concluded that there had been no change in Hitler's view of Britain after all.[54]

Raeder's astonishing reliance on Hitler's assurance to him persisted throughout most of the remainder of the summer. Despite the very tense state of Germany's relations with Britain, France, and Poland, the *Gneisenau* embarked on a lengthy training voyage in June, armed largely with practice ammunition. That same month, Raeder assured the commander of the Minesweeping Forces, Friedrich Ruge, that he could go on leave without fear of a crisis. The next month, when Dönitz expressed the worries of his U-boat officers that war with Britain was imminent, Raeder promised to convey their concern to Hitler. The head of the navy returned on July 22, with the soothing answer that their fears were groundless; Dönitz went on leave as well. By August, however, the international situation had become so tense that even Raeder was beginning to take certain precautionary measures. On August 15, he recalled Dönitz from leave, and four days later the navy began deploying two *Panzerschiffe* and a number of U-boats in the Atlantic and North Sea, where they would be ready should the unexpected happen and hostilities break out with the West. But Raeder seems to have shared to the very end Hitler's illusion that the West would not resort to war for Poland. After Hitler's eleventh-hour address to the leading officers of the Wehrmacht at Berchtesgaden on August 22, the admiral appears to have concluded that the British and French would confine their response to a German attack on Poland to economic sanctions, or that Ribbentrop's departure for Moscow that same day would bring another Hitlerian masterstroke that would dispel the clouds of war altogether. Raeder's optimism evidently affected others at the Seekriegsleitung: when Fleet Commander Hermann Boehm complained that the dispositions of the fleet only made sense if the British and the French were not going to intervene, Captain Fricke noted in the margin: "That is precisely the point! It *is* highly unlikely."[55] The miracle for which Raeder hoped was not forthcoming. To be sure, Britain and France were distressed by the news of the Nazi–Soviet Nonaggression Pact of August 23, 1939, but they stood by their pledges to Poland just the same. On September 1, the ancient predreadnought *Schleswig-Holstein* opened fire on the Polish fortifications at Westerplatte, and German armies crossed the Polish frontier. Two days later Britain and France declared war on Germany.

Notes for Chapter 7

1 For an exhaustive treatment of German foreign policy during this period, see Gerhard L. Weinberg, *The Foreign Policy of Hitler's Germany*, 2 vols (Chicago, 1970–1980), 2, *passim*. Other accounts include Klaus Hildebrand, *Deutsche Aussenpolitik 1933–1945: Kalkül oder Dogma?* (Stuttgart, 1971), Hans-Adolf Jacobsen, *Nationalsozialistische Aussenpolitik 1933–1938* (Frankfurt, 1968), and Norman Rich, *Hitler's War Aims*, 2 vols. (New York, 1973–1974). As will become evident in the course of this chapter, my interpretation of National Socialist foreign policy is heavily dependent upon Andreas Hillgruber's concept of a *Stufenplan*, whereby Hitler, after consolidating his power at home and rounding out Germany's borders in Central Europe by a series of lightning campaigns against isolated opponents, hoped to lead the Reich to world power status in two main stages. The first of these entailed the acquisition of continental hegemony by seizing vast amounts of *Lebensraum* in the east. The second stage consisted of the conquest of an African empire and the creation of a strong fleet with Atlantic bases such as the Azores and the Cape Verde Islands. This stage would elevate the Reich to the position of one of four remaining world powers alongside Britain, Japan, and the United States. According to Hitler's program, the next generation of Germans would battle the United States in a "struggle of the continents" for world hegemony. For this, see Andreas Hillgruber, *Deutschlands Rolle in der Vorgeschichte der beiden Weltkriege* (Göttingen, 1967), pp. 68–69; also Andreas Hillgruber, *Die gescheiterte Grossmacht: Eine Skizze des Deutschen Reiches 1871–1945* (Düsseldorf, 1980), pp. 77–107.

2 Jost Dülffer, *Weimar, Hitler und die Marine: Reichspolitik und Flottenbau 1920–1939* (Düsseldorf, 1973), pp. 391–400.

3 The London Protocol of November 6, 1936, which Germany adopted seventeen days later, required submarines to give warning and to allow the crews of unescorted merchant vessels to abandon ship before attacking them.

4 Dülffer, *Hitler und die Marine*, pp. 418–419.

5 By 1936, Japan, Italy, France, and Russia were undertaking rather ambitious naval building programs which made the likelihood of continued restraint on the part of the remaining naval powers, Germany, Britain, and the United States, exceedingly problematical.

6 For this, see Gerhard Schreiber, "Zur Kontinuität des Gross- und Weltmachtstrebens der deutschen Marineführung," *Militärgeschichtliche Mitteilungen*, 2/1979, pp. 101–171.

7 Dülffer, *Hitler und die Marine*, pp. 400–401.

8 For this, see James Thomas Emmerson, *The Rhineland Crisis, 7 March 1936: A Study in Multilateral Diplomacy* (London, 1977).

9 For the role of colonies in National Socialist foreign policy, see Klaus Hildebrand, *Vom Reich zum Weltreich: Hitler, NSDAP und koloniale Frage 1919–1945* (Munich, 1969).

10 Dülffer, *Hitler und die Marine*, pp. 410–412.

11 Ibid., pp. 402–406; Michael Salewski, *Die deutsche Seekriegsleitung 1935–1945*, 3 vols (Munich, 1970–1975) 1, pp. 18–19.

12 For the navy's participation in the Spanish Civil War, see Manfred Merkes, *Die deutsche Politik im spanischen Bürgerkrieg 1936–1939*, 2nd edn, rev. (Bonn, 1969), especially pp. 58, 144–152, 276–292. Other works of interest include Hans-Henning Abendroth, *Hitler in der spanischen Arena* (Paderborn, 1973), *passim*; and Gerhard Schreiber, *Revisionismus und Weltmachtstreben: Marineführung und deutsch-italienische Beziehungen 1919–1944* (Stuttgart, 1978), pp. 95–106.

13 Merkes, *Politik im Bürgerkrieg*, pp. 145–146; Abendroth, *Hitler in der spanischen Arena*, pp. 137–155.

14 On May 29, 1937, Republican aircraft attacked the "pocket" battleship *Deutschland*, killing thirty-one and wounding seventy-five officers and men. Two days later, the *Deutschland*'s sister ship, *Scheer*, bombarded the town of Almeria in reetaliation. On June 18, the cruiser *Leipzig* reported that she had been hit by a torpedo but that it had not detonated. Merkes, *Politik im Bürgerkrieg*, pp. 276–292.

15 Salewski, *Seekriegsleitung*, 1, pp. 28–31.

16 D. C. Watt, "Anglo-German Naval Negotiations on the Eve of the Second World War," *Journal of the Royal United Service Institution*, 103 (May 1958), pp. 205–206.

17 Dülffer, *Hitler und die Marine*, p. 435.

18 Ibid., pp. 440–442.

19 Ibid., pp. 442–443; Salewski, *Seekriegsleitung*, 1, pp. 35–36.

20 Dülffer, *Hitler und die Marine*, pp. 446–447.

21 The following four paragraphs are based on the minutes of the meeting taken by Colonel Friedrich Hossbach, which are reprinted in *Documents on German Foreign Policy* (hereafter cited as *DGFP*), D, Vol. 1, No. 19. A thorough analysis of the "Hossbach Memorandum" is provided in Weinberg, *Foreign Policy*, 2, pp. 35–41. For a critical evaluation of the most important literature on the conference, see ibid., 2, p. 35, n. 61.

22 Erich Raeder, *Mein Leben*, 2 vols (Tübingen, 1956–1957), 2, pp. 149–150; Dülffer, *Hitler und die Marine*, p. 447.

23 See ibid., p. 451.

24 On January 12, 1938, the 60-year-old Blomberg married a considerably younger woman named Eva Gruhn. It subsequently became known that the new Frau von Blomberg had a colorful past, having posed for pornographic pictures, and the field marshal was forced to resign on January 27. The fullest account of this often-told story is given in Harold C. Deutsch, *Hitler and His Generals: The Hidden Crisis, January–June 1938* (Minneapolis, Minn., 1974), pp. 78–133. The response of Blomberg's naval adjutant, Lieutenant Commander Baron Hubertus von Wagenheim,

to the news of the general's humiliation sheds considerable light on the naval officer corps' conception of "honor" under Raeder. With Raeder's specific approval, Wagenheim followed the honeymoon couple to Rome and told Blomberg he ought to part with his wife or put a bullet through his head. Wagenheim then offered the general a pistol. Blomberg refused, and went on to enjoy seven happy years of marriage before his death by natural causes in 1946. Ibid., pp. 122–123, 127.

25 Deutsch, *Hitler and His Generals*, pp. 134–215; Robert J. O'Neill, *The German Army and the Nazi Party, 1933–1939* (London, 1966), p. 142. For contrasting interpretations of the connection between the discussion of November 5 and the Fritsch Crisis, see Hermann Gackenholz, "Reichskanzlei, 5. November 1937," in *Forschungen zu Staat und Verfassung: Festgabe für Fritz Hartung* (Berlin, 1958), pp. 59–84; and Peter Kielmannsegg, "Die militärisch-politische Tragweite der Hossbach Besprechung," *Vierteljahrshefte für Zeitgeschichte*, 8 (July 1960), pp. 268–274.

26 Klaus-Jürgen Müller, *Das Heer und Hitler: Armee und nationalsozialistisches Regime 1933–1940* (Stuttgart, 1969), p. 280. Fritsch eventually returned to his regiment as a volunteer and was killed in action near Warsaw on September 22, 1939. Many writers have argued that the general actively sought death in battle, but the most recent study by Gerd Brausch argues convincingly against this interpretation. "Der Tod des Generalobersten Werner Freiherr von Fritsch," *Militärgeschichtliche Mitteilungen*, 1/1970, pp. 95–112.

27 Müller, *Das Heer und Hitler*, pp. 290, 293; Deutsch, *Hitler and His Generals*, pp. 127–129.

28 For the history of the *Anschluss*, see Ulrich Eichstädt, *Von Dollfuss zu Hitler: Geschichte des Anschlusses Österreichs 1933–1938* (Wiesbaden, 1955).

29 Dülffer, *Hitler und die Marine*, pp. 461–464; Salewski, *Seekriegsleitung*, 1, p. 40.

30 For the diplomacy of the Czechoslovakian crisis from May until October 1938, see Weinberg, *Foreign Policy*, 2, pp. 313–464.

31 Dülffer, *Hitler und die Marine*, pp. 468–469; Salewski, *Seekriegsleitung*, 1, p. 41.

32 Here, too, the Kriegsmarine was doubtless haunted by its past. In 1914, the Imperial Navy was eight battleships and thirteen cruisers behind in the schedule that Tirpitz had foreseen for it. Holger H. Herwig, *Luxury Fleet: The Imperial German Navy, 1888–1918* (London, 1980), p. 92.

33 Müller, *Das Heer und Hitler*, p. 316, n. 66. Excerpts from Heye's memorandum are reprinted in Helmut Krausnick, "Vorgeschichte und Beginn des militärischen Widerstandes gegen Hitler," in *Vollmacht des Gewissens* (Frankfurt am Main, 1960), pp. 311–315. There is some confusion as to whether Heye's study predated Guse's (which will be analyzed subsequently), but the exact timing of the two studies is not important for present purposes, for both studies found their way into Raeder's hands at approximately the same time.

34 Müller, *Das Heer und Hitler*, p. 317, n. 68; Dülffer, *Hitler und die Marine*, p. 476; Krausnick, "Vorgeschichte des Widerstandes," pp. 316–317.

35 Kurt Assmann, *Deutsche Schicksalsjahre: Historische Bilder aus dem Zweiten Weltkrieg und seiner Vorgeschichte* (Wiesbaden, 1950), p. 45, maintains that Raeder did submit a memorandum to Hitler. Raeder's own memoirs make no mention of this, and in an interview with Carl-Axel Gemzell in 1960, Heye asserted that Raeder had expressly refused to take part in any approach to the Führer: *Raeder, Hitler und Skandinavien: Der Kampf*

für einen maritimen Operationsplan (Lund, 1965), p. 171, n. 30. See also Salewski, *Seekriegsleitung*, 1, p. 45, n. 26.

36 Müller, *Das Heer und Hitler*, p. 330.

37 For this, see Boris Celovsky, *Das Münchener Abkommen von 1938* (Stuttgart, 1958).

38 Dülffer, *Hitler und die Marine*, p. 491.

39 The text of the revised version of Heye's study, "Seekriegführung gegen England und die sich daraus ergebenden Forderungen für die strategische Zielsetzung und den Aufbau der Kriegsmarine," is given in Salewski, *Seekriegsleitung*, 3, pp. 27–63. For Salewski's interpretation of the study, see ibid., 1, pp. 45–51.

40 Gemzell, *Raeder, Hitler und Skandinavien*, pp. 84–104; Salewski, *Seekriegsleitung*, 1, pp. 51–57; Dülffer, *Hitler und die Marine*, pp. 481–486, 492.

41 Dülffer, *Hitler und die Marine*, pp. 492–494.

42 Raeder, *Mein Leben*, 2, pp. 126–127; Dülffer, *Hitler und die Marine*, pp. 494–497.

43 Dülffer, *Hitler und die Marine*, pp. 497–498.

44 Ibid., pp. 497–501. The designation "Z Plan" comes from the navy's practice of assigning letters to the various building plans. In December 1938, the Seekriegsleitung had already contemplated "Bauplan X" and "Bauplan Y."

45 Ibid., pp. 499–502; Salewski places Hitler's decision on January 29. *Seekriegsleitung*, 1, pp. 59–60.

46 Gemzell, *Raeder, Hitler und Skandinavien*, p. 94. Four additional *Panzerschiffe* had evidently been added to the eleven projected by Raeder on December 9, 1938, to bring the total to fifteen.

47 And indeed, not just the British! A number of historians have argued that with the "Z fleet" Hitler was already looking ahead to the struggle for world hegemony with the United States. For this, see Dülffer, *Hitler und die Marine*, p. 569, and Holger H. Herwig, *Politics of Frustration: The United States in German Naval Planning 1889–1941* (Boston, Mass., 1976) pp. 193–194.

48 Dülffer, *Hitler und die Marine*, pp. 198, 517; Salewski, *Seekriegsleitung*, 1, pp. 63–64.

49 This realization had been clear to virtually everyone in the know for quite some time. On March 3, 1939, however, Britain informed Germany of British intended naval construction over the next four years. It was not nearly enough to allow the building program that the Kriegsmarine was now planning to remain within the bounds of the 35 per cent limit. Salewski, *Seekriegsleitung*, 1, pp. 59–60.

50 Dülffer, *Hitler und die Marine*, p. 517.

51 Weinberg, *Foreign Policy*, 2, p. 555. The diplomatic developments of the period from March 15 to September 1, 1939, have been treated by numerous writers. In addition to the works cited above (note 1, this chapter), see Walther Hofer, *Die Entfesselung des Zweiten Weltkrieges: Eine Studie über die internationalen Beziehungen im Sommer 1939*, 3rd edn, (Frankfurt, 1964).

52 Max Domarus, *Hitler, Reden und Proklamationen, 1932–1945*, 2 vols (Munich, 1965), 2, pp. 1118–1127; Raeder maintains that he was surprised by the news of the termination of the agreement. *Mein Leben*, 2, p. 163. The exact timing of the announcement might have caught him by surprise, but the basic decision to abrogate the agreement most assuredly did

not. Dülffer, *Hitler und die Marine*, p. 518; Salewski, *Seekriegsleitung*, 1, p. 80.

53 Dülffer, *Hitler und die Marine*, p. 540.
54 *DGFP*, D, Vol. 4, No. 433; Raeder, *Mein Leben*, 2, p. 163.
55 The quotation is from Salewski, *Seekriegsleitung*, 1, p. 82. For the navy's role in the final phase of the Polish crisis, see Raeder, *Mein Leben*, 2, pp. 163–166; Friedrich Ruge, *In vier Marinen* (Munich, 1979), p. 187; Dülffer, *Hitler und die Marine*, pp. 542–543.

8

'Dying Gallantly,' September 1939– January 1943

On September 3, 1939, a gloomy Erich Raeder noted in the war diary of the Seekriegsleitung:

> Today the war against England and France, which the Führer had previously assured us we would not have to confront until 1944 and which he believed he could avoid up until the very last minute, began . . . .
>
> As far as the Kriegsmarine is concerned, it is obvious that it is not remotely ready for the titanic struggle against England. To be sure, the brief period of time that has elapsed since the Agreement of 1935 has witnessed the creation of a well-trained and well-conceived force of U-boats, of which approximately twenty-six are currently ready for Atlantic operations, but these boats are still far too few to exert a *decisive* influence upon the war. The surface forces, moreover, are so weak and so few in number vis-à-vis the British fleet that the only course open for them—presupposing their active employment—is to show that they know how to die gallantly and thereby to create the basis for an eventual rebirth in the future.[1]

Raeder's assessment was frank beyond even his usually severe standards. Moreover, it was fully borne out by the material situation of the Kriegsmarine. At the beginning of September 1939, the navy's surface fleet consisted of two fast battleships (the *Scharnhorst* and *Gneisenau*, both of which were still going through their "working up" exercises), three *Panzerschiffe*, one heavy cruiser, six light cruisers, and thirty-four destroyers and torpedo-boats. The U-boat arm was scarcely better off, numbering only fifty-seven submarines, of which less than half were suitable for operations in the Atlantic.[2] Nor were the prospects of reinforcement very encouraging. The heavy cruiser *Blücher* would join the fleet that same September, but after that there would be a long dry spell until the Reich's first fully combat-worthy battleships, the *Bismarck*

187

and *Tirpitz*, and another heavy cruiser, *Prinz Eugen*, would be ready for action. Other ships were under construction, but whether any of these could be completed (much less manned) was anyone's guess.[3]

In view of the situation confronting the Kriegsmarine, Raeder had justifiable grounds for pessimism. He was nonetheless determined that the navy would make the most of its meager resources and that it would not, as in the First World War, squander opportunities by a policy of inaction. Accordingly, in the opening months of the war, the Service's small U-boat force would wage an active campaign against Allied commerce, initially according to Prize Law, later on with fewer restrictions. Meanwhile, the Kriegsmarine's surface forces would also pursue an aggressive, "double-pole" strategy aimed primarily at Great Britain. The navy's *Panzerschiffe* and, subsequently, a number of auxiliary cruisers would attack British commerce over the vast reaches of the ocean and, if possible, divert British forces from the waters around Great Britain. At the same time, the Kriegsmarine's remaining surface vessels would exploit the diversion to reduce the Royal Navy's numerical superiority by frequent and successful forays into the North Sea.[4]

Through this aggressive strategy the naval high command hoped to persevere until Germany's land and air forces could turn from Poland, which was crushed within a month, and secure victory over Britain and France. But there also appeared to be a second motive, more political than military, behind Raeder's emphasis upon the aggressive use of the fleet. After years of extolling to Hitler the benefits of sea power, it was now essential that the Service vindicate the hopes that it had raised in Hitler's mind. Thus, the following spring Raeder urged his commanders to take aggressive action in words strikingly similar to those of the previous September:

> The great aim that the Führer has set forth for the German nation requires the utmost exertion in all places . . . A navy which undertakes daring actions against the enemy and suffers losses through this will be reborn on an even larger scale. If it has not fought this action, then its existence will be threatened after the war.[5]

Raeder left his subordinates no doubt as to his views on the matter. Those officers who boldly pressed home their attacks on the enemy were rewarded with high praise and military honors. Following Günther Prien's celebrated destruction of the British battleship *Royal Oak* in October 1939, for example, both he and his crew were flown to Berlin, where Hitler personally decorated him with the Knight's Cross.[6] On the other hand, those officers who displayed less initiative soon encountered difficulties. The same autumn as Prien's success, the skipper of the *U-53* was swiftly removed from command when he failed to use his submarine in a sufficiently aggressive manner.[7] Nor was Raeder's "offensive drive" confined to relatively junior officers.[8] In early 1940 Raeder replaced Admiral Wilhelm Marschall with Admiral Günther Lütjens when Marschall failed to show sufficient energy as

Fleet Commander. No sooner had Lütjens taken command than his cautious employment of the fleet likewise incurred Raeder's criticism. The head of the navy, it seems, wanted action, and neither high rank nor long-established friendship were to stand in the way of this.[9]

Yet it was difficult at times to determine whether a commander had fully exploited the possibilities available to him in the conduct of a given operation. A good case in point concerned Hans Langsdorff, captain of the *Graf Spee*. After a moderately successful commerce-raiding campaign in the South Atlantic, the *Graf Spee* was damaged by British cruisers in December 1939 during the Battle of the River Plate. Langsdorff took the *Graf Spee* to Montevideo, Uruguay, for repairs. Given seventy-two hours by Uruguayan authorities to clear port, Langsdorff decided to scuttle the *Panzerschiff* rather than risk its falling into British hands. After taking care that his crew was safely interned in Buenos Aires, Argentina, he committed suicide.[10]

The untimely end of the *Graf Spee* placed Raeder in an uncomfortable position. Publicly, Hitler expressed his approval of Langsdorff's decision to scuttle; privately, he admitted that he was "very upset" that the ship had gone down without attempting to inflict additional damage upon the enemy. Moreover, the self-destruction of the vessel was bound to bring back memories of the unfortunate fate of the High Sea Fleet at Scapa Flow some twenty years before. Was the navy making a tradition of scuttlings? Not so, Raeder hastened to assert. In a circular dated December 22, 1939, he described to the officer corps the dilemma that Langsdorff had faced and expressed his conviction that the captain had done everything possible to defend the honor of the flag. The peculiar circumstances of the *Graf Spee*, he continued, did nothing to alter the guiding principle that the "German warship fights until the last shell with the full commitment of its crew until it is victorious or until it goes under with banners flying."[11]

Developments in the spring of 1940 gave the officers and men of the Kriegsmarine ample opportunity to prove themselves worthy of Raeder's charge. Since the defeat of Poland the previous September, the Wehrmacht high command had been concerned with preparations for Operation Yellow, the forthcoming invasion of France and the Low Countries. Throughout the fall and winter of 1939–1940, though, German authorities were also beginning to receive disturbing reports of impending Allied action along the Reich's northern flank, in Scandinavia. Allied operations in this area could pose a serious threat for Germany. A British occupation of Norway would not only seal the entrance to the Baltic, thereby tightening the naval blockade of the Reich; it would also impede the vital flow of Swedish iron ore to Germany, particularly during the winter months, when roughly 50 per cent of that ore was shipped through the Norwegian port of Narvik. Moreover, once entrenched in Norway, the Allies could threaten the Swedish ore fields directly or develop other potentially harmful strategic initiatives.[12]

Raeder was well aware of these dangers. Indeed, in prewar studies, the naval high command had raised the possibility of a preemptive strike into Scandinavia, but had ultimately concluded that, given the Kriegsmarine's present weakness, Norway's continued neutrality was preferable to German occupation.[13] By the late fall of 1939, however, it appeared less and less likely that Norway would or could maintain its neutrality in the face of Allied pressure. The outbreak of the so-called "Winter War" between Finland and the Soviet Union on November 30 raised the possibility that the Allies might dispatch an expeditionary force across Norway to aid the Finns and that they might occupy parts of Norway in the bargain. In view of this, Raeder began to evaluate possible countermeasures. On December 11, he met in Berlin with Vidkun Quisling, the head of the Nasjonal Samling, the tiny Norwegian equivalent of the NSDAP. Quisling expressed his willingness, given the proper circumstances, to overthrow the present Norwegian government and to work with the Germans in the ostensible goal of maintaining Norwegian neutrality.[14] Raeder informed Hitler of this the following day, but advised caution since the Norwegian's motives were uncertain. Although Hitler subsequently had several meetings with Quisling, both he and Raeder appear to have concluded that Norway's continued neutrality was preferable to any alternative. For the moment, the only thing to do was to hold the Kriegsmarine in readiness to counter possible Allied intervention in Scandinavia. Nevertheless, in January 1940, Raeder also ordered contingency plans to be prepared for a preemptive invasion of Norway.[15]

From this point on, both Raeder and Hitler appear to have wavered between an aggressive solution to the Norwegian problem and the continued maintenance of the status quo. In February 1940, the British attack upon the German supply ship *Altmark* in Norwegian territorial waters and the liberation of 299 Allied merchant seamen who had been held captive aboard that vessel made it clear that the Royal Navy was willing to violate Norwegian neutrality.[16] On the other hand, the conclusion of a peace treaty between the Soviet Union and Finland the following month removed one pretext for Allied intervention in Scandinavia. Nevertheless, Raeder remained convinced that a major Allied undertaking in the north was inevitable. Each day that the Kriegsmarine waited for this meant another day in which its vessels would be diverted from the vital campaign against enemy shipping in the Atlantic. On March 26, therefore, the admiral met with Hitler and argued that, since the navy would have to act sooner or later, it was better that Germany undertake preemptive action in Scandinavia as soon as possible. This argument evidently persuaded the Führer, for during the same conference he set the date of *Weserübung*, the invasion of Norway and Denmark, for the first part of April.[17]

The ensuing campaign proved to be one of the most successful combined services operations of the Second World War.[18] Despite overwhelming British naval superiority, the Kriegsmarine, through a combination of surprise and daring, succeeded in landing substantial ground forces in Norway and on the Danish islands on April 9. Without realistic possibilities of resistance, the Danes surrendered the same day.

In Norway, the German army and air force pushed steadily northward against Norwegian and Allied opposition so that by early June, when the king and government fled to Great Britain, all of mainland Norway was under German control. The price the navy paid for this success was considerable; ten destroyers were lost at Narvik, and three cruisers, including the recently commissioned heavy cruiser *Blücher*, were sunk in separate operations. Nevertheless, the Seekriegsleitung had reckoned on extensive losses, and the gains seemed worth the price. Operation Weserübung had secured Germany's northern flank and opened the way for a more aggressive campaign against British sea communications. Perhaps most important, at least in the eyes of the naval high command, was the splendid impression that the fleet had made upon Hitler; as early as April 10, the Führer conveyed his recognition of the "great achievement" of the navy. It was small wonder, therefore, that Raeder subsequently chose to describe the Scandinavian campaign as "the operation which will remain *the* feat of arms by the Kriegsmarine in this war."[19]

Raeder would certainly have preferred for the navy to have remained in the limelight for as long as possible. As it turned out, the Service's accomplishments in the north were swiftly overshadowed by even more momentous developments in the west: on May 10, 1940, the Wehrmacht's long-awaited invasion of the Low Countries and France began. This time it was the army and the air force's turn to shine. In less than two months, Luxembourg, the Netherlands, Belgium, and, to the surprise of military experts everywhere, France succumbed to the might of the Wehrmacht. In contrast to the Scandinavian campaign, the Kriegsmarine's direct contribution to this latest and most astonishing series of German successes was relatively minor. Nevertheless, the conquest of France offered vastly improved strategic opportunities for the navy. Not only did France's eclipse remove the bulk of the French navy from the forces opposing the Kriegsmarine; it also encouraged Fascist Italy to throw in its lot with the Reich, so that the Royal Navy now faced a potential Italian threat in the Mediterranean.[20] Equally significant to the Kriegsmarine was the sudden and unexpected availability of numerous French bases along the English Channel, the Breton Peninsula, and the Bay of Biscay. Just as the recent conquest of Norway placed the navy in a position to outflank Great Britain in the north, so the acquisition of French bases—the second half of Admiral Wolfgang Wegener's strategy from the 1920s—placed the Kriegsmarine within easy striking distance of Britain's vital southwestern approaches.

Perhaps most important, however, was the simple fact that Britain now stood alone against Germany. How different the situation was from the previous September, when Raeder had so pessimistically weighed the navy's chances! To be sure, the navy still faced a long and bitter struggle, but the odds against it had diminished markedly in the first ten months of the war. Perhaps one final campaign would topple the British or bring them to the conference table where a favorable peace could be obtained. Then Raeder and his subordinates would be able to return to the construction of the *Weltmachtflotte* that had been so rudely interrupted by the outbreak of the war.

Indeed, although Great Britain was as yet unvanquished, it was to the postwar fleet and the postwar world that many of Germany's naval leaders turned their attention. Some preliminary sketches of these problems already existed. In the winter of 1939–1940, for example, before the Wehrmacht's lightning campaigns in Scandinavia and the west had extended the navy's freedom of action, the Seekriegsleitung had requested a study of the probable requirements of a postwar fleet. By January 1940, an overview was ready. Proceeding from the assumption that Germany would be "the predominant power on the European continent," the author, in all likelihood Captain Kurt Fricke, the chief of the Seekriegsleitung's Operations Division, envisioned a ten- to twelve-year building program that would provide the Reich with a fleet of 37 battleships, 10 to 12 aircraft carriers or cruisers with flight decks, 130 other cruisers of various types, 250 destroyers, 250 submarines, and over 1,100 torpedo-boats, minesweepers, and auxiliary vessels. The logistical support necessary for this fleet would be immense, and the report foresaw Kriegsmarine bases in Norway, Denmark, the Channel Coast, and in the colonies that Germany would conquer. The author added that, depending upon circumstances, the demands that might be placed upon the navy (and hence the necessary number of ships) might be even greater.[21]

The report of January 1940 provided only the broadest outline for the future German empire and the navy's tasks therein. A memorandum prepared in the summer of 1940 for one of Raeder's briefings for Hitler refined the picture considerably. The author of the report, probably the Seekriegsleitung's Captain Heinz Assmann, presupposed that Germany would be the predominant power on the continent and that the economic resources of the north, west, and southeast would be available to the Reich. The author also envisioned a central African empire for Germany stretching from the Atlantic to the Indian Ocean. Given Germany's immense power, he argued, the participation of either a Scandinavian or a western continental state in a coalition against the Reich was out of the question. Britain's future relations with Germany were as yet undetermined, but it seemed safe to assume that, having been driven from the continent, Britain would probably ally with the United States. The consequences of this were clear: the two "Anglo-Saxon powers" would spare no effort to maintain or to enhance their sea power and would thereby become the natural enemies of the Reich. Germany would therefore have to become a naval power of the first order. This, of course, was what champions of the navy had been advocating for decades. As the author of the report expressed it: "With this step a centuries-long development of German sea power, which has been hindered by numerous errors and miscalculations in the past, will be brought to a definite conclusion."[22]

In a separate report compiled in June 1940, Kurt Fricke foresaw a similarly glorious future for the new *Weltreich* and described a policy of outright annexations, protectorates, and client states that would leave every Western European nation save Britain totally dependent upon Germany. Fricke's African empire was the largest envisioned to date, linking Senegal in the northwest with the Belgian Congo in the south and former German East Africa in the east. In order to protect the seaborne communications between these colonies and the homeland, the navy would also take possession of numerous island bases in the Atlantic and Indian Oceans. Fricke noted that German possession of Iceland would bring additional strategic advantages to the navy.[23]

Soon other officers were busily adding their favorite items to the navy's "wish list." Both Heinz Assmann and Rear Admiral Otto Schniewind, Raeder's Chief of Staff, were dissatisfied with Fricke's suggestion that Germany dominate Norway through indirect means, and insisted instead that the Reich retain a naval base at the Norwegian port of Trondheim. In a separate memorandum, an unidentified naval officer detailed the bases that he hoped the navy would gain in Africa and on offshore islands. In addition to bases in Togo, Cameroon, and East Africa, all of which had formerly belonged to Imperial Germany and which would presumably form the core of National Socialist Germany's new overseas empire, the officer foresaw German acquisition, either through conquest or exchange, of Dakar, Conakry (Guinea), Douala (French Cameroons), Pointe Noire and Boma (French Equatorial Africa), Zanzibar, Mombassa, Kilindoni, Diego Suarez, Fernando Po, São Thomé, St Helena, Ascension, Pemba, the Comoro Islands, Reunion, the Seychelles, Mauritius, and "the remaining small islands in the same areas which are of significance to naval warfare." Fricke submitted a similarly detailed list to the Foreign Office and, for good measure, added Iceland, the Faeroe Islands, the Azores, and, possibly, the Canary Islands.[24]

Each of the above memoranda reflected the naval high command's increasingly ravenous appetite for territory. Nevertheless, it was Rolf Carls, the commander of Naval Group North, who carried naval fantasies concerning the postwar world to their most extreme conclusions. In an undated memorandum, most likely from the summer of 1940, he described the purpose of the present war as the elevation of Germany to a world power, the achievement of unimpeded access to the seas, the weakening of France, and the reduction of the British Empire to the point where it was roughly the same size as the emerging German *Weltreich*. To achieve this, Carls was willing to employ draconian measures. Denmark, Norway, Holland, and the Flemish-speaking parts of Belgium would enter a German-dominated federation. The Walloonian part of Belgium, Greater Luxembourg, and substantial parts of France—Lorraine, Artois, Picardy, Normandy, and Brittany—would be demilitarized and formed into German protectorates along the lines of Bohemia and Moravia. France's African empire would be divided among Germany, Italy, and, to some extent, Spain, whereas France's navy would be reduced to a quarter of the size of the Kriegsmarine. If the present war resulted in a German victory over Great Britain, then Britain would likewise suffer substantial territorial losses, including the secession of South Africa from the British Empire and the end of the British protectorate over Egypt. Britain's postwar fleet would be about one-half the size of Germany's navy.[25]

Carls was also anxious to extend Germany's power into parts of the globe that his fellow officers had neglected. In the north, he added Greenland, the Shetlands, and the Channel Islands to the navy's "possessions." In the south, his eye fixed upon Walvis Bay and the former German colony of Southwest Africa. Carls was willing to concede British Somaliland and Djibouti (French Somaliland) to the Italians, but he hoped that Germany would acquire Aden and Socotra in the Near East as well as all British oil concessions in Persia. The Reich would probably not demand Ceylon from the British, but in order to assure communication with the East Indies—which Germany would get from the Dutch and, in the case of North Borneo, from the British—the navy would have to obtain the Cocos Islands. German consideration for the expansionist desires of Japan would probably necessitate the Reich's forgoing any Indonesian colonies east of the Moluccas, but Carls was apparently satisfied that his modest empire would be sufficient for the needs of the Reich. As he concluded his cartographical tour de force he argued:

> Taken together, such demands may sound fantastic, but they follow automatically from the constellation of states which, in my opinion, will result from the war and from the necessary rounding out of colonial holdings which will secure Germany's right to its share of the globe for all time. The renunciation of territory in the Mediterranean, in America, and in the East Asian-Japanese sphere, which I likewise find to be absolutely necessary, even constitutes a conscious act of self-restraint on our part .... The colonial empires left to France and above all England give them enough strength, along with Italy, to maintain their existence and power within the limits we wish for them. In my opinion this is both necessary and proper for a balancing of global power.[26]

The difficulty with all of these speculations, of course, was that Great Britain, the Reich's sole remaining adversary in the summer of 1940, was still unwilling to come to terms with Germany. This unexpected British tenacity was certainly disturbing to Hitler. Despite all evidence to the contrary (and despite the intentions of his admirals, who clearly had no intention of respecting the integrity of the British Empire), the Führer evidently continued to count on some sort of a "deal" with Great Britain. But British stubbornness was, if possible, even more disturbing to Raeder than to Hitler. Now that the army had conquered France, it was up to the navy to render Britain receptive to political accommodation or, barring this, to prepare the way for a cross-channel invasion of the island kingdom. And this was precisely the rub, for given the Kriegsmarine's numerical inferiority vis-à-vis the Royal Navy, there was little likelihood that the Service could accomplish either of these two objectives within the foreseeable future.

Erich Raeder was too clever a politician to admit this state of affairs to his Führer. Hitler, for his part, was all too aware that the navy's predicament with respect to Britain likewise indicated the essential bankruptcy of his own *Englandpolitik*: for if the British persisted, there was little that he could do to make them see the light of day. Accordingly, in the summer of 1940, both men assumed a dilatory attitude toward the cross-channel invasion of Britain (Operation "Sea Lion") in the apparent hope that some outside development would rescue each of them from their respective difficulties.[27] To be sure, on June 20, 1940, Raeder bravely expressed the navy's willingness to carry out "Sea Lion," but he added the proviso that Hermann Göring's Luftwaffe must first secure air superiority over the English Channel.[28] In similar fashion, the navy continued with such matters as the modification of Rhine River barges into landing craft, the compilation of debarkation schedules, and the analysis of tidal flows, just in case "Sea Lion" might some day prove both necessary and feasible.

Yet from the very beginning, both Raeder and Hitler hoped that some alternative to a cross-channel invasion would present itself. Perhaps the British would come to their senses and recognize the generosity of the Führer's offer to "guarantee" the British Empire. Perhaps the navy could inflict enough damage on Britain's merchant shipping to force the British into negotiations. Or perhaps—and this was a possibility that must have seemed a double-edged sword to Raeder, given Hermann Göring's confident boast that the air force could successfully assume many of the navy's tasks—the vaunted Luftwaffe could bomb the British into submission. Whatever the case, the longer Hitler and Raeder waited for these hopes to materialize, the less likely Operation "Sea Lion" became. German sailors might continue with their lusty renditions of the popular hit, *Wir Fahren Gegen Engelland*; Operation "Sea Lion" itself might remain on the books for purposes of propaganda, deception, or as a last resort to be undertaken in the "indefinite future." In fact, as early as June 30, 1940, Adolf Hitler's fertile mind was beginning to seize upon a different solution to the problem of Great Britain, one that, rather typically, involved massive armies rather than navies. This decision would come as a bitter disappointment to Raeder. And yet there was an ironic twist to Hitler's new plan that ought to have awakened at least a faint measure of recognition in the historian Erich Raeder. Like the great mariners of the fifteenth and sixteenth centuries who had confounded popular wisdom by sailing west to reach the east, Hitler would attempt to humble his western adversary, Great Britain, by a thrust eastward, into the Soviet Union. In short, "Sea Lion" was giving way to "Barbarossa."[29]

Raeder made one final attempt to interest Hitler in another approach to the British problem. In September 1940, on two separate occasions, he dangled the grandiose prospect of a Mediterranean alternative to both "Sea Lion" and "Barbarossa" before the Führer. According to

Raeder's scheme, German, Italian, Spanish, and, possibly, Vichy French forces would seize Gibraltar and Suez and drive the British from the Mediterranean. If possible, Axis forces would also turn the Canary Islands, the Azores, and the Cape Verdes Islands into bases of operation against Britain and, if it chose to intervene, the United States. From these new vantage points the Kriegsmarine, bolstered by the Italian fleet and new construction from the fatherland, would wage a final, victorious campaign against British shipping. Hitler was evidently impressed, and for a time he actually toyed with Raeder's "Mittelmeer" program. Eventually, however, the Führer returned to "Barbarossa."[30]

Hitler's decision in favor of a land campaign against the Soviet Union would have fateful consequences for the Kriegsmarine. For a brief moment in the summer and fall of 1940, it had appeared as if, at long last, the problem of confronting a first-class maritime power was going to force the German dictator to address the needs of his navy. Hitler's decision for "Barbarossa" at the expense of "Sea Lion" or the Mediterranean alternative dashed these hopes. To be sure, the navy would continue its campaign against British commerce; indeed, it eventually commissioned U-boats and light surface vessels in numbers that had seemed impossible only a few years before. But after the decision for "Barbarossa," it was clear that, until the conquest of the Soviet Union, the army would assume priority in the allocation of Germany's resources.[31] The navy was once again the stepchild of the Wehrmacht.

Yet with or without "Barbarossa," the demands on the Service continued unabated. As "Sea Lion" receded from the realm of possibility and as the Luftwaffe's promise to humble Britain turned up empty, the war against British shipping (*Handelskrieg*) assumed that much more importance for the survival of the Third Reich. A myriad of other concerns—the administration of occupied territories, the orchestration of propaganda, and the indoctrination of the Service's own personnel—likewise consumed the attention of the officer corps. Here, too, the Service often faced daunting problems.

One area in which the navy encountered difficulties concerned occupation policies for territories under German control. An instructive case in point was Norway, where, for various reasons, the navy felt a strong proprietary interest. The invasion of April 1940 could scarcely have been mounted without the navy, which, in turn, had paid dearly in gaining Norway. In addition, the strategic importance of Norway for attacking Britain's northern flank (and, after "Barbarossa," for interdicting the flow of Lend-Lease material to the Soviet Union), lent it immense significance for the prosecution of the war at sea. Linked with these considerations, moreover, was the head of the navy's personal interest in the fate of Norway, for in the early years of the war, at least, Raeder and his closest advisor on Scandinavian affairs, Admiral Hermann Boehm, tended to see Raeder as the spiritual father of *Weserübung*.[32]

Unfortunately, the Kriegsmarine's claim to a certain preeminence in the administration of Norway was bound to lead to complications with Hitler's political representative there, Reichskommissar Joseph Terboven.[33] In particular, the navy's highest-ranking officer in Norway, Admiral Boehm, soon fell out with Terboven over the Reichskommissar's use of terror in dealing with the Norwegian Resistance. "It is self-evident," Boehm wrote Raeder in April 1941, "that men who ally themselves with England must be eliminated. Nevertheless, I consider such measures that (might) have been used in Poland to be politically incorrect in a land that is supposed to be won over to friendship." The following September, Boehm expressed his disapproval to Terboven when the Reichskommissar sentenced two Norwegian labor union leaders to death in retaliation for a strike.[34] A month later Boehm informed Raeder that he could not understand the German occupation authorities' moral outrage at the acts of Norwegian partisans. The Norwegians, Boehm confided, were merely acting in the same way that German patriots had acted in the past. Whether Boehm shared this observation with Terboven is uncertain. Whatever the case, the Reichskommissar's policies remained unchanged, reaching a low point on October 6, 1942, when Terboven had ten prominent citizens of Trondheim executed as "atonement" for recent acts of sabotage there. In the days immediately following, a further twenty-four Norwegians fell victim to Terboven. According to Boehm, the navy was unable to prevent the Reichskommissar's brutal reprisals, even though they occurred in what was essentially the navy's backyard, the port of Trondheim.[35]

Boehm and Terboven also clashed over the future political relationship between Norway and Germany.[36] Although in retrospect there seems to be little difference in the ends that the two men sought—both wanted a Norway that was politically and militarily dependent upon the Reich—there was at least a shade of difference between the way the two men hoped to accomplish this goal. Terboven occasionally spoke of a "Greater Germanic Reich" that would bind Norway and other Nordic countries into a (presumably) free and honorable federation with their fellow "Aryan" brethren in Germany, but as often as not he administered Norway without regard for Norwegian national sensitivity. In 1940, for example, Terboven took the provocative step of quartering German officials in the Storting, the Norwegian parliament building. That same year the Reichskommisar requisitioned the Crown Prince's official residence and made it into his own. Nor was Terboven the only high-ranking party official to view Norway as little more than a conquered province. In January 1941, the visiting SS leader, Heinrich Himmler, expressed similar views on Norway when he informed Boehm: "Here we stand, and from here we shall never depart! Right, Herr Admiral?"[37]

Boehm certainly had no intention of seeing the navy leave Norway. He nevertheless hoped that German concessions to Norwegian national pride would make occupation less odious and in turn pave the way for a less one-sided "association" than that envisioned by Terboven and Himmler. He also hoped that the Reich's authorities would eventually find "some great goal that with time might be suitable for winning the

Norwegians over as friends."[38] Although such a prescription required no great stroke of insight, it certainly offered a more promising point of departure for Norwegian-German friendship than Terboven's reprisals. The problem, as Boehm would soon discover, was to find that "great goal" that would bring Norwegians and Germans together.

Boehm began working for reconciliation as early as December 1940, when he called for the swiftest possible conclusion of a peace treaty between Norway and Germany, followed by the normalization of relations between the two states. According to Boehm's formula, an offensive and defensive alliance (*Schutz- und Trutzbündnis*) would replace Norway's present subordinate status. Once Norway would agree to this, a special representative of the Führer (presumably someone other than Terboven) would assume responsibility for Norwegian affairs. German officials would vacate the most important public buildings in Norway, and the Norwegian flag would be raised once again. Boehm also suggested that Norwegian army units be formed as a symbol of Norwegian sovereignty. These units would not take part in the present hostilities with Britain, and for the remainder of the war Norway would remain ostensibly neutral. Germany would continue, however, to exploit Norway's resources as long as the war lasted. Thereafter, Norway would become a voluntary member of a Germanic *Bund* and would be permitted to form air and naval units which, unlike the army units, would be integral parts of the larger navy and air force of the *Bund*.[39]

In subsequent months, both Boehm and his adjutant, Commander Richard Schreiber, returned to the admiral's musings of December 1940, each time with the same results. Norway would receive the trappings of sovereignty and enjoy the greatest possible freedom of action in internal affairs. At the same time, however, since Norway must never again be used in what Boehm and Schreiber perceived as British "intrigues" against the fatherland, Norway would have to remain within the German sphere of influence, permitting a German (or "Germanic," if one considers Boehm's vision of a German-Scandinavian *Bund*) military presence.[40] In other words, Norway would be free to make its own decisions, so long as these favored Germany.

It was, of course, one thing to call for a voluntary Norwegian participation in a Greater Germanic *Bund* and quite another thing to achieve it in reality. And despite their rather phantasmagorical speculations as to the future of Norway, both Boehm and Schreiber occasionally appear to have realized this truth. Thus in April 1941, in the course of calling for voluntary Norwegian participation in a Germanic *Bund*, Boehm confessed to Raeder that he was uncertain how this cooperation could be attained. He knew only that the methods tried thus far would not work. After the invasion of the Soviet Union in June 1941, Boehm appears to have hoped that Hitler's much ballyhooed crusade against Bolshevism might provide the "great goal" that the admiral had been seeking to unite Germany with Norway and the other Scandinavian countries. In October 1941, for example, he wrote in excited tones about a "Germanic bloc which would stand inviolable between the Russian, Asiatic *Volk* in the east and the democratic Western powers on the other side." But that same month, Schreiber, who was no less enthralled by such prospects than his superior, admitted that this vision of Nordic solidarity presupposed a complete reorientation of the present attitude of most Norwegians toward Germany. German victory in the present war, Schreiber noted, would certainly encourage many Norwegians toward a more friendly attitude to the Reich. Until this victory could be attained, however, the only thing German authorities could do was to allow cooperative Norwegians a tiny measure of "independence" in order to prove that they were not simply German puppets.[41]

It was on this matter—the problem of "cooperation" or, to use a word more colored by contemporary history, "collaboration"—that German naval and political leaders in Norway most clearly differed. And the primary question at issue was the use or nonuse of the man whose very name has become synonymous with the word "collaborator," Major Vidkun Quisling. Since his meeting with Raeder and Hitler in December 1939, the Norwegian had not been entirely inactive. When German troops invaded Norway the following April, Quisling, with Hitler's blessings, had declared himself the head of the new regime. His mishandling of the coup, however, and his manifest unpopularity with the majority of Norwegians almost immediately gave the German dictator second thoughts about the major. Thus, within a week of the invasion, German diplomats prevailed upon Quisling to resign as the head of government and began efforts to utilize other, less objectionable Norwegians. Until June 1940, German statesmen, including Terboven, even hoped to entice the Norwegian king, Haakon VII, or one of his relatives, to return to Oslo and reign as a German puppet. It was only after these and other hopes had faded that Reich leaders began to reconsider Quisling. Nevertheless, many German political figures, especially Terboven, retained grave reservations concerning the major.[42]

A number of the navy's leaders, by contrast, held a consistently high view of Quisling. Raeder, for example, was impressed with the major's personal reliability, describing him as a "very upright, trustworthy man, typical of the somewhat dour Norwegian, but intelligent," whose sole liability was his insufficient mastery of German.[43] Even after German authorities removed him as Prime Minister, therefore, Raeder continued to push him as Minister of Defense in the collaborationist government. From this position, Raeder hoped, Quisling would court prominent Norwegians and eventually lay the foundations for closer Norwegian-German cooperation. Accordingly, Raeder sought to "display" Quisling and to let him take credit for whatever popular measures that occupation forces undertook. Unfortunately, Raeder's suggestions went unheeded, for the major was initially excluded from the new Cabinet.

In September 1940, however, Hitler opted for a new tack with regard to Norway. Reichskommissar Terboven announced the formal deposition of King Haakon, the dissolution of all parties except the Nasjonal

Samling, and the formation of a new government dominated by that party. Although Terboven's lingering reservations concerning Quisling still precluded his inclusion in the new Cabinet, the major, as head of the Nasjonal Samling, appeared to have recouped at least some of the power that had been wrested from him the previous April.[44]

Nevertheless, Norwegian affairs continued to perplex Raeder. In October 1940, he wrote Boehm that he had the impression that the "Quisling people" were not always loyally supported by German authorities. In early December, Boehm responded with his own assessment in favor of Quisling. Although the Quisling movement was still relatively weak, it seemed self-evident to Boehm that the best way to deal with the situation was to encourage the Nasjonal Samling as the one party that had supported the Germans through "thick and thin." The admiral conceded that a number of obstacles—strong monarchical feelings, centuries of pro-British sentiment, and the all too evident presence of German occupation forces—hampered the major's efforts to win Norway for the Reich. Nevertheless, Boehm felt that German authorities could foster Quisling's work if, rather than looking at Norway through the eyes of conquerors, they could show that the Nasjonal Samling stood for the good of Norway.[45]

Raeder passed Boehm's suggestions on to Hitler in mid-December. On December 21, the head of the navy assured Boehm that the Führer had read the report with great interest. Unfortunately, a number of the Reich's civilian leaders appear to have concluded that Boehm was taking an undue interest in politics. That same month, Hans Lammers, Hitler's chief of the Reich Chancellery, noted a recent remark by Quisling to the effect that the Norwegians would prefer to see Boehm, rather than General Nikolaus von Falkenhorst, as the supreme Wehrmacht representative in Norway. Lammers saw this as evidence that Boehm was pursuing an independent course from Falkenhorst and Terboven. Raeder suggested rather disingenuously that Quisling had been misunderstood (here Quisling's poor command of German came to the advantage of the navy!) and asserted that Boehm had always refrained from involving himself in politics.[46]

By the end of 1940, therefore, Boehm and Terboven, the highest naval and political German representatives in Norway, were on a collision course. On December 28, Boehm wrote Raeder about the increasing friction between the Reichskommissar and himself and criticized Terboven's neglect of Quisling.[47] Terboven, for his part, appears to have complained to Hitler about Boehm's intervention in his affairs. Sensing danger, Raeder urged caution on Boehm:

> Since the R.K. [Reichskommissar] is apparently laying some mines, I would suggest that for the time being you behave as circumspectly as possible in political matters so that I can pursue the goals that I have confided to you. It goes without saying that I approve of the policy that you have described to me with respect to politics, and I shall always defend it before the Führer.[48]

Despite Raeder's admonition, Boehm's difficulties with Terboven continued. In January 1941, the two men disagreed publicly in front of visiting SS leader Heinrich Himmler, over the relative importance of Norwegian national feeling. In April Boehm and Schreiber sent reports to Raeder that were highly critical of Terboven's handling of Quisling. And in the summer and fall of 1941, both Boehm and Schreiber suggested forcefully that Terboven should place all his hopes on Quisling.[49]

Under normal circumstances, the Reichskommissar could have been expected to resist the navy's challenges to his authority. Hitler, however, not Terboven, was the ultimate arbiter of Norwegian affairs, and by early 1942 the Führer was also ready for a change in German policy. Whether influenced by the constant pressure of the naval officers, by Alfred Rosenberg's continued support of Quisling,[50] or by one of his own flashes of intuition, Hitler appears to have concluded that the Nasjonal Samling and Quisling represented the only hope of winning Norwegians over to the New Order in Europe. On January 23, 1942, therefore, Terboven at last invited Quisling to take formal control of a new government. Quisling obliged on February 1, taking the portfolios of defense and foreign affairs in the bargain.[51] The naval officers—Raeder, Boehm, and Schreiber—had good reason to celebrate. After two years of effort, their protégé would now be given his chance. It remained only for Vidkun Quisling to justify the many hopes that had been placed in him.

Alas, this ultimately proved to be beyond the poor major's capabilities. Despite a few cosmetic changes in the months that followed, most Norwegians had little difficulty in recognizing Quisling for what he was. He was thus no more successful than Terboven at winning Norway for Hitler, and, although Quisling continued to head the collaborationist government for the duration of the war, he gradually lost interest even in the limited functions that fell beneath his purview. Perhaps because of this, there was a curious reconciliation of sorts between the two old adversaries, Quisling and Terboven. As one authority on the subject has suggested: "The less Quisling interfered in the practical management of Norwegian affairs, the better Terboven liked him."[52]

Yet if Terboven ultimately resolved at least some of his outward differences with Quisling, the same could not be said of the Reichskommissar's relationship with Quisling's two patrons, Raeder and Boehm. The more evident German failure in Norway became, the more Terboven sought to place the blame for this upon the admirals. In December 1942, for example, Terboven complained bitterly to Boehm's chief of staff, Rear Admiral Fein, that because of the machinations of the Kriegsmarine, the political situation in Norway was virtually irretrievable. The admirals likewise continued to complain about Terboven, though with little success. According to Raeder, his inability to secure a change in Norwegian policy was one of the reasons for his resignation as head of the navy in January 1943. Boehm persisted, pressing for Terboven's removal as Reichskommissar even after his own retirement from active duty in March 1943. At a meeting with Hitler the following September, the admiral took up the issue of Norway in considerable detail. According to Boehm, Hitler listened without interruption for seventy-five minutes (surely a record for the Führer!) as the admiral described Terboven's "ruinous policy." Hitler's response was instructive vis-à-vis National Socialist occupation policies: the Führer thanked his admiral politely and then dismissed him. Terboven remained in power in Norway until the bitter end.[53]

The matter of Norway, then, proved to be a troublesome point of contention between naval and party officials. Another source of difficulties between the Party and the Kriegsmarine concerned the formulation and dissemination of propaganda. The naval high command was certainly aware of the value of a well-coordinated propaganda campaign. Successful propaganda could maintain morale on the home front; it was also useful in influencing neutral opinion and in discouraging and misleading the enemy. Moreover, as the war continued, it was clearly essential that Hitler be apprised of the Kriegsmarine's services for the fatherland. Unfortunately, in these tasks, as in so many others, the navy found that it operated under disadvantages that did not confront the other branches of the Wehrmacht.[54]

The navy's handicaps in the realm of propaganda emerged most graphically at the highest level of the military's propaganda campaign in the so-called *Wehrmachtberichte*, short communiqués which were issued every day to the press and radio by the Oberkommando der Wehrmacht (OKW) and which gave a brief summary of military developments over the past twenty-four hours. Each branch of the Wehrmacht submitted its own reports, which were then modified or abridged to fit the available space or, on occasion, to put a more favorable interpretation upon events. Understandably, the commanders of the army, navy, and air force were at pains to see that their particular branch was not neglected. Unfortunately, because the Kriegsmarine's warships usually operated under radio silence, the results of most missions were not announced until the return of the vessel to port. Consequently, there were often times when the navy had little to report, and on occasion there were days when the navy—alone among the services—was not mentioned at all. The army and especially the air force, by contrast, tended to mention the most trivial accomplishments in order to keep their branches in the public eye. Sea warfare consequently received less coverage in the *Wehrmachtberichte* than did air or land warfare.[55]

Yet the *Wehrmachtberichte* were not the only matters in which the Service encountered difficulties with its propaganda campaign. Naval officers also ran into problems with the correspondents that Joseph Goebbels' Propaganda Ministry assigned to cover the Kriegsmarine's exploits. The Service's relationship with the "propaganda troops," as these reporters were called, was an uncomfortable one from the beginning. Although propaganda units were formed for the army and air force in 1938, neither the Propaganda Ministry nor the naval high command appear to have been overly enthusiastic about similar units for the Kriegsmarine at that time.[56] Indeed, it was not until the spring and summer of 1939 that the navy, acting at the urging of the Wehrmacht high command, began to show an interest in propaganda troops. After some delay, on June 15, 1939, the Kriegsmarine announced its intention to form two propaganda companies (one for each of the Naval Stations) and urged all subordinate units to cultivate "an understanding and friction-free cooperation" with these latest additions to the Service.[57]

Unfortunately for intra-service harmony, a number of obstacles hampered the smooth integration of the propaganda troops into the Kriegsmarine. As with earlier arrangements concerning the war correspondents for the army and air force, Goebbels' Propaganda Ministry provided the "specialists" (writers, photographers, radio broadcasters, and technicians) while the navy furnished the "military personnel" (company commanders, drivers, secretaries, and cooks). As a result, the first propaganda units were a hodgepodge of conscripts, elderly reservists, and a few enthusiastic reporters.[58] Because of its role in providing the "specialists," the Propaganda Ministry often sought to extend its influence into matters (discipline, for example) that normally would have fallen to the navy alone. Disputes also occurred over the censorship and presentation of news pertaining to the navy. To complicate the matter, the Oberkommando der Wermacht (OKW) took an interest in virtually all aspects of the propaganda units as well, which meant that the Propaganda Ministry, the Kriegsmarine, and the OKW were frequently involved in a three-way tug-of-war over the navy's war correspondents.[59]

The practical difficulties of covering the war at sea also hampered the "friction-free cooperation" between regular naval personnel and "propaganda troops" to which the high command had appealed. Space aboard the Kriegsmarine's vessels was always at a premium, and in the early years of the war, at least, few if any of the reporters could make a contribution to the day-to-day operation of the vessel to which they were assigned. In addition, security considerations made many commanders reluctant to allow reporters on board their vessels. Moreover, despite Raeder's desire that all branches of the navy appear frequently in the public eye, the high command initially thought it best to prohibit war correspondents from visiting U-boats and to limit direct contacts between reporters and submarine personnel. By January 1940, these restrictions had evidently been relaxed, but war correspondents continued to complain that their activities were severely handicapped by Kriegsmarine officers. Ship commanders rarely took the initiative in inviting reporters aboard, and, when they did issue invitations, they restricted the correspondents' movement, thereby hindering effective reportage.[60]

Nor were matters improved by the use of the so-called *Sonderführer* in the propaganda units. This designation was the result of an arrangement whereby the Propaganda Ministry's reporters were given the provisional ranks of noncommissioned officers or lieutenants in the Kriegsmarine. In due time, the *Sonderführer* were expected to undergo regular training that would transform them into "real" noncommissioned officers or, in the case of the lieutenants, into reserve officers in the navy. The designation of *Sonderführer* would then lapse. Unfortunately, reporting assignments and frequent transfers often prevented attendance at the reserve officer training courses, which meant that some lieutenants (S) (for *Sonderführer*) were still in evidence as late as 1943.[61]

In theory, the presence of a group of what were essentially civilians in uniform ought not to have mattered very much. In practice, however, the *Sonderführer* almost immediately encountered the prejudices of what one of their number subsequently termed "the right honorable company of dark blue jackets," that is, the regular navy. Veterans of the Kriegsmarine tended to see the war correspondents as babes in the wood when it came to the navy, and the behavior and appearance of a number of the *Sonderführer* did little to allay this suspicion. Some *Sonderführer* appear to have "forgotten" to wear their *Sonderführer* insignia, thereby giving added credence to the suspicion that they were merely masquerading as "real" officers. Others were physically unfit, whereas still others so peppered their reports with party jargon as to exhaust the patience of all but the most sympathetic of the regular officers.[62] And nearly all of the propaganda soldiers had a great deal to learn about the navy of Erich Raeder.

Indeed it was the last of these considerations that probably most fully explains the difficulties that the *Sonderführer* encountered in their dealings with the regular officers of the Kriegsmarine. Thus in June 1940, a regular naval officer, a certain lieutenant (j.g.) Reymann, complained that a photographer from the First Naval Propaganda Company had displayed no knowledge of naval affairs and had behaved very awkwardly during a visit to the Germania Werft at Kiel. Reymann added that the man's photographs left something to be desired as well. The following year, the commander of Naval Propaganda Detachment West determined that one of his *Sonderführer*, a Dr Nonnenbruch, would have to be dismissed from the Service because his "nonmilitary appearance" precluded his acceptance by sailors at the front. And in December 1941, Karl Dönitz became enraged because a war correspondent embroidered a pep talk to workers at a Mannheim steelyard with a series of hair-raising and improbable experiences aboard the U-boats. Presumably, the reporter's "revolver propaganda," as Dönitz described it, did not meet the august standards that the leader of the U-boat force sought to set for his men.[63]

Other *Sonderführer* offended the regular officer corps through their exaggerated sense of their own importance. In May 1941, for example, the head of the Naval Personnel Department, Admiral Conrad Patzig, encountered a suggestion that the *Sonderführer* attend special accelerated courses rather than burden them with the usual requirements that were made of all reserve officers in the Kriegsmarine. Patzig's response was icy. He insisted that the correspondents continue to undergo the same training as the other officers, "so that they will be reserve officers in fact as well as appearance." Any departure from this rule would tend toward the creation of what Patzig sarcastically termed a "war correspondent reserve officer corps" which would wear the same uniform as the other branches of the Kriegsmarine but which would otherwise have no professional connection with them. To implement the proposal would risk turning the "membership" of the correspondents in the navy into a "farce, pure and simple."[64]

A similar case of *Sonderführer* effrontery occurred in the fall of 1941, when the commanding admiral of the Norwegian north coast, Vice Admiral Leopold Siemens, ordered the war correspondent troop at Trondheim to move from their present comfortable quarters into an old Norwegian army barracks. Although there are indications that the admiral was already no friend of the war correspondents—he had supposedly made little use of them and had spoken disparagingly of their services—the indignant letter of the troop commander, a lieutenant Pfeiffer, to his superiors at the Wehrmacht Propaganda Department at Potsdam could scarcely have generated much sympathy among the regular naval officers. Pfeiffer was miffed that Vice Admiral Siemens did not have the time to discuss the propaganda troop's accommodations with him personally, referring the matter to his chief of staff instead. The lieutenant also complained bitterly that the new quarters were completely unsuited for the war correspondents. The washroom was "really primitive," containing only a tin trough and a shower, with no separate facilities for the officers' private use. There were no proper toilets, but only an outdoor latrine. There was no kitchen, and if one were installed it would take up one of the barracks' nine rooms. Pfeiffer then listed his requirements, which, in view of the conditions then prevailing at Trondheim, must have sounded well-nigh utopian: his small troop needed five officers' rooms, three noncommissioned officers' rooms, two rooms for the enlisted men, one composition room, two photo laboratories, one common room, one equipment room, one storage room, one kitchen, and a three-car garage. Only in this way, Pfeiffer concluded, could his correspondents "prepare their material and recover in quiet and comfort, so as to be ready for their next mission."[65] Unfortunately, there is no record of the navy's response to Pfeiffer's demands. Anyone familiar with the Service's cramped vessels must surely have wondered from which *salon* the good lieutenant had sauntered. Not surprisingly, nothing was done to ease Pfeiffer's predicament before the troop was transferred out of Trondheim that December.

Yet not all of the difficulties with the *Sonderführer* were confined to trivialities. A number of more serious cases concerned the worthiness of the *Sonderführer* to wear the uniform of the Kriegsmarine. Some of these involved apparent cowardice in combat or in crisis situations.[66] Others concerned transgressions in civilian life which came to light after investigations into the backgrounds of the war correspondents. Thus in late October 1941, a lieutenant (S) was stricken from the list of reserve officer candidates on account of a prior conviction for sodomy.[67] One month later another lieutenant (S), Walter Selss, was dismissed from the navy for numerous prior convictions for forgery. Nor were all of the disheartening revelations concerning the war correspondents restricted to the distant past. In November 1942, *Sonderführer* Joseph Vidau was charged with stealing from his comrades, dereliction of duty, and disregard for security matters, while the following December yet another lieutenant, Heinz von Rebeur-Paschwitz, was removed from *Sonderführer* status and confined to a hospital to determine whether he was, as suspected, a kleptomaniac.[68]

In the face of these and other discoveries[69] concerning the past and present activities of some of the war correspondents, many regular naval officers must have wondered what was happening to their Service. Concerning as they did a foreign and easily identifiable element within the navy, these incidents must surely have aroused the impression that the corps was opening its ranks to the dregs of German society. And if other officers chose to convey their disapproval by a stubborn refusal to cooperate with the reporters or a studied aloofness from them, at least one high-ranking officer chose to confront the problem head-on. In June 1941, the commander of the North Sea Naval Station noted that since the beginning of the war the Naval Propaganda Detachment West had promoted eighty-two war correspondents to *Sonderführer* status. After noting that it had already proven necessary to dismiss two of these *Sonderführer* from the navy, the admiral went on to question whether all of these appointments were necessary. The behavior of the *Sonderführer*, he asserted, frequently damaged the Service's good name, "as a number of unpleasant incidents have already shown." Continued indiscriminate promotion of *Sonderführer*, he alleged, was a danger to the appearance of the officer corps and to the proper maintenance of discipline.[70]

Thus the relationship between the regular navy and the war correspondents proved to be a difficult one. Yet it would appear that despite these difficulties, the "propaganda troops" were gradually incorporated into Raeder's "naval family," for, as the war wore on, many reporters saw or professed to see a slow but steady increase in the willingness of Kriegsmarine commanders to take them on board during combat missions. One explanation for this was doubtless the growing awareness among regular officers that, whatever objections they might have against the propaganda troops, they were nevertheless performing useful work for the navy. Another was the virtual disappearance of the troublesome status of *Sonderführer* as the majority of the war correspondents completed their military training courses and became full-fledged reserve officers in the Kriegsmarine. Nor was the change from *Sonderführer* to reserve officer merely a cosmetic one. With experience many of the correspondents learned to contribute at least something in emergency situations, particularly aboard the Service's minesweepers and *Schnellboote*, where an extra gunner or ammunition handler came in handy. Indeed, various correspondents earned the Iron Cross, First or Second Class, and at least one correspondent even managed to win appointment to the executive officers' training program through his exertions.[71]

The price that the war correspondents paid for this initiation as true "front soldiers," however, was a heavy one. As early as October 1941, the commander of Naval Propaganda Detachment North noted that since the beginning of the war, 10 per cent of the detachment's reporters had been killed or were missing in action.[72] In due time, these losses would mount considerably. Yet even this rather sobering realization contributed to the gradual integration of the propaganda troops into the rank and file of the navy, for there was nothing like the awareness of shared dangers and shared sacrifices to blur the distinction between the professional soldier and the civilian.

While the war correspondents played a vital part in popularizing the navy to the German public, in another area—the indoctrination of the Service's own personnel—their role was much more limited. Initial discussions concerning the formation of the propaganda units left little doubt that *Truppenbetreuung*, which encompassed such matters as indoctrination and the maintenance of morale within the Service, was to remain the exclusive province of the navy. When one overly enthusiastic propaganda commander sought to undertake this task on his own, he was swiftly reminded that this did not pertain to his duties.[73] The navy was clearly determined to keep the direction of *Truppenbetreuung* in the hands of "insiders."

In the first months of the war, this task was left largely to the initiative of individual unit commanders. In the spring of 1940, however, a department for *Wehrbetreuung* was created within the Allgemeines Marinehauptamt under Commander Erich Frühling to coordinate the navy's efforts in this regard.[74] At the same time, a *Wehrbetreuungsoffizier* was appointed from among the Service's active or reserve officers for each Kriegsmarine vessel, and for company-sized and larger land units. The duties of the *Wehrbetreuungsoffizier* varied with the size of the unit. At the higher levels, the officer might devote his attention exclusively to matters of *Wehrbetreuung*; in smaller commands, he would be responsible for more traditional functions as well.

Wehrbetreuung itself encompassed a number of concerns, many of which were fairly conventional. Remembering the Service's failures in the realm of leadership during the Great War, Frühling and his assistants sought to make sure that the off-duty hours of naval personnel were filled with activity. Professional entertainers and films were sent from base to base, and the sailors were urged to take up such matters as singing and drama on their own. The Service also encouraged athletics and gardening as worthwhile recreational activities to relieve the monotony of life in the rear echelons. At sea, the possibilities were more limited, but Frühling saw to it that even the smallest vessels of the fleet received a varied and up-to-date selection of books and magazines for off-duty reading. Finally, Frühling encouraged individual unit commanders to do their utmost to maintain morale by giving lively lectures which either stressed the importance of each man's doing his duty or else attempted to place the day-to-day developments of the war into a larger perspective.

As one officer noted at the time, however, the subject of *Wehrbetreuung* was not exhausted by such matters as "*Kdf, Kino, Bastelei*" (Strength through Joy programs, cinema, and hobbies).[75] Political indoctrination also played an important role in the activities of the *Wehrbetreuungsoffiziere* from the beginning.[76] At the first general session for *Wehrbetreuungsoffiziere* at Berlin in December 1940, for example, Frühling set the tone for future conferences in his opening address.[77] The Party's general dismay over the urbanization of Germany, its emphasis upon the "monumental tasks" that would confront the *Volk* upon the victorious conclusion of the war, and its concern for the crucial role of ideology in understanding all aspects of human endeavor, in politics, economics, and history, were all reflected in the course of Frühling's remarks. Perhaps most striking, however, was Frühling's Social Darwinist explanation of the relations between states. "Struggle," he intoned, "which is the lot of the soldier, is also the life's work of every being in nature . . . . Every species of animal which is for any length of time inferior to another similar species in its willingness to fight, its intelligence, cleanliness, or conscientiousness is inevitably condemned to death by this inferiority." In similar fashion, the strengths and weaknesses of each individual, when added together into a national pool, would spell victory or defeat in the struggle between nations. In view of these considerations, each German sailor bore immense responsibilities, not simply as a combatant but as a progenitor of the race. Addressing the latter point, Frühling admonished: "A soldier, for example, who goes triumphantly into an enemy land but who then renders himself impotent by contracting a venereal disease has, for his part, lost the war for his *Volk*."[78]

It was the task of the *Wehrbetreuungsoffiziere* to incorporate these and other insights into their messages to the troops. Frühling expected the highest degree of initiative in this regard. As he drew to a conclusion, he exhorted his audience to whip the Kriegsmarine's sailors into crusaders for National Socialism:

> We want to turn as many sailors as possible into conscious and enthusiastic bearers of the Idea and into fanatical adherents of its realization. We aim at personalities with personal conviction, who will carry out the tasks of our *Volk* to the very end, even if they are alone, without witnesses, and without leaders at distant and forlorn posts.[79]

Frühling's remarks, spoken in December 1940, were a striking prefiguration of the *Götterdämmerung* mentality of April 1945. At the same time, however, both Frühling and his audience must have been aware that the transformation that they sought within the navy would not be an easy one. Not only were many of the *Wehrbetreuungsoffiziere* as yet unfamiliar with their new duties; in the early years of the war the notion of *"wehrgeistige Führung"* or "spiritual leadership" in the ideological sense still went against the grain of many officers who believed, rightly or wrongly, that they had been trained in a tradition of unpolitical soldiership. It was small wonder, therefore, that in his concluding address at the same December session on *Wehrbetreuung*, Frühling's superior, Admiral Walter

Warzecha, encouraged the *Wehrbetreuungsoffiziere* to go to their tasks with "open hearts" but at the same time cautioned that there would be skeptics in the Kriegsmarine who doubted the efficacy of their new form of leadership.[80]

Despite these difficulties Warzecha and Frühling were determined to proceed with their plans for the navy. In one area—the generation of reading material on "spiritual leadership"—the two men showed particular energy. When Frühling became responsible for *Wehrbetreuung* in the spring of 1940, virtually the only work that purported to offer any insight in this matter was Siegfried Sorge's *Marineoffizier als Führer und Erzieher*.[81] By November 1941, however, when the second general conference on *Wehrbetreuung* took place, the first new contributions to what eventually became a fairly extensive literature on the subject were already beginning to appear.

As with Sorge's earlier work, much of the new material was of a fairly conventional nature, combining common sense with traditional insights into the art of leadership. In view of this, some of the initial efforts to impart a National Socialist coloring to the navy's "spiritual leadership" must have appeared rather lame. In a pamphlet drawn up for the second session on *Wehrbetreuung*, for example, about the best Captain Friedrich Ruge could do on the subject of National Socialism was to make the usual stock reference to the Party's service in providing "a very strong central idea for the entire Wehrmacht and the entire *Volk*."[82] The contributions of the highly successful commander of the auxiliary cruiser *Atlantis*, Captain Bernard Rogge, were equally unconvincing in this regard. For him, National Socialism was largely "common good before individual good" and "one for all and all for one."[83] In their comments on *Wehrbetreuung*, moreover, both Ruge and Rogge occasionally raised potentially embarrassing questions concerning both the navy's and the Party's recent past. Ruge, for example, reawakened painful memories of the Service's failures in leadership by urging the aspiring young officer to read Joachim Ringelnatz's polemic on the Imperial Navy, *Als Mariner im Weltkrieg*, so that the mistakes described therein could be avoided in the future.[84] Rogge likewise recommended Ringelnatz and suggested Erich Maria Remarque's *All Quiet on the Western Front*, Theodore Plivier's *Des Kaisers Kulis*, and Lothar Persius' *Menschen und Schiffe in der kaiserlichen Flotte* for insight into the negative lessons from the *Kaiserreich*. Unfortunately, Rogge added, the works of these authors, all of whom were leftists, pacifists, or both, were virtually unobtainable in Germany.[85] Nor was Rogge's oblique reference to Joseph Goebbels' book burnings the only offense against National Socialist etiquette that the commander of the *Atlantis* committed in his musings on "spiritual leadership." In the same address, Rogge appears to have stated that the older National Socialists were in part "crass egoists" and "pompous asses" and complained about the "HJ [Hitler Youth] sickness" evident among younger Germans. Other officers had an easier time incorporating National Socialist ideology into their works on *Wehrbetreuung*. Captain Rudolf Krohne's "Der Kommandant auf kleinem Fahrzeug," which appeared in 1941, was especially interesting, for he maintained that the sailor's naval experience was a perfect example of National Socialism in practice:

> There is scarcely any form of association in which all of the elements of National Socialist ideology are more applicable than aboard a small vessel. A well-directed front boat is a model of National Socialist management. The daily operation of the boat offers a thousand opportunities to make practical application of National Socialist thought and, what is absolutely the same thing, of the officer's way of looking at things.

And, as Krohne added later: "to be an officer means and must always mean that one is at the same time a model National Socialist."[86]

Occasionally, the Service's activities in the realm of *Wehrbetreuung* could take a rather surprising turn. A common complaint within the navy was that the younger officers usually lacked any sort of training in practical psychology when it came to dealing with their men.[87] Yet, when the navy commissioned a short primer, "Führung und Soldatenseele," to redress this deficiency, the author almost immediately forsook the bounds of traditional psychology in favor of a livelier discourse on race, blood, and soil. Outward differences among the races, he maintained, were merely manifestations of deeper differences in the racially formed soul, which in turn impelled the races of the world in different directions. Race, however, was not the only determining factor in the relations between nations; the *Volk* lived in constant interaction with the environment, "with the soil and everything that comes from it: tree, bush, and animal." If this contact with the soil was lacking, then the individual became a "rootless city dweller" with a "stunted soul." But if the land formed the *Volk*, the *Volk* also formed the land. This, the author averred, explained the Germans' sense of uneasiness in eastern Europe: "There no German can take up any feeling with the landscape, for it has been formed by the soul of men who are racially alien to us. The German soul must first conquer this landscape and then mold it before we can find a relationship in common with it."[88]

Thus the Service gradually developed a body of literature on the subject of "spiritual leadership." And the more serious the situation facing the Reich became, the more men like Frühling, Warzecha, and their commanding admiral, Raeder, sought to use this new ideological "weapon" as a means of countering Germany's increasing military and personnel inferiority vis-à-vis the Allies. Indifference or lightheartedness on the part of Kriegsmarine officers was not to be tolerated. When Warzecha, for example, discovered a tendency on the part of some sailors to view the *Wehrbetreuungsoffizier* as little more than a "movie and recreation man," he moved energetically to set matters straight at the next session on "spiritual leadership" in November 1941. There was far more to *Wehrbetreuung* than mere entertainment, the admiral asserted. Nor did he accept some officers' argument that "spiritual leadership" diverted them from other, more essential tasks. According to Warzecha, the benefits derived from *Wehrbetreuung* more than compensated for lost time in other areas and would assume more importance the longer the war lasted.[89]

Raeder shared Warzecha's favorable assessment of *Wehrbetreuungsoffiziere*. At the same session in November 1941, he, too, complained that the Service was not employing all the possibilities that were available in this area and urged the *Wehrbetreuungsoffiziere* to create the proper warriors to accomplish the Führer's great aims.[90] Raeder's most open endorsement of the new emphasis on ideological leadership, however, came a little over a year later, at a session on *Wehrbetreuung* in January 1943.[91] By that time, the fortunes of war were beginning to turn against Germany, and Raeder's own resignation was scarcely two weeks away. Perhaps it was these twin considerations—the gravity of the situation confronting the Reich and Raeder's own desire to place his final stamp upon the Kriegsmarine before it passed from his control—that prompted the admiral's comments on *Wehrbetreuung*.

After a few introductory remarks surveying the material and personnel difficulties facing the navy, Raeder moved swiftly to the crux of his message. The present war, he told his audience, was a war of ideologies. That being the case, it was in Germany's favor that the tenets of National Socialism had penetrated the entire *Volk*. It was likewise essential that the officer corps recognize this fact and use it as a source of tremendous "moral strength." Later in the address, Raeder indicated exactly how ideology could fulfill this role. Not only did a common ideology facilitate the officer's task in explaining to his men the reasons why Germany was fighting and what the nation stood to gain or lose in the war; common ideology also fostered within the officer corps the as yet unrealized unity of opinion that Raeder deemed essential for the achievement of Germany's aims.[92]

Those were the most obvious contributions that sound ideological schooling could make. There was, however, another side to the war of ideologies that Raeder also recognized. Especially in the east, in the campaign against the Soviet Union, the German soldier and sailor faced an ideologically tough enemy, who made resourceful use of propaganda, both to encourage his own troops and to discourage those of the Axis. Under these circumstances, it was no longer enough to deny enemy reports; the German officer must inculcate his soldiers with the proper beliefs. Accordingly, ideological leadership was a vital task that was of equal importance with traditional military duties. Indifference to this feature of *Wehrbetreuung* had no place in the navy and must be eliminated "root and branch." As Raeder expressed it: "We cannot win the war against a fanatical enemy with the old principle of 'live and let live.'"[93]

Thus Raeder called for the addition of ideological fervor to the navy's arsenal. Granted that this placed still greater burdens upon the already hard-pressed officers of the Kriegsmarine; the commanding admiral felt confident that the demands of Führer and fatherland fully justified every new exertion. Indeed, as he warmed to his topic, Raeder reminded his officers that it was these considerations that were of paramount importance:

> Do not think only of the present day or the present war; think instead of the millennia in which the German nation has already struggled and of the centuries that lie before us and require a wise use of all our resources from this day on .... Remember, therefore, the most important axiom in the thoughts of our Führer and Supreme Commander; it is not the individual, the family, or the clan that count, but the *Volk* and the *Volk* alone. That which serves it is good; that which harms it is bad. The *Volk* incorporates our highest goals. Its thousand-year tasks and struggles extend unto the heights from which divine providence directs all life.[94]

Such, then, were Raeder's views on the utility of *Wehrbetreuung*. The degree to which the rank and file of the Kriegsmarine adhered to these and other exhortations is, of course, a matter of debate. Since the Second World War, apologists for the navy have steadfastly maintained that the Service was scarcely touched by National Socialist ideology. In the early years of the war, however, Allied officers often drew very different conclusions about the ideological toughness of captured naval personnel. In the fall of 1940, for example, interrogation of the crew of Lieutenant Commander Hans Jenisch's *U-32* revealed that the prisoners "were all fanatical Nazis and hated the British intensely, which had not been so evident in previous cases." Similarly, in February 1941, the British interrogator of the crew of *U-70* noted that morale was high and that "the usual undigested propaganda was repeated *verbatim ad nauseam*." On the other hand, when Commander Otto Kretschmer, one of the top U-boat "aces," was captured the following month, his political opinions were found to be "less extreme Nazi than had been assumed." Likewise, his first officer, Lieutenant Commander Hans Jochen von Knebel Döberitz, admitted to his captors that he was ashamed of many features of National Socialism and that his outward behavior had merely been a facade.[95] All in all, however, such cases of open disillusionment would appear to have been relatively rare, at least in the early part of the war. Even if some officers did harbor doubts about the rectitude of Germany's cause, one suspects that few of them were going to divulge their uncertainties, either to their captors or to their brother officers in the Kriegsmarine.

Privately, though, some naval officers *were* beginning to see a more disturbing side of the National Socialist regime. As noted earlier, both Raeder and his primary advisor on Norwegian matters, Hermann Boehm, were deeply troubled by Reichskommissar Terboven's bloody reprisals against Norwegian civilians in 1941 and 1942. Raeder also displayed at least some signs of unease over the draconian measures that Hitler adopted in dealing with Allied commandos in October 1942. To be sure, the head of the navy dutifully passed the so-called "Commando Order" (calling for the merciless elimination of enemy commando units and the immediate delivery of any surviving prisoners to almost certain death at the hands of Himmler's *Sicherheitsdienst*) on to the Service with barely a comment. But when two British marines were captured at Bordeaux, France, the following December and executed without trial by a naval firing squad, Raeder noted in the Seekriegsleitung's war diary that this was "an innovation in international law since the soldiers were wearing uniforms."[96]

Raeder's laconic comment may or may not have been intended as a veiled criticism of the National Socialist regime. But at least two naval officers did compose lengthy, if at times unconventional, memoranda that revealed their unease over certain developments in Germany.

In July 1941 an experienced destroyer commander, Commander Hans Erdmenger, prepared a twenty-five-page memorandum in which he addressed a variety of "pedagogical and spiritual" problems confronting the fatherland.[97] His analysis was nothing if not wide-ranging. To facilitate the government's restoration of the farming sector and to combat the oft-lamented "flight from the land," Erdmenger urged Reich authorities to pay greater attention to the "biologic-dynamic" farming methods of Dr Erhardt Bartsch, who was said to have derived spectacular results from the use of natural rather than artificial fertilizers. To counteract the increasing poverty of German religious life, the naval officer suggested that the government might wish to rehabilitate the "Christian Society" (*Christengemeinschaft*) of Pastor Friedrich Rittelmeyer, which the Gestapo had suppressed the previous June. Erdmenger assured his superiors that, unlike most modern Christian sects which had their origins in Britain or the United States, Dr Rittelmeyer's followers represented a "purely German renewal movement," which strongly emphasized the duties that fell upon all "creative" Germans.

Erdmenger reserved his most interesting comments, however, for the Reich government's campaign against the followers of Dr Rudolf Steiner, the founder of the anthroposophist movement. Although Erdmenger viewed Steiner as a good German—so immersed in Goethe that he ultimately came to "think original 'Goethese' himself"—he was disturbed that Steiner's followers had come under attack by the Gestapo for their alleged connection with freemasonry, officially prohibited in Germany since 1935. Erdmenger viewed this as a tragic misunderstanding, especially since Steiner had been among the first to take up the fight against freemasonry during the First World War.

How was this confusion possible? To Erdmenger, the answer lay in the freemasons' and Dr Steiner's mutual interest in the supernatural. Yet in marked contrast to the freemasons, Dr Steiner had been careful not to abuse his powers in this realm and had used them for the greater good of the *Volk* instead. Unfortunately, Erdmenger asserted, the good doctor's enemies, "freemasons and Jesuits," were alarmed that he had shed light on supernatural matters and had consequently sought to discredit him, thereby rendering his work valueless for the fatherland.

In Erdmenger's view, recent developments in Germany lent added urgency to his message. On May 10, 1942, Deputy Führer Rudolf

Hess had undertaken an unauthorized one-way mission to Scotland allegedly to restore peace between Britain and Germany. Goebbels' Propaganda Ministry reacted to this astonishing news by suggesting that Hess had been suffering recently from severe physical pain and that he had temporarily taken leave of his senses.[98] But Erdmenger suspected a more sinister force at work: quite possibly Allied specialists in the occult had misused their power to control Hess' actions from afar. Rather than ignore the work of Steiner, therefore, the Reich would be well advised to make use of it. Perhaps those followers of Steiner who were most familiar with the doctor's work on long-distance control (*Fernbeeinflussung*) could aid the Gestapo in its efforts to combat the "criminal" tactics of the Allies. Should the Gestapo ignore this opportunity, should the regime persist in its ill-advised campaign against the Steiner movement, then Western freemasonry would have rendered its most deadly enemy in Germany impotent.

In July 1942, another naval officer, Engineer Commander Otto König, expressed slightly more down-to-earth reservations concerning National Socialism in an address at the Wesermünde Naval School.[99] To be sure, many of König's remarks on spirit, discipline, and professional training echoed the navy's standard line on Party/Service relations. König found it an advantage, for example, that Germany had in National Socialism "a very strong, sustaining [*tragende*] idea for the entire Wehrmacht and the entire *Volk*." He likewise assumed the basic compatibility between military ways of thinking and National Socialism.

Yet König also noticed some disturbing features of National Socialism, particularly in the way it was molding German youth. The products of the Hitler Youth, he observed, tended to be arrogant. They thought they knew everything, whereas in fact they knew practically nothing. Tact and good manners left much to be desired and were sometimes even ridiculed by the younger generation. The concepts of "mine" and "yours" were "only very loosely perceived," as the widespread scrounging of naval equipment and theft of personal belongings indicated. A tendency toward untruthfulness was also currently more prevalent among the cadets than had been the case in the past.

These character failings, however, were only part of the picture. An unwillingness to own up to one's deeds and insubordination were also disturbingly evident in the younger generation. König cited a personal example in which a midshipman coolly informed a superior officer in front of his troops that the older man had no right to give him a particular order. Although the cadet was technically correct, his attitude was disturbing, and König suspected that the midshipman cared more about the rights of a German soldier than the duties. Indeed, subsequent inquiry revealed that the cadet could not even recall one of the seven duties of a German soldier. Yet within five months of this episode, König complained, the midshipman in question had ostensibly proven his worth through some 'daredevil' stunt aboard a U-boat and gotten himself promoted to officer's rank. König doubted the suitability of this sort of man for the officer corps: "In ninety out of a hundred cases these people will be a cancer for discipline and training."

Other problems further complicated the training of young officers. According to König, women and alcohol played a disproportionate role in the lives of the cadets. Table manners and saluting also stood in need of improvement. Finally, König lamented the highly exaggerated sense of honor evident among a sizeable number of officer candidates: "Punishments, rules, or even corrections for any kind of mistake cause [the cadet] to feel that his honor has been called into question. He assumes the role of the misunderstood youth, and today it is no longer an oddity when young officer candidates, consumed by an exaggerated sense of honor, commit suicide over utter trivialities."

König offered no immediate solutions to the problems he outlined in his address. He did, however, feel that the navy would have to place renewed emphasis on character, ethics, and morality as it trained the new generation of German naval officers. What is interesting in this regard is that König presumably believed that this was possible within the context of National Socialism. Curiously, this linked König to his brother officer and fellow critic, the eccentric Commander Erdmenger, for despite their criticism of certain isolated features of the regime, neither of the two men questioned the fundamental legitimacy of National Socialism. Rather, Erdmenger called for the partial rehabilitation of the anthroposophist movement so that its followers could strengthen the very regime that persecuted them. Similarly, König sought to teach proper soldierly values to the spoiled brats of the Hitler Youth so that the Third Reich could survive and (presumably) produce new generations of HJ boys. Thus although both officers detected a particular shortcoming within National Socialism, each assumed that shortcoming to be an anomaly rather than part of the essence of the regime. The answers to the problems raised by National Socialism, it seemed, could be found in the perfection of its doctrines rather than in their repudiation.

It is, of course, impossible to say how representative Erdmenger's or König's sentiments were of the naval officer corps as a whole or to what degree their views circulated among the higher levels of command. In a curious way, though, the two men's views did anticipate a more fundamental change in the navy, one which would in time bring the Service into closer alignment with that National Socialism which both König and Erdmenger apparently still thought capable of perfection. When the change came, however, it was completely to overshadow the musings of these two relatively junior officers, for it concerned the highest leadership of the Kriegsmarine itself.

Predictably, the impetus for change was provided by that most sensitive of issues in Raeder's navy, the question of the "big ships." Since the loss of the *Bismarck* in May 1941, the surviving heavy units of the fleet had played an increasingly minor role in the war. To Hitler, this suggested the essential bankruptcy of one half of Raeder's "double-pole" strategy—the use of surface ships to complement the submarine campaign against Allied convoys—and it raised the question

215

of whether the Reich might use the men and resources tied up in the surface fleet more profitably elsewhere. Raeder, for his part, could maintain (in private at least) that the inaction of the fleet was due to the very restrictions that Hitler imposed upon its use. The Führer, it seems, wanted successes from the big ships but was unwilling to see them take the necessary risks that might bring those successes. Wherever the responsibility lay, one thing was certain: after the spectacular return of the *Scharnhorst, Gneisenau,* and *Prinz Eugen* from their exposed position at Brest, France, to safer waters in February 1942, the greater part of the surface fleet stayed at port, either in the fatherland or in Norway. Increasingly, the fleet's inactivity, so reminiscent of the Imperial Navy, threatened to undermine the delicate understanding between Hitler and his grand admiral.

A number of events in the fall and early winter of 1942 further exacerbated relations between the two men. In November, the navy, along with Hitler and the rest of the high command, was taken by surprise by Operation Torch, the Anglo-American invasion of French North Africa. Although Hitler could scarcely single out the navy for failing to foresee what he had likewise failed to anticipate, the Führer's response—the occupation of southern France—ran counter to Raeder's longstanding desire to bring the Vichy government into a closer partnership with the Reich against Britain. Just as important, the scuttling of the Vichy fleet on November 27 removed a potentially valuable force that Raeder had sought, however unrealistically, to use against the Allies in the Mediterranean. In short, the events in the Mediterranean that fall represented the final demise of Raeder's strategy for that region and suggested that, in the future, the Führer would be less inclined than ever to consider his advice.[100]

Developments in northern Europe, however, brought about the final break between the two men. By November 1942, the increasingly desperate situation of the German Sixth Army at Stalingrad underlined the need for more effective naval interdiction of Lend-Lease shipments to the Soviet Union. Unfortunately for Raeder, two planned sorties by heavy units of the fleet that month either failed to materialize or else inflicted only exceedingly modest damage upon Allied shipping. When a third sortie, consisting of the heavy cruisers *Lützow* and *Hipper* as well as six destroyers, was undertaken in late December, both the army's urgent situation in the east and the tempting nature of the target, a weakly defended convoy, created an atmosphere of high expectation at the Seekriegsleitung and at Hitler's headquarters near Rastenburg.[101]

The course of the ensuing naval action in the Barents Sea on December 31, 1942, initially seemed to favor the Germans.[102] The *Hipper* and *Lützow* engaged the convoy's destroyers in a spirited exchange of gunfire, and the commander of a shadowing U-boat radioed headquarters that the entire horizon was lit with red. Shortly thereafter, Admiral Oskar Kummetz, the commander of the German task force, radioed that he was breaking off the action. The Seekriegsleitung evaluated these messages cautiously, suggesting that it looked as if good results had been obtained. Upon receiving the same transmissions from the north, Hitler chose to put an even more optimistic interpretation upon them and promptly informed his New Year's guests that a great naval victory had been won. Raeder's representative at Rastenburg, Admiral Theodor Krancke, did not want to dampen the Führer's enthusiasm on this of all evenings and accordingly said nothing.[103]

In reality, Hitler's jubilation was somewhat premature. To be sure, the *Hipper* and *Lützow* had engaged the convoy's escort, but the unexpected arrival of two British light cruisers and the inherent difficulties of fighting in Arctic waters in the dead of winter had frustrated Kummetz's plans to close with the convoy. After a very confused encounter that cost the British a destroyer as well as a minesweeper and the Germans a destroyer, Kummetz reluctantly broke off the engagement. Operating under radio silence, the German task force was unable to report further details of the battle until the following afternoon, New Year's Day, 1943. By that time, an impatient Hitler had already learned from a British radio broadcast that the Royal Navy had won a defensive victory and that the convoy's transports were unscathed. The dawning of this highly unwelcome news sent Hitler into a tirade, and he seized the occasion to browbeat the nearest available naval officer, the unfortunate Admiral Krancke, with the failings of the navy. The big ships were useless, the Führer averred, and it was his "unalterable decision" that they be stripped of their guns and scrapped. Raeder was ordered to the Wolf's Lair immediately to carry out the Führer's wishes.[104]

Fortunately for Raeder, the collection of reports on the most recent sortie (and perhaps the desire to give Hitler time to compose himself) delayed the admiral's arrival at Rastenburg until January 6. By that time, the Führer's temper had cooled somewhat, but not so much as to preclude the delivery of a classic Hitler monologue lasting one and a half hours to Raeder, General Wilhelm Keitel, and two stenographers. Hitler began by criticizing the haphazard way in which he had been informed of the most recent engagement in the Barents Sea. He then launched into a more comprehensive diatribe on the navy's failings, both past and present. With the exception of the submarines, Hitler averred, the entire history of the navy—the High Sea Fleet, the 1918 Revolution, the mass scuttlings at Scapa Flow, and the experiences of the present war—was one of failure. He repeated his earlier assertion to Krancke that the big ships were worthless and suggested that the air protection that they required could be employed more usefully elsewhere. Accordingly, the ships were to be decommissioned and their guns employed as shore batteries.[105]

Hitler's merciless attack on the navy represented the repudiation of Raeder's entire life's work. The admiral's reaction was predictable; after requesting and receiving a private session with the Führer, he tendered his resignation as head of the navy. According to Raeder's account—the only record of the session—Hitler softened his stand somewhat, saying that he had merely meant to criticize the heavy units of the fleet. Yet, given the vehemence of Hitler's earlier remarks and Raeder's own sensitivity to criticism, particularly on the issue of the big ships, there could be no question of his consenting to stay in office. It remained only for the two men to agree upon a successor and to carry out the transfer of command in such a way that neither the navy nor the regime would suffer a further loss of prestige. The latter commodity, it seems, was in rather short supply in Germany in the winter of Stalingrad.[106]

As it turned out, an inner logic provided for the swift resolution of both of these questions. By January 1943, Raeder was nearing his sixty-seventh birthday and was no longer in the best of health. He had been at the helm of the navy for fourteen tumultuous years, nearly ten of which had been spent under Adolf Hitler. Raeder's retirement as head could therefore be portrayed as a well-deserved reward for a decade of service to the Third Reich. Nor was the regime at a loss to find a convenient date to honor the grand admiral. January 30, 1943, the tenth anniversary of the National Socialist *Machtergreifung*, was chosen as the official day for Raeder to relinquish his command and assume the purely ceremonial position of General Inspector of the Navy.[107]

The matter of a successor was a slightly more delicate matter. Upon Hitler's request Raeder proposed two men, either General Admiral Rolf Carls or Admiral Karl Dönitz, for consideration as head of the navy. Currently the supreme commander of the Northern Naval Forces, Carls was an advocate of a balanced fleet, a man very much in the Raeder mold. Dönitz, by contrast, was known largely as a U-boat man. Especially over the past year, his open criticism of the Seekriegsleitung's handling of the submarine force had roused Raeder's ire, but if Hitler was indeed determined to scrap the big ships, then Dönitz was the logical choice to head the navy. Once again logic won out, and on January 30, 1943, Dönitz assumed command of the Kriegsmarine. One era had ended; another was beginning.[108]

Notes for Chapter 8

1 Quoted in Michael Salewski, *Die deutsche Seekriegsleitung 1935–1945*, 3 vols, (Munich, 1970–1975), 1, p. 91. A useful guide for the daily events of the war at sea during the Second World War is Jürgen Rohwer and Gerhard Hümmelchen, *Chronology of the War at Sea 1939–1945*, 2 vols (New York, 1972–1974).

2 These figures are taken from Friedrich Ruge, *Der Seekrieg: The German Navy's Story 1939–1945* (Annapolis, Md, 1972). Ruge includes the latecomer *Blücher* in his tally for heavy cruisers.

3 In fact, the *Bismarck*, *Prinz Eugen*, and *Tirpitz* were the last major additions to the surface fleet. For the fate of the uncompleted ships, see Jost Dülffer, *Weimar, Hitler und die Marine: Reichspolitik und Flottenbau 1920–1939* (Düsseldorf, 1973), p. 571. Curiously, the name of one of the unfinished cruisers, the *Lützow*, lived on in the Kriegsmarine, for after the loss of the *Graf Spee* in December 1939, an apprehensive Hitler ordered the *Deutschland* rechristened as *Lützow* in order to preclude a national loss of prestige should the ship be lost in action.

4   For the "double-pole" strategy, see Salewski, *Seekriegsleitung*, 1, pp. 65–66, 158–159, and 514.

5   Quoted in Salewski, *Seekriegsleitung*, 1, p. 523.

6   Peter Padfield, *Dönitz: The Last Führer* (New York, 1984), pp. 201–202.

7   Bundesarchiv-Militärarchiv, Freiburg, West Germany (hereafter cited as BA-MA), RM 7/91, "Kurzbericht 'U-53,' 'U-49' vom 2. 12. 1939."

8   This characterization of Raeder's strategy from BA-MA, N 172/3 Nachlass Boehm, Letter of Eberhardt Weichold to Boehm, January 12, 1960.

9   Salewski, *Seekriegsleitung*, 1, pp. 206, 211.

10 For the *Graf Spee's* voyage and destruction, see Edward P. von der Porten, *The German Navy in World War II* (New York, 1969), pp. 48–58.

11 Salewski, *Seekriegsleitung*, 1, p. 164, n. 140; BA-MA, RM 7/91, "Der Ob.d.M. B. Nr. 7437 geh. 22. Dez. 1939."

12 For an analysis of the possibilities open to the Allies in Scandinavia, see Carl-Axel Gemzell, *Hitler, Raeder und Skandinavien: Der Kampf für einen maritimen Operationsplan* (Lund, 1965); also Norman Rich, *Hitler's War Aims*, 2 vols (New York, 1973–1974), vol. 1, pp. 133–135.

13 Salewski, *Seekriegsleitung*, 1, pp. 176–177.

14 For Quisling's earlier career see Paul M. Hayes, *Quisling: The Career and Political Ideas of Vidkun Quisling, 1887–1945* (Bloomington, Ind., 1972). For the meeting itself see ibid., pp. 160–161; also Hans-Dietrich Loock, *Quisling, Rosenberg, und Terboven* (Stuttgart, 1970), pp. 218–219. A record of the meeting is reproduced in Gerhard Wagner (ed.), *Lagevorträge des Oberbefehlshabers der Kriegsmarine vor Hitler 1939–1945* (Munich, 1972), p. 59.

15 Wagner, *Lagevorträge*, p. 61; Salewski, *Seekriegsleitung*, 1, pp. 178–179. The dates of Hitler's meetings with Quisling are a matter of dispute. Hayes, *Quisling*, p. 354, gives their most likely dates as December 13 and December 18.

16 For the *Altmark* "affair," see von der Porten, *German Navy*, pp. 60–61.

17 Wagner, *Lagevorträge*, p. 86.

18 For the German campaign in Scandinavia, see Walter Hubatsch, *"Weserübung." Die deutsche Besetzung von Dänemark und Norwegen 1940* (Göttingen, 1960).

19 Wagner, *Lagevorträge*, p. 93; Salewski, *Seekriegsleitung*, 1, p. 191.

20 For the navy's role in Plan Yellow, see Hans-Adolf Jacobsen and Jürgen Rohwer, "Planungen und Operationen der deutschen Kriegsmarine im Zusammenhang mit dem Fall 'Gelb,'" *Marine-Rundschau*, vol. 57 (1960), pp. 65–78. For the possibilities as well as the perils (for the addition of Italy as an active ally was by no means an unmixed blessing for the navy) of the changed situation as of summer 1940, see Salewski, *Seekriegsleitung*, 1, pp. 219–234, 271–313; also Gerhard Schreiber, *Revisionismus und Weltmachtstreben: Marineführung und deutsch-italienische Beziehungen 1919–1944* (Stuttgart, 1978), *passim*.

21 BA-MA, RM 7/94 B. Nr. 1, Skl III a, 17907/40, Berlin, January 1940.

22 Reprinted in Salewski, *Seekriegsleitung*, 3, pp. 122–130.

23 Reprinted in ibid., pp. 106–108.

24 See ibid., pp. 107, n. 9, 114–115.

25 Reprinted in ibid., pp. 108–114.

26 Ibid.

27 For "Sea Lion," see Walter Ansel, *Hitler Confronts England* (Durham, NC, 1960); Karl Klee, *Das Unternehmen "Seelöwe:" Die geplante deutsche Landung*

in England 1940 (Göttingen, 1958); and Ronald Wheatley, *Operation Sea Lion; German Plans for the Invasion of England, 1939–1942* (Oxford, 1958).

28 Ansel, *Hitler Confronts England*, pp. 100–104.

29 Hitler issued the decisive directive for "Barbarossa" on December 18, 1940. As early as June 1940, however, he was contemplating an invasion of the Soviet Union as a way out of his dilemma vis-à-vis Britain. For the interrelationship between "Sea Lion" and "Barbarossa," see Rich, *Hitler's War Aims*, vol. 1, pp. 159–164, 209–210; also *Das deutsche Reich und der Zweite Weltkrieg*, 2, pp. 375ff.

30 Salewski, *Seekriegsleitung*, 1, pp. 271–353, especially 271–287.

31 For the Kriegsmarine's persistent oil shortage, see Wilhelm Meier-Dörnberg, *Ölversorgung der Kriegsmarine 1935–1945* (Freiburg, 1973).

32 BA-MA, N 172/4 Nachlass Boehm, "Unterlagen für eine kommende Besprechung mit dem Reichskommissar im Anschluss an meine Unterredung mit ihm vom 30. Januar 1941;" also Richard Schreiber's "Politischer Bericht" of April 7, 1941; and Boehm to Raeder, February 5, 1942.

33 For Terboven's career prior to becoming Reichskommissar, see Loock, *Quisling, Rosenberg, und Terboven*, pp. 335–339.

34 BA-MA, N 172/4 Nachlass Boehm, Boehm to Raeder, April 7, 1941; Hermann Boehm, *Norwegen zwischen England und Deutschland* (Lippoldsberg, 1956), pp. 137–138.

35 BA-MA, N 172/4 Nachlass Boehm, Boehm to Raeder, October 6, 1941. Boehm, *Norwegen*, pp. 159–160.

36 For German plans for Scandinavia, see Hans-Dietrich Loock, "Zur 'grossgermanischen' Politik des Dritten Reiches," *Vierteljahrshefte für Zeitgeschichte*, 8 (1960), pp. 37–63.

37 BA-MA, N 172/1 Nachlass Boehm, Raeder to Boehm, June 4, 1940; BA-MA, N 172/3 Nachlass Boehm, Boehm to Raeder, October 6, 1941.

38 BA-MA, N 172/4 Nachlass Boehm, "Gedanken zur politischen Lage," December 9, 1940.

39 Ibid.

40 See BA-MA, N 172/4 Nachlass Boehm, Boehm to Raeder, January 8, 1941; Boehm to Raeder, April 7, 1941; also Schreiber's report "Die politische Lage in Norwegen, 28. 9. 1941;" Schreiber's "Anlage zum Bericht vom 6. X. 41;" and Boehm, *Norwegen*, p. 136.

41 BA-MA, N 172/4 Nachlass Boehm, Boehm to Raeder, April 7, 1941; Boehm to Raeder, October 6, 1941; "Anlage zum Bericht von 6. X. 41."

42 Hayes, *Quisling*, pp. 210–245, 252, 259.

43 BA-MA, N 172/1 Nachlass Boehm, Raeder to Boehm, June 4, 1940.

44 Hayes, *Quisling*, pp. 265–266

45 BA-MA, N 172/1 Nachlass Boehm, Raeder to Boehm, October 30, 1940; BA-MA, N 172/4 Nachlass Boehm, "Gedanken zur politischen Lage," December 9, 1940.

46 BA-MA, N 172/1 Nachlass Boehm, Raeder to Boehm, December 21, 1940.

47 BA-MA, N 172/4 Nachlass Boehm, Boehm to Raeder, December 28, 1940.

48 BA-MA, N 172/1 Nachlass Boehm, Raeder to Boehm, December 30, 1940.

49 BA-MA, N 172/4 Nachlass Boehm, "Unterredung Kommandierender Admiral Norwegen mit RK am 30. Januar 1941 in Skaugum;" Boehm

to Raeder, April 7, 1941; "Politischer Bericht," April 7, 1941; Boehm to Raeder, June 12, 1942; "Anlage zum Bericht von 6. X. 41."

50 For the continuing efforts of Rosenberg and the navy on behalf of Quisling after 1941, see Loock, *Quisling, Rosenberg, und Terboven, passim.*

51 Hayes, *Quisling*, pp. 277–278; see also the notes from Raeder's conference with Hitler on January 22, 1942, in Wagner, *Lagevorträge*, p. 348.

52 For Quisling's subsequent efforts to administer Norway, see Hayes, *Quisling*, pp. 278–297.

53 Boehm, *Norwegen*, pp. 159–165. Boehm reports that he subsequently heard that Hitler later told a member of his inner circle that, in the quarrel between Boehm and Terboven, the admiral was correct. Boehm, however, also notes that Terboven remained at his post and adds: "Why Hitler did not remove the R.K. is a matter for speculation." Ibid., p. 165. Perhaps it was because Terboven's views of power politics and occupation measures were much closer to those of the Führer than Boehm suspected.

54 There is a substantial literature on the formulation of propaganda by and for the Wehrmacht during the Second World War. For the Wehrmacht as a whole, see Hasso von Wedel, *Die Propagandatruppen der Deutschen Wehrmacht* (Neckargemünd, 1962); also Erich Murawski, *Der deutsche Wehrmachtbericht, 1939–1945. Ein Beitrag zur Untersuchung der Geistigen Kriegführung. Mit einer Dokumentation der Wehrmachtberichte von 1. 7. 1944 bis zum 9. 5. 1945*, 2. Auflage. (Boppard, 1962). For aspects of the navy's role in the propaganda campaign, see Günther Heysing, *Propagandatruppen der deutschen Kriegsmarine. Teil 1. Juni 1939 bis Juni 1940. Versuch einer Dokumentation* (Hamburg, 1964).

55 Murawski, *Der deutsche Wehrmachtbericht*, pp. 40–41, 51.

56 For the early history of the propaganda troops, see Wedel, *Propagandatruppen*, pp. 17–25; Heysing, *Propagandatruppen der Kriegsmarine*, p. 5.

57 BA-MA, RW 4/194 Oberkommando der Kriegsmarine A II b 1419/39, June 15, 1939.

58 BA-MA, RW 4/194 Oberkommando der Kriegsmarine A II b 1419/39, June 15, 1939, Anlage I, "Richtlinien für die mob. mässige Aufstellung von Propaganda-Kompanien bei der Kriegsmarine." For the composition of the propaganda units, see Heysing, *Propagandatruppen der Kriegsmarine*, p. 8.

59 For an example of this, see the exchanges concerning photographer Friedrich Böltz between March 30, 1941 and August 12, 1942 in BA-MA, RW 4/199.

60 Wedel, *Propagandatruppen*, p. 133; BA-MA, RW 4/194 OKM M I 3419, September 16, 1939; R V Nr. 34/40 (22/50), January 27, 1940; BA-MA, RW 4/275 Mar. Prop. Abt. Nord B. Nr. 328/42, April 19, 1942; BA-MA, RW 4/197 Oberkommando der Wehrmacht WPr (VIIb) B. Nr. 952/41, February 28, 1941.

61 For the general provisions regarding the *Sonderführer*, see Heysing, *Propagandatruppen der Kriegsmarine*, pp. 8–9.

62 Ibid., pp. 9–10, 38; BA-MA, RM 35 III/102 Marinegruppenkommando Süd B. Nr. 21, July 24, 1941; Wedel, *Propagandatruppen*, pp. 134–135.

63 Heysing, *Propagandatruppen der Kriegsmarine*, p. 69; BA-MA, RW 4/200 Mar. Prop. Abt. West B. Nr. 31941/41, July 18, 1941; Befehlshaber der Unterseeboote B. Nr. 4110 A4, December 19, 1941.

64 BA-MA, RW 4/199 Marine Propaganda Abteilung West B. Nr. 1771/41, May 8, 1941; OKM MPA IV B. Nr. 244/41, May 29, 1941.

65   BA-MA, RW 4/202 Bericht über Unterkunft Trupp Drontheim, November 11, 1941.

66   In April 1942, for example, Admiral Hermann Boehm demanded the dismissal of an older lieutenant (S), Gerhard-Ludwig Milau, because of Milau's conduct the previous December when the transport plane in which he had been travelling had been forced to ditch in Oslo Fjord. According to the report of one eyewitness, Milau's frantic behavior in the plane's rubber boat prevented the occupants from bringing another survivor aboard. This and the lieutenant's screaming and whimpering, even after a rescue boat appeared, convinced Boehm that Milau was not worthy to be an officer in the Kriegsmarine. Boehm only grudgingly revised his opinion after the doctor who had treated the *Sonderführer* testified that, since Milau was nearly dead from exposure at the time this had happened, there was nothing all that unusual about his behavior. For this, see the lengthy exchange between Boehm, the Inspektion des Bildungswesens, and other parties in BA-MA, RW 4/208, beginning April 1, 1942.

67   BA-MA, RW 4/202 Mar. Prop. Abt. Nord B. Nr. 1174/41, October 1, 1941. The culprit remained with the propaganda troops as an enlisted man.

68   BA-MA, RW 4/202 OKM AMA/M Wehr I c B. Nr. 16054/41, November 21, 1941; BA-MA, RW 4/207 Fernschreiben of November 11, 1942; BA-MA, RW 4/209 Inspektion des Bildungswesens B. Nr. 6549, December 12, 1942.

69   See the cases of *Sonderführer* Koglin (BA-MA, RW 4/201 Mar. Prop. Abt. Südost B. Nr. 453, September 4, 1941); *Sonderführer* Arenz (BA-MA, RW 4/203 Mar. Prop. Abt. West B. Nr. 1614/41, September 9, 1941); and *Sonderführer* Hans Järisch (a number of exchanges in BA-MA, RW 4/202, beginning August 3, 1941, and concluding September 17, 1941).

70   BA-MA, RW 4/199 Marinestation der Nordsee B. Nr. P22101 P I, June 13, 1941.

71   Heysing, *Propagandatruppen der Kriegsmarine*, pp. 8–9. For cases of Iron Crosses being awarded, see BA-MA, RW 4/202 Mar. Prop. Abt. Nord B. Nr. 1066/41, September 13, 1941; also BA-MA, RW 4/203 Mar. Prop. Abt. Nord B. Nr. 1247/41, October 12, 1941; also the case of Friedrich Böltz in BA-MA, RW 4/199. For the case of the war correspondent (Rudolf Schmidt) entering the executive officers' training program, see BA-MA, RW 4/208 Inspektion des Bildungswesens der Marine B. Nr. 6898-ROA/K 1 b, December 5, 1942.

72   BA-MA, RW 4/203 Mar. Prop. Abt. Nord B. Nr. 1247/41, October 12, 1941.

73   BA-MA, RW 4/194 OKW/WPr I b, "Ergebnis der Besprechung über Prop. Organisation für Kriegsmarine am 31. 3. 39;" Reichsministerium für Volksaufklärung und Propaganda RV Nr. 34/39 (22140–20), October 5, 1939.

74   This and the following paragraph are based on Erich Frühling's two-part overview, "Wehrbetreuung bei der Kriegsmarine im zweiten Weltkrieg," Sonderdruck aus *MOV-Nachrichten*, Nr. 9/44 and 10/44, Bonn-Bad Godesberg, September and October 1969. Frühling has provided the Bundesarchiv-Militärarchiv with photocopies of much of the material used in *Wehrbetreuung*. For this see BA-MA, MSg/296; MSg/297; MSg/298 Sammlung Erich Frühling.

75 "Tagung für Befehlshaber und Kommandeure der Kriegsmarine beim OKM, Berlin, vom 12. bis 15. Januar 1943. Einleitung durch den Hauptamtschef des Allgemeinen Marinehauptamtes Admiral Warzecha," in BA-MA, MSg/297 Sammlung Frühling.

76 The conclusions that I have drawn in reading the material assembled by Frühling differ considerably from his own. For Frühling, expressions of "Heil Hitler" or indebtedness to the NSDAP are not to be taken as indications of political opinion. BA-MA, MSg/297 Sammlung Frühling, p. 7. As will be seen, I tend to take these comments at their face value and, in addition, place considerable emphasis on cases in which the arguments of naval officers closely paralleled those espoused by the Party.

77 Erich Frühling, "Wege geistiger Betreuung bei der Einheit. Auszug aus einem Vortrag vor den Wehrbetreuungsoffizieren der Kriegsmarine in Berlin im Dezember 1940," in BA-MA, MSg/297 Sammlung Frühling.

78 Ibid., pp. 2, 9–11.

79 Ibid., p. 12.

80 "Ansprache des Hauptamtschefs des Allgemeinen Marinehauptamtes des OKM Konteradmiral Warzecha. Gehalten als Schlussansprache bei der Tagung der Wehrbetreuungsoffiziere der Kriegsmarine in Berlin, 9. bis 11. Dezember 1940," in BA-MA, MSg/297 Sammlung Frühling.

81 See above, Chapter 6.

82 Friedrich Ruge, "Erziehung zum Führer. Vortrag bei der Tagung für Befehlshaber und Kommandeure der Kriegsmarine in Berlin vom 6. bis 8. November 1941," p. 5, in BA-MA, MSg/297 Sammlung Frühling.

83 Bernard Rogge, "Voraussetzungen für den Offiziersberuf. Ausarbeitung für die Inspektion des Bildungswesens der Marine, 1942," pp. 5–6, in BA-MA, MSg/298a Sammlung Frühling.

84 Ruge, "Erziehung zum Führer," pp. 7–8. There was apparently little danger of Ruge endorsing Ringelnatz's angry critique of the navy. According to the final, published version of the captain's address, Ruge and his subordinates took the motto, "Never again Ringelnatz," as the inspiration for their work in *Wehrbetreuung* during the winter of 1939/40 in Cuxhaven. Ibid., p. 8. In a postwar interview with Michael Salewski, Ruge maintained that this claim was added without his knowledge.

85 Bernard Rogge, "Erfahrung in der Wehrbetreuung eines Hilfskreuzers. Notizen zum Vortrag, gehalten 1942 auf der Befehlshabertagung in Berlin im Oberkommando der Kriegsmarine," p. 1, in BA-MA, MSg/298a Sammlung Frühling.

86 Rudolf Krohne, "Der Kommandant auf kleinem Fahrzeug," pp. 22, 56, in BA-MA, MSg/297 Sammlung Frühling.

87 See, for example, Ruge, "Erziehung zum Führer," p. 7.

88 "Führung und Soldatenseele," pp. 16, 18, in BA-MA, MSg/297 Sammlung Frühling.

89 "Einleitung durch den Hauptamtschef des Allgemeinen Marinehauptamtes Vizeadmiral Warzecha. Tagung für Befehlshaber und Kommandeure der Kriegsmarine beim OKM, Berlin, vom 6. bis 8. November 1941," pp. 7–10, in BA-MA, MSg/297 Sammlung Frühling. See also, "Tagung für Befehlshaber und Kommandeure der Kriegsmarine beim OKM, Berlin, vom 12. bis 15. Januar 1943. Einleitung durch den Hauptamtschef des Allgemeinen Marinehauptamtes Admiral Warzecha," p. 5, in BA-MA, MSg/297 Sammlung Frühling.

90 "Tagung für Befehlshaber und Kommandeure der Kriegsmarine beim OKM, Berlin, vom 6. bis 8. November 1941. Schlusswort des Oberbefehlshabers der Kriegsmarine Grossadmiral Dr. h.c. Raeder," pp. 4–5, 8, in BA-MA, MSg/297 Sammlung Frühling.

91 "Schlussansprache des Oberbefehlshabers der Kriegsmarine Grossadmiral Dr. h.c. Raeder auf der Tagung für Befehlshaber und Kommandeure der Kriegsmarine beim OKM, Berlin, 12. bis 15. Januar 1943," in BA-MA, MSg/297 Sammlung Frühling.

92 Ibid., pp. 7, 10–11, 13–14.

93 Ibid., pp. 9–10.

94 Ibid., p. 13.

95 Padfield, *Dönitz*, p. 226.

96 For the text and distribution of the "Commando Order," see International Military Tribunal, *Trial of the Major War Criminals before the International Tribunal*, 42 vols (Nuremberg, 1947–1949), 26, Document 498-PS, pp. 100–101; also ibid., 34, Document 179-C, pp. 772–773. For the Bordeaux incident, see ibid., Document 176-C, pp. 747–766; also ibid., 39, Document U57-UK, p. 124. Raeder's entry in the war diary (reprinted in ibid., 35, Document 658-D, p. 325) actually predated the execution of the commandos by two days, as they were given a stay of execution for purposes of interrogation.

97 BA-MA, RM 6/93, "Oberkommando der Kriegsmarine. *M* Korvettenkapitän Erdmenger über erzieherische und religiöse Fragen."

98 For Hess's flight to Scotland see John Toland, *Adolf Hitler*, 2 vols (Garden City, NY, 1976), 2, pp. 757–765.

99 BA-MA, N 582/3 Nachlass Werner Bräckow, "Erziehung des jungen Offiziere . . ." June 23, 1942.

100 Salewski, *Seekriegsleitung*, 2, pp. 147–184.

101 Ibid., pp. 194–199. For this and the subsequent events leading to Raeder's resignation, see Michael Salewski, "Von Raeder zu Dönitz: Der Wechsel im Oberbefehl der Marine," *Militärgeschichtliche Mitteilungen*, 2/1973, pp. 101–146.

102 For a description of the battle, see Stephen W. Roskill, *The War at Sea, 1939–1945*, 3 vols (London, 1954–61), 2, pp. 291–299.

103 Salewski, *Seekriegsleitung*, 2, pp. 199–201.

104 Ibid., p. 201.

105 Wagner, *Lagevorträge*, pp. 453–454 provides a record of the conference. See also Raeder, *Mein Leben*, 2, pp. 286–288.

106 Wagner, *Lagevorträge*, pp. 454–455; Raeder, *Mein Leben*, 2, pp. 289–290.

107 Wagner, *Lagevorträge*, pp. 454–455.

108 Raeder, *Mein Leben*, 2, p. 290.

9

For Führer and Fatherland

On January 30, 1943, Erich Raeder addressed the Kriegsmarine for the last time as commander-in-chief. His parting comments were largely unremarkable—a few observations on the current state of the war, a rather innocuous rendering of the official reasons for his retirement, and a heartfelt expression of his gratitude for the past services of the officers and men of the navy. Those who had expected something more memorable from the grand admiral, a final assessment of the Raeder era from the old man, must have been disappointed. Yet for two brief moments in the address, Raeder did manage to leave the realm of the banal. In one passage he expressed his lingering bitterness over the material disadvantages that the navy had faced in the war. Curiously, his resentment appeared to be directed more at the privileged position of the army and the Luftwaffe than at Germany's enemies, and he called for the maintenance of sound discipline and unity of opinion within the Kriegsmarine as a means of redressing this imbalance. Elsewhere he addressed the navy's relationship with National Socialism. It had been his accomplishment, Raeder asserted, to bring the navy "smoothly and completely" into the service of the Führer and the Third Reich. Continuing in this vein he noted:

> This was possible only because, despite all outside efforts to influence it, the training of the navy [in the Weimar Republic] derived from an inner attitude that was itself truly National Socialist. For this reason we did not have to change, but could become followers of the Führer with open hearts. I find it particularly satisfying that the Führer has always attributed this to me, and I would like to ask all of you to see to it that the navy remains a strong and reliable support of the Führer in this regard.[1]

Raeder, then, appeared to leave the achievement of parity within the Wehrmacht and continued service to Adolf Hitler as his final charges to the Kriegsmarine. Indeed, the departing admiral may well have intended for these twin concerns to go hand in hand, for the service to the Führer that he implored might well bring parity as a reward. Were this indeed Raeder's intent, then he could scarcely have wished for a more suitable successor than the one Hitler had chosen, for few within the navy more

225

aptly combined the defense of their own turf with service to a superior than Karl Dönitz.

The new commander-in-chief of the navy was in many respects the antithesis of his predecessor.[2] Just over 51 years old in January 1943, Dönitz was a full fifteen years younger than Raeder. He brought a resultant energy to the navy that greatly exceeded that of Raeder, particularly the Raeder of more recent years. The differences between the two men, however, encompassed more than simply age. Although Dönitz had held important ship- and shore-based commands outside of the submarine fleet, his eight-year tenure as head of Germany's underwater branch between 1935 and 1943 marked him first and foremost as a U-boat man. His U-boat experience, in turn, would color his administration of the whole navy. Although just as authoritarian in his own way as Raeder, he brought a certain informality of style from the submarine force to the navy as a whole. He also brought an impatience with both theory and established ways of doing things and an enthusiasm for his own measures, however unconventional, to the myriad of problems facing the Kriegsmarine. These last two characteristics—impatience and enthusiasm—became evident as early as February 5, 1943, when Dönitz issued his first major directive after taking command:

1 It is a question of winning the war. Considerations of how the navy should appear after the war have no value.
2 The sea war is the U-boat war.
3 All has to be subordinated to this main goal.[3]

Dönitz wasted no time in placing his stamp upon the Kriegsmarine. Within a matter of weeks he completed an administrative shake-up that sent many of the familiar faces from the Raeder era into retirement or to less important commands. Kurt Fricke gave way to Wilhelm Meisel as chief of staff of the Seekriegsleitung and assumed the inconsequential position of supreme commander of Group South. Erich Schulte-Mönting, Raeder's personal staff chief, was likewise replaced by Hans von Davidson. Nor were Dönitz's actions confined to Berlin, for Hermann Boehm, the Commanding Admiral Norway, and Rolf Carls, the Fleet Commander, soon made way for Dönitz's appointees and joined Raeder in retirement. In all of the above cases, the replacements were experienced, highly professional officers. It is interesting to note, however, that none of the new appointees was known for his independent judgement. Dönitz, it appears, was determined to have obedience from below.[4]

Dönitz's relationship with his own superior, however, was as yet imprecise when he assumed command of the navy that January. In the past, with his characteristic enthusiasm for the task at hand, Dönitz had paid only scant attention to the larger questions of politics, concentrating instead on the U-boat war. Now, though, he would have to devote his attention to the needs of the entire navy rather than the submarine fleet alone. This, in turn, was bound to involve him in the larger questions of politics.

Dönitz's first significant excursion into the latter realm concerned the fate of the battleships. As a champion of the U-boat, Dönitz had initially agreed with Hitler's decision to scrap the big ships, but upon reflection, the head of the navy changed his mind. The battleships, Dönitz came to believe, still tied down some enemy vessels, and scrapping them would free only minimal amounts of men and material for the U-boat force. Conversations with the new Fleet Commander, Otto Schniewind, on February 22 strengthened Dönitz in his position. He told Schniewind, though, that arguments based on the battleships' defensive role, either as a "fleet in being" or in resisting an Allied invasion of Norway, would not persuade Hitler to change his mind; only an active, offensive role manifesting "the strong will to strike the enemy" could achieve this aim.[5]

Four days later Dönitz met with Hitler to secure his permission to retain the big ships. There were still opportunities for action against Allied convoys to the Soviet Union, he told the Führer, and in view of the worsening situation in the east, he felt it the navy's duty to use every means possible, including sorties by the surface fleet, to relieve the front. Hitler repeated the charges that he had earlier made to Raeder; the days of the big ships were over, and he needed the steel and nickel that would come from scrapping them more than he needed them to fight. When Dönitz reiterated his position that the capital ships could still contribute to the war, however, Hitler apparently relented. He agreed to the transfer of the *Scharnhorst* to strengthen the *Tirpitz*'s battle group in northern Norway and asked, doubtless with some resignation, how long it would be before he could expect offensive operations. Dönitz assured him that three months would suffice. Although still unconvinced, Hitler responded: "You can have six months. Then you will come to me and see that I was right."[6]

Thus the "U-boat fanatic," as Dönitz later termed himself,[7] gained a stay of execution for the surface fleet. The consequences of his success with Hitler on February 26 ultimately encompassed far more than the fate of the fleet alone. By "saving" the battleships—the most visible embodiment of German sea power—Dönitz solidified his standing with those traditionalists within the Service who were still suspicious of the "U-boat man." Two weeks after the meeting of February 26, for example, one officer wrote enthusiastically: "Perhaps December 31, 1942, was not the last chapter in the history of German navalism [*Flottengedanken*] after all." Raeder likewise ultimately came to view Dönitz's retention of the surface fleet as one of his great successes.[8]

Yet all of this came at a price. Even if Dönitz had "saved" the battle fleet from the scrap yard, this was only on the condition that it be used. The circumstances of war and Hitler's continuing "generosity" might—indeed did—ultimately allow the surface ships more than the six months that the Führer initially considered sufficient to prove or disprove their utility to the war effort. But given the overwhelming numerical superiority of the Allies in ships and planes and their clear edge in RADAR, one might well have wondered whether there were realistic chances for success for the German battleships by 1943. As will be seen, the tragic fate of the *Scharnhorst* and the *Tirpitz* suggests that it would have been far better for the officers and men of these vessels if Dönitz had been less persuasive with the Führer on February 26.

There was, moreover, a larger price that Dönitz would pay for his success with Hitler that winter. The admiral might well congratulate himself that, for once at least, the Führer had altered a decision. He might well conclude that Hitler was open to suggestions and that he would make concessions to the navy. Yet Hitler rarely gave anything without a quid pro quo, and now that he had consented to Dönitz's wishes, the admiral would have to give something in return. Dönitz's "repayment" for the Führer's support of the navy in February 1943 and in the two years that followed would take a variety of forms. It was most evident, though, in the enthusiastic and steadfast support that Dönitz gave Hitler as Germany's fortunes waned.

This, of course, provides the final contrast between Dönitz and Raeder. For all his hopes that Hitler would serve the navy's ends, and for all his professions of loyalty to National Socialism, there was always something rather artificial about Raeder's relationship with the Führer and the Party. The parallels that he sought to draw between party history and navy history were often strained, and his own relationship with Hitler, even in the best of times, was hampered by the world of differences that separated the Imperial officer from the Bohemian corporal. Dönitz, too, was a former officer of the Imperial Navy, but he seemed drawn to Hitler. Perhaps this affinity was a function of the two men's relative closeness in age. Perhaps it reflected both men's unbridled ambitions. Or perhaps, as Dönitz's most recent biographer has suggested, there was simply something in Dönitz's personality that made him look for a repository for his utter faith and loyalty.[9] Whatever the case, Dönitz's support of Hitler appears to have been unquestioning, unrestrained, and from the heart.

One striking manifestation of the changed relationship between Führer and admiral under Dönitz was in the increased frequency of the latter's visits with Hitler in comparison to Raeder's. Raeder's visits to Führer headquarters had always been something of an ordeal for the admiral, and he consequently sought to make them as infrequent and as short as possible. Dönitz came more often, especially at the beginning of his tenure, and he was evidently more easily influenced by the prevailing mood there.[10] Moreover, the atmosphere surrounding Hitler was itself beginning to change by the time Dönitz took command. The winter of 1942/1943, the winter of the Allied demand for unconditional surrender at Casablanca and the defeat at Stalingrad, produced a visible hardening of determination within Germany's political leadership that the war would be fought to the end. As Joseph Goebbels informed the nation at the Berlin Sportpalast on February 18, the struggle was now one of total war. In his new position as head of the navy, Dönitz first reflected and then embodied the new atmosphere.[11]

Dönitz's response to Goebbels' speech on total war provides a good case in point. The war diary of the Seekriegsleitung described the address as the "blast of a trumpet" and added that "only the German Wehrmacht and the German *Volk* possess, with their allies, the power to save Europe from the threat confronting it. Total war is the order of the day."[12]

This realization, in turn, gave renewed importance to the need to support Hitler. Here, too, Dönitz proved to be the loyal subordinate. On April 20, 1943—Hitler's fifty-fourth birthday—Dönitz announced that the Kriegsmarine's gift that day was its pledge of "constant battle readiness and an untiring fighting spirit."[13] Later, in August 1943, Dönitz was thinking in even more glowing terms:

> The huge force which the Führer radiates, his unshakable confidence, his far sighted judgement of the situation in Italy have made it plain during these days what very poor little sausages we all are in comparison with the Führer, and that our knowledge, our vision of things outside our restricted sphere, is fragmentary. Anyone who believes he can do better than the Führer is foolish.[14]

Dönitz, for one, was not about to second guess Hitler. On the contrary, his actions in 1943 and early 1944 suggest that he took his own strictures to the navy concerning unquestioning obedience to Hitler's orders quite seriously. When Hitler committed Axis forces to maintaining a North African bridgehead in Tunisia, Dönitz energetically seconded this measure. He instructed the German naval command in the Mediterranean to use every means available, including cutters and luxury yachts if necessary, to master the British submarine threat to the resupply of Axis forces. When resupply by surface vessels proved insufficient, Dönitz offered three submarines to carry petrol, even though their total carrying capacity was an inconsequential 30 cubic meters of fuel. And when the Italian naval command held back its forces, ostensibly for the forthcoming battles for Sicily and the Italian mainland, Dönitz urged immediate action:

> A sacrifice of the fleet for this task [the retention of Tunis] makes more sense than saving it for later tasks . . . The navy cannot simply opt out while the other branches of the armed forces fight it out at a desperate post. . . . The choice is either to hold Tunis, which means that the navy must throw in everything, or lose the Panzer Army. The supreme command has ordered that Tunis must be held. Naval Command is convinced that this is the only possible decision.[15]

Dönitz, then, was among the most stalwart supporters of Hitler's decision to hold in North Africa. Although militarily senseless—as the spring of 1943 wore on it became increasingly evident that the Tunisian bridgehead was untenable—such a policy at least prevented the Luftwaffe and the army, both still smarting from the débâcle at Stalingrad, from placing the onus for the coming Axis defeat on the navy. Perhaps for this reason, Dönitz's exhortations for last-minute heroics continued until the end in Africa. As late as May 5, 1943, he ordered the Kriegsmarine forces in the Mediterranean to throw everything into the support of the bridgehead, without regard for losses or future operations, so that the Axis forces could defeat the "exhausted" enemy. Although Tunis fell to the Allies five days later, Dönitz's efforts were not lost on Hitler. Looking back on the Axis collapse in North Africa, the Führer opined: "We must recognize that the new German naval command accomplished as much as was humanly possible. If everyone had worked as hard earlier it would probably have turned out differently for us."[16]

Tunis, however, was merely the first in a series of opportunities for Dönitz to display his fidelity to Hitlerian principles of war. Over the next year, successive Axis reverses would reveal a pattern wherein Dönitz equalled or, on occasion, exceeded his Führer in the determination to hold one position after another at all costs. Thus, in August 1943, while Hitler wavered and Army Staff Chief Alfred Jodl urged evacuation of the Axis bridgehead in Sicily, Dönitz committed himself unconditionally to the retention of the island. Similarly, between October 1943 and April 1944, Dönitz consistently and rather ostentatiously supported Hitler's dogged refusal to evacuate Axis troops from the Crimean peninsula before they were overrun by the Soviets. And finally, it was Dönitz who reinforced Hitler in his refusal to allow Army Group North to withdraw along the Baltic in 1944 and thereby shorten its overextended front. Among other things, the two men reasoned, Russian possession of the Baltic states would jeopardize the flow of Swedish iron ore to Germany and threaten the Kriegsmarine's U-boat training program in the Baltic. Army Group North would have to stay where it was.[17]

Leaders of the army might well have objected that it was easy enough for Dönitz to champion a policy of no retreat when it was largely army troops who paid the price. But Dönitz's unrelenting approach to war also characterized his conduct of the war at sea. Indeed, from the spring of 1943 onward, when Allied numerical superiority and improved Allied use of RADAR and aircraft at last turned the tide against the submarine, Dönitz's exhortations to fight on regardless of losses became a familiar feature of naval life. Thus in May 1943, as U-boat losses mounted catastrophically, Dönitz urged his subordinates to put their "ingenuity, ability and hard will" against the enemy's technological advantages. Continuing, he noted:

> Commanders in the Mediterranean and Atlantic have proved that even today the enemy has weak spots everywhere and that in many cases the enemy devices are not nearly so effective as they appear at first sight if one is determined, despite all to achieve something."

Later that month Dönitz sought to shame U-boat commanders into more aggressive action: "If there is anyone who thinks that fighting convoys is

no longer possible, he is a weakling and no real U-boat commander. . . .
Be hard, draw ahead and attack."[18]

Ultimately, after the loss of thirty-eight submarines in exchange for
a paltry forty-two merchant vessels that May, even Dönitz had to admit
defeat and allow a "temporary" withdrawal of the U-boat force from the
North Atlantic into quieter waters.[19] Nevertheless, subsequent orders by
the head of the navy continued to strain the bounds of rationality. In June
1943, for example, he expressed his disapproval after the commander
of a sinking U-boat unsuccessfully sought to get enemy aircraft to
cease fire by waving a white towel from the bridge of the vessel.
Although in retrospect the submarine commander's motives seemed
entirely reasonable (he apparently hoped to get the stricken boat closer
to the coast of Africa to facilitate the crew's rescue), Dönitz noted that
his action contradicted the navy's regulations in "Service on Board"
and "Directions for the Commanders of Ships and Vessels of the
Navy Abroad." He announced, therefore, that he would hold the
young commander responsible for his actions after his return from
enemy captivity. In the meantime, the officer corps was to be reminded
regularly that the honor of the flag was more important than individual
lives and that neither vessels nor land formations of the Kriegsmarine
were to use the white flag. To do so merely disgraced the vessel and
its crew.[20]

Dönitz's watchword that summer, therefore, was one of resolution in
the face of all odds. This obligation, in turn, applied equally to the army,
the navy, and the fatherland as a whole. Thus in August 1943 he echoed
Hitler's view that everything depended upon holding out stubbornly.
Germany, the admiral maintained, was much better off with regard to
food than it had been in 1918. "In addition," he continued, "we have the
great plus of the unity of the German people. This is our most precious
possession and must be carefully preserved." This unity, however, was
apparently not absolute, for in the same address Dönitz expressed his
belief that there were those in Germany who lacked "hardness" and
who were easily inclined to criticism, "without being able to do better
themselves or even to comprehend the whole picture."[21]

Dönitz evidently felt that he knew how to deal with this sort of
people. The month after his address he issued an "Order Against
Habitual Criticism and Grumbling" wherein he threatened to court
martial those who openly imparted their own "miserable attitude"
within the navy. Once again he emphasized the contribution that
Hitler and National Socialism had made in laying the firm foundations
for the unity of the *Volk*. In this phase of the war, he said, it was the
navy's duty to protect this precious unity not only through "toughness,
patience, and determination" but also through "fighting, work and
silence."[22]

"Determination," "silence," "unquestioning obedience to orders,"
above all "hardness." All of these qualities had figured—and figured
prominently—in the navy of Erich Raeder. In the past, though, these
attributes, so familiar to the political vocabulary of National Socialism,

had shared center stage with other considerations. Now these qualities appeared to drive all others from the field.

Two events from the last months of 1943 illustrate exactly how circumstances were changing. In October Dönitz evidently attended the now infamous "Gauleiters' Conference" at Posen during which Himmler first revealed details of the extermination of the Jews to a broader audience within the Party. The head of the navy apparently never commented on the speech; indeed, he never acknowledged that he had been present at Posen at all.[23] Nevertheless, after October Dönitz could scarcely complain that he was uninformed about the true nature of the regime. From that date, whatever illusions he harbored concerning Hitler and National Socialism were largely of his own making.

Two months later Dönitz revealed how untroubled he was by the secret he had learned at Posen. On December 17, 1943, he delivered his most enthusiastic endorsement of the Movement thus far when he told a group of senior naval officers that he was "a firm adherent of ideological schooling."[24] It was not enough merely to fulfill one's duty to the letter of the law; true fulfillment of duty occurred only when one's heart and "entire inner conviction" entered into the action. "It is therefore necessary," Dönitz continued, "that the soldier bring his spiritual and moral power and his willpower to the task at hand." Uniform ideological training was a must, and every dualism, every deviation from this dictum, was a weakness.

Dönitz understood the implications of this increased commitment to ideological purity. In the same address he noted the absurdity of suggesting that the navy should be apolitical. On the contrary, since the soldier was the very embodiment of the state in which he lived, the navy would have to adopt ideological training "with the deepest conviction." The Soviets, he reminded the audience, had already gone this route. The Kriegsmarine had no alternative than to do likewise: "We can win this struggle only if we go at our task with a holy zeal, with unremitting fanaticism."

Dönitz's own analysis of the war reflected precisely the ardor that he urged on his audience. It was fortunate for Germany, the admiral asserted, that the Führer had adopted the only possible strategy and had seized sufficient space on the continent for the Reich to hold off the Soviets and endure the Anglo-American blockade. It was equally fortunate that the home front remained strong. Allied attacks had not broken civilian morale, he maintained, and the enemy's clumsy demand for unconditional surrender had only strengthened German resolve. Borrowing heavily from the Propaganda Ministry's skillful manipulation of German fear concerning Allied plans for Germany, he added: "If the enemy says to a nation: 'Tomorrow you lose the war, and then twenty-five million Germans will be shipped to the Urals for twenty-five years,' then this is the stupidest thing he can say to a nation." Such an attitude, Dönitz affirmed, merely made the nation more determined to win.

Far from being discouraged, therefore, Dönitz professed optimism. The men of the Kriegsmarine had only to concentrate on their twin tasks of "tonnage warfare" and the defense of Fortress Europe against amphibious assault. The navy would hold its posts "with fanaticism" when the hour of decision came; the surface fleet would be used if the opportunity presented itself. In the meantime, however, it was up to the navy's leaders to tap the Service's human resources and to weld their men into an "ideological, spiritual whole."

Thus Dönitz sketched the path he expected the navy to follow in the years to come. It was, of course, an open question whether the officers of the Kriegsmarine would embrace the principles of ideological warfare with the same enthusiasm as their commander. As will be seen shortly, a number of officers spurned Dönitz's example, even as they continued to serve in the navy of the Third Reich. But willingly or unwillingly, enthusiastically or unenthusiastically, they continued to serve. Coupled with their commander's increased emphasis on aggressive, unremitting, ideological war, their obedience in itself was bound to create an explosive situation within the navy.

No single episode more graphically illustrates just how volatile the combination of ideologically tinged leadership and obedience to orders could be than the fate of the *Scharnhorst* that same December.[25] For most of the past year that vessel and the other ships of Battle Group North had been inactive, as the head of the navy sought vainly for an effective way to employ the surface fleet against the Allies.[26] The six-month stay of execution that Hitler had originally granted for the big ships the previous February had come and gone, without a suitable opportunity arising for their employment. When the Anglo-Americans resumed Arctic convoys to the Soviet Union in November 1943, however, the time at last seemed ripe to undertake a surface sortie against the enemy.

The obstacles to Axis success that winter were admittedly numerous. Two of Battle Group North's heavy vessels, the *Tirpitz* and *Lützow*, were unavailable for action, leaving the *Scharnhorst* as the single capital ship available for the "fleet." The long Arctic nights, moreover, hampered reconnaissance by the Luftwaffe and favored the Allies in any engagement involving RADAR. Perhaps because these obstacles made a sortie unlikely, the commander of Battle Group North, Admiral Oskar Kummetz, had gone on leave, entrusting command to his deputy, Vice Admiral Erich Bey. But even in his absence, Kummetz cast a shadow over the operations of Battle Group North. Still smarting from Hitler's stinging critique of his cautious conduct of the engagement the previous New Year's Eve, Kummetz had earlier stated that, unless he were called off by his superiors, the next time he went into battle he would fight through to the end.[27] Dönitz, it appears, was not the only officer thinking of heroics in the face of impossible odds.

Yet it was Bey who would command in Kummetz's absence. He, too, had adopted a fatalistic attitude toward a fleet operation. On November 22 he had expressed his doubts over the feasibility of a surface sortie but had also noted that, since the high command had not ruled out such an operation, it was his duty to prepare for one. Success, he said, would depend upon luck and the enemy making a mistake. Then, in a masterpiece of wishful thinking (or was it perhaps simply resignation?), he added that the experiences of the war, "which have given us success in spite of our weakness, allow us to hope that luck will again be on our side."[28]

Of Dönitz's own attitude there can be little doubt. Hitler's condition for "saving" the battle fleet the previous February had been that it be used. For the past ten months the primary theme in Dönitz's messages to the units at the front, whether to the Service's escort vessels in the Mediterranean, the U-boat fleet on the high seas, or the support units ashore, had been steadfast determination in the face of virtually hopeless odds. In the admiral's mind there was no reason to exclude the surface fleet from these same considerations. Thus when German intelligence detected an Arctic convoy on December 18, Dönitz and his chief of staff, Wilhelm Meisel,[29] spurred the *Scharnhorst* into action. It scarcely seemed to matter that Arctic weather grounded the Luftwaffe and drove the *Scharnhorst*'s escort of five destroyers into port, that the location of enemy covering forces was unknown, or that three admirals—Otto Klüber (Commanding Admiral of Arctic Waters), Schniewind, and Bey—had recently advised against the action. On Christmas Day, 1943, the *Scharnhorst* departed for its final mission. Dönitz instructed Bey not to end the battle with a "half success;" at the same time he left Bey free to break off the engagement at his own discretion if heavy enemy units appeared.[30]

The resulting action was among the most tragic in the history of the Kriegsmarine. Bey dutifully sought the enemy convoy, but ran into heavy Allied covering forces instead. Fighting essentially "blind" and with virtually no idea of what confronted him, Bey was unable to escape, and the lonely *Scharnhorst* was hunted down and battered by a host of Allied vessels. On the morning of December 26, 1943, Bey sent a final message: "We shall fight to the last shell. Heil Hitler!"[31] Minutes later the *Scharnhorst* went under, taking with her all but thirty-six of her crew of nearly 2,000.

Thus the *Scharnhorst* joined the *Graf Spee* and the *Bismarck* on the list of ships that succumbed to the British after valiant but lonely fights. If the disaster tempted Hitler to say "I told you so" to his admiral, there is no evidence of it in the record of the conversations between Hitler and Dönitz in the days following the sinking. Nor was there any repetition of the ugly scene the previous January, when the unpleasant news of the aborted New Year's Eve engagement had led to the final break between Raeder and the Führer. Instead, Hitler contented himself with some mild criticisms of the way the *Graf Spee*, the *Bismarck*, and, most recently, the *Scharnhorst* had been handled tactically. Might it not have been better, he asked, if the vessels in question had chosen to fight it out in their first encounter with the enemy rather than seeking safety in flight? Dönitz responded that, in the most recent case at least, the *Scharnhorst*'s commander had received orders not to end the operation with a half success. Dönitz then suggested that perhaps the problem lay in the way Bey had chosen to conduct the battle. There the matter ended, for neither Hitler nor Dönitz cared to pursue Bey's responsibility any further. Whatever his shortcomings as a commander, the vice admiral had at least known how to die properly.[32]

Dönitz's own responsibility in sending a technologically outmoded battleship to fight alone against a host of enemy vessels apparently did not come up in the conversations with Hitler.[33] To be sure, the fate of the *Scharnhorst* suggested to Dönitz that, unless better RADAR equipment could be installed upon the Kriegsmarine's heavy units, there would be few opportunities to use them against the Anglo-Americans. Despite this realization, however, the admiral still hoped to find some way to use the big ships against Allied convoys in the north, and he immediately initiated plans to send the *Prinz Eugen* to take the *Scharnhorst*'s place in Norway. Presumably, if conditions permitted, the *Prinz Eugen* would try to repeat the *Scharnhorst*'s performance, this time with better luck.[34]

Thus Dönitz appeared to learn little from the most recent disaster or, for that matter, from the larger events from his first year at the head of the Service. He remained the arch advocate of offensive action in the face of hopeless odds and of unyielding defense, no matter how exposed the position. If his actions often defied rational thought, this is only to suggest that Dönitz was not thinking. Rather, as one authority has noted, he was "not fighting with his head, but with his blood, behaving not as a rational commander but as a National Socialist, convinced like Hitler that willpower and fanaticism would make up for numerical inferiority."[35]

Dönitz maintained the same tenor in the year to come. In February 1944, for example, he informed the officer corps that, while there was no reason why the commander of a sinking vessel should not save himself, provided he had done his duty, the same could not be said for those officers who enjoyed *Seebefehlshaber* status:

> The deportment of a *Seebefehlshaber* demands higher standards than those of a ship's commander. The dignity and the high position of a flag officer place particular obligations upon this man. A *Befehlshaber* who goes under with his command will live on in the history of the German *Volk* as the embodiment of the highest soldierly values and the best German fulfillment of duty. Through his hero's death he provides the greatest service for the warlike attitudes of following generations of soldiers and for their education as soldiers.[36]

The *Befehlshaber*, however, were not the only ones in the Service with obligations, for rank and file had duties too. That spring, as the Wehrmacht braced for the expected cross-channel invasion by the Allies, Dönitz reminded the navy of what this duty entailed. The admiral expected every sailor in the Kriegsmarine to throw himself relentlessly into the fight, "whether on land, where not a single meter of territory may be surrendered, or at sea, where only the most determined effort, without regard for saving the ship and without hesitation in the face of unfavorable odds, can lead to victory." Those soldiers who did not give their utmost, Dönitz added, would be "ignominiously eradicated."[37]

A glorious death to inspire future generations of Germans; relentless determination to hold every meter of ground; ruthless eradication of those who proved weak. More and more Dönitz came to sound like Hitler. And indeed, there now came times when the head of the navy was called upon to substitute for his Führer. In March 1944, for example, when Hitler's deteriorating health prevented him from reviewing the annual Heroes' Memorial Day parade, he asked Dönitz to deputize for him. The grand admiral did not disappoint his Führer. In a speech preceded by Beethoven's *Coriolan* overture he spoke of the "merciless struggle" in which the Fatherland was engaged. On the one hand was the united German *Volk*; on the other, a host of enemies who, in their materialism and their "degraded Jewish enslavement" were determined to exterminate Germany. Germany would endure, Dönitz assured the audience. The home front and the fighting front, he said, stood united as never before, thanks to the unifying force of National Socialism. Without the Movement's "uncompromising ideology" the Reich would have long ago been permeated with the "disintegrating poison of Jewry" and been delivered over to "the pitiless destruction of our enemy." With ideological unity and unshakable loyalty to the Führer, however, National Socialist Germany would be invincible.[38]

Thus the head of the navy confidently predicted victory in the spring of 1944. One wonders, of course, to what degree the officers and men of the Kriegsmarine shared their commander's conviction. Did they continue to nourish serious hopes for victory by this relatively late date in the war? Did they share Dönitz's increasing emphasis on the advisability, indeed the necessity of waging an ideological war? Or did they continue to serve in the Kriegsmarine for other reasons?

These are admittedly difficult questions to answer. Few military establishments actively encourage their soldiers to pose questions such as these, and the Kriegsmarine was certainly no exception. Given the political and naval leadership's pathological suspicion of "defeatism" by that stage of the war, moveover, any open discussion of Germany's chances for victory was bound to be risky at best. And the sheer size of the navy, which had mushroomed into a force of approximately 27,500 officers, 23,000 officer candidates, and 735,000 noncommissioned officers and enlisted men, makes any generalization exceedingly hazardous.[39] Individual examples can, however, reveal the range of responses to the tone their commander was setting for the navy.

A number of officers, including some from Dönitz's immediate entourage, were clearly disturbed by the direction that the war was taking by the late summer of 1943. That August, while Dönitz and the Führer were speaking confidently of the victory that would come when the unwieldy enemy coalition collapsed, Captain Werner Pfeiffer, the keeper of the official war diary at the Seekriegsleitung, presented a far gloomier assessment to the head of the navy. It was highly doubtful, he argued, whether the Reich could still attain victory by military means alone, for the reverses of the past year had transformed Germany from a "hammer" into an "anvil." Pfeiffer then hinted in a few carefully chosen words (for this was still officially taboo) that Germany ought to consider a separate peace with one or more of its enemies. Not surprisingly given his mood that August, Dönitz declined to pass this suggestion on to the Führer.[40]

Three months later Pfeiffer again tried to inject a note of realism into Dönitz's assessment of the war, this time concerning the more limited but still highly sensitive matter of troop withdrawals. Pfeiffer suggested that, given the enemy's increasing strength and the Reich's own unwieldy defensive perimeter, it might make sense to evacuate nonessential areas such as the Crimea, the Aegean, the Baltic States, and northern Norway so that their garrisons could defend more vital areas elsewhere. Again Dönitz rejected Pfeiffer's suggestion, this time rather bluntly. The evacuation of the Crimea, the admiral indicated, was "out of the question" whereas giving up northern Norway was "not subject to discussion."[41]

Other officers encountered a similar rigidity on the part of the naval high command that fall and winter. In October 1943 Captain Konrad Weygold, the Kriegsmarine's liaison officer at Army High Command, expressed his sense of foreboding concerning the forthcoming Soviet winter offensive and proposed that the navy divert some of its resources from the battle in the Atlantic to bolster the eastern front. Between January and July 1944 Captain Heinz Assmann, the navy's representative at the Führer's headquarters, intermittently supported army efforts to secure Hitler's permission to withdraw Army Group North to a more defensible position in the Baltic. Neither Weygold nor Assmann were any more successful in gaining their commanding admiral's ear than Pfeiffer.[42] Nevertheless, these men's efforts to secure a change, however tentative they might have been, do suggest that at least some within the navy were unwilling to assume their commanding admiral's uncritical posture vis-à-vis the Führer.

Other officers, however, appear to have been more susceptible to the message emanating jointly from Hitler and Dönitz. The example of Wilhelm Meisel, the chief of staff at the Seekriegsleitung, suggests that it must have been particularly difficult for those in daily contact with Dönitz to resist the force of his personality, for as early as June 1943, Meisel was thinking in terms that were remarkably similar to his admiral.[43] The time of "cabinet wars" in which neither sustenance nor overpopulation played a role was over, he informed an audience of senior officers. Modern war pitted entire nations against one another and was accordingly fought by different rules. In this respect, he suggested, Germany could learn a lesson from its present enemies:

We must not forget that in the USA the grandfathers of the current generation were witness to the extermination of the native inhabitants, that in Russia, which has been completely robbed of its Germanic upper class since 1917, the primal, Asiatic-Mongolian methods of the steppes are the rule in treating lands and people, and that the peoples of Central Europe currently under German control mean no more than 'natives' to the sanctimonious Englishmen.[44]

The same address reveals other parallels between Meisel and Dönitz. Meisel's contention that recent German reverses on the Eastern Front would at least make the neutral powers and the states under German occupation more aware of the danger of a Bolshevik victory suggests that he, too, could draw optimistic conclusions from even the most adverse of circumstances. Nor did he yield anything to Dönitz when it came to anti-Semitism. It was the "vengeful Jew," Meisel suggested, that was really behind the coalition arrayed against Germany. He evidently supported measures to deal with Jewish influence whenever possible, for in the same address he lamented the Hungarian government's reluctance to impose "something like the Nuremburg Laws" on its Jews. He likewise criticized Marshal Antonescu of Rumania for delaying his country's solution to the Jewish question.[45]

Meisel was not the only officer to attribute Germany's current misfortunes to the Jews. In October 1944, another of Dönitz's immediate entourage, Personal Staff Chief Hans von Davidson, interpreted Sweden's recent prohibition of German merchant ships from entering Swedish waters as a sign of Sweden's "fear of and dependence upon international Jewish capital."[46] Likewise, for Admiral Hans-Georg von Friedeburg, the new Commanding Admiral of U-boats, the presence of Jewish blood was evidently sufficient to explain both the defection to the Soviets of the army's General Lindemann and the Gestapo's punitive measures against the general's family.[47] It was a holdover from the Raeder era, though, who apparently drew the most radical anti-Semitic conclusions. In May 1943 and again in January 1944, Kurt Fricke, the former chief of staff at the Seekriegsleitung who was now serving as commander of Navy Group South, suggested that if other efforts to halt Jewish emigration via ship from Rumania failed, the Kriegsmarine should seize the ships outside of Rumanian territorial waters and cause them and their "entire complement" to "disappear." This proposal, so contrary to the unofficial code of the sea that virtually every German sailor respected, was apparently too much even for Dönitz, for the Seekriegsleitung took no action on Fricke's suggestion. Indeed, on one occasion, the head of the navy even provided an escort for a Jewish refugee vessel. On the other hand, neither Dönitz nor any one else at naval headquarters called Fricke to account for his proposal.[48]

Fricke at least confined himself to thoughts rather than actions. But the example of another officer, Lieutenant Commander Heinz Eck, demonstrates how, amid his commanding admiral's calls for ruthlessness, hardness, and iron resolution, the behavior of an officer in the heat of battle could result in barbaric deeds as well.

On January 18, 1944, the submarine *U-852* left Kiel under Eck's command. Although Eck was an experienced minesweeper commander, this was his first patrol aboard a submarine. The patrol came, moreover, at a time when the war was going badly for the U-boat force and when the danger of visual or electronic detection by Allied vessels and aircraft was acute. Accordingly, Eck and his crew were operating under considerable pressure.

On March 13, *U-852* torpedoed and sank the Greek steamer *Peleus*. Eck ordered the submarine to surface and, for the next five hours, proceeded to cruise through the quite considerable wreckage, murdering the ship's survivors with machine guns, pistols, and hand grenades. Included among the "executioners" aboard the *U-852* were the submarine's watch officer, its engineer, and its doctor. Eck subsequently justified this extraordinary measure to his crew on the grounds that it was essential to remove all traces of the attack (even as *U-852* left bullet-riddled rafts and timber floating amid the wreckage!) and that it was important to "think of our wives and children who die as the victims of air attack at home."[49]

After the war, men who knew Eck were hard pressed to account for his actions; his "crew" comrades from the Naval School generally remembered him as a quiet, upright, and competent officer.[50] Eck likewise appears to have had difficulty explaining his actions, maintaining stubbornly to an Anglo-Greek tribunal that he had felt it necessary to remove any signs of the attack and denying steadfastly that he had superior orders from Dönitz or anyone else for his action. Perhaps the most complete explanation for this gruesome incident would be that, in the heat of battle and in the hate-ridden atmosphere that his commanding admiral's rhetoric had helped to create by 1944, something in the lieutenant commander snapped and he lost control. Unlike the case of Fricke, however, there was no superior to restrain him at the front. Eck ultimately paid for his lapse into barbarism with his life.

These few examples, then, suggest that there were a variety of responses to the changing atmosphere within the navy by the summer of 1944. A few officers came to question particular directives from Führer headquarters or from naval high command, especially when these orders impinged upon their areas of specialty and when they were seen as demonstrably harmful to Germany's war effort. Others embraced the irrational element in National Socialism, with its call to racial hatred, ruthlessness, and, ultimately, barbarism. Still others apparently continued in the routine that they were in and simply chose not to think about the regime at all.

One final example from this period of the war, however, suggests that there was a fourth type of response to National Socialism within the navy. In an undated address to naval officers at Bad Homburg vor der Höhe, Admiral Hermann Boehm sought to put the war into its broader historical perspective.[51] Germany, he maintained, was sandwiched between three powerful adversaries: France, its hereditary enemy; the "Anglo-Saxon nation" (presumably Britain *and* the United States), which selfishly refused to allow any other nation to engage in friendly trade and competition; and the Soviet Union. The Soviets, the admiral suggested, were merely the most recent in a series of Asiatic intruders into central Europe. Whether it was against the Huns in the fifth century, or the Arabians, Magyars, Mongols, or Turks in the centuries that followed, it had been the lot of Germanic defenders to turn back these incursions. Now, Boehm suggested, Germany faced a new invader, the "mongrelized race of Russians," who came this time on tanks rather than horses. The fatherland was fighting for its very existence, Boehm noted, and it was foolish to complain about sacrifices. Victory was all that counted.

In this respect, at least, Boehm's message scarcely differed from that of Karl Dönitz or, for that matter, from Joseph Goebbels. But in two particular passages, whether intentionally or unintentionally, the admiral's address hit a strangely discordant note. At one point he appeared to caution against the reigning atmosphere of ethnocentrism and fanaticism in Germany by urging his audience to recognize the worth of historical research, even if written by Germany's enemies, and to avoid the "exaggerated dogmatism" to which the German was "so easily inclined." There was, Boehm suggested, more truth in British Admiral Lord Fisher's simple maxim, "Strike first, strike hard, and strike everywhere," than there was in any number of long-winded analyses by German scholars of where tactics end and strategy begins. In another passage, Boehm evidently sought to counter the belief, now elevated to a nearly universal truth in National Socialist propaganda, that commitment and determination would triumph over everything. His listeners, Boehm cautioned, should beware of clichés. It was all well and good to note Admiral Albrecht von Stosch's familiar adage that men, not ships, fought, but there were limits even to this. Rather, Boehm noted: "I go along with the Führer in the view that only the best in weapons and material are good enough for the soldier. The mocking comment of the Philosopher King, Frederick the Great, that God is usually on the side of the biggest battalions, is only saying the same thing."

Clearly Boehm's own message was not free from clichés or from paradox. His call for greater attention to the work of foreign scholarship was couched in an anti-intellectualism that would have done credit to Hitler, Göring, or Goebbels. His choice of Fisher's maxim, so simple, so direct, so seductive, clearly resembled Dönitz's own approach to war. Nevertheless, in carefully choosing both the maxim to question (von Stosch's hoary adage) and the men to question it (the Führer and his idol!), Boehm may well have been seeking to convey much more to his audience than initially met the eye.

All of which suggests a certain ambivalence toward the regime on the part of Boehm. The admiral, after all, was a staunchly patriotic German who, as a sailor had welcomed Hitler's rearmament of the Reich with open arms. His vision of the current war at times approached apocalyptic levels, and he certainly had no desire to see a German defeat, particularly at the hands of the Soviet Union. On the other hand, Boehm's experience with Reichskommissar Joseph Terboven in Norway between 1940 and 1943 had given him ample opportunity to know the brutality of the National

Socialist regime at first hand, even in a supposedly "kindred" land. The admiral, moreover, was a thoughtful, if occasionally naive, man who was not afraid to search for answers. Unfortunately, the truth had been difficult to come by in National Socialist Germany for quite some time; nor was it as easy to discover within the navy by 1944 as it once might have been. It is not surprising, therefore, that the picture that Boehm formed of the Third Reich was characterized both by insight and self-delusion. In his confusion, Boehm's example may have been the most typical of all.

The foregoing examples, then, suggest a variety of responses to the changing atmosphere in the navy by the summer of 1944. Yet whatever the differences that separated a Pfeiffer from a Meisel or an Eck from a Boehm, on one issue they were unanimous: each continued to accept the National Socialist regime as the legitimate government of Germany. In this respect their example was typical of the overwhelming majority of the naval officer corps. After all, the entire training of the navy emphasized obedience. Every officer had personally sworn an oath of unconditional obedience to Adolf Hitler. The navy had labored far too long under the stigma of 1918 for its officers to seriously consider rebellion now.

It is not surprising, therefore, that the news of Colonel Claus Schenk Graf von Stauffenberg's abortive attempt to assassinate Hitler on July 20, 1944, filled most Kriegsmarine officers with a mixture of incredulity and indignation that grew all the more as the extent of the army officer corps' complicity in the plot became evident.[52] The army, heir to a 300-year tradition of service to the state, had turned on its leader at a moment when the fatherland was facing the most extreme crisis in its history. The navy's response, therefore, was simple and predictable. Dönitz flew immediately to Hitler's side at Rastenburg and promised him the unconditional support of the Kriegsmarine. At Paris, one of the centers for the conspiracy, Admiral Theodor Krancke, the commander of Naval Group West, intervened energetically if somewhat superfluously against the conspirators. Elsewhere Kriegsmarine assistance was unnecessary, and in most cases the navy simply stood to arms while loyal troops from the army and the SS disarmed the conspirators. Hitler, however, did not fail to notice the contrast between the army and the navy, for in the aftermath of the failed coup he crowed: "Not a single one of these criminals belongs to the navy. Today it has no Reichpietsch in it."[53]

Strictly speaking, Hitler was not entirely correct. It soon became evident that two individuals at the Seekriegsleitung, International Law Advisor (Oberstabsrichter) Berthold von Stauffenberg (Colonel Stauffenberg's brother) and Commander Alfred Kranzfelder, were deeply involved in the conspiracy. There was also the case of the discredited *Abwehr* chief, Admiral Wilhelm Canaris, whose earlier contacts with the Allies now led to his arrest after July 20. Canaris, however, had scarcely belonged to the navy after 1935, and he, Kranzfelder, and Berthold von Stauffenberg were apparently dismissed as aberrations and left to their fate.[54] Certainly Dönitz had no interest in emphasizing these men's roles, even as examples for the navy not to follow.

On the contrary, the head of the navy's response in the days that followed was to present the Service as a monolithic bloc of loyal soldiers, as indeed it largely was.[55] Thus on the evening of the *Putsch* Dönitz sent the following address to the Kriegsmarine:

> Men of the navy! The treacherous attempt on the life of the Führer fills each and everyone of us with holy wrath and bitter rage toward our criminal enemies and their hirelings. Providence spared the German people and their armed forces this unimaginable misfortune. In the escape of the Führer we see additional proof of the righteousness of our cause. We will therefore unite more firmly behind the Führer! We will fight still harder until victory is ours![56]

The following day Dönitz issued another proclamation, stressing again the "holy wrath and extravagant fury" and adding for good measure that it was an "insane, small clique of generals" who had pursued this folly. He called upon his subordinates to remain true to their oaths and instructed them to follow only the naval chain of command, "so that errors through false instructions will be impossible." The navy, he added, should destroy everyone who revealed himself as a traitor.[57]

With these measures Dönitz's own initial anger appears to have cooled. But in the days that followed, the armed forces undertook further steps to display their loyalty to the regime. On July 23 the Wehrmacht adopted the party salute as a sign of what Dönitz described as its "unshakable commitment to National Socialist ideology."[58] Later that year membership by soldiers in the Party became permissible.[59] Although the final impetus for these steps evidently stemmed from the Wehrmacht high command rather than from the navy, there is no reason to suspect that Dönitz was displeased by them or that his own compliance was simply pro forma. On the contrary, he had spoken as early as December 1943 about the absurdity of suggesting that the soldier should be unpolitical. In this respect, therefore, the events of July 20 and the days that followed primarily served as a catalyst in a process that had been well underway since long before.

Accordingly, when Dönitz delivered his own lengthy catechism on the *Putsch* to the Service's frontline commanders on August 24, few who heard or read his comments could have been surprised, for they merely reiterated what he had been saying for more than a year.[60] The head of the navy heaped scorn on both the methods and motives of the conspirators. They had imagined that the concentration camps held "stalwart citizens" who had innocently run afoul of the regime. In reality, Dönitz averred, 99 per cent of the inmates were "professional criminals" whose incarceration merited the thanks of every upstanding German. The conspirators had also mistaken the nature of Allied war aims. Allied victory, Dönitz argued, would mean that millions of Germans would be shipped eastward to restore the damage that Axis forces had caused there.

In Dönitz's view there was only one way to avert this catastrophe. The German soldier would have to leave politics to those who understood it and array himself "fanatically behind the National Socialist state." The alternative was a return to the days of Weimar, something Dönitz refused to contemplate. As he told his commanders: "I would rather eat dirt than see my grandchildren grow up in the filthy, poisonous atmosphere of Jewry or to see the cleanliness of today's public art, culture, and education ... return to Jewish hands." The commanding admiral expected similar determination from his subordinates. Those who would not or could not embrace this "fanatical willingness to face death [*Sterbenkönnen*]" were not fit to be officers and would have to disappear.

The months that followed the failure of the *Putsch* witnessed the continuation of the war in all its bitterness. At sea the Kriegsmarine attempted valiantly but vainly to stem the flow of Allied reinforcements into Europe. On land the Service's support units and coastal artillery sought bravely to bolster an army that was reeling under the onslaught of the Anglo-Americans and the Soviets alike. In coming to the aid of the army, Kriegsmarine personnel once again displayed their resolution and, on occasion, their devotion to the new principles of war. Thus in September 1944 Rear Admiral Friedrich Frisius, the naval commandant of the isolated German garrison at Pas de Calais, complained of his army counterpart's lack of initiative in seeking combat and contrasted the growing tendency of army personnel to desert to the Allies with his sailors' good record in that regard. Then, after noting rather casually that two of the big coastal artillery batteries under his command would soon be cut off, he added tersely: "I am convinced that they will sell their lives dearly."[61]

Others took similar pride in the accomplishments of their own troops and similar umbrage at the behavior of the army. That same September Commander Wilhelm Ambrosius, who had led a group of sailors in the recent retreat across France, complained that his men had rarely seen any army units on foot as they had hobbled across the countryside, and that when they had seen them, there had been few officers in evidence. On the other hand, he continued, his unit had seen quite a few trucks drive by with only an army officer or official, a driver, and a big load of baggage on board. The crowning blow for his footsore detachment, however, had occurred when they had encountered some of the volunteers from the Indian Legion, a force recruited primarily from Indian prisoners of war in Germany with the ostensible aim of liberating India from the British. The navy had heard that the Legion had fought well in France, Ambrosius noted, and the sailors readily acknowledged their claim to be fellow soldiers. When elements of the Legion had "rolled by" the dusty column of sailors in trucks, however, the sight of these "in part very Negroid types" had simply been too much for Ambrosius' "racially conscious" men.[62]

The Eastern Front also offered examples of Kriegsmarine resolution that fall. In October, Davidson, Dönitz's staff chief, noted the successful withdrawal of naval forces up the Danube valley and their eventual linkage with army troops in Serbia. Davidson took this as a sign that "energetic leadership can master seemingly impossible situations." In contrast with the previous year, Dönitz was also apparently willing to sanction skillfully conducted withdrawals by this stage of the war, for he personally decorated the engineer officer responsible for the operation, Rear Admiral Paul Zieb, with the German Cross in Gold.[63]

Thus Kriegsmarine officers continued to display their dogged determination to continue as the year 1944 drew to a close. And the naval high command was certainly willing to furnish reasons to continue fighting. In March 1944 one Seekriegsleitung report adopted one of Hitler's stock interpretations when it noted that Britain's initial aim in going to war with Germany—preventing a single power from dominating the continent—was now being frustrated by the emerging might of the Soviet Union. The report also suggested that Britain was becoming a satellite of the United States. In September Davidson issued similar circulars which again emphasized the differences separating the Allied powers from one another. And in October he drew hope from two lengthy speeches that Winston Churchill and Anthony Eden had recently delivered in Parliament. The very fact that both men so strongly emphasized inter-Allied unity, Davidson observed, actually suggested that there were cracks in the Allied coalition.[64]

Nor were inter-Allied difficulties the only signs of hope that the naval high command detected by the end of 1944. In September Davidson professed to see a stabilization in the Eastern Front after General Heinz Guderian had taken command. He also wrote enthusiastically about the immense forces that the Kriegsmarine's own U-boats were tying down—supposedly 3,800 airplanes, 1,210 destroyers and escort vessels, and 635,000 men. Southern England and London, he added, were suffering from a rain of V-1 and V-2 weapons. All of this, he suggested, underlined the need for tenacity:

> History shows numerous examples in which strong leadership has mastered the most difficult, even apparently hopeless situations. We have that kind of leadership today. Our situation, therefore, is full of opportunity. The Kriegsmarine may take especial pride in the knowledge that one day, while Germany defends itself against enemies on all sides, the navy's task will again be to sortie forth from its confines, reclaim the offensive, and attack the enemy.[65]

Promises of new and better weapons supplemented the wishful thinking emanating from the naval command. In this regard, at least, the Kriegsmarine did have something more substantial to hope for than in the previous year, when one officer had drawn up a memorandum entitled "Fantasy: A Weapon."[66] The head of the navy, for example, was pursuing a number of measures, including the use of 12,000 concentration camp inmates as construction workers, to accelerate the production of conventional weapons. By late 1944, moreover, German designers were feverishly completing two vastly improved submarine designs, the Type XXI and the smaller Type XXIII, which might offset the overwhelming advantages that the Allies currently enjoyed in submarine warfare. There was also hope that the experimental "Walter" U-boat, with its phenomenal underwater speed of 24 knots, could regain the initiative at sea.[67]

By the end of 1944 those with recent experience at the front could readily see how slender these hopes were. As a confidential naval circular from December makes clear, however, there were even ways to downplay the significance of first-hand information if the occasion warranted it. Commenting on the Allied bombing of German cities, the author of the report noted a tendency of soldiers and sailors to put more faith in the letters of their loved ones than in official pronouncements. He hastened to add, however, that whatever information an individual had, he still lacked an overview of the war and could therefore not make definitive pronouncements. The situation at home was serious, the author continued, but there was no reason to make it worse than it actually was. Every soldier could rest assured that everything possible was being done to combat the Allied raids.[68]

This argument—that the individual sailor or soldier could not see the total picture and should therefore concentrate exclusively on his own assignment—also became a recurring theme in the naval high command's directives in the final months of the war. But what of those who wavered in their commitment to the cause or who, for various reasons, remained unconvinced by their superiors' outward show of confidence? What of those who tried to assess Germany's current situation even when they lacked the lofty overview available to the Führer and his advisors, both civilian and military? Perhaps there were a number of officers who were privately inclined to yield to these temptations as Germany's situation became more and more hopeless. If so, the fate of one retired naval officer in the fall of 1944 ought to have been sufficient to send most of the doubters away from their speculation and back to the task at hand with a vengeance.

On October 1, 1944, Heinrich Theede, a retired commander in the paymasters branch, entered the Hansa Hotel in Kiel and invited two noncommissioned officers to have a glass of wine with him.[69] Theede was apparently depressed at the time, and when the conversation turned to politics, he began to criticize one after another of Hitler's closest advisors. He then took up Hitler's own contributions to the war. The Führer, he asserted, was a good politician and had accomplished much in rebuilding Germany in the 1930s, but he was also responsible for the defeats at El Alamein and Stalingrad. He ought to keep his hands off the armed forces and leave that to the professionals. When his table companions suggested that the Führer had also won victories in Poland, France, and the Balkans, Theede replied that the generals had won them and that Hitler had merely taken the credit.

Theede's remarks were reported to higher authorities (by whom is uncertain), and he was eventually tried, convicted, and sentenced to death for "defeatism." The navy's National Socialist Leadership Staff then circulated the news of his fate throughout the navy. Although this in itself was nothing new—all three branches of the Wehrmacht routinely gave notice of death sentences for any number of real or imagined crimes—both the publicity within the navy and the editorializing that accompanied Theede's case were indicative of how the atmosphere in the Service was changing by the end of 1944. Neither Theede's service at the time of the First World War, nor his status as a retired officer, nor the relative triviality of his remarks (he had, after all, praised the Führer as a politician, if not as a soldier!) were allowed to save him. On the contrary, the author of the circular announcing Theede's fate maintained that his action constituted a particularly severe form of defeatism precisely because he was a soldier. That he had been depressed at the time, the report continued, altered nothing, and his execution as a common criminal was entirely appropriate.

Theede's example, of course, was scarcely typical for the officers of the Kriegsmarine. On the contrary, whatever their motivation, the overwhelming majority within the officer corps served steadfastly and silently as the war approached its conclusion. As the case of Lieutenant Commander Karl Müller suggests, moreover, at least a few of them continued to believe in the possibility of ultimate victory. On the night of September 18-19, 1944, Müller, a holder of the Knight's Cross, was captured by British naval personnel after his and two other S-boats were sunk in the English Channel by enemy motor torpedo boats.[70] Slightly over two months later, on December 1, he was exchanged for a badly wounded English captain. Between the time of his capture and his exchange, however, Müller was able to observe conditions in Great Britain, converse extensively with a number of British and American soldiers and sailors, and, on at least one occasion, ride around London in civilian clothes. When he returned to active duty with the Kriegsmarine, his written observations on his experience in the camp of the enemy must have made fascinating reading for all who saw them.

Müller was particularly interested in the questions that two brothers named Walker, one a lieutenant commander in the Royal Navy, the other a soldier in the Royal Marines, asked him in one of the initial interrogations. They were particularly interested, he noted, in the Jewish question, in youth education, in information about alleged atrocities by the Gestapo and the *Sicherheitsdienst* (SD), and in "what the British believe is the Party's tyrannical rule over the German people." It was amazing, Müller continued, that his two British inquisitors seemed to think that few Germans really supported National Socialism: "The idea of the unity between Party, State, and *Volk* was completely unfathomable to these people."

Müller, on the other hand, felt that he could see through the British rather easily. Underneath the Walker brothers' outward show of confidence in victory, Müller detected signs of uncertainty. The brothers seemed concerned over the increasing danger of the Soviet Union. And there were certainly signs that the war was exerting a strain on the British economy, for from the threadbare state of the average Londoner's clothes it was clear to Müller that the shortages on the British home front were greater than in Germany.

Later in his stay Müller was turned over to the Americans and held at a camp at "Moreton bei Oxfort" [*sic*]. Müller clearly preferred the company of the British to that of his new hosts, and he was particularly disturbed at the "deplorable" way the Americans were treating twenty-six German girls and women, apparently nurses, from the hospitals at Brest. The women could exercise only three hours a day, he complained, and they were compelled to live together in a single room. "The reasons for keeping these girls and women behind barbed wire," he added, "are beyond me."

American treatment of male POWs also apparently left something to be desired. Although the Americans provided sufficient food, they disregarded the Geneva Convention on a number of minor points. The guards also did not like it when fellow prisoners saluted each other with the National Socialist or "slave" salute, as one American major termed it. Given this harassment, Müller observed, it was useful to know the provisions of the Geneva Convention, "especially since a large number of the American camp personnel are Jews who emigrated from Germany either shortly before or shortly after the National Socialist Revolution."

The least pleasant feature of Müller's captivity, however, occurred just before his exchange, when he and some other German officers were flown across the Channel and quartered overnight at Rennes, France. To quote directly from Müller's rather peevish report:

> The accommodations made a mockery of all the provisions of the Geneva Convention. We spent the night in a windowless old shed without a table or chairs. We had to sleep on wooden benches. We only had two blankets to keep out the cold. I had no luck when I protested against this kind of treatment, which was hardly surprising since the commander, a first lieutenant, was a Jew.

It was with these rather jaundiced memories of Allied captivity that Lieutenant Commander Müller returned to the service of the fatherland. His report raises a number of tantalizing questions. One wonders, for example, if the lieutenant commander ever paused to consider the bitter irony of his description, so replete with righteous indignation, of his last night in enemy captivity, or if he, an officer of the Third Reich, had even the slightest inkling of the crimes that his government had committed and would commit in the name of Germany and National Socialism. One wonders as well whether Müller's commander-in-chief, Dönitz, ever read his report. Might not Dönitz, in turn, have brought it to the attention of the Führer, as a confirmation of the weakening will of the British or, more importantly, as proof of the navy's own relentless determination? Whatever the answers to these questions, one thing seems certain: In his ideological toughness and his apparently unbroken confidence in German victory, Lieutenant Commander Karl Müller was precisely the type of man that Dönitz was seeking as the war approached its finale.

Dönitz's own determination, of course, remained as strong as ever. Thus on New Year's Day, 1945, he sent the following message to the Kriegsmarine:

> Comrades! A fateful year lies behind us. It has brought the German nation severe tests, but it has also spared us the life of the Führer. His genius alone has mastered every crisis.
>
> The German people stand with iron discipline behind him. His will shows the Kriegsmarine the way as well. We will attack the enemy with unquestioning readiness in the coming year, wherever we find him. Fanatical daring will carry us to victory.[71]

But Dönitz's oratory notwithstanding, by the New Year both the navy and the fatherland were beginning to crack under the multiplicity of burdens they were bearing. There was scarcely a major city within the Reich that had not been bombed severely. At the frontier, after some initial successes in the Ardennes, Germany's last major land offensive of the war had turned into a disaster, consuming the few strategic reserves that were still available to the army. At sea the loss of France had deprived the U-boat force of its most advanced bases, leaving only Germany or Norway as effective sally ports from which to continue the "tonnage war," a war which in itself had been a losing proposition since mid-1943. The Kriegsmarine's one remaining capital ship, the *Tirpitz*, had at last succumbed to Royal Air Force bombers in November 1944, leaving what remained of the surface fleet fit only for action against the qualitatively inferior Soviet fleet in the Baltic.

This, however, by no means exhausted the litany of difficulties facing the Kriegsmarine. Indeed, the perceptive observer might well have noted that one of the unseen costs of ideological accommodation by 1945 was the necessity of fighting through the mass of red tape that fidelity to party pronouncements entailed. One presumes, for example, that most officers had more pressing matters to worry about in the last year and a half of the war than the social or racial pedigrees of their subordinates' prospective wives, but the naval high command continued to lavish attention on this apparently vital issue. Thus in January 1944 a naval circular noted the distressing number of cases in which armed forces personnel had asked their commanders' permission to marry "unsuitable" brides—either prostitutes, or women who were mentally unstable, sterile, or considerably older than their prospective bridegroom. The navy condemned this cavalier disregard for the "demographic/political meaning of marriage" and called upon unit commanders to instruct their men in the proper choice of a bride.[72] Later that year the navy took up the thorny question of whether those few "half-breed" Jews (*Mischlinge*) who had been permitted to serve in the Wehrmacht through certain exceptions to the law would be permitted to marry. The Marinewehramt declined to make a general ruling and suggested that permission would probably be granted on a case-by-case basis, depending upon whether the individual in question proved himself worthy of treatment as an Aryan.[73] And finally, in February 1945, naval authorities noted with dismay that, despite all instruction to the contrary, German sailors generally chose the less worthy type of bride when they married women from "racially kindred nations." Superiors, therefore, were to redouble their efforts in directing their men toward more suitable choices and approve only marriages with "racially and biologically worthy maidens."[74]

However trivial such matters were, they were also time-consuming for the officers who had to administer them. And although one wonders whether many officers really took the time to lecture their subordinates about the "demographic/political" advisability of finding the right girl, there were evidently times by the winter of 1944/45 when the Kriegsmarine was indeed hard pressed to balance the conflicting demands of service at the front, technical training, and ideological schooling. There were limits, after all, to what even the most committed of individuals could give to the Service. Thus a report on staff officer training from February 1945 noted that five of the thirteen participants at a recently completed course at the Naval Academy at Bad Homburg vor der Höhe had arrived as much as three weeks late due to pressing needs elsewhere and that one officer had to leave early after only fourteen weeks of instruction.[75] The officers' state of health, moreover, was "only mediocre" [*recht mässig*], mostly on account of war wounds or exhaustion from service at the front. Neither wounds, nor fatigue, nor the pressing demands of the Service, though, were allowed to interfere with the political education of the officers. Rather, the participants left the Naval Academy in the middle of the course for a five-day workshop for NS-Führungsoffiziere (NSFO) at the Berlin suburb of Bernau. There the officers received instruction on such topics as "General Racial Teaching," "The Racial and Biological Situation of Germany," "The English Enemy," "The Bolshevik Enemy," "National Socialist Ways of Life," "July 20, 1944," and "National Socialist Leadership of Troops."

Exactly how much importance the participants placed on this ideological instruction is unclear. The navy's educational establishment apparently felt it to be sufficiently important to reserve slightly over 10 per cent of the total time spent in preparing staff officers for topics of this sort. The thirty-eight classroom hours consumed in ideological training, moreover, rivaled the time spent on tactics (fifty hours) and staff training [*Führungsstabsdienst*] (forty-seven and a half hours), and they equalled the time spent on logistics, naval history, torpedo weapons, and blockade warfare combined. On the other hand, there are indications that the officer responsible for evaluating the curriculum at the Naval Academy may have nursed doubts about the wisdom of interrupting the technical training of future staff officers with a five-day excursion into the realm of ideology. As his delicately worded assessment of the NSFO course at Berlin-Bernau reads:

As necessary and as useful as participation at such a course might seem, its nature does not really quite fit into the framework of the Academy. Quite apart from the fact that an ever larger number of the participating officers have already been assigned to NSFO courses, the highly select and for the most part intellectually open minded officer of the Academy is somewhat out of place in the very large and rather mixed circles at an NSFO course. As was discussed with the leader of the NSF class, it would probably serve the Naval Academy better if individual, tried and true speakers from the NS leadership visited the Academy every so often. There they could meet with the small circle of staff officer trainees on a more intimate basis and take up matters of interest that fall outside of the special lecture topic.

One wonders whether the author of the foregoing remarks was sincerely interested in having a bevy of political speakers descend upon the Marineakademie. Perhaps he was merely paying lip service to the idea of Party/Service unity; by this stage of the war it was certainly the prudent thing to do. Perhaps he inwardly questioned the utility of his work and wondered whether there was any point at all in training staff officers for the future, much less in worrying about their political education. But if he did despair during that last winter of the war, his attitude was certainly not shared by his commander-in-chief.

On the contrary, Dönitz continued to exude optimism on virtually every front. That December he informed Hitler of his intention to send ten or fifteen naval officers to Japan so that they could reacquaint themselves with fleet operations and prepare for the eventual rebirth of the Reich's own naval might. On January 3 the admiral waxed enthusiastic about the possibility that the midget submarines that the Kriegsmarine was currently deploying might sink upwards of 100,000 tons of Allied shipping monthly. And in February 1945 he took heart in the revolutionary qualities of the new Type XXI and XXIII submarines, confiding to Hitler that the "mighty sea power of the Anglo-Saxons" would be "essentially powerless" against them.[76]

None of this was lost on Hitler. On February 27 Goebbels commented in his diary on the "fine impression" that the admiral had made upon the Führer. Two weeks later the Propaganda Minister wrote: "What a difference between Dönitz and Göring. Both have suffered a severe technical setback in their own arm of service. Göring resigned himself to it and has gone to the dogs. Dönitz has overcome it."[77]

The behavior of other officers helped to reinforce Hitler's favorable opinion of the navy in the closing months of the war. By the spring of 1945 the Kriegsmarine was fully engaged in the resupply of isolated garrisons along the Baltic coast. Later, as army resistance began to crumble in the face of the final Soviet onslaught, the navy would embark on an even more arduous task, evacuating thousands of soldiers and civilians from the east. Given Hitler's aversion to retrograde movements of any kind, however, it is perhaps not surprising that it was an admiral who stood his ground who most caught the attention of the Führer that spring. In March 1945 Admiral Friedrich Hüffmaier, the naval commander of the isolated (and almost totally insignificant) Channel Islands, suggested that, by adopting a policy of drastic confiscation and severely reduced consumption, he could hold the islands until the end of the year. This evidently made a most favorable impression upon Hitler, for when Hüffmaier subsequently found himself in disagreement with his army counterpart concerning the defensibility of the islands, Hitler relieved the army commander and ordered that *all* fortress commanders in the west should be *Marineoffiziere*. Conveniently forgetting the *Graf Spee*, Hitler opined: "Many fortresses have been given up, but no ships were ever lost without fighting to the last man."[78]

Dönitz was determined to maintain the esteem which his subordinates' and his own determination had won for the navy. That March the Führer declared as dishonored any soldier who fell into enemy hands who was not wounded or otherwise able to prove that he had done his utmost in battle; on March 8 the Marinewehramt applied this to the navy without a comment, even though the decree envisioned the withdrawal of any support or entitlements from the innocent families of the men so "dishonored." When Hitler established summary court martials to deal with deserters, Dönitz supplemented the measure with his own instructions to the naval police, encouraging them to take the most drastic actions. Those "scoundrels" who failed to show the proper resolution, he said, were to be strung up with the placard: "Here hangs a traitor who by his low cowardice allows German women and children to die instead of protecting them like a man."[79]

Thus the head of the navy sought to maintain the struggle to the bitter end. On April 11 he reviewed the reasons for continued fighting in a "secret order" to the Kriegsmarine. It was largely a tired reprise of the admiral's arguments over the past two years. The navy was fighting, he suggested, to prevent the Bolsheviks from exterminating large numbers of Germans and exporting countless others as slaves to the Soviet Union. The Führer had recognized this threat long ago and had adopted the only possible course in attacking the Soviets before they could attack Germany. A "hate blind" Churchill and an uncomprehending Europe had prevented him from accomplishing his aims, Dönitz averred, but soon, "at the latest in a year's time," Germany's neighbors would see that the Führer was "the single statesman of stature in Europe." Dönitz then repeated the familiar instructions to the navy from previous years. The honor of the flag was sacred. Every ship was to go down with honor. Those commanders who lacked the spiritual strength to carry through would have to give way to "harder" warriors. The deeds of the present would someday be judged by posterity.[80]

Yet Dönitz was still not willing to abandon all matters to the judgment of posterity, even at this late date in the war. Rather, at times he clearly acted as if the future of the Kriegsmarine and the Reich could be counted in years rather than in weeks. Thus on April 19, 1945, he announced his approval of the actions of a zealous petty officer from the auxiliary cruiser *Cormoran* who had quietly done away with fellow prisoners of war in a camp in Australia on the grounds that they were Communists. Dönitz was determined to promote the man to officer rank the moment he returned from captivity.[81]

The following day—April 20, Hitler's fifty-sixth birthday—and again on April 21, Dönitz paid his final visits to the Führer. Unfortunately, there is no contemporary record of what passed between the two men at this time. What is evident is that after securing Hitler's permission to leave Berlin, Dönitz moved westward with his staff to the Baltic city of Plön.[82] There, while Reichsmarschall Göring and Reichsführer Himmler desperately vied with one another to arrange an unauthorized truce with the Western Allies that would save their positions and enable the Reich to continue fighting the Soviets in the east, Dönitz continued the struggle unabated. Perhaps it was this final display of fidelity amid the seemingly monumental ingratitude of both Göring and Himmler that for the last time drew Hitler's favorable attention toward the admiral. Or perhaps it was more the cumulative effect of over two years of unquestioning obedience in the face of what were now seen to be hopeless odds that prompted the Führer's final token of approval for the head of the navy. Whatever the explanation, in his final testament of April 29, 1945, Hitler named Grand Admiral Dönitz his successor as Reich Chancellor and War Minister.[83] The following day, as the first of the "revolutionary" Type XXI U-boats set forth on its first and only wartime mission, Hitler shot himself.

Given the chaotic conditions then reigning in what was left of the Third Reich, it took almost a full day before final confirmation of Hitler's suicide could filter through to Dönitz. The news of the Führer's death probably came as no surprise to the head of the navy; the revelation of Hitler's final testament naming the admiral his successor, on the other hand, was stunning.[84] Dönitz had certainly expected rewards for his obedience over the past few years: verbal recognition of his and the navy's accomplishments and allocation of resources for the Service's behalf. But it had apparently never occurred to him that Hitler's final "reward" would be to name him Chancellor and War Minister. In retrospect, of course, the Führer's decision appears far less astonishing. Given his comments in recent months, the "desertion" of Göring and Himmler, and the clear intention of Goebbels not to survive his master, there were few trusted supporters to whom Hitler could turn. But at the time it appeared that, after a career characterized by one stunning reversal of policy after another, Hitler had saved one of the biggest surprises of his life for the end.

And yet Dönitz's own behavior over the ensuing weeks represented no less startling a reversal of character than Hitler's.[85] To be sure, the admiral initially announced that the struggle against "Bolshevism" would continue unabated. The war against the Western powers would likewise continue until Britain and the United States permitted Germany a free hand to deal with the Soviet Union.[86] But having announced these intentions, Dönitz, the arch advocate of unremitting struggle, sought to end the war as quickly as possible.

A number of explanations have been offered for this remarkable "sea change." One biographer of Dönitz has pointed out how Hitler's death and his own assumption of power clarified what had lately become an impossible command relationship in the mind of the admiral. Increasingly in the past weeks, authority in Berlin had been divorced from responsibility in the field. Now Dönitz had authority *and* responsibility.[87] And in a curious way, Hitler's allocation of responsibility to perhaps the most turf conscious of his remaining paladins may have had one salutary (although entirely unintended) effect. Once Dönitz assumed power, it was no longer possible for the self confessed "little sausage" of years past to retreat into his own narrow specialty (*Ressort*) and leave the "larger picture" to the Führer. In this respect, Dönitz's final *Ressort* was now Germany itself, and by May 1945 even he could have had no illusions: the end was at hand.

The chaotic conditions in the navy, the one institution in the Reich about which Dönitz did have first-hand knowledge in May 1945, may also have played a role in the admiral's decision to surrender. To be sure, even in the last days of the war there were signs of a willingness on the part of many *Seeoffiziere* and their subordinates to fulfill their duty to the utmost. In the east, Kriegsmarine personnel continued the evacuation of German sailors and civilians for another nine days, often under the most difficult of conditions and in the face of the gravest risks. In the U-boat force, moreover, there were still a few diehard commanders who were willing to brave even the most daunting odds with their crews. And in the west a few isolated garrisons continued to hold out stubbornly, patiently awaiting orders from either the new head of state (Dönitz) or his successor at Naval Command, Admiral Hans-Georg von Friedeburg.[88]

Elsewhere, however, there were signs that the navy was also at the end of its tether. In March, one Kriegsmarine crew had deserted with its boat to Sweden. In April, only the last-minute arrival of an SS detachment and summary executions had prevented the members of the small navy garrison at Helgoland from turning the island over to the British. In early May there were renewed signs of trouble in the same area when the commanding admiral of the Helgoland Bight reported very low morale among civilians and Wehrmacht personnel, large numbers of absences without leave (presumably due to desertion), and, in at least two cases, refusal to obey orders aboard Kriegsmarine vessels in Cuxhaven.[89]

Perhaps the most disturbing signs of dissolution, however, came from Norway. On May 4 Seaman Second Class Novak of minesweeper *M 253* was sentenced to death and immediately executed for a variety of offenses. Among other things, Novak had called the continuing war effort "insanity" and had characterized the Anglo-Americans as "human beings." Nor had he helped his case by expressing (presumably some time before April 30) his desire to murder the Führer or by drunkenly crowing, somewhat prematurely it turned out, that "no Nazi pig could lay a hand on him." Novak's execution did not put an end to the troubles aboard *M 253*, for the following day three more of the boat's enlisted men were executed for listening to Allied radio broadcasts, welcoming

Soviet successes, and plotting to remove unpopular superiors from their commands. Two other men were sentenced to six years' imprisonment for failing to report the conspiracy aboard *M 253*, and two other sailors deserted. These developments, so reminiscent of the last days of the Imperial Navy in 1918, prompted swift reaction on the part of the naval high command, which removed the commander of *M 253*, a Lieutenant Commander Fromme, from command on the grounds that he had made grave mistakes in leadership.[90]

Given the overall situation of the fatherland, however, it was clear that even the best in leadership could not preserve order for much longer. On May 4, therefore, Dönitz bowed to the inevitable and initiated the final process of surrender. That same day he ordered Germany's remaining U-boat commanders to cease hostilities. The U-boat men, he added consolingly, were both "undefeated and spotless," and their fallen comrades had "sealed with death their loyalty to Führer and Fatherland."[91] Three days later, National Socialist Germany surrendered unconditionally to the Allies at Rheims, France.

The behavior of the naval officers over the hectic days that followed revealed a kaleidoscope of human responses. A few diehards in the U-boat force refused to accept defeat directly and opted to take their boats to distant Argentina or Japan. Most submarine commanders, however, either brought their boats back to Germany for surrender or took them to Allied ports. The behavior of naval officers on land reveals a similar disparity of responses. Admiral Frisius, the commander of "Fortress Dunkirk," radioed a final message of loyalty to the fatherland from his "brave, undefeated garrison" and then marched his men into captivity.[92] Most officers and men, though, appear to have surrendered without fanfare, if possible to the British or the Americans, or else simply went home.

For the naval high command, however, there remained the laborious business of winding up the war. For sixteen days after the capitulation at Rheims, Dönitz's government maintained a precarious existence as it oversaw the transfer to the Allies of the few remaining areas under German control—primarily Norway, Denmark, parts of Schleswig-Holstein and Holland, and the so-called "Bavarian Redoubt." For a few more days, therefore, Dönitz continued to cling to the outward attributes of power, arriving every day at the naval school in Flensburg, the new seat of the "government," in a large armored Mercedes to preside over "Cabinet" meetings. At times he even spoke as if there was a future for the Movement. Thus, in a secret address to officers at Flensburg on May 11, he conceded that it was possible that Germans would have to abolish some features of National Socialism and that the Allies might do away with still more. Nevertheless, it was up to every one of his listeners to become the most diligent guardians of "the best and most noble features" of the Movement, particularly its strong sense of national community.[93]

Publicly, though, Dönitz took steps to distance himself from the regime. In subsequent discussions with the Allies, for example, he found it useful to emphasize his role as commander-in-chief of the Wehrmacht rather than his position as Führer or head of state. Likewise, he maintained to Germans and non-Germans alike, that the navy, the Wehrmacht, and even parts of the SS had emerged from the war with unstained escutcheons.[94]

In the process, the admiral's old ability to deny reality again came to the fore. Thus, when the Allies insisted that the swastika banner be lowered from those garrisons remaining under German control, Dönitz, the champion of total war, insisted that this be undertaken with all the ceremonies of a bygone era, as though the navy, Germany, and the world could be miraculously transported back to the age of "cabinet wars." Similarly, when Allied newspapers and radio broadcasts began revealing the gruesome details of the concentration camps, the admiral informed the officers and men of the navy that this had nothing to do with them. To be sure, he did announce that the misdeeds that "allegedly" occurred in the camps would be "sharply condemned." But in his view the safeguarding of "professional criminals [the concentration camp inmates] in time of war" had been a legitimate exercise of state authority.[95] Later, on May 17 and May 20, he informed General Rooks, the American chief of the Allied Control Commission now present at Flensburg, that the stories of the concentration camps were "largely exaggerated and were propaganda."[96]

Reality set in on the morning of May 23, when Rooks summoned Dönitz, Jodl, and Friedeburg to his quarters aboard the liner *Patria* in Flensburg harbor. In a short statement the American informed his visitors that the acting German government was dissolved and that they were to be taken into custody as prisoners of war. Dönitz took the news calmly, Jodl somewhat less so, but both men soon packed their bags for a journey that would eventually lead them to the prisoners' dock at Nuremberg. Friedeburg did not accompany them. Instead he returned to his quarters to gather his luggage, wrote a letter to his wife, and then asked permission to use the bathroom. Once inside he locked the door and swallowed a vial of poison. Within minutes the last commander of the Kriegsmarine was dead.[97]

Notes for Chapter 9

1 Bundesarchiv-Militärarchiv, Freiburg, West Germany (hereafter cited as BA-MA), RM 7/97, "Ansprache des Grossadmiral Raeder zur Niederlegung des Oberkommandos am 30. Januar 1943."

2 Dönitz described his own life in *Zehn Jahre und zwanzig Tage*, in *Mein wechselvolles Leben*, and in *40 Fragen an Karl Dönitz*. Biographies include Walter Görlitz, *Karl Dönitz: Der Grossadmiral* (Göttingen, 1972) and Peter Padfield, *Dönitz: The Last Führer* (New York, 1984). Fundamental to an understanding of Dönitz's conduct of the war is Michael Salewski's *Die deutsche Seekriegsleitung 1935–1945*, 3 vols (Munich, 1970–1975), 2, *1942–1945*.

3 Quoted in Salewski, *Seekriegsleitung*, 2, p. 226.

4   For Dönitz's personnel changes and the personalities of his appointees, see ibid., pp. 238–245.

5   Ibid., pp. 232–235.

6   Gerhard Wagner (ed.), *Lagevorträge des Oberbefehlshabers der Kriegsmarine von Hitler 1939–1945* (Munich, 1972), pp. 470–472; Salewski, *Seekriegsleitung*, 2, p. 238.

7   See BA-MA, K 10–2131, "Grossadmiral Dönitz. Schlussansprache auf der Tagung für Befehlshaber der Kriegsmarine in Weimar," December 17, 1943.

8   Salewski, *Seekriegsleitung*, 2, p. 237; Erich Raeder, *Mein Leben*, 2 vols (Tübingen, 1956–1957), 2, p. 291; Karl Dönitz, *Zehn Jahre und zwanzig Tage* (Bonn, 1958), pp. 308, 371.

9   Padfield, *Dönitz*, p. 268.

10 See, for example, Captain Konrad Weygold's postwar analysis of this phenomenon in BA-MA, N 328/53 Nachlass Weygold, "Aus dem Zusammenwirken von Marine und Heer im 2. Weltkrieg," p. 10.

11 For Dönitz's political inexperience, see Salewski, *Seekriegsleitung*, 2, p. 246. For Goebbels' speech, see G. Moltmann, "Goebbels Reden zum totalen Krieg am 18. Februar 1943," *Vierteljahrshefte für Zeitgeschichte*, 12, No. 1 (January 1964), pp. 13–43.

12 Salewski, *Seekriegsleitung*, 2, p. 246.

13 BA-MA, RM 8/65, "Laufende Befehle," April 20, 1943. See also a similar message from the following year in BA-MA, RM 8/66, "Laufende Befehle," April 20, 1944.

14 Wagner, *Lagevorträge*, p. 538. It is impossible to concur with Wagner's contention that this assessment had "nothing to do" with Dönitz's attitude toward the ideology of National Socialism.

15 Salewski, *Seekriegsleitung*, 2, pp. 257, 264–265.

16 Ibid., pp. 266–268.

17 Wagner, *Lagevorträge*, pp. 531–536; Salewski, *Seekriegsleitung*, 2, pp. 383–400, 454–455.

18 Quoted in Padfield, *Dönitz*, pp. 297–299.

19 These figures for Atlantic sinkings are from Friedrich Ruge, *Der Seekrieg: The German Navy's Story 1939–1945* (Annapolis, Md, 1972), p. 306. Jak P. Mallmann Showell, *The German Navy in World War Two: A Reference Guide to the Kriegsmarine, 1935–1945* (London, 1979), p. 47, gives a figure of forty-two U-boats as the overall Kriegsmarine losses for the month of May.

20 BA-MA, RM 7/98 1 Skl Nr. 18142/43g, June 17, 1943.

21 Wagner, *Lagevorträge*, p. 537.

22 BA-MA, RM 7/98 Oberkommando der Kriegsmarine, AMA Nr. 480, September 9, 1943.

23 For Dönitz's probable presence at Posen, see Padfield, *Dönitz*, pp. 322–326.

24 BA-MA, K 10–2131, "Grossadmiral Dönitz. Schlussansprache auf der Tagung für Befehlshaber der Kriegsmarine in Weimar," December 17, 1943.

25 For a detailed analysis of the decision to "unleash" the *Scharnhorst*, see Salewski, *Seekriegsleitung*, 2, pp. 324–346. Older works on the *Scharnhorst* include Karl Peter, *Schlachtkreuzer Scharnhorst: Kampf und Untergang* (Berlin, 1951); Heinrich Bredemeier, *Schlachtschiff Scharnhorst* (Jungenheim, 1962); and M. Ogden, *The Battle of the North Cape* (London, 1962).

26   One exception to the general inactivity was a raid on the Allied weather station at Spitzbergen between September 6 and 9, 1943, by the *Scharnhorst*, the *Tirpitz*, and nine destroyers.

27   Salewski, *Seekriegsleitung*, 2, p. 320.

28   Quoted in ibid., p. 332.

29   Dönitz spent Christmas Eve and part of Christmas Day in Paris at a yuletide celebration for U-boat personnel. In his absence Meisel urged the *Scharnhorst* sortie in the strongest possible terms. Salewski, *Seekriegsleitung*, 2, pp. 335–338.

30   Ibid., pp. 334–342.

31   Quoted in Padfield, *Dönitz*, p. 344.

32   For the record of Hitler's and Dönitz's first meeting in the aftermath of the *Scharnhorst* disaster, see Wagner, *Lagevorträge*, pp. 565–569.

33   There was, however, muted criticism of Dönitz within the Service. Salewski, *Seekriegsleitung*, 2, pp. 342–343.

34   Wagner, *Lagevorträge*, pp. 565, 567, 572.

35   Padfield, *Dönitz*, p. 291.

36   See the copy of Dönitz's directive dated February 10, 1944 in BA-MA, RM 7/99.

37   BA-MA, RM 7/1099 B. Nr. 1/Skl 13321/44, April 10, 1944.

38   Padfield, *Dönitz*, p. 351.

39   These figures, giving the approximate strength of the navy as of June 1, 1944, are in BA-MA, RM 7/99 Mar Wehr Tr Ia B Nr. 2912/44, June 29, 1944.

40   See Pfeiffer's memorandum of August 20, 1943, reprinted in Salewski, *Seekriegsleitung*, 3, pp. 364–371; also Salewski's analysis in ibid., 2, pp. 373–374.

41   See the text of Pfeiffer's memorandum of November 20, 1943, in ibid., 3, pp. 372–379; also Salewski's analysis in ibid., 2, pp. 388–389.

42   Ibid., 2, pp. 453–465.

43   This, of course, should not rule out the possibility of reciprocal influence between Meisel and Dönitz.

44   BA-MA, RM 7/97, "Vortrag des Chefs des Stabes der Seekriegsleitung bei der Besprechung der Oberbefehlshaber in Berlin am 8. Juni 1943."

45   Ibid.

46   BA-MA, RM 7/100, "Kurzlage ObdM Nr. 4," October 10, 1944.

47   See the exchange of letters dated August 7, August 21, August 31, and September 2, 1944, between Hans-Georg von Friedeburg and Heinrich Himmler in National Archives Microcopy No. T-175, "Records of the Reich Leader of SS and Chief of the German Police."

48   Salewski, *Seekriegsleitung*, 2, pp. 444–445.

49   Padfield, *Dönitz*, p. 355.

50   Eric Christian Rust, "Crew 34: German Naval Officers under and after Hitler" (PhD dissertation, University of Texas at Austin, 1987), p. 248.

51   BA-MA, N 172/38 Nachlass Boehm, "Vortrag vor den Führergehilfen im Bad Homburg." The date for this address would be sometime between late 1943, when the Marinekriegsakademie was transfered to Bad Homburg vor der Höhe, and the fall of 1944.

52   The most comprehensive account of the German opposition to Hitler is Peter Hoffman's *The History of the German Resistance, 1933–1945* (Cambridge, Mass., 1977). For the navy see Walter Baum, "Marine, Nationalsozialismus und Widerstand," *Vierteljahrshefte für Zeitgeschichte*, 11 (January 1963), pp.

16–48. Salewski, *Seekriegsleitung*, 2, pp. 432–448, and Padfield, *Dönitz*, pp. 364–379, provide important analyses of the problem of resistance in the navy. For the attitudes of numerous naval officers toward the *Putsch*, see Rust, "Crew 34," pp. 278–282.

53 Padfield, *Dönitz*, p. 374; Albert Speer, *Spandauer Tagebücher* (Frankfurt, Berlin and Vienna, 1975), p. 507.

54 Berthold Stauffenberg and Kranzfelder were condemned as traitors by a "Peoples Court" and executed on August 10, 1944. Canaris survived until April 9, 1945, when he was hanged at Flossenbürg prison.

55 A number of other officers were apparently aware of some features of the assassination plot. Two of them, Fregattenkapitän Dr Sydney Jessen and Commander Otto Mejer were subsequently arrested. Jessen managed to convince the Gestapo that he had merely heard rumors that a *Putsch* was in the offing. Baum, "Widerstand," p. 44. Mejer was freed after Werner Pfeiffer intervened on his behalf. Salewski, *Seekriegsleitung*, 2, p. 436.

56 Reprinted in BA-MA, RM 8/66, "Laufende Befehle," July 20, 1944.

57 The text of this speech is quoted extensively in Padfield, *Dönitz*, p. 373.

58 RM 8/66, "Laufende Befehle," July 23, 1944.

59 Manfred Messerschmidt, *Die Wehrmacht im NS Staat: Zeit der Indoktrination* (Hamburg, 1969), p. 429.

60 This and the following paragraph are from Salewski, *Seekriegsleitung*, 2, pp. 640–648. See also Padfield, *Dönitz*, pp. 374–379.

61 BA-MA, RM 7/158, Letter from Frisius to the Oberbefehlshaber des Marineoberkommandos Nordsee, September 17, 1944.

62 BA-MA, RM 7/137, "Bericht über den Rückmarsch der Marschgruppe Ambrosius (2. Minensuchflottille) durch den französischen Raum." See also the reports of Captain Edward Wegener on the retreat through France in BA-MA, RM 35 III/129, Lageübersicht des Marine Gruppenkommandos West, "Rückblick Monat August 1944" and "Rückblick Monat September 1944."

63 BA-MA, RM 7/100, "Kurzlage ObdM Nr. 4," October 10, 1944.

64 BA-MA, RM 7/1099 "Einige Bermerkungen zur englischen Frage," March 28, 1944; also two reports entitled "Kurzlage des ObdM Nr. 1," and "Kurzlage des ObdM Nr. 2," both dated September 21, 1944 and "Kurzlage des ObdM Nr. 4," October 10, 1944, in BA-MA, RM 7/100.

65 BA-MA, RM 7/100, "Kurzlage des ObdM Nr. 2," September 21, 1944.

66 See BA-MA, RM 7/97, "Phantasie—eine Waffe," Anlage zu B. Nr. 1. Skl. I Op. 17637/43.

67 For these measures, see Padfield, *Dönitz*, pp. 381, 387.

68 BA-MA, M/304 Mar Wehr/NSF Nr. 913, "Vertrauliche Nachrichten des nationalsozialistischen Führungsstabes der Kriegsmarine."

69 Theede's actions are described in ibid.

70 For this and the following, see BA-MA RM 7/131, "Bericht über den Verlust der Boote S 200, S 183, und S 702 in der Nacht vom 18–19. 9. 1944 und über die Eindrücke in englischer Gefangenschaft vom 19. 9. bis 1. 12. 1944."

71 BA-MA, RM 8/67, "Laufende Befehle," January 1, 1945.

72 BA-MA, RM 8/66, "Laufende Befehle," January 22, 1944.

73 BA-MA, RM 8/66, "Laufende Befehle," May 15, 1944.

74 BA-MA, RM 8/67, "Laufende Befehle," January 22, 1944 and May 15, 1944; BA-MA, RM 8/68, "Laufende Befehle," February 28, 1945. In principle, the latter directive added, only marriages with Germans were *really* desired.

75 This and the following from BA-MA, RM 6/103, "Bericht über den 4. Kriegslehrgang vom 2. Oktober 44 bis 14. Februar 45," February 14, 1945.
76 Wagner, *Lagevorträge*, pp. 621, 630; Padfield, *Dönitz*, p. 382.
77 See Goebbels' diary entries for February 28 and March 14, 1945, in *Joseph Goebbels Tagebücher 1945. Die letzten Aufzeichnungen* (Hamburg, 1977), pp. 55–56, 248.
78 Padfield, *Dönitz*, p. 389.
79 See BA-MA, "Massnahmen bei unehrenhafter Gefangennahme," March 14, 1945; Padfield, *Dönitz*, p. 392.
80 Lengthy excerpts from this directive are given in Padfield, *Dönitz*, pp. 393–397.
81 Ibid., p. 398.
82 For Dönitz's activity during this period, see Padfield, *Dönitz*, pp. 399–401.
83 Hitler's Political Testament is reprinted in Goebbels, *Tagebücher 1945*, pp. 550–555.
84 Padfield, *Dönitz*, p. 407.
85 For Dönitz's actions as head of state, see Walter Lüdde-Neurath, *Regierung Dönitz: die letzten Tage des Dritten Reiches* (Göttingen, 1953) and Marlis G. Steinert, *Capitulation 1945* (London, 1969).
86 The text of Dönitz's radio broadcast of May 1, 1945, is reprinted in Goebbels, *Tagebücher 1945*, p. 557.
87 See Padfield, *Dönitz*, pp. 409, 414.
88 Dönitz appointed Friedeburg head of the navy on May 1, the same day he received news of Hitler's death. Salewski, *Seekriegsleitung*, 2, p. 547.
89 Ibid.; BA-MA, RM 7/854 Kdr. Adm. Deutsche Bucht, Eingang Violett III, May 4, 1944; Padfield, *Dönitz*, p. 393.
90 BA-MA, RM 7/854 MBBS 0320 Abschrift MOK Norwegen GKdos 04008 FIII.
91 Padfield, *Dönitz*, p. 419.
92 Ibid., p. 420; Salewski, *Seekriegsleitung*, 2, p. 556. For the experiences of one of the boats that sailed to Argentina, see Heinz Schaeffer, *U-977: 66 Tage unter Wasser* (Wiesbaden, 1950).
93 Padfield, *Dönitz*, p. 431; Salewski, *Seekriegsleitung*, 2, p. 558.
94 Padfield, *Dönitz*, pp. 427–428.
95 BA-MA, RM 7/854 MA 1734, May 14, 1945; MOK Ost F I 137, May 14, 1945.
96 Padfield, *Dönitz*, p. 430.
97 Ibid., pp. 431–435.

Epilogue and Conclusion

With the arrest of Karl Dönitz and the death of Hans-Georg von Friedeburg on May 23, 1945, the official history of the Kriegsmarine came to a close. In the weeks that followed the officers and men of the navy were scattered to the four winds. Ironically, many of those sailors with minesweeping experience continued their dangerous trade in the newly organized German Minesweeping Administration (GM/SA), an agency which operated under British auspices but which enjoyed considerable internal autonomy. A period of captivity in Allied camps ranging from a few weeks to several years awaited most other officers. Judging from the experiences of Crew 34, treatment at the hands of the Allies varied from generous (in the case of the British) to severe (the French and the Russians), with the Americans falling somewhere in between. By the end of 1947, most officers had returned from captivity and were ready to begin their lives anew.[1]

A different fate awaited the two surviving former heads of the navy. Dönitz remained in Allied captivity after the dissolution of his regime at Flensburg on May 23, 1945. His predecessor, Raeder, was arrested by the Soviets later that summer and was initially taken to Moscow. The two grand admirals eventually met again as defendants before the International Military Tribunal at Nuremberg, where each was charged on three counts: "Conspiracy to Wage Aggressive War," "Waging Aggressive War," and "War Crimes."[2]

Both men vigorously asserted their innocence. Dönitz flatly stated that the indictments at Nuremberg had nothing to do with him and were merely "typical American humor."[3] Raeder likewise maintained that he knew nothing of German atrocities and that he had a "clear conscience" to his friend and correspondent, Hermann Boehm.[4] Nevertheless, on October 1, 1946, the tribunal found Raeder guilty on all three counts and sentenced him to life imprisonment. The tribunal acquitted Dönitz of conspiring to wage aggressive war but sentenced him to ten years' imprisonment for waging an aggressive war and committing war crimes.

The two men served most of their respective sentences at Spandau prison in Berlin. As it turned out, Raeder's advanced age and poor health resulted in his release from Spandau in September 1955. Dönitz joined him as a free man the following year, ten years to the day after his original condemnation at Nuremberg. There is no indication that the years at Spandau did anything to soften either man's resentment over his conviction. On the contrary, in their memoirs and in their public statements both men vociferously maintained both their innocence and that of the navy of the crimes that had been committed under National Socialism. The blame for the latter, they maintained in virtual unison, fell upon Hitler and his *political* advisors—especially Ribbentrop, Goebbels, Himmler, and Göring. As admirals they had concentrated exclusively on the needs of the navy.[5]

Yet even if one accepts the argument that the needs of the Service deserved their sole attention, the two admirals' records under the National Socialist dictatorship constitute a telling commentary on their leadership. After all, the *raison d'être* of Raeder's style of leadership—his "very tight rein"—after 1928 was the assumption, both spoken and unspoken, that he knew how to represent the navy's needs to the politicians. During the last years of the Weimar Republic and the first years of the National Socialist dictatorship Raeder gradually refined this conception to a very simple formula whereby the navy's self-interest (*Ressortegoismus*) became the highest measure of political wisdom. In the short run the admiral was not disappointed. After the Anglo-German Naval Agreement of 1935 it seemed as if the navy would receive the men and matériel commensurate with the needs of a major sea power. But Raeder "purchased" this growth for the navy only at tremendous cost: by displaying absolute loyalty to the Hitler state, by renouncing any independent judgment in the larger questions of policy, both foreign and domestic, and by naively accepting Hitler's assurance that the Kriegsmarine would not face a major naval power until 1943 at the earliest. As Raeder noted, when war came in 1939, the Kriegsmarine was utterly unprepared to fight it.

Despite other differences with Raeder, Dönitz's approach to the leadership of the navy was essentially the same as his predecessor's, but with one added twist. Whereas Raeder confined himself to naval affairs out of calculation, Dönitz evidently did so out of conviction, secure in his knowledge of Hitler's "genius." Thus in August 1943 Dönitz likened himself to a "little sausage" next to the Führer. One year later, in the wake of July 20, 1944, he insisted that the soldier had to leave politics to those who understood it. Given the strength of the massive enemy coalition facing the Reich by the summer of 1944, Dönitz might well have questioned his Führer's grasp of politics and grand strategy. He chose not to and thereby prolonged a war that Germany had long since lost all hope of winning.

Yet if the premature outbreak of war or the senseless prolongation of the struggle illustrate both admirals' shortcomings as leaders, they also provided grim vindication of their abilities on another plane. For the Second World War gave Raeder's and Dönitz's subordinates ample opportunity to follow Raeder's injunction of September 3, 1939, and "die gallantly." Whether it was in the narrow fjords of Norway or in the vast expanses of the Atlantic, the warships of the Kriegsmarine duly went down to their watery graves as ordered. This time, in marked contrast to October and November 1918, the officers and men of the German navy chose to fight to the bitter end. And this time, when revolt shook the homeland in July 1944, it was the army and not the navy which appeared to crack under the strain of war.

What accounts for the differences between the navy of Wilhelm II and that of Adolf Hitler? One could argue with considerable persuasiveness that it was the navy's remembrance of its misfortunes during the First World War—Raeder's "silent oath" that there would never be another November 1918—that molded the response of the Service's officers and men to the catastrophe of the Second World War. An equally convincing case could be made that it was the increased threat to the security and, indeed, the survival of the Reich, especially after Casablanca and Stalingrad, that made the navy fight so doggedly. Wilson's Fourteen Points, after all, would appear to have been far more appealing to would-be negotiators than the twin specters of Russian "Bolshevism" and unconditional surrender. Or, one could also argue that the officers of the Kriegsmarine had simply learned the art of leadership far more thoroughly than had their counterparts in the Imperial Navy.

There is a strong element of truth to each of these explanations; taken together, they go far toward explaining the difference between the navy's experiences in the First World War and those of the Second. Yet, so great was the navy's determination to fight on regardless of the odds and so great were the ensuing losses—roughly 70 per cent of the submariners, to take the extreme example, ultimately failed to return—that one suspects that there was another element present in the make-up of the mature Kriegsmarine as well, one that Michael Salewski has termed *Menschenverführung* (the seduction of men) rather than simply *Menschenführung* (the leadership of men). It is in this area, it would seem, that the impact of National Socialism was critical.

The Party's influence assumed a variety of forms. In a very real sense, it provided the link between the divergent forces outlined above which collectively account for the navy's determination to pursue the war at all costs. Party ideology, for example, reinforced the Service's painful memory of the German Revolution of 1918 with its demand that retribution be meted out to the "November criminals" who had subverted the fleet and the fatherland. Joseph Goebbels' Propaganda Ministry tirelessly exploited the fear of unconditional surrender to spur the officers and men of the Kriegsmarine on to greater and greater sacrifices. And, in a curious way, the Party's cherished notion of *Volksgemeinschaft*, of the essential unity and community of the nation, did much to counteract whatever residual tensions might have existed between officers and men, and thereby facilitated the task of leadership.

Nor was this all. In the totalitarian state of National Socialist Germany, the teachings of the Party served as the ideological bond that united the "front soldier" of myth and legend with *Volk* and family in the distant homeland. The efforts of Tirpitz's Fatherland Party notwithstanding, there had been nothing remotely comparable to this in the First World War. And, finally, the repeated pronouncements of the Party provided the most immediate source for the seemingly endless supply of stock phrases—"extreme readiness for battle," "fighting to the last shell," and "sinking with banners flying," to name but a few—that accompanied the officers and men of the navy on their desperate voyages. It is highly probable that many of the Service's personnel were put off by such high-flown rhetoric, and that they did their duty in spite of the Party's message, rather than because of it. But for others, there can be little doubt that it was the essential unity of the Party's and the navy's messages that kept them at their posts in the dark days of 1944 and 1945.

At the same time, however, one would be well advised to remember that the increasing unity of Party and Kriegsmarine evident by the latter stages of the war had not always been present. In the days before the *Machtergreifung*, many officers had been distinctly skeptical concerning Adolf Hitler's claim to embody the will of the *Volk*. Even after the National Socialist seizure of power on January 30, 1933, there had been many within the Service who had been suspicious of some or all of the Party's actions. Until early 1935, there had been serious altercations with the SA and the SS. The memory of these confrontations faded only slowly in the minds of the combatants. Moreover, throughout the latter half of the 1930s, there were those within the navy who were deeply disturbed by the Party's increasingly vicious campaigns against the Churches and the Jews, and others, such as Günther Guse and Hellmuth Heye, who were at least willing to question the basic postulates of Hitlerian foreign policy.

It had been Erich Raeder's task to see that none of these doubts disturbed the overall policy of accommodation between Party and Kriegsmarine. Between January 1933 and January 1943, the admiral patiently drew upon the examples of his predecessors, of Tirpitz and Scheer from the Imperial Navy, and of Trotha, Behncke, and Zenker from the Reichsmarine. To his subordinates, Raeder continually emphasized the pressing necessity of obedience to orders from above and of loyalty to the New Order. To the public at large, he stressed the historical connection (for the most part bogus) between Party and Service and the strong ties uniting fleet and fatherland. And, at the Reich Chancellery and at Berchtesgaden, he tirelessly sought to develop Hitler's appreciation for the uses of the navy in peace and war.

Raeder's undertaking was by no means an easy one. Privately, he continued to nurse doubts about the justice of many of the Party's domestic policies. The persecution of the Jews troubled him not a little; the Party's campaign against the Churches caused him greater concern. And always, there remained the nagging fear at the back of Raeder's mind that Germany's volatile Führer would somehow turn against the Service and destroy the life's work of the admiral.

Yet, if Raeder had his private reservations about the legitimacy of National Socialism, he rarely, if ever, revealed them. For the decade that he served Adolf Hitler, Raeder had nothing but public praise for the Party and its Führer. If, in retrospect, the admiral's enthusiasm for the Movement paled in comparison with that of a number of his contemporaries in the armed forces—men such as Werner von

263

Blomberg, Walther von Reichenau, and Wilhelm Keitel—it must have nevertheless looked genuine enough to many of Raeder's subordinates. The more ambitious of them took the cue from their commander and embraced the Party. His successor, moreover, would go far beyond Raeder's position. Raeder's interest in National Socialism, after all, had always remained a means toward a greater end, for in the final analysis, there was room for only one all-embracing concern in Raeder's scheme of things, and he had found that long ago when he had first entered the navy. Dönitz, being of a somewhat livelier cast of mind, had room for more than one gospel at a time. He would embrace National Socialism unreservedly.

Notes for Epilogue and Conclusion

1 Eric Christian Rust, "Crew 34: German Naval Officers under and after Hitler" (PhD dissertation, University of Texas at Austin, 1987), pp. 312–320.
2 For an overview of Dönitz at Nuremberg, see Peter Padfield, *Dönitz: The Last Führer* (New York, 1984), pp. 435–468.
3 Quoted in Ann Tusa and John Tusa, *The Nuremberg Trial* (New York, 1984), p. 132.
4 Bundesarchiv-Militärarchiv, Freiburg, West Germany (BA-MA), N 172/19 Nachlass Boehm, Raeder to Boehm in prisoner of war postcard composed on July 24, 1946.
5 For Raeder's and Dönitz's memoirs see above, "Introduction," note 6.

Bibliography

Archival Material: Bundesarchiv-Militärarchiv, Freiburg, West Germany

AKTEN

Five collections from the documentary holdings of the Bundesarchiv-Militärarchiv were essential in exploring the naval officer corps in the National Socialist era. Perhaps most revealing of the changing relationship between Service and Party are the navy's day-to-day circulars and announcements, which were known variously as *Bekanntmachungen* or *Laufende Befehle* and are preserved in the collection RM 8 (Kriegswissenschaftliche Abteilung der Marine). Collections RM 6 (Oberbefehlshaber der Kriegsmarine) and RM 20 (Marinekommandoamt) contain a wealth of information, ranging from the high command's efforts to combat suspected subversion by the German Communist Party in the early 1930s to its frantic efforts to staff the burgeoning fleet in the late 1930s. Collection RW 6 (OKW/Alegemeines Wehrmachtamt) offered insight both into inter-service rivalries between the three branches of the armed forces and into the navy's often troubled relations with the SA and the SS. Information about the Service's experimentation with the naval propaganda units during the Second World War came from collection RW 4 (OKW/Wehrmachtführungsstab).

NAVAL REGULATIONS

Marineverordnungsblatt, 1930–1945.

Besondere Marine Bestimmungen, 1935–1945.

Nordseestationstagesbefehle, 1939–1945.

Ostseestationstagesbefehle, 1935–1945.

M. Dv. Nr. 49 "Bestimmungen für den Dienst an Bord." Berlin, 1925.

M. Dv. Nr. 49 "Bestimmungen für den Dienst an Bord, Heft II: Der innere Dienst des Schiffes und seine Reglung, Nachdruck 1941."

RM D4 67c "Ergänzungsbestimmungen für die Ingenieuroffiziere der Marine vom 24. März 1927." Berlin, 1927.

RM D4 67 Heft 1 "Ergänzungsbestimmungen für die Offizierslaufbahnen für die Kriegsmarine vom 30. September 1938."

RM D4 67a "Seeoffizier-Ergänzungsbestimmungen vom 24. Juli 1926. Neudruck 1931."

RM D4 M. Dv. Nr. 67f "Dienstvorschrift für die Marineschule Flensburg-Mürwik." Berlin, 1930.

RM D4 M. Dv. Nr. 67h "Vorschrift für die Ausbildung der Freiwilligen bzw. Kadetten der Seeoffizier-Ingenieuroffizier-Sanitätsoffizier- und Zahlmeisterlaufbahnen der Reichsmarine." Berlin 1930.

RM D4 M. Dv. Nr. 67i "Vorschrift für die Ausbildung der Fähnriche auf den Sonderlehrgängen und im praktischen Dienst an Bord der Schiffe." April 21, 1931.

RM D4 67n "Erganzungsbestimmungen für die Offizierslaufbahnen in der Kriegsmarine vom 30. September 1938."

NACHLÄSSE AND SPECIAL COLLECTIONS

MSg 296–298. Erich Frühling "Wehrbetreuung bei der Kriegsmarine im Zweiten Weltkrieg."
N 165 Nachlass Groos.
N 172 Nachlass Boehm.
N 239 Nachlass Levetzow.
N 316 Nachlass Weichold.
N 328 Nachlass Förste.
N 374 Nachlass von Friedeburg.
N 548 Nachlass Fuchs.
N 582 Nachlass Bräckow.

Published Documents and Official Histories

Germany, *Documents on German Foreign Policy, 1918–1945*, Series C, 1933–1937; Series D, 1937–1945 (Washington: U.S. Government Printing Office 1957–).

Germany, Ministry of Marine, *Fuehrer Conferences on Matters Dealing with the German Navy*, 7 vols (Washington, DC: U.S. Navy Department, 1947).

Germany, Ministry of Marine, *Der Krieg zur See, 1914–1918*, 22 vols (Berlin: E. S. Mittler & Sohn, 1922–1966).

International Military Tribunal, *Trial of the Major War Criminals before the International Tribunal*, 42 vols (Nuremberg: US Government Printing Office, 1947–1949).

Wagner, Gerhard (ed.), *Lagevorträge des Oberbefehlshabers der Kriegsmarine vor Hitler 1939–1945* (Munich, 1972).

Memoirs, Diaries and Published Papers

Baden, Prinz Max von, *Erinnerungen und Dokumente*, edited by Golo Mann and Andreas Burckhardt (Stuttgart: Ernst Klett Verlag, 1968).

Boehm, Hermann, *Norwegen zwischen England und Deutschland* (Lippoldsberg: Klosterhaus, 1956).

Dönitz, Karl, *Mein wechselvolles Leben* (Göttingen: Musterschmidt, 1968).

Dönitz, Karl, *Memoirs: Ten Years and Twenty Days* (London: Weidenfeld & Nicholson, 1959)

Dönitz, Karl, *Zehn Jahre und zwanzig Tage* (Bonn: Athenäum-Verlag, 1958).

Dönitz, Karl, *40 Fragen an Karl Dönitz* (Munich: Bernard & Graefe, 1979).

François-Poncet, André, *The Fateful Years: Memoirs of a French Ambassador in Berlin* (New York: Harcourt Brace and Company, 1949).

Gessler, Otto, *Reichswehrpolitik in der Weimarer Zeit* (Stuttgart: Deutsche Verlags-Anstalt, 1958).

Goebbels, Joseph, *Joseph Goebbels Tagebücher 1945. Die letzten Aufzeichnungen* (Hamburg: Hoffmann und Campe, 1977).

Goebbels, Joseph, *Vom Kaiserhof zur Reichskanzlei*, 36th edn. (Munich: Zentralverlag der NSDAP, 1942).

Hossbach, Friedrich, *Zwischen Wehrmacht und Hitler 1934–1938*, 2nd edn. rev. (Göttingen: Vandenhoeck & Ruprecht, 1965).

Keitel, Wilhelm, *Generalfeldmarschall Keitel: Verbrecher oder Offizier? Erinnerungen, Briefe, Dokumente des Chef OKW*, edited by Walter Görlitz (Göttingen: Musterschmidt, 1961).

Noske, Gustav, *Erlebtes aus Aufstieg und Niedergang einer Demokratie* (Offenbach-Main: Bollwerk Verlag, 1947).

Noske, *Von Kiel bis Kapp* (Berlin: Verlag für Politik und Wirtschaft, 1920).

Puttkamer, Karl-Jesko von, *Die unheimliche See: Hitler und die Kriegsmarine* (Vienna and Munich: K. Kuhne, 1952).

Raeder, Erich, *Mein Leben*, 2 vols (Tübingen: Verlag Fritz Schlichtenmayer, 1956–1957).

Raeder, Erich, *My Life* (Annapolis, Md: Naval Institute Press, 1960).

Ruge, Friedrich, *In vier Marinen* (Munich: Bernard & Graefe, 1979).

Scheer, Reinhard, *Deutschlands Hochseeflotte im Weltkrieg* (Berlin: August Scherl, 1920).

Speer, Albert, *Spandauer Tagebücher* (Frankfurt, Berlin and Vienna: Propyläen, 1975).

Tirpitz, Alfred von, *Erinnerungen* (Leipzig: K. F. Koehler, 1919).

Tirpitz, Alfred, *Politische Dokumente*, 2 vols (Stuttgart and Berlin: Cotta, 1924–1926).

Weizsäcker, Ernst von, *Die Weizsäcker Papiere*, 2 vols, edited by Leonidas E. Hill (Berlin: Propyläen Verlag, 1974–1982).

Books

Abendroth, Hans-Henning, *Hitler in der spanischen Arena* (Paderborn: Ferdinand Schöningh Verlag, 1973).

Abshagen, Karl Heinz, *Canaris* (London: Hutchinson, 1956).

Absolon, Rudolf, *Die Wehrmacht im Dritten Reich*, 4 vols (Boppard am Rhein: Harald Boldt Verlag, 1969–).

Ansel, Walter, *Hitler Confronts England* (Durham, NC: Duke University Press, 1960).

Aronson, Schlomo, *Reinhard Heydrich und die Frühgeschichte von Gestapo und SD* (Stuttgart: Deutsche Verlags-Anstalt, 1971).

Assman, Kurt, *Deutsche Schicksalsjahre: Historische Bilder aus dem Zweiten Weltkrieg und seiner Vorgeschichte* (Wiesbaden: E. Brockhaus Verlag, 1950).

Bauer, Werner, *Geschichte des Marinesanitätswesens bis 1945* (Berlin: E. S. Mittler & Sohn, 1958).

Bennecke, Heinrich, *Die Reichswehr und der "Röhm Putsch"* (Munich: Gunter Olzog Verlag, 1964).

Berghahn, Volker R., *Der Stahlhelm: Bund der Frontsoldaten, 1918–1935* (Düsseldorf: Droste Verlag, 1966).

Berghahn, Volker R., *Der Tirpitz-Plan. Genesis und Verfall einer innenpolitischen Krisenstrategie unter Wilhelm II* (Düsseldorf: Droste Verlag, 1971).

Bird, Keith W., *Weimar, The German Naval Officer Corps and the Rise of National Socialism* (Amsterdam: B. R. Grüner, 1977).

Born, Karl Erich, "Die Politischen Testamente Friedrichs des Grossen," in *Seemacht und Geschichte: Festschrift zum 80. Geburtstag von Friedrich Ruge* (Bonn-Bad Godesberg: MOV Verlag, 1975).

Bracher, Karl Dietrich, *Die Auflösung der Weimarer Republik*, 3rd edn. (Villingen: Ring Verlag, 1960).

Bracher, Karl Dietrich, *The German Dictatorship* (New York: Praeger, 1970).

Bracher, Karl Dietrich; Sauer, Wolfgang; and Schulz, Gerhard, *Die nationalsozial-istische Machtergreifung*, 2nd edn (Cologne: Westdeutscher Verlag, 1960).

Bräckow, Werner, *Die Geschichte des deutschen Marine-Ingenieuroffizierkorps* (Oldenburg and Hamburg: Stallings, 1974).

Bredemeier, Heinrich, *Schlachtschiff Scharnhorst* (Jungenheim: Koehlers Verlags-gesellschaft, 1962).

Buchheim, Hans, *Glaubenskrise im Dritten Reich: Drei Kapitel Nationalsozialistischer Religionspolitik* (Stuttgart: Deutsche Verlags-Anstalt, 1953).

Bund der Deckoffiziere, *Deckoffiziere der Deutschen Marine; Ihre Geschichte 1848–1933* (Berlin: private publication, 1933).

Carsten, F. L., *The Reichswehr and Politics 1918 to 1933* (Oxford: Clarendon Press, 1966).

Caspar, Gustav Adolf, *Die sozialdemokratische Partei und das deutsche Wehrproblem in den Jahren der Weimarer Republik* (Frankfurt: E. S. Mittler, 1959).

Celovsky, Boris, *Das Münchener Abkommen von 1938* (Stuttgart: Deutsche Verlags-Anstalt, 1958).

Conway, John S., *The Nazi Persecution of the Churches, 1933–1945* (New York: Basic Books, 1968).

Craig, Gordon A., *The Politics of the Prussian Army, 1640–1945*, rev. edn (New York: Oxford University Press, 1964).

Czisnik, Ulrich, *Gustav Noske: Ein sozialdemokratischer Staatsmann* (Zürich and Frankfurt: Musterschmidt, 1969).

Deák, István, *Weimar Germany's Left-Wing Intellectuals: A Political History of the Weltbühne and Its Circle* (Berkeley, Calif: University of California Press, 1968).

Deist, Wilhelm, "Die Aufrüstung der Wehrmacht," in *Das deutsche Reich und der Zweiten Weltkrieg*, 10 vols (Stuttgart: Deutsche Verlags-Anstalt, 1979-). Vol. 1: *Ursachen und Voraussetzungen der deutschen Kriegspolitik* (1979), pp. 371–532, by Wilhelm Deist, Manfred Messerschmidt, Hans-Erich Volkmann and Wolfram Wette.

Deist, Wilhelm, *Flottenpolitik und Flottenpropaganda: Das Nachrichtenbureau des Reichsmarineamtes 1897–1914* (Stuttgart: Deutsche Verlags-Anstalt, 1976).

Deist, Wilhelm, *Militär und Innenpolitik im Weltkrieg*, 2 vols (Düsseldorf: Droste Verlag, 1970).

Deist, Wilhelm, *The Wehrmacht and German Rearmament* (London: Macmillan, 1981).

Deutsch, Harold C., *Hitler and His Generals: The Hidden Crisis, January-June 1938* (Minneapolis, Minn.: University of Minnesota Press, 1974).

Diehl, James M., *Paramilitary Politics in Weimar Germany* (Bloomington, Ind.: Indiana University Press, 1977).

Domarus, Max, *Hitler, Reden und Proklamationen, 1932–1945*, 2 vols (Munich: Süddeutscher Verlag, 1965).

Dülffer, Jost, "Die Reichs- und Kriegsmarine 1918–1939," in *Handbuch zur deutschen Militärgeschichte*, 5 vols (Munich: Bernard & Graefe, 1964–1979), Vol. 4, pp. 337–488.

Dülffer, Jost, *Weimar, Hitler und die Marine: Reichspolitik und Flottenbau 1920–1939* (Düsseldorf: Droste Verlag, 1973).

Ehrenreich, Bernd, *Marine-SA: Das Buch einer Formation* (Hamburg: Hanseatische Verlagsanstalt, 1935).

Eichstädt, Ulrich, *Von Dollfus zu Hitler: Geschichte des Anschlusses Österreichs 1933–1938* (Wiesbaden: Fritz Steiner Verlag, 1955).

Emmerson, James Thomas, *The Rhineland Crisis, 7 March 1936: A Study in Multilateral Diplomacy* (London: Temple Smith, 1977).

Erger, Johannes, *Der Kapp-Lüttwitz-Putsch: Ein Beitrag zur deutschen Innenpolitik 1919/20* (Düsseldorf: Droste Verlag, 1967).

Fest, Joachim, *Hitler* (New York: Harcourt Brace Jovanovich, 1974).

Foertsch, Hermann, *Der Offizier in der neuen Wehrmacht* (Berlin: R. Eisenschmidt, 1935).

Foertsch, Hermann, *Schuld und Verhängnis: Die Fritsch-Krise im Frühjahr 1938 als Wendepunkt in der Geschichte der nationalsozialistischen Zeit* (Stuttgart: Deutsche Verlags-Anstalt, 1951).

Forstmeier, Friedrich, "Zur Rolle der Marine im Kapp Putsch," in *Seemacht und Geschichte: Festschrift zum 80. Geburtstag von Friedrich Ruge* (Bonn-Bad Godesberg: MOV Verlag, 1975).

Gackenholz, Hermann, "Reichskanzlei, 5. November 1937," in *Forschungen zu Staat und Verfassung: Festgabe für Fritz Hartung* (Berlin: Duncker & Humbolt, 1958).

Gemzell, Carl-Axel, *Organization, Conflict, and Innovation: A Study of German Naval Strategic Planning, 1888–1940* (Stockholm: Esselte Studium, 1973).

Gemzell, Carl-Axel, *Raeder, Hitler und Skandinavien: Der Kampf für einen maritimen Operationsplan* (Lund: CWK Gleerup, 1965).

Giese, Friedrich, *Von Scapa Flow zur Kriegsmarine Grossdeutschlands* (Berlin: Verlag "Die Wehrmacht," 1939).

Giese, Friedrich, *Wie werde ich Offizier der Kriegsmarine?* (Berlin: E. S. Mittler & Sohn, 1937).

Görlitz, Walter, *Karl Dönitz: Der Grossadmiral* (Göttingen: Musterschmidt, 1972).

Grenville, J. A. S., *The Major International Treaties 1914–1973: A History and Guide with Texts* (New York: Stein and Day, 1974).

Gröner, Erich, *Die deutschen Kriegsschiffe 1815–1945*, 2 vols (Munich: J. F. Lehmanns Verlag, 1966).

Güth, Rolf, *Die Marine des deutschen Reiches 1919–1939* (Frankfurt: Bernard & Graefe, 1972).

Güth, Rolf, "Die Organisation der deutschen Marine in Krieg und Frieden 1913–1939," in *Handbuch zur deutschen Militärgeschichte 1648–1939*, 5 vols (Munich: Bernard & Graefe, 1964–1979). Vol. 4, pp. 263–336.

Hayes, Paul M., *Quisling: The Career and Political Ideas of Vidkun Quisling, 1887–1945* (Bloomington, Ind.: Indiana University Press, 1972).

Herwig, Holger H., *The German Naval Officer Corps: A Social and Political History, 1890–1918* (Oxford: Clarendon Press, 1973).

Herwig, Holger H., *Luxury Fleet: The Imperial German Navy, 1888–1918* (London: Allen & Unwin, 1980).

Herwig, Holger H., *Politics of Frustration: The United States in German Naval Planning, 1889–1941* (Boston, Mass.: Little, Brown, 1976).

Heye, Hellmuth, *Die Deutsche Kriegsmarine: Aufgaben und Aufbau* (Berlin: Junker und Dünnhaupt Verlag, 1939).

Heysing, Günther, *Propagandatruppen der deutschen Kriegsmarine. Teil 1. Juni 1939 bis Juni 1940. Versuch einer Dokumentation* (Hamburg, 1964).

Hildebrand, Klaus, *Deutsche Aussenpolitik 1933–1945: Kalkül oder Dogma?* (Stuttgart: Kohlhammer Verlag, 1971).

Hildebrand, Klaus, *Vom Reich zum Weltreich: Hitler, NSDAP und koloniale Frage 1919–1945* (Munich: Wilhelm Fink Verlag, 1969).

Hillgruber, Andreas, *Deutschlands Rolle in der Vorgeschichte der beiden Weltkriege* (Göttingen: Vandenhoeck & Ruprecht, 1967).

Hillgruber, Andreas, *Die gescheiterte Grossmacht: Eine Skizze des Deutschen Reiches 1871–1945* (Düsseldorf: Droste Verlag, 1980).

Hinsley, F. H., *Hitler's Strategy* (Cambridge: Cambridge University Press, 1951).

Hitler, Adolf, *Hitlers Zweites Buch: Ein Dokument aus dem Jahr 1928*, edited and introduced by G. L. Weinberg (Stuttgart: Deutsche Verlags-Anstalt, 1961).

Hitler, Adolf, *Mein Kampf* (Munich: Franz Eher Verlag, 1940).

Hofer, Walther, *Die Entfesselung des Zweiten Weltkrieges: Eine Studie über die internationalen Beziehungen im Sommer 1939*, 3rd edn, (Frankfurt: Fischer Bücherei, 1964).

Hoffman, Peter, *The History of the German Resistance, 1933–1945* (Cambridge, Mass.: MIT Press, 1977).

Hofmann, Hanns Hubert (ed.), *Das deutsche Offizierkorps 1860–1960* (Boppard am Rhein: Harald Boldt Verlag, 1980).

Höhne, Heinz, *Canaris: Patriot im Zwielicht* (Munich: C. Bertelsmann Verlag, 1976).

Horn, Daniel, *The German Naval Mutinies of World War I* (New Brunswick, NJ: Rutgers University Press, 1969).

Horn, Daniel (ed.), *War, Mutiny and Revolution in the German Navy: The World War I Diary of Seaman Richard Stumpf* (New Brunswick, NJ: Rutgers University Press, 1967).

Hubatsch, Walther, *Der Admiralstab und die obersten Marinebehörden in Deutschland 1848–1945* (Frankfurt: Bernard & Graefe, 1958).

Hubatsch, Walther, *"Weserübung." Die deutsche Besetzung von Dänemark und Norwegen 1940* (Göttingen: Musterschmidt, 1960).

Hürten, Heinz (ed.), *Zwischen Revolution und Kapp Putsch: Militär und Innenpolitik 1918–1920* (Düsseldorf: Droste Verlag, 1977).

Ingrim, Robert, *Hitlers glücklichster Tag: London, am 18. Juni 1935* (Stuttgart: Seewald, 1962).

Jacobsen, Hans-Adolf, *Nationalsozialistische Aussenpolitik 1933–1938* (Frankfurt: Alfred Metzner Verlag, 1968).

Kennedy, Paul M., *The Rise of the Anglo-German Antagonism 1860–1914* (London: Allen & Unwin, 1980).

Klee, Karl, *Das Unternehmen "Seelöwe:" Die geplante deutsche Landung in England 1940* (Göttingen: Musterschmidt, 1958).

Kluge, Ulrich, *Soldatenräte und Revolution: Studien zur Militärpolitik in Deutschland 1918/19* (Göttingen: Vandenhoeck & Ruprecht, 1975).

Krausnick, Helmut, "Vorgeschichte und Beginn des militärischen Widerstandes gegen Hitler," in *Vollmacht des Gewissens*, 2 vols (Frankfurt am Main: Alfred Metzner Verlag, 1960). Vol. 1, pp. 177–384.

Krüger, Gabriele, *Die Brigade Ehrhardt* (Hamburg: Leibniz Verlag, 1971).

Loock, Hans-Dietrich, *Quisling, Rosenberg, und Terboven* (Stuttgart, 1970).

Lüdde-Neurath, W., *Regierung Dönitz: die letzten Tage des Dritten Reiches* (Göttingen: Musterschmidt, 1953).

McBain, Howard Lee, and Rogers, Lindsay, *The New Constitutions of Europe* (Garden City: Doubleday, 1923).

Marder, A. J., *From the Dreadnought to Scapa Flow: The Royal Navy in the Fisher Era, 1904–1919*, 5 vols (London: Oxford University Press, 1961–1970).

Martienssen, Anthony, *Hitler and His Admirals* (New York: E. P. Dutton and Company, 1949).

Maser, Werner, *Hitlers Briefe und Notizen* (Düsseldorf: Econ Verlag, 1973).

Meier, Kurt, *Die Deutschen Christen: Das Bild einer Bewegung im Kirchenkampf des Dritten Reiches* (Halle, Saale: M. Niemeyer, 1964).

Meier, Kurt, *Kirche und Judentum: Die Haltung der evangelischen Kirche zur Judenpolitik des Dritten Reiches* (Göttingen: Vandenhoeck & Ruprecht, 1966).

Meier-Dörnberg, Wilhelm, *Ölversorgung der Kriegsmarine 1935–1945* (Freiburg: Rombach, 1973).

Meier-Welcker, Hans, *Seeckt* (Frankfurt: Bernard & Graefe, 1967).

Merkes, Manfred, *Die deutsche Politik im spanischen Bürgerkrieg 1936–1939*, 2d edn, rev. (Bonn: Ludwig Röhrscheid Verlag, 1969).

Messerschmidt, Manfred, *Die Wehrmacht im NS Staat: Zeit der Indoktrination* (Hamburg: R. v. Decker's Verlag, 1969).

Milatz, Alfred, "Das Ende der Parteien im Spiegel der Wahlen 1930 bis 1933," in *Das Ende der Parteien 1933*, pp. 741–793, edited by Erich Matthias and Rudolf Morsey (Düsseldorf: Droste Verlag, 1960).

Müller, Klaus-Jürgen, *Das Heer und Hitler: Armee und nationalsozialistisches Regime 1933–1940* (Stuttgart: Deutsche Verlags-Anstalt, 1969).

Murawski, Erich, *Der deutsche Wehrmachtbericht, 1939–1945. Ein Beitrag zur Untersuchung der Geistigen Kriegführung. Mit einer Dokumentation der Wehrmachtberichte von 1. 7. 1944 bis zum 9. 5. 1945*, 2nd edn (Boppard: Harald Boldt, 1962).

Niemann, Alfred, *Revolution von Oben—Umsturz von Unten: Entwicklung und Verlauf der Staatsumwälzung in Deutschland 1914–1918* (Berlin: Verlag für Kulturpolitik, 1927).

Ogden, M., *The Battle of the North Cape* (London: W. Kimber, 1962).

O'Neill, Robert J., *The German Army and the Nazi Party, 1933–1939* (London: Cassell, 1966).

Orlow, Dietrich, *The History of the Nazi Party: 1919–1933* (Pittsburgh, Penn.: University of Pittsburgh Press, 1969).

Padfield, Peter, *Dönitz: The Last Führer* (New York: Harper & Row, 1984).

Papke, Gerhard; Black, Hans; Matuschka, Edgar Graf von; and Wohlfeil, Rainer, *Untersuchungen zur Geschichte des Offizierkorps: Anciennität und Beförderung nach Leistung* (Stuttgart: Deutsche Verlags-Anstalt, 1962).

The Persecution of the Catholic Church in the Third Reich: Facts and Documents, translated from the German (London: Burns & Oates, 1940).

Peter, Karl, *Schlachtkreuzer Scharnhorst: Kampf und Untergang* (Berlin: E. S. Mittler, 1951).

Philbin, Tobias R., *Admiral von Hipper: The Inconvenient Hero* (Amsterdam: B. R. Grüner, 1982).

Picker, Henry, *Hitlers Tischgespräche im Führerhauptquartier 1941–1942* (Stuttgart: Seewald Verlag, 1963).

271

Porten, Edward P. von der, *The German Navy in World War II* (New York: Thomas Y. Crowell, 1969).

Post, Gaines, Jr, *The Civil-Military Fabric of Weimar Foreign Policy* (Princeton, NJ: Princeton University Press, 1973).

Prien, Günther, *Mein Weg nach Scapa Flow* (Berlin: Im deutschen Verlag, 1940).

Rabenau, Friedrich von, *Seeckt: Aus seinem Leben 1918–1936* (Leipzig: v. Hase & Koehler Verlag, 1940).

Rahn, Werner, *Reichsmarine und Landesverteidigung 1919–1928: Konzeption und Führung der Marine in der Weimarer Republik* (Munich: Bernard & Graefe, 1976).

Reuter, Ludwig von, *Scapa Flow: Das Grab der deutschen Flotte*, 2nd edn, rev. (Leipzig: K. F. Koehler, 1921).

Rich, Norman, *Hitler's War Aims*, 2 vols (New York: Norton, 1973–1974).

Ritter, GGerhard A. and Miller, Susanne (eds), *Die deutsche Revolution 1918–1919* (Frankfurt and Hamburg: Fischer Verlag, 1969).

Rohwer, Jürgen and Hümmelchen, Gerhard, *Chronology of the War at Sea, 1939–1945*, 2 vols (New York: Arco, 1972–1974).

Roskill, Stephen, *Naval Policy between the Wars*, Vol. 1: *The Period of Anglo-American Antagonism, 1919–1929*, Vol. 2: *The Period of Reluctant Rearmament, 1930–1939* (New York: Walker, 1968–1976).

Roskill, Stephen, *The War at Sea, 1939–1945*, 3 vols (London: HMSO, 1954–1961).

Ruge, Friedrich, *Der Seekrieg: The German Navy's Story 1939-1945* (Annapolis, Md, 1972).

Ruge, Friedrich, *Scapa Flow 1919: The End of the German Fleet* (London: Allan, 1973).

Ryder, A. J., *The German Revolution of 1918: A Study of German Socialism in War and Revolt* (Cambridge: Cambridge University Press, 1967).

Salewski, Michael, *Die deutsche Seekriegsleitung 1935–1945*, 3 vols (Munich: Bernard & Graefe, 1970–1975).

Salewski, Michael, "Menschenführung in der deutschen Kriegsmarine 1933-1945," in *Menschenführung in der Marine* (Herford and Bonn: E. S. Mittler & Sohn, 1981), pp. 83–103.

Salewski, Michael, "Das Offizierkorps der Reichs- und Kriegsmarine," in *Das Deutsche Offizierkorps, 1860–1960*, edited by Hanns Hubert Hofmann (Boppard am Rhein: Harald Boldt Verlag, 1980).

Schaeffer, Heinz, *U-977: 66 Tage unter Wasser* (Wiesbaden: Limes Verlag, 1950).

Schottelius, Herbert, and Deist, Wilhelm (eds), *Marine und Marinepolitik im kaiserlichen Deutschland, 1871–1914* (Düsseldorf: Droste Verlag, 1972).

Schreiber, Gerhard, *Revisionismus und Weltmachtstreben: Marineführung und deutsch-italienische Beziehungen 1919–1944* (Stuttgart: Deutsche Verlags-Anstalt, 1978).

Showell, Jak P. Mallmann, *The German Navy in World War Two: A Reference Guide to the Kriegsmarine, 1935–1945* (London: Arms and Armour Press, 1979).

Snyder, Louis L., *Encyclopedia of the Third Reich* (New York: McGraw Hill, 1976).

Sorge, Siegfried, *Der Marineoffizier als Führer und Erzieher* (Berlin: E. S. Mittler & Sohn, 1937).

Steinberg, Jonathan, *Yesterday's Deterrent: Tirpitz and the Birth of the German Battle Fleet* (London: Macdonald, 1965).

Steinert, Marlis G., *Capitulation 1945* (London: Constable, 1969).

Temperley, H. W. V., ed., *A History of the Peace Conference of Paris* (London: H. Fronde, and Hodder & Stoughton, 1920–1924).
Toland, John, *Adolph Hitler*, 2 vols (Garden City, NY: Doubleday & Company, 1976).
Tusa, Ann, and Tusa, John, *The Nuremberg Trial* (New York: Atheneum, 1984).

Vogelsang, Thilo, *Reichswehr, Staat und NSDAP* (Stuttgart: Deutsche Verlags-Anstalt, 1962).

Wacker, Wolfgang, *Der Bau des Panzerschiffes "A" und der Reichstag* (Tübingen: Mohr Verlag, 1959).
Waite, Robert G. L., *Vanguard of Nazism: The Free Corps Movement in Postwar Germany, 1918–1923* (New York: W. W. Norton, 1969).
Wedel, Hasso von, *Die Propagandatruppen der Deutschen Wehrmacht* (Neckargemünd: Kurt Vowinkel, 1962).
Weinberg, Gerhard L., *The Foreign Policy of Hitler's Germany*, 2 vols, Vol. 1: *Diplomatic Revolution in Europe 1933–1936*, Vol. 2: *Starting World War II, 1937–1939* (Chicago: University of Chicago Press, 1970–1980).
Wheatley, Ronald, *Operation Sea Lion; German Plans for the Invasion of England, 1939–1942* (Oxford: Clarendon, 1958).
Wheeler-Bennett, John W., *The Nemesis of Power: The German Army in Politics 1918–1945* (London: Macmillan, 1953).
Wrobel, Kurt, *Die Volksmarine Division* (Berlin: Verlag des Ministeriums für Nationale Verteidigung, 1957).

Zieb, Paul, *Logistiche Probleme der Kriegsmarine* (Neckargemünd: Kurt Vowinkel Verlag, 1961).
Zienert, Josef, *Unsere Marineuniform: Ihre geschlichtliche Entstehung seit den ersten Anfängen und ihre zeitgemässe Weiterentwicklung von 1816 bis 1969* (Hamburg: Helmut Gerhard Schulz Verlag, 1970).
Zipfel, Friedrich, *Kirchenkampf in Deutschland, 1933–1945: Religionsverfolgung und Selbstbehauptung der Kirche in der Nationalsozialistischen Zeit* (Berlin: Walter de Gruyter and Co., 1965).

Articles

Angress, Werner T., "Das deutsche Militär und die Juden im Ersten Weltkrieg," *Militärgeschichtliche Mitteilungen*, 1/1976, pp. 77–146.

Baum, Walter, "Marine, Nationalsozialismus und Widerstand," *Vierteljahrshefte für Zeitgeschichte*, vol. 11 (January 1963), pp. 16–48.
Bird, Keith W., "The Origins and Role of German Naval History in the Inter-War Period 1918–1939," *Naval War College Review*, vol. 32 (March-April 1979), pp. 42–58.
Brausch, Gerd, "Der Tod des Generalobersten Werner Freiherr von Fritsch," *Militärgeschichtliche Mitteilungen*, 1/1970, pp. 95–112.
Brennecke, Fritz, "Die deutsche Kriegsmarine im Jahre 1935," *MOV-Nachrichten*, vol. 18, no. 2 (1936), pp. 9–13.

Brennecke, Fritz, "Marine Zahlmeister, 1867–1967," *MOV-Nachrichten*, vol. 16 (1967), pp. 273–274.

Czisnik, Ulrich, "Die Unruhen in der Marine 1917/18," *Marine-Rundschau*, vol. 67 (1970), pp. 641–664.

Deist, Wilhelm, "Die Politik der Seekriegsleitung und die Rebellion der Flotte Ende Oktober 1918," *Vierteljahrshefte für Zeitgeschichte*, vol. 14 (October 1966), pp. 341–368.
Deist, Wilhelm, "Die Unruhen in der Marine 1917/18," *Marine-Rundschau*, vol. 68 (1971), pp. 325–343.
Drascher, Wahrhold, "Zur Soziologie des deutschen Seeoffizierkorps," *Wehrwissenschaftliche Rundschau*, vol. 12, no. 10 (1962), pp. 555–569.

Ebert, Paul, "Seefahrt, Lebensraum und Rasse," *MOV-Nachrichten*, vol. 18 (November 1, 1936), pp. 349–353.

Forstmeier, Friedrich, "Stellung und Disziplinarbefugnisse des Ersten Offiziers an Bord von Kriegsschiffen der deutschen Marine, 1847–1945," *Marine-Rundschau*, vol. 66 (1969), pp. 39–50.

Herwig, Holger H., "The First German Congress of Workers' and Sailors' Councils and the Problem of Military Reform," *Central European History*, vol. 1 (June 1968), pp. 150–165.
Herwig, Holger H., "From Kaiser to Führer: The Political Road of a German Admiral, 1923–1933," *Journal of Contemporary History*, vol. 9 (April 1974), pp. 107–120.

Jacobsen, Hans-Adolf and Jürgen Rohwer, "Plannungen und Operationen der deutschen Kriegsmarine im Zusammenhang mit dem Fall 'Gelb,'" *Marine-Rundschau*, vol. 57 (1960) pp. 65–78.

Kennedy, Paul M., "Tirpitz, England and the Second Navy Law of 1900: A Strategical Critique," *Militärgeschichtliche Mitteilungen*, 2/1970, pp. 33–58.
Kielmannsegg, Peter, "Die militärisch-politische Tragweite der Hossbach Besprechung," *Vierteljahrshefte für Zeitgeschichte*, vol. 8 (July 1960), pp. 268–274.

Loock, Hans-Dietrich, "Zur 'grossgermanischen' Politik des Dritten Reiches," *Vierteljahrshefte für Zeitgeschichte*, vol. 8 (January 1960), pp. 37–63.

Marschall, Wilhelm, "Marine, Nationalsozialismus und Widerstand," *MOH-Nachrichten*, vol. 12 (1963), pp. 105–108.
Mau, Hermann, "Die 'Zweite Revolution'—Der 30. Juli 1934," *Vierteljahrshefte für Zeitgeschichte*, vol. 1 (April 1953), pp. 119–137.
Moltmann, G., "Goebbels Reden zum totalen Krieg am 18. Februar 1943," *Vierteljahrshefte für Zeitgeschichte*, vol. 12, No. 1 (January 1964), pp. 13–43.

Ruge, Friedrich, "Ausbildung zum Seeoffizier," *Marine-Rundschau*, vol. 37 (1932), pp. 101–110.
Ruge, Friedrich, "Erich Raeder zum hundertsten Geburtstag: Seeoffizier—Oberbefehlshaber—Mensch," *Marineforum*, vol. 51 (1976), pp. 91–92.

Salewski, Michael, "Marineleitung und politische Führung 1931-1935," *Militärgeschichtliche Mitteilungen*, 2/1971, pp. 113–158.

Salewski, Michael, "Selbstverständnis und historisches Bewusstsein der deutschen Kriegsmarine," *Marine-Rundschau*, vol. 67 (1970), pp. 65–88.

Salewski, Michael, "Von Raeder zu Dönitz: Der Wechsel im Oberbefehl der Marine," *Militärgeschichtliche Mitteilungen*, 2/1973, pp. 101–146.

Sandhofer, Gert, "Dokumente zum militärischen Werdegang des Grossadmirals Dönitz," *Militärgeschichtliche Mitteilungen*, 1/1967, pp. 59–81.

Sandhofer, Gert, "Das Panzerschiff 'A' und die Vorentwürfe von 1920 bis 1928," *Militärgeschichtliche Mitteilungen*, 1/1968, pp. 35-62.

Schreiber, Gerhard, "Zur Kontinuität des Gross- und Weltmachtstrebens der deutschen Marineführung," *Militärgeschichtliche Mitteilungen*, 2/1979, pp. 101-171.

Steinert, Marlis G., "Die alliierte Entscheidung zur Verhaftung der Regierung Dönitz," *Militärgeschichtliche Mitteilungen*, 2/1986, pp. 85–99.

Stern, Howard, "The *Organisation Consul*," *Journal of Modern History*, vol. 35 (March 1963), pp. 20–32.

Stockfisch, Dieter, "Der Marineoffizier als Führer und Erzieher: Gedanken zu einem Offizierhandbuch aus der Kriegsmarine," *Marineforum*, vol. 50 (1975), pp. 156–157.

Vogelsang, Thilo, "Neue Dokumente zur Geschichte der Reichswehr 1930–1933," *Vierteljahrshefte für Zeitgeschichte*, vol. 2 (October 1954), pp. 397–436.

Watt, Donald C., "The Anglo–German Naval Agreement of 1935: An Interim Judgment," *Journal of Modern History*, vol. 28 (June 1956), pp. 155–175.

Watt, Donald C., "Anglo–German Naval Negotiations on the Eve of the Second World War," *Journal of the Royal United Service Institution*, vol. 103 (May and August, 1958), pp. 201–207, 384–391.

Wegener, Edward, "Selbstverständnis und historisches Bewusstsein der deutschen Kriegsmarine," *Marine-Rundschau*, vol. 67 (1970), pp. 321–340.

Wiedersheim, William A., "Officer Personnel Selection in the German Navy, 1925–1945," *United States Naval Institute Proceedings*, vol. 73 (April 1947), pp. 445–449.

Dissertations and Manuscripts

Fechter, Helmut, "Admiral Hans Fechter," Manuscript, Kempten, West Germany, 1979.

Lewis, Wallace L., "The Survival of the German Navy 1917–1920: Officers, Sailors and Politics," PhD dissertation, University of Iowa, 1969.

Mills, Arthur H., "Bloodhound of the Revolution: Gustav Noske in German Politics 1918–1920," Masters thesis, Vanderbilt University, 1973.

Peter, Karl, "Seeoffizieranwärter-Ausbildung in Preussen/Deutschland, 1848-1945," Manuscript, Militärgeschichtliches Forschungsamt, Freiburg, West Germany, n.d.

Rust, Eric Christian, "Crew 34: German Naval Officers under and after Hitler," PhD dissertation, University of Texas at Austin, 1987.

Sauer, Wolfgang, "Das Bündnis Ebert-Groener. Eine Studie über Notwendigkeit und Grenzen der militärischen Macht," PhD dissertation, Free University of Berlin, 1957.

Schubert, Helmut, "Admiral Adolf von Trotha (1868–1940). Ein Versuch zur historischen-psychologischen Biographik," PhD dissertation, University of Freiburg, 1976.

Stöckel, Kurt, "Die Entwicklung der Reichsmarine nach dem Ersten Weltkrieg, 1919–1935: Åusserer Aufbau und innere Struktur," PhD dissertation, Göttingen University, 1954.

Werner, Andreas, "SA und NSDAP. SA: 'Wehrverband,' 'Parteitruppe' oder 'Revolutionsarmee'? Studien zur Geschichte der SA und der NSDAP, 1920–1933," PhD dissertation, University of Erlangen/Nuremberg, 1964.

Index

279